The Scots P

Founded on Wood's ed. of Sir Rob__

Peerage of Scotland; containing an historical and

genealogical account of the nobility of that kingdom

(Volume IX)

Editor

James Balfour Paul

Alpha Editions

This edition published in 2020

ISBN : 9789354036958

Design and Setting By
Alpha Editions
www.alphaedis.com
email - alphaedis@gmail.com

EDITORIAL NOTE

THIS, the concluding volume of the *Scots Peerage*, completes a work, the first volume of which was published in 1904. It contains, in the first place, a long list of *addenda et corrigenda*: the latter may, it is hoped, serve to put right some at all events of the actual errors which have occurred in the work; the former, and they are the larger class of the two, contain a good deal of information which has come to light since the publication of the several articles. The editor has to thank many kind correspondents and contributors for information supplied, and especially he may name his friends Mr. J. Maitland Thomson, LL.D., and Col. the Hon. R. E. Boyle, both of whom have been unremitting in their helpful endeavours to increase the usefulness and accuracy of the *Peerage*. Nobody is more aware of the many shortcomings of this work than the editor himself, but perhaps he may be allowed to claim that at all events it is an advance on what has gone before. No doubt, with increased facilities of investigation and the further publication of national records and the contents of private charter-chests, a future generation may be able to produce a fuller and still more accurate account of individual families, but it is hardly probable that a history of the Scottish Peerage on a scale similar to that of the present work will be attempted for many years to come.

The full and elaborate Index, with which the greater part of this volume is occupied, is the work of Mrs. Alexander Stuart, who has brought towards its completion an enthusiasm, energy, and ability which are beyond all praise. Not only does it contain a list of between forty and fifty thousand names, but each person is definitely described by the mention of his or her title, occupation, or relationship. In itself, indeed, the Index forms a valuable compendium of Scottish family history, which will be found useful even without reference to the pages of the *Peerage*. But it goes without saying that such an Index doubles the usefulness of a work like the present. It is not often that an editor meets with a compiler who is so fully in accord with him as to the standard to be aimed at in an index, and who is so capable of carrying it to a successful conclusion. It is difficult for the editor adequately to express the obligations he is under to Mrs. Stuart for her services in this matter.

The Index has been compiled on the following principles:—

1. A Peerage title is given, in capitals, with its holders in alphabetical order, and their respective wives.

2. If the name of the title is changed, *e.g.* from Lyon to Glamis, it is given a separate heading.

3. The surname of the holder of a Peerage title is given in capitals with the various Peerages, in alphabetical order, pertaining to it.

4. After Peers, owners of lands are given in alphabetical order; those of the same Christian name are put in chronological order.

5. Ordinary persons then come in alphabetical order and according to the paging in the volumes.

6. Women are given under their maiden names: if married, as ' wife of ——'; if unmarried as ' dau. of ——.'

7. As a rule, children who died in infancy are not inserted.

In taking leave of a task which has been a congenial if a somewhat strenuous one for the last twelve years, the editor has to express his appreciation of the amicable relations which have subsisted between him and his contributors (some now, alas, beyond the reach of acknowledgments). It is a pleasure to have worked with such colleagues.

JAMES BALFOUR PAUL.

EDINBURGH, *June* 1914.

ADDENDA ET CORRIGENDA

ADDENDA ET CORRIGENDA

VOL. I.

KINGS OF SCOTLAND

p. 4, l. 26, for 'Annandale,' read 'Carrick (vol. ii. p. 433).'

p. 4, l. 2 from foot, after Bohun, insert 'father of the first,' after 'Hereford' insert 'of that family (*Complete Peerage*).'

p. 6, l. 29, for '17 January,' read '28 January (*Scottish Kings*, p. 97).'

p. 8, l. 19, for '1547' read '1347.'

p. 9, l. 6, after '1362,' add 'She had left King David on account of his infidelity, and received Hertford Castle from King Edward as a residence.'

p. 10, l. 2, after 'St.,' insert 'Florent de.'

p. 10, l. 3, for 'Brittany' read 'Anjou.'

p. 10, l. 12, for 'Brittany' read 'Touraine.'

p. 10, l. 21, after 'Priory of,' insert 'Lehon, a Priory of the abbey of.'

p. 10, l. 22, for 'title' read 'tithe.'

p. 12, l. 2, after 'known,' add 'Walter had also a daughter, *Margaret*, buried at Paisley (*Regist. de Passelet*, 74).'

p. 12, l. 5, after 'Eva,' add note, 'Her name was certainly Eva (*Reg. Prior S. Andree*, 257), but her parentage is unknown.'

p. 12, l. 9, after 'leaving,' add 'issue,' and delete 'at least two sons.'

p. 12, between ll. 12 and 13, add

'3. *Leonard*, designed son of Alan, Steward of the King of Scots, who is noted in the *Liber Vitæ* of Durham as bestowing a bezant yearly on the convent, was probably also a son (*Illustrations of Scottish History*, 18).

4. *Avelina*, who was, in 1200, carried off by Duncan, son of Gilbert, afterwards Earl of Carrick (Hoveden, *Rolls Series*, iv. 145).'

p. 12, l. 24, delete 'He appears to have died soon after 13th June 1292,' and insert 'He was summoned by Edward I. to attend him into France, 1st September 1294, and died soon after that date.'

p. 12, between ll. 36 and 37, insert

'7—— a daughter, married to Donald Lord of the Isles. *See* Isles.'

p. 12, l. 37, for '7' read '8.'

p. 14, l. 23, for '1326' read '1327.'

Note.—Bower, the only authority, is so confused at this point that he may be read to mean either year. Walter witnessed several royal charters after 9 April 1326, the latest being dated 31 March 1327 (Polmaise Charter-Chest).

p. 15, l. 4 from foot, after ' her,' add 'who was buried in the church of the Blackfriars of Perth (*Blackfriars of Perth*, 38).'

p. 17, ll. 26 and 27, delete 'about the year 1367,' and insert 'Papal dispensation, dated 13 March 1365-66' (cf. vol. vii. 37).'

p. 18, l. 16, for '1409' read '1405.'

p. 18, l. 17, after 'Kennedy;[4]' add 'In July 1409 there was a papal dispensation for her marriage with Sir William Cunningham of Kilmaurs (cf. vol. iv. 230).'

p. 18, l. 17, delete 'third,' and insert 'on 13 November 1413 she was married.'

p. 19, l. 16, after '1496,' add note, 'The Duchess Eleanor's arms are still in the Burg at Meran. See Baillie-Grohman's *The Land in the Mountains.*'

p. 22, l. 36, for 'John, Lord Gordon' read 'John, styled Lord Gordon.'

p. 22, l. 3 from foot, for 'Isabella' read 'Agnes.'

p. 22, l. 2 from foot, after 'Buchan,' add 'afterwards Countess of Bothwell (see charter cited in *Geneaologist*, N.S., viii. 185, 186).'

p. 23, l. 4, after 'Barthélemy,' insert 'She was living 22 August 1560.'

p. 24, l. 9, after 'He,' insert 'was born about 1529, as a dispensation granted by Pope Clement vii. on 30 August 1534 states that he was then in his fifth year (*Sixth Report Hist. MSS. Com.*, 670) and.'

p. 24, l. 5 from foot, after 'Coldingham,' insert 'He was born about 1531 (Dispensation *ut cit.*).'

p. 24, ll. 4 and 5 from foot, delete '28 December 1561,' and insert '11 January 1561-62 (*Cal. of Scot. Papers*, i. 590).'

p. 25, l. 7, after 'Whithorn,' insert 'He was born about 1533 (Dispensation *ut cit.*).'

p. 29, l. 15, after 'Maria,' insert note, 'Her name was originally Henrietta only, as recorded in the baptismal register at Exeter. She took the name of Anna on joining the Roman Catholic faith when she married the Duke of Orleans' (*ex inform.* Hon. James Hope).

ABERCORN

p. 37, l. 27, after '1543' add note, 'Claud was probably baptized June 1546. (Cf. *Treasurer's Accounts*, viii. 461.)'

p. 39, l. 19, for '24,' read '29.'

p. 39, ll. 27, 28, delete 'High Treasurer of Scotland.' William Hamilton, though frequently so styled never appears to have held this office. He does not appear even to have been a knight.

p. 39, l. 28, delete 'March,' and insert 'a few days before 18 February (*Complete Peerage*, viii. 488).'

p. 40, l. 13, for '1662,' read '1622,' and add '(contract dated 20 July 1619) (*Reg. of Deeds*, ccxciv. 160).'

p. 40, note 3, l. 4 from foot, for 'Robert Lauder of the Bass,' read 'Maurice Lauder of Dunbar.'

p. **42**, l. 11, after 'issue,' add 'Warrant for his burial in Holyrood Church 17 April 1696 (*Privy Council Acta*).'

p. **42**, ll. 20 and 21, delete 'Campbell,' and insert after of, 'Sir Archibald Campbell of Glencarradale' (cf. vol. v. 504).'

p. **47**, l. 7. Boyd of Trochrig gives the date of Lord Abercorn's death as Monday, 2 April 1618 (Bannatyne Club *Misc.*, i. 289). The date in the text is taken from his funeral entry in the Lyon Office.

p. **47**, l. 17, after 'Hamilton,' delete comma, and insert full stop. 'He chose curators 19 July 1621, his next-of-kin on the father's side being Sir George Hamilton of Greenlaw and Sir Frederick Hamilton; on the mother's side, William Boyd of Bonshaw and Adam Boyd of Templeton (*Acts and Decreets*, ccclvi. 103).'

p. **48**, l. 21, after 'contract,' add 'She was buried in Holyrood church on or after 9 June 1696 (Warrant in *Privy Council Acta*).'

p. **49**, l. 24, delete 'William Lenthall of Burford, in the county of Oxford, Speaker in the House of Commons in the Long Parliament,' and insert 'Sir John Lenthall, Marshal of the King's Bench, by Hester, daughter of Sir Thomas Temple, first Baronet of Stowe, which Sir John was the Speaker's brother (*Complete Peerage*, viii. 253).'

p. **54**, l. 34, for '1735' read '1735-36.'

p. **54**, l. 2 from foot, delete 'at Paris, 17 March 1731, was buried in the Scots College there,' and insert 'in Dublin, 6, was buried in St. Patrick's Cathedral there 9, March 1730-31. Michel, on whose authority the statement in the text was given, is wrong, and the inscription he quotes must belong merely to a memorial tablet.'

p. **55**, l. 28, delete the notice of John Hamilton, and insert 'John Hamilton was made a major-general in 1690-91, and died a prisoner in Dublin of wounds received at the battle of Aughrim. He married at Sixmile Bridge, co. Clare, in January 1690, Elizabeth M'Can, daughter of Glesney M'Can by Eleanor, daughter of William Folliard. They had an only child, *Margaret*, who became a chanoinesse of Poussay, in Lorraine, of which her cousin, Elizabeth de Gramont, was Abbess. She married, first, 16 September 1715, Pierre, Comte de Réance, etc.; and, secondly, 18 July 1718, François Philippe, Comte de Marmier, and had a son, Philippe François, created Marquis de Marmier 1740, from whom the present Marquis de Marmier descends (*ex. inform.* G. D. Burtchaell, Esq., Athlone Pursuivant).'

p. **62**, l. 15, after 'son,' insert 'She had a pardon for violating the Acts of Parliament against marriage with Papists in December 1734 (Signet Bills, Public Record Office).'

p. **63**, l. 17, for 'in November' read '13 October.'

p. **63**, l. 2 from foot, for 'eighty' read 'seventy.'

p. **64**, l. 23, after '1789,' insert 'the Patent, a most unusual one, as neither her father nor any of his issue could have succeeded to the title, was obtained with great difficulty through the influence of her cousin, the first Marquess, with whom she was on terms of intimacy. The King was most averse to granting it (Cf. Wraxall's *Posthumous Memoirs*, 163, and Lady Charlotte Bury's *Diary*, ii. 157).'

p. 68, l. 28, after 'Jane,' insert 'Gore.'

SANDILANDS, LORD ABERCROMBIE

p. 75, l. 17, for 'third' read 'fourth.'

p. 75, last line, after 'Garden,' add 'He was killed at the battle of Pinkie, 1547, and his widow married, secondly, John Shaw of Broich (*Exch. Rolls*, xviii. 468; *Acts and Decreets*, xxii. 397).'

p. 76, l. 24, after 'Janet,' insert 'natural.'

p. 76, l. 25, for 'Andrew' read 'Patrick (see *Reg. Mag. Sig.*, 13 April 1541).'

p. 76, last line, after 'Pittedie,' add 'married Isobel Cuninghame and left a son and heir *John*, who was served heir to his father 26 May 1610 (*Fife Retours*).'

p. 76, note 14, for 'xxxiii.' read 'lxxxiii.'

p. 77, after l. 11, add

'9. *Isobel*, married, before 12 December 1562, to John Boswell of Balmuto (*Reg. Mag. Sig.*, 2 March 1562-63). By contract dated 28 October 1554, he had become bound to marry Grisel or Isobel, whichever he pleased, when he had completed his fourteenth year (*Reg. of Deeds*, i. 249).'

p. 77, l. 21, after 'had,' add 'besides *James*, accidentally killed at St. Andrews in April 1574 by George, son of John Shaw of Lethangie, both being children (*Reg. Sec. Sig.*, lvi. 140).'

p. 77, note 4, for '393' read '293.'

p. 78, l. 15, delete 'before June 1593,' and insert 'contract 1590 (*Reg. of Deeds*, clxviii. 227).'

p. 78, l. 18, after 'William,' insert 'married Catherine Cranstoun (*Reg. of Deeds*, ccccxxxii. 47), and had a son *William*, and a daughter, married to James Carstairs (*Ibid.*, Dlix. 327). He is also said to have had an eldest son, *John*, of Rashiehill, father of another John, father of John of Breadshaw, whose son Thomas was served heir of Sir James Sandilands of St. Monance, first Lord Abercrombie (*sic*), brother-german of his great-great-grandfather, in 1734 (Canongate Services of Heirs). Thomas's claim to be Lord Abercrombie was rejected by the House of Lords in 1739 (*Stewartiana*, 127).'

p. 78, l. 24, delete whole line.

p. 78, l. 25, after 'Catherine,' insert 'married (contract 5 April 1628) to Mr. Adam, son of Adam Bothwell of Glencorse, and died before 21 March 1632 (cf. vol. iv. 435).'

p. 78, l. 27, after 'Jean,' insert 'Died 1647, Mr. Andrew, her brother, being served heir to her 26 January 1648 (Fife Sheriff-Court Books).'

p. 78, ll. 31 and 32, delete 'and predeceased his father, dying in 1644 or 1645,' and insert 'was alive 1 January 1645 (*Reg. of Deeds*, Dlix. 326).'

p. **79,** l. 2, after 'Catherine,' insert 'married to Sir Robert Dalzell, first Baronet of Glenae (discharge for tocher dated 20 June 1644, *Reg. of Deeds,* Dlvii. 70).'

p. **79,** after l. 3, insert

'7. *Mary,* baptized 9 May 1638 (Canongate Reg.), probably iden-tical with that Marion who calls herself sister of James, Lord Aber-crombie, and daughter of Dame —— Carnegy and Sir James Sandi-lands, in a deed renouncing certain rights she had over lands belonging to her brother, which she had apprised. The date is 17 November 1658, and at that time she was "appearand" wife of Mr. David Lyall, minister of Banchory-Devenick, afterwards of Aberdeen and Mont-rose, where he died in 1696' (*ex inform.* Dr. W. A. Macnaughton, Stonehaven ; deed recorded in Register of Bonds, etc., Sheriff-Court Books, Stonehaven).'

p. **79,** l. 4, for 'father's' read 'mother's.'

p. **79,** l. 5 from foot, for 'Crichton,' read 'Lichtoun.'

p. **80,** l. 22, after 'Falkland,' insert 'Lord Abercrombie ultimately divorced his wife, apparently on 13 March 1663 (*Edin. Com. Decreets,* but the Decreet is not engrossed in the Register). On 18 October 1663 he produced extract of his divorce before the kirk-session of Kinneff, and was thereafter contracted and proclaimed with Christian Fletcher (Kinneff Register).'

p. **81,** l. 17, for 'VII.' read 'II.'

p. **81,** l. 31, after 'proper,' insert 'on a chief azure three mullets of the first.'

ABERDEEN

p. **83,** l. 28, for 'Lomnay' read 'Lonmay.'

p. **87,** l. 27, after 'Charles,' insert 'apprenticed to Bailie George Reid, merchant, Edinburgh, 6 July 1659 (Edinburgh Apprentice Register).'

p. **89,** l. 22, delete '7 May 1691,' and insert '1694 (*ex inform.* Hon. Vicary Gibbs).'

p. **89,** ll. 26, 27, delete 'died before June 1709,' and insert 'was buried 16 December 1708 (*Complete Peerage,* s.v. Eglinton).'

p. **90,** l. 28, for '1 April,' read '25 April.'

p. **90,** l. 29, delete 'Anna.'

p. **90,** l. 31, for 'pence,' read 'pounds.'

p. **91,** l. 6, after 'thirdly,' insert 'banns proclaimed at Bellie 15 Novem-ber 1729.'

p. **91,** l. 8, after '1791,' insert 'and was buried in St. Cuthbert's Church-yard, Edinburgh.'

p. **93,** l. 18, for '1793,' read '1795.

p. **95,** l. 34, after 'Morton,' add note, 'The present wife is reckoned agreeable and clever, but how unlike her predecessor in beauty and charm (Lady Charlotte Bury's *Diary*).'

p. 100, last l. after 'daughter,' insert '*Henrietta.*'

p. 102, l. 22, after 'in,' insert 'March.'

p. 103, l. 9, after 'George,' insert 'entered Douai College 5 November 1685, aged ten. Studied Philosophy at Paris, and became a religious, but renounced in 1699.'

'4. *Patrick*, entered Douai 10 April 1681, aged nine.'

p. 103, l. 10, delete '4,' and insert '5.'

p. 103, l. 10, after '*John,*' insert 'entered Douai 5 November 1685, aged eight (*Records of Scots Colleges*).'

p. 103, l. 11, delete '5,' and insert '6.'

p. 103, l. 14, after '1698,' insert 'for adultery with a Frenchman Lavelette or Laballot (*Consistorial Processes*, Scot. Rec. Soc., No. 86).

p. 103, l. 15, delete 'succeeded his father 1681 and on,' and insert 'entered Douai 10 April 1681, aged eleven. Became a religious (probably Jesuit) at Rome, "a sweet youth and humble like the dust of the street" (*Letters of James, Earl of Perth*, Camden Soc., 1845, p. 18). On 4 September 1694 Aboyne was in Scotland, having been captured on his return from France, and sent down from London on bail. He was, 19 October 1694, confined to one of the houses of Glamis or Castle Lyon, whichever the Earl of Strathmore should be residing at for the time (*Privy Council Acta*). On'.

p. 103, line 16, after '1698,' insert 'he.'

p. 103, l. 27, after 'married,' insert 'as his first wife.'

p. 103, l. 28, after 'Kinnaird,' insert 'She was dead before 3 November 1731 (*Consistorial Processes*, Scot. Rec. Soc., No. 293).'

p. 103, last line, after 'married,' insert '20 June 1724 (*Complete Peerage*).'

p. 104, l. 6, after 'Glentanner,' insert 'born 19 June 1728.'

p. 104, l. 12, after 'Baronet,' insert 'She died 31 March and was buried at Restalrig 6 April 1803 (Restalrig Reg.).'

p. 104, l. 15, after 'company,' insert 'Born 8 July 1765, died 26 December 1832.'

p. 104, l. 16, after 'R.N.', insert 'Born 9 April 1769, died 23d August 1799, and was buried at Restalrig (*Ibid*).'

p. 104, l. 17, delete 'died young,' and insert 'was buried at Restalrig, 23 February 1781 (*Ibid.*).'

p. 104, l. 18, after 'Clementina,' insert 'born 6 May 1763.'

p. 104, l. 18, delete 'at Exmouth, 13 December 1801, aged 33,' and insert 'after 9 July 1804, when she was served heir to her mother.'

p. 104, l. 20, after '*Grace,*' insert '*Margaret*, born 27 September 1766.'

p. 104, l. 22, after 'Lockhart,' insert 'born 1732.'

p. 104, l. 26, after 'first,' insert '25 April 1753.'

p. 104, l. 26, after 'Levi,' insert 'She died *s.p.* 17 March 1754.'

p. 104, l. 26, delete 'and,' and insert 'He married.'

p. 104, l. 26, after 'secondly,' insert '4 October 1770.'

p. 104, l. 27, after 'Portsmouth,' insert 'She died 29 May 1813, having thrown herself out of the window in the house of her daughter, Mrs. Williams, 39 Somerset Street, Portman Square. They had seven children, of whom four came of age (*Notes and Queries*, 10 S. ix. 449; x. 38).'

p. 104, l. 28, delete 'and left,' and insert 'By his second wife he had issue :—'

p. 104, l. 29, after 'Gordon,' insert 'born 28 July 1775.'

p. 104, l. 30, after 'Gordon,' insert 'born 9 May 1780, was in the Royal Artillery, and afterwards in the 56th Regiment. He was living in 1828 at Laverstock, Salisbury. For an account of the elopement of these two brothers with Mrs. Lee, see Bulloch's *Earls of Aboyne*, App.'

p. 104, l. 31, after ' (3) *Catherine*,' insert ' (4) *Caroline*, died at Exmouth, 13 December 1801.'

p. 104, l. 41, for 'CHARLES,' read 'GEORGE.'

p. 104, last line, after 'Catherine,' insert 'born at Holyrood 31 March 1760, and died at Restalrig 5 June 1764 (Restalrig Reg.).'

p. 105, l. 2, delete '26 May 1766,' and insert 'at the Castle de la Tour, in the Pays de Vaud, 23 May 1786 (*Rambles about Bath*, 317).'

p. 105, l. 4, for '23 April' read '14 May (Reg. St. George's, Hanover Square).'

p. 105, l. 20, for 'CHARLES' read 'GEORGE.'

p. 105, ll. 11 and 12, delete 'Royal Scots, the 113th Regiment, and 3rd Foot Guards,' and insert 'the 22nd Foot and Grenadier Guards (*Army Lists*).'

AIRLIE

p. 106, l. 23, for 'Kynmethan,' read 'Kinminethen.'

p. 111, after l. 16, insert

'4. *Henry*, a natural son, had a dispensation to take orders and hold two benefices, 30 July 1405 (*Reg. Avenion.*, 320, 604). He was provided to the canonry and prebend of Tulynestyn in Aberdeen Cathedral, 19 August 1413 (*Cal. Pet. to the Pope*, i. 600).'

p. 113, l. 22, delete 'or William Lord Seton.'

p. 113, l. 23, after 'statement,' add 'He certainly married Isobel Forbes, who survived him. On 1 August 1489, she executed a revocation of deeds done by him in prejudice of her rights (*Aberdeen Burgh Sasines*).'

p. 114, delete ll. 7 and 8.

p. 114, l. 27, delete 'is known to have,' and insert after married, 'secondly, before May 1478.'

p. 114, l. 28, after '1486.7' insert 'She was the widow of William, second Lord Graham, and daughter of William, second Earl of Angus, and by her he had a son, *Oliver* (*Reg. de Aberbrothock*, ii. 176, 300).'

p. 114, l. 34, delete ' *Walter*, stated to be,' and insert ' *Oliver*, who was.' After Balfour, insert 'He married Felicia Fentoun (*Reg. de Aberbrothock*, ii. 176, 300, 390).'

p. 114, note 5, add 'He was dead three and a half years before 2 May 1508 (Aberdeen Sheriff Court Diet Book, vol. i. at date).'

p. 115, after l. 5, insert

'7. *Thomas* (probably by first marriage), bailie in a Sasine 8 July 1483 (Bamff Charters).'

'8. *Margaret* (by first marriage), married, contract 10 April 1482, to Gilbert Ramsay younger of Bamff (*Ibid*). She is incorrectly given in the text as belonging to the previous generation.'

p. 115, ll. 6, 11, and 17, for '7, 8, 9,' read '9, 10, 11.'

p. 117, l. 19, delete 'previous to the Reformation,' and insert 'before 15 May 1556 (See writ in Protocol Book of James Harlaw, f. 114).

p. 117, after l. 29, add

'(2) *Janet*, married (contract 14 October 1572) to James Anderson, maltman, burgess of Perth (*Reg. of Deeds*, xl. 277). In 1577 she is called Thomas's daughter and heir, and there is mention of *John Ogilvie* of Easter Bogside, brother and heir of tailzie of Archibald, Thomas's lawful son (*Acts and Decreets*, lxxi. 311). His retour to Archibald was, however, reduced, February 1578-79 (*Ibid.*, lxxv. 25).'

p. 117, l. 31, for '(2),' read '(3).'

p. 117, last l., after 'James,' insert 'fifth.'

p. 118, l. 20, after 'to,' insert 'Thomas, son of.'

p. 118, l. 29, after 'husband,' insert 'and as his second wife.'

p. 118, l. 30, delete '1574,' and insert '1 October 1578.'

p. 122, l. 3, after 'Montgomerie,' insert 'daughter of Robert Montgomerie in Haltoun, and Euphame Guthrie, his wife (Brechin Com. Deeds at Forfar, 14th March 1594-95 : cf. *Reg, Mag. Sig.*, 8 May 1601).'

p. 122, l. 25, for 'instituting,' read 'substituting.'

p. 122, l. 29, delete 'before 1588,' and insert '11 November 1581, with great solemnity and triumph, in Holyrood House.'

p. 123, l. 8, after 'Newbigging,' insert 'styled second son in 1620 (*Reg. of Deeds*, cccxx. 41).'

p. 124, l. 15, after 'died,' delete 'soon afterwards,' and insert 'in 1666 (*Reg. of Retours*, xxxix. 183).'

p. 125, l. 3, for '*Helen*' read '*Elizabeth*.'

p. 125, l. 3, after 'married,' insert 'as his first wife.'

p. 125, l. 6, after 'good,' add 'She died in 1654, after a lingering illness (Oxenfoord Writs).'

p. 127, after l. 30, insert

'(3) *Elizabeth*.

(4) *Helen*, married, at Edinburgh, 4 March 1759, to Roger Robertson of Ladykirk (Wood's Douglas's *Peerage*), with issue.'

p. 128, l. 14, delete '1813,' and insert '1803. Testament recorded 5 April 1803.'

p. 129, l. 8, after 'first,' insert 'on or before 31 May 1648.'

p. 129, l. 13, after 'Inshewan,' insert 'She raised an action of divorce against her husband in 1798 (*Consistorial Processes*, Scot. Rec. Soc., No. 1133).'

p. 130, l. 23, after '1835,' insert 'and was buried in the Canongate Churchyard.'

p. 130, l. 24, after '1838,' insert ' at 6 Heriot Row, Edinburgh.'

p. 130, l. 6 from foot, for '1838,' read '1831.'

p. 130, l. 4 from foot, delete '*s.p.*'

p. 131, l. 16, after 'Alderley,' insert note, 'Nature but rarely moulds such a nature in which knowledge, intelligence, and charity are so excellently blended and combined (Lady Dorothy Neville's *Reminiscences*, 156).'

AIRTH

p. 137, l. 25, after '1612,' add note, 'In *Reg. Mag. Sig.* (30 July 1613, the date of this contract is given as 30 January 1610.'

p. 137, l. 28, delete 'alive in 1683,' and insert 'died in 1687 or 1688.'

p. 137, l. 5 from foot, after 'Bramhall,' insert 'Archbishop of Armagh.'

p. 137, l. 4 from foot, after ' *Eleanor*,' insert 'born 17 January 1661-62 (Parish Register, St. Peter's, Drogheda, Ireland).'

p. 137, l. 4 from foot, after 'married,' delete remainder of sentence, and insert 'licence 15 February 1682, to Arthur, afterwards Sir Arthur Rawdon, Bart., and died 17 March 1710, and was buried at St. Andrew's, Dublin (*Complete Baronetage*).'

p. 138, l. 6, after '*Archibald*,' insert 'baptized 25 April 1631 (Canongate Reg.).'

p. 138, note 1. The reference is ' *Reg. of Deeds*, DXXiv. 358.'

p. 138, note 2, for 'lii.' read ' Dlii.'

p. 139, l. 22, for '1632' read '1633 (*Gen. Reg. Sas.*, xxxvii. 188, 191).'

p. 141, l. 17, for 'charter' read 'warrant.'

p. 141, l. 34, after 'married,' insert 'contract 13 December 1681, tocher 4000 merks (*Stirlings of Keir*, 172).'

p. 141, l. 4 from foot, delete 'prior to 28 April 1677,' and insert 'in November 1661 (*Privy Council Decreta*, 25 June 1674).'

p. 141, l. 3 from foot, after '1684,' insert 'for adultery with Robert Ross, younger of Auchlossen (*Edin. Com. Consist. Decreets*, i. 1).'

p. 142, l. 1. *Note.*—The correct date of the second marriage of the Earl of Airth and Menteith with Katherine Bruce was 4 April 1685 (Edinburgh Reg.). It was solemnised by warrant of the Bishop of Edinburgh to Mr. Alexander Ramsay.

p. 142, l. 25, after 'married,' insert 'in 1686 (*Privy Council Decreta*, 21 July 1691).'

p. 142, l. 26, after 'issue,' insert 'buried at Arbuthnott, 19 April 1699.'

p. 142, l. 4 from foot, for 'on' read 'in.'

p. 144, l. 9, after 'Surrey,' insert 'her footman and the co-respondent in the divorce case' (*Consistorial Processes*, Scot. Rec. Soc., No. 1005).'

p. 145, l. 19, after 'husband,' add 'with three other children :—'

ALBANY

p. 149, l. 1, for 'six' read 'seven.'

p. **149,** ll. 11 and 12, delete 'and, secondly, to Robert Stewart of Lorne, by both of whom,' and add

'4. *Joanna,* married to Sir John Stewart of Ennerme [Innermeath], as is shown by a commission from Pope Benedict XIII. to the Bishop of St. Andrews to dispense with the marriage, dated at Avignon 5 Kal. October Anno 3 (A.D. 1397) (*Regesta Avenionensia,* 303, f. 556). They had issue.'

p. **149,** l. 13, for '4' read '5.'

p. **149,** l. 14, 'delete 'before February 1407-8,' and insert, '8 May 1402' (cf. vol. vii. 242).

p. **149,** l. 15, after 'secondly,' insert 'before 1406 (cf. vol. iv. 334).'

p. **149,** l. 17, for '5' read '6.'

p. **149,** l. 19, for '6' read '7.'

p. **150,** l. 20, after 'married,' insert 'first, a lady whose Christian name was Joanna, but whose surname is not stated. She is referred to as his former wife in the dispensation, dated 9 June 1392, for the marriage of Murdac and Isobel (*Regesta Avenion.,* 269, f. 397). She may have been a Douglas, as explained in vol. v. 342 *n.* He married, secondly' (etc., as in text).

p. **150,** l. 26, after '1421,³' add 'Robert had dispensation on 4 May 1414 to marry Euphemia Stewart, Countess of Strathearn (*Reg. Avenion.,* 344, f. 670), but the marriage did not take place.'

p. **150,** l. 29, after 'papal,' insert 'dispensation on 5 September 1415, for a marriage with Euphemia Stewart, Countess Palatine of Strathearn, they being in second and third degrees from the common stem and in the third and fourth degrees of affinity (*Regesta Avenion.,* 335, f. 649). She had been contracted to his brother Robert. Walter had another' (dispensation, as in text).

p. **153,** l. 10, after 'Breadalbane,' add 'He had another daughter, *Janet,* married to Thomas Charteris of Kinfauns, but divorced from him (*Acts and Decreets,* xiii. 129, 344).'

p. **153,** l. 28, after 'Arran,' insert 'and had issue a son *James.*'

p. **153,** l. 29, after '1542,' add 'Margaret Stewart survived Sir Patrick and became the wife and widow of David Ross of Balnagown, who died in 1527 (*Acta Dom. Conc.,* xxxvii. f. 180 (189)).'

p. **153,** l. 3 from foot, for 'd'Bouillon' read 'de Bouillon.'

p. **154,** l. 28, delete '8,' and insert 'contract 13 (*L'Art de verifier les dates,* ii. 372).'

ALTRIE

p. **159,** l. 3, for '13 July 1594' read '18 March 1595-96 (Benholm Charters).'

p. **159,** l. 10, for '1556' read '1566 (*Reg. of Deeds,* viii. 361).'

p. **159,** l. 12, after '1584),' add 'She was divorced from him, and in 1617 was the wife of James Allardes (Slains Charters ; see Riddell's *Tracts,* 114).'

p. **159**, l. 13, delete 'prior to 28,' and insert 'contract 25.'

p. **159**, l. 17, after '*Margaret*,' delete 'and secondly,' and insert 'John
Erskine died 21 October 1592, and she was married, secondly, before 1
February 1596-97 (Benholm Charters).'

p. **159**, l. 18, for 'ninth,' read 'tenth.'

ANGUS

p. **167**, l. 10, for 'Richard, the son of a,' read 'the son of a Richard.'

p. **168**, l. 2, delete '1246,' and insert '2 December 1247, before which date
she had married Richard of Dover, son of Richard Fitzroy, a natural
son of King John. By him she had issue a son *Richard* and a
daughter *Isabel*, afterwards wife of David, Earl of Athol (*Genealogist*,
new series, xxii, 109).'

p. **168**, l. 10, delete 'in,' and insert 'before 8 November (Patent Rolls).'

p. **168**, l. 11, after 'issue,' add 'He married Elizabeth, daughter of Alexander Cumyn, Earl of Buchan. She died in 1369 (cf. vol. ii. 256).'

p. **168**, l. 17, delete 'in 1325,' and insert '30 March 1325 and was buried in
the Abbey of Newminster. He married, first, before 20 September 1303,
Lucy, daughter, and in her issue heir of Sir Philip de Kyme of Kyme,
co. Lincoln, by Joan, daughter of Sir Hugh de Bigod, Chief Justiciar
of England; and, secondly, Alianore ——, who survived him and
married, secondly, before 16 August 1327, Sir Roger Mauduit of Eshot
and Bockenfield, co. Northumberland. She died 31 March 1358' (Article
by G. W. Watson in *Genealogist*, N.S. vol. xxvi. p. 193).'

p. **168**, l. 18, delete 'and,' and insert 'Earl Robert.'

p. **168**, l. 25, delete 'in,' and insert '6 or 7 January 1380-81.'

p. **168**, l. 25, after 'without,' insert 'surviving.'

p. **168**, l. 26, after 'issue,' insert 'He married, first, Joan, daughter of Sir
Robert Willoughby d'Eresby. She died 13 July 1350, and he married,
secondly, before October 1369, Maud, only daughter of Sir Thomas de
Lacy of Cockermouth. She survived him and married, secondly, before
1 May 1383, as his second wife, Henry Percy, first Earl of Northumberland, and died *s.p.s.* 18 December 1398 (*Genealogist, ut supra*).'

p. **170**, l. 24, for 'William' read 'John.'

p. **171**, l. 2, and note 1, 'This is the only known son of Earl Thomas.
Douglas, followed by the *Complete Peerage*, gives him a son Thomas,
Earl of Angus from 1361 to 1377, but his statement is founded on wrong
premises.'

p. **173**, l. 7 from foot, for '1409' read '1405.'

p. **173**, l. 5 from foot, after 'third,' insert '13 November 1413.'

p. **174**, l. 5 from foot, for '1435' read '1436.'

p. **175**, l. 10, for 'three' read 'four.'

p. **175**, l. 10, after 'sons,' insert 'and a daughter.'

p. **175**, after l. 23 insert

'4. *Hugh*, who, in a Papal Bull of 7 June 1455, is said to be brother-
german of the then Earl of Angus, in the twentieth year of his age, and in

the second and third degrees of consanguinity with James, King of
Scots (*Reg. Vaticana*, cccclxxvii. 141). He had several provisions to
canonries, etc., between 1449 and 1455, was archdeacon of St. Andrews
in 1458 (*Reg. Mag. Sig.*), and rector of St. Andrews University 1466
(*Reg. of Papal Petitions*, 590, 116).'

5. *Helen*, married, first, to William, second Lord Graham; secondly,
to James, first Lord Ogilvie of Airlie (see addenda to Airlie article).'

p. 178, l. 5, delete '3 *Anne* to issue,' and insert 'The wife of William,
second Lord Graham, was named Helen, and was a sister, not a
daughter of Earl George.'

p. 178, ll. 8, 10, 13, 17, 22, and 23, for '4, 5, 6, 7, 8, 9,' read '3, 4, 5, 6, 7, 8.'

p. 178, l. 28, after 'father,' insert 'comma,' and add 'to whom he was
served heir 12 April 1468 (*Harl. MS.*, 6443).'

p. 180, l. 15, for 'at' read 'on.'

p. 183, l. 1, delete 'before May 1468,' and insert 'on 4 March 1467-68.'

p. 184, l. 14, after 'was,' insert 'Margaret, daughter of John Carmichael
of Meadowflat, to whom and his children by her he granted a Bond of
Provision 28 January 1553-54 (*Acts and Decreets*, x. 164). He married,
thirdly.'

p. 185, l. 2, after 'Keith,' add 'Agnes was married (contract 14 January
1571-72) to William Hay of Urie (*Reg. Sec. Sig.*, xli. 45). They were
divorced before 1587 (*Reg. of Deeds*, xxviii. 125).'

p. 185, line 5, after 'Katherine,' insert 'She was married to John Carmichael, Captain of Crawford (*Harl. MS.*, 6443).'

p. 185, l. 16, delete 'in September 1522,' and insert 'between 10 September, when his will was executed, and 15 September 1522, when it
received probate (Small's *Poetical Works of Gavin Douglas*, i. p. cxvii;
Scottish Historical Review, ii. 63).'

p. 186, note 4, after '149,' add, 'but see vol. iv. p. 406, where further details
as to the Herries marriage are given.'

p. 188, l. 23, delete 'in 1560,' and insert 'on 12 December 1573, when her
liferent was reserved in a charter to her grandson (*Reg. Mag. Sig.*, at
date).'

p. 192, line 22, after 'first,' insert 'contract 26 June 1509 (Buccleuch
Charter-Chest).'

p. 192, l. 25, after 'Tudor,' insert 'whom he married 4 (or 6) August 1514
at the Church of Kinnoull (*Scottish Kings*, at date)' and.'

p. 192, l. 27, after 'wife,' insert 'whom he married before 9 April 1543
(*Reg. Mag. Sig.*, at date).'

p. 193, l. 6, after 'and,' insert 'by, it is said, a daughter of Stewart of
Traquair.'

p. 193, l. 4 from foot, after 'first,' insert 'contract 19 January 1567-68
(*Acts and Decreets*, xlii. 22).'

p. 196, l. 6 from foot, delete 'in the beginning of 1587. In July,' and
insert '12 July 1587, and in the same month (*Hatfield Col.*, iii.
268).'

p. 196, l. 4 from foot, for 'seventh Earl of,' read 'eighth Lord.'

p. 196, l. 2 from foot, after '1583,' insert note, 'The exact date of Robert Douglas's death is doubtful. See *post*, vol. vi. 550.'

p. 197, l. 3, after '*Margaret*,' delete remainder of sentence, and insert 'who was served heir of line to her father 13 July 1590 (*Reg. of Deeds*, xlvi. 142A). She was alive in 1591 (*Ibid.*, xxxvii. 276; *Harl. MS.*, 6442).'

p. 198, l. 26, after 'Gavin,' insert 'styled of Raquarrall.'

p. 198, l. 32, after 'married,' insert 'first, contract 27 October 1598 (*Reg. of Deeds*, cccxxxi. 211) Jean, sister of Robert Menzies, burgess of Aberdeen, and widow of Gilbert Menzies of Auldquhat; secondly.'

p. 199, l. 1, delete 'who,' and insert 'entered Douai College in 1596 and afterwards went to Rome, where he graduated in philosophy in 1598 (*Records of Scots Coll.*, 7). He.'

p. 199, l. 12, after 'married,' insert 'contract 5 January 1567-68, (*Aberdeen Hornings*, 25 June 1584).'

p. 204, l. 26, delete 'in,' and insert '11 September.'

p. 205, l. 3 from foot, after 'Isabel,' insert 'baptized 21 May 1642 (Canongate Reg.). She was the third daughter by the second marriage (*Lanark Sasines, Upper Ward*, i. 134). She was.'

p. 206, l. 6, after 'daughter,' insert 'She died 8 January 1713.'

p. 206, last line, delete 'or about 15,' and substitute 'Tuesday 16 (MS. [1659] by his widow at Kilkerran).'

p. 207 l. 3, delete 'In,' and insert 'On 26 April.'

p. 207, after l. 10, insert
'2. *Charles*, baptized 9 February 1637 (Canongate Reg.).'

p. 207, l. 11, for '2' read '3.'

p. 207, l. 15, for '3' read '4'; after 'death,' delete remainder of sentence, and insert 'Baptized 1 April 1655, and buried in April 1656 (*Ibid*).'

p. 207, l. 17, for '4 and 5' read '5 and 6.'

p. 207, after l. 18, insert
'7. *Ann*, baptized 8 January 1650 (*Ibid*).'

p. 207, l. 19, for '6' read '8.'

p. 208, l. 11, after 'Dundee,' add 'On the abolition of heritable jurisdictions, the Duke received £5104, 5s. 1d. as his compensation for the regalities of Kirriemuir, Abernethy, Selkirk, Jedburgh Forest, Bonkle and Preston, Bothwell, Douglas and Dudhope (*Treasury Money Book*, xliii. 149, P.R.O.).'

p. 208, l. 15, insert at beginning of line, 'He was engaged to the daughter of widow Jack, a taverner in Perth, but this was apparently broken off (Lamont's *Diary*).'

p. 210, l. 5, for 'August' read 'April.'

p. 211, l. 2, delete 'in' and insert 'on 1.'

p. 211, line 6, after 'beautiful,' insert note, 'Her "beauty" was doubtful, but she was very free and outspoken, and quite a character. She was the last of the nobility to be attended by halberdiers when going about the country. When she visited, she left her dress behind her as a present. She left certain estates to Archibald Douglas and other

heirs of entail to be called Douglas Support; and provided that the
person succeeding should bear the name and arms of Douglas, with
the addition of a woman with a child in her arms and a snake under
her feet: but these have never been officially recorded. There was a
picture at Douglas of her holding a medallion of Archibald in her right
hand and a pair of scales in her left. On a pedestal the heads of Lords
Mansfield and Camden, and, crouching on the ground in an attitude
of terror, a figure with a mask in his right hand, supposed to be the
Duke of Hamilton.'

p. 213, l. 25, after 'Macdowall,' read '(*sic* in Lyon Register, but probably
for Galloway).'

MURRAY, EARL OF ANNANDALE

p. 220, ll. 12, 13, 'for John, Master of Maxwell,' read 'Maister John of
Maxwell.'

p. 221, l. 18, for 'sixth' read 'fifth.'

p. 221, l. 22, for 'seventh' read 'sixth.'

p. 222, note 13, for '218' read '281.'

p. 224, l. 19, after 'married,' insert 'contract 2 January 1547 (*Acta Dom.
Conc. et Sess.*, xxvi. 36).'

p. 226, l. 9, delete 'Drumlanrig,' and insert 'Hawick.'   See vol. vii.
129.

p. 228, l. 11, delete 'in,' and insert '22 (Sir Thomas Hope's *Diary*).'

p. 229, ll. 21, 22, delete 'and Lord St. John of Torphichen in the county of
Perth.'

JOHNSTONE, EARL OF ANNANDALE

p. 236, l. 25, for 'whom' read 'who.'

p. 239, l. 10, after 'issue,' delete 'a son, Adam Scott,' and add 'two
sons, *Robert* and *Adam*.   Robert, the elder, was infeft in the lands of
Rysholm, co. Ayr, as heir to his mother,10 November 1541 (Sasine in Kel-
burn Charter-Chest). She had died in 1524 (*Acts and Decreets*, vi. 111,
26 January 1551). Robert died before 19 January 1549, when his brother
Adam sold Wamphray, with his father's consent (*Reg. Mag. Sig.*, 24
January 1549).'

p. 245, l. 31, delete '1576,' and insert 'in 1598, as she is referred to in a
writ of 1 November in that year (*Reg. Sec. Sig.*, lxx. f. 90).'

p. 246, l. 2 from foot, after 'will,' delete remainder of paragraph, and
insert 'She married, first, John Carmichael, younger of Meadowflat;
secondly, William Weir, younger of Stonebyres; and, thirdly, William
Livingston of Jerviswood (cf. vol. viii. 371).'

p. 247, l. 7, for '1570' read '1570-71.'

p. 248, l. 7, delete 'at a date which has not been ascertained,' and
insert 'about March 1543-44 (*Treasurer's Accounts*, viii. 267).'

p. 248, l. 2 from foot, after '1577,' add 'She was married, secondly, to
Alexander (Abernethy), sixth Lord Saltoun, and thirdly, in or before

1589, to William, son of Mark Ker, Commendator of Newbattle (cf. vol. vii. 412; v. 455).'

p. 254, l. 25, after '1609,' delete to end of paragraph, and insert 'She was dead before 1624 (*Gen. Reg. Inhibs.*, 22 November 1624).'

p. 258, l. 4, after 'residence,' add note, 'See a sonnet on him by Arthur Johnston in *Musa Latina Aberdonensis*, vol. ii. p. 46 (New Spalding Club).'

p. 258, l. 15, after 'Carnegie,' insert 'They were married in the Kirk of Holyroodhouse, 25 February 1647 (Canongate Reg.).'

p. 258, l. 16, after 'year,' add 'Her will is dated 4 July 1648.'

p. 263, l. 8, after 'Annandale,' add 'But apparently he was buried in Greyfriars, Edinburgh, 30 July 1672 (Greyfriars' Burial Reg.).'

p. 264, l. 16, for 'fifteenth' read 'eighteenth.'

p. 264, l. 16, after 'issue,' insert 'Albert Johnstone Campbell, who died April 1907, the last male of the Campbells of Glen Saddell and Newfield, is said to have claimed through Lady Mary, as heir of line, the Annandale and Hartfell Peerages.'

p. 264, after l. 29, insert 'There is a tradition that there was a daughter, Christian, who made a runaway match with James Willison, in Elvanfoot, first writing to him proposing marriage, and then riding with him to Edinburgh, where they were married. See a note on the family of Black of Over Abington by W. G. Black, Glasgow, p. 9. The name, however, does not appear in the Edinburgh Marriage Register.'

p. 265, l. 1, for 'these' read 'the.'

p. 268, l. 28, after 'Westerhall,' insert 'He was killed at Carthagena, 1741.'

p. 268, l. 28, for '1772' read '1762.'

ARBUTHNOTT

p. 273, last l., delete 'another son,' and insert 'his grandson.'

p. 280, l. 13, after 'Ilk,' insert 'with issue (*Ninth Rep. Hist. MSS. Com.*, 192).'

p. 280, l. 25, delete 'prior to February 4, 1576, when his,' and insert 'in January 1573. His.'

p. 280, l. 26, after 'recorded,' insert '4 February 1576.'

p. 280, l. 28, after '*James*,' insert 'Collector of Cess for Angus and Mearns (*Reg. of Deeds*, vii. 196).'

p. 281, note 13, after '*Origines*,' insert
'In 1469 Guille Arbutnot was an Archer of the Scots Guard in France (Forbes Leith, i. 162).'

p. 282, l. 30, after 'first,' insert 'prior to 5 August 1468.'

p. 285, l. 5 from foot, delete '1626,' and insert '1 March 1642 (*Aberdeen Reg. of Inhibitions*).'

p. 285, after l. 3 from foot, insert
'iii. *Mr. Peter*, designed brother german to Mr. Andrew Arbuthnott,

heir apparent of Little Fiddes, on 6 January 1597-98, was pedagogue to Lord Thirlestane in 1607, obtained a Crown charter of certain lands in Lauderdale 1 April 1633 (*Reg. Mag. Sig.*), and died *s.p.*'

p. 285, l. 2 from foot, for 'iii.' read 'iv.'

p. 286, l. 1, after 'Fiddes,' insert 'married, first, Sara Strachan; and, secondly, Janet Gordon, who survived him.'

p. 286, l. 2, delete 'by his wife, Janet Gordon,' and insert 'issue.'

p. 286, l. 9 from foot, for '¹¹' read '¹⁰.'

p. 286, l. 7 from foot, after '¹¹,' insert 'He was a merchant in Dundee. He was twice married, and died in 1690, leaving by his first wife, Janet Gordon, who died in 1680, James, Alexander, and Elizabeth, to whom their uncle Patrick was served tutor at law (*Retours*).'

p. 286, l. 5 from foot, after '1651,' insert 'became a Writer to the Signet in 1678, and died 6 March 1704.'

p. 286, l. 2 from foot, for 'and' read 'He.'

p. 287, l. 32, for 'Robert' read 'Henry.'

p. 288, l. 17, after '1532, 'add 'He had letters of legitimation 15 February 1530-31 (*Reg. Sec. Sig.*, viii. 237).'

p. 290, l. 7 from foot, delete '13 April 1558,' and insert 'in September 1553.'

p. 290, note 7, delete note and insert '*Treasurer's Accounts*, vol. x.'

p. 292, l. 6, after 'Andrew,' insert 'apprentice with James Dalziel, merchant and bailie of Edinburgh, 14 March 1610. He is.'

p. 292, l. 13, after '(5),' insert '*Mr.*'

p. 292, l. 26, after 'Arbuthnott,' add 'In confirmation as executor dative to his mother he is designed Mr. Robert Arbuthnott at the Kirk of Fordoun.'

p. 293, l. 6, after 'secondly,' insert 'as his second wife.'

p. 293, l. 21, for '1557' read '1557-58.'

p. 294, l. 5, after 'first,' insert 'contract 8 October 1556.'

p. 296, note 12, after 'vol.', insert 'xvi.'

p. 297, l. 6, after '16,' delete to end of paragraph and insert '*Margaret*, married, before 1582, to David Ogilvy of Persie (*Reg. of Deeds*, cccxxi. 141; see also *Laing Charters*, 1053). She died 10 June 1614 (St. Andrews Tests., 25 June 1614).'

p. 297, l. 21, delete 'Crown.'

p. 299, l. 27, after 'Elizabeth,' insert 'eldest daughter (*Forfar Sasines*, ii. 72).'

p. 300, l. 26, delete '20.'

p. 300, l. 27, after 'recorded,' insert '31 May 1619 and.'

p. 301, l. 27, after 'on,' insert '31.'

p. 302, l. 12 from foot, for 'Torlairtoun' read 'Tortairstoun.'

p. 302, l. 6 from foot, before 'Melville,' insert 'Richard.'

p. 303, l. 16, delete 'born,' and insert 'baptized 4 April.'

p. 303, l. 18, delete 'born 1657,' and insert 'baptized 20 October 1654 (Kinneff Reg., *ex inform.* W. A. Macnaughton, M.D.).'

p. 306, l. 17, after 'died,' insert '13 August.'

p. 308, l. 19, after 'peculiar,' insert 'She died 4 November 1692 (*Ibid.*).'

p. 309, l. 8, after 'Elizabeth,' insert 'died 16 April 1755 (Aberdeen *Com. Reg.*, 3 February 1768).'

p. 309, l. 11, after 'Ann,' insert 'died 15 February 1777 (*Annual Register*).'

p. 310, l. 12, after 'first,' insert 'contract 20 and 21 January 1687 (*Part. Reg. Sas. Aberdeen and Kincardine*, xii. 468).'

p. 310, l. 13, after 'secondly,' insert 'contract 8 September 1694 (*Part. Reg. Sas. Aberdeen and Kincardine*, xv. 113; *Gen. Reg. Sas.*, xci. 408).'

p. 310, l. 15, after 'Anne,' insert '(or Agnes)'; after 'married,' insert 'contract 20 and 25 November 1693 (*Part. Reg. Sas. Aberdeen*, xiv. 463).'

p. 310, l. 34, delete '*William*, who both,' and insert '*William Henry*, baptized 13 February 1691 (Canongate Reg.). Both he and his immediate elder brother.'

p. 311, after line 6, insert
  '11. *Janet*, " sister to the present Viscount Arbuthnott," died at Prestonpans, July 1706 (Funeral Entry Lyon Office).'

p. 312, ll. 4 and 5, delete 'in 1710,' and insert '8, and was buried 10 May 1710 in the Abbey there (*Complete Peerage*).'

p. 313, l. 1, for '*prisc fideiœ*,' read '*priscœ fidei*.'

p. 313, l. 32, after 'married,' insert 21 April 1769.'

p. 314, l. 5, after 'married,' insert '27 December 1775.'

p. 314, l. 32, for '1808' read '1805.'

p. 315, l. 6, after 'had,' insert 'with other issue.'

p. 315, l. 17, for 'Thomson' read 'Morison.'

p. 315, l. 21, after '1888,' insert 'married, 21 November 1911, to N. D Beatson Bell, C.I.E.'

p. 315, l. 32, after 'Madras,' insert 'retired 1908. Married Gertrude Forbes, daughter of C. E. F. Nash, Barrister-at-law, with issue.'

p. 315, l. 36, for '1891,' read '1894,' and insert 'John Sinclair, born 1898; Donald Charles, born 1902; Hugh Forbes, born 1906.'

p. 315, l. 37, delete 'Margaret, born 1896,' and insert 'Anne, Eliza Mary. Mary Frances Clementina.'

p. 315, l. 2 from foot, after 'of,' insert '(1) James Vaughan Allen of Inchmartine; and (2).'

p. 315, last line, after '1902,' add 'without issue. She died 1904.'

p. 316, l. 3, after '1903,' insert 'without issue.'

p. 316, l. 24, after '1847,' insert 'He died 1906, unmarried.'

p. 317, l. 5, for 'wyverns' read 'dragons.'

ARGYLL

p. 320, l. 11, delete 'first.'

p. 320, note 2, for '204' read '203*.'

p. 321, note 6, delete 'Robertson's *Index*, 14,' and insert '*Cal. Doc. Scot.*, ii. 200.'

p. 323, l. 25, delete 'His only recorded wife is,' and insert 'He married, first, before 1303, the younger daughter of Andrew Crawford (*Cal. of Docs. Scot.*, ii. 1406); and, secondly.'

p. 324, l. 22, for 'Robert, Lord Erskine' read 'Sir Robert Erskine.'

p. 327, ll. 7 and 6 from foot, delete 'said to have been married, first, to John Macdonald, Earl of Ross,' and insert 'married, first, to John, eldest son of John, Lord of the Isles.'

p. 327, l. 6 from foot, after 'Lennox,' insert 'Her first marriage is referred to in a dispensation for her second, dated 30 March 1373 (Theiner, p. 348, No. 700; cf. vol. v. of this work, p. 340).'

p. 329, l. 11, after '326,' add ' "Sir" John or Ian Campbell was rector of Kilmartin, and as "frater noster" witnessed, on 4 June 1414, a charter of his brother Duncan at "Innyschonelle" Castle (Argyll Charter-Chest).'

p. 329, l. 20, after 'Lochwinnoch,' insert 'Kildalvan, Dunloskin.'

p. 329, after line 29, insert

'6. *Patrick*, a priest, who, as vicar of Kilmartin, and brother to Duncan Cambell, Lord de Cambell and Lord of Lochawe, witnessed a charter at Inchconnell Castle, 20 November 1420 (Argyll Charter-Chest).

7. *Celestine*, who, along with his brother Patrick, witnessed a charter 6 July 1403 (*Ibid.*).'

p. 329, l. 30, for '6' read '8.'

p. 329, after l. 32, insert

'9. *Mor.* On 30 May 1393 there was a mandate to the Bishop of Sodor to grant dispensation for the marriage of Hector Macgilleoin and Mor, daughter of Colin Cambel of Sodor and Argyll dioceses who had married although in the third and fourth degrees of consanguinity (*Reg. Avenion.*, cclxxii. 403).'

p. 329, l. 34, delete 'sometimes called Neil.'

p. 331, l. 5 from foot, after 'secondly,' insert '(under dispensation of date 17 January 1422-23, they being in the second and third degrees of affinity and third and fourth of consanguinity (*Cal. Papal Letters*, vii. 259).'

p. 331, l. 2 from foot, delete 'born c. 1406.'

p. 331, note 9, for '187,' read 'p. clxxvii.' and add 'Marcellina was still alive in February 1419-20, when she and her husband were granted the privilege of a portable altar (*Cal. Papal Letters*, vii. 336).'

p. 332, l. 20, after '1440,' add 'probably before 1439.'

p. 332, ll. 23 and 24, delete 'this last unless she was a natural daughter,' and insert 'of either of these marriages. He probably did marry Mariota of the Isles, daughter of Sir Donald, Lord of the Isles and Ross, as, on 13 February 1419-20, the Pope granted a dispensation for their union, as though they were betrothed they could not marry without his permission (*Ibid.*, vii. 151). She is probably the Mariota of the Isles, who about 1439 married Alexander Sutherland of Dunbeath (*The Thanes of Cawdor*, 16).'

p. 334, l. 2 from foot, for '*Margaret*,' read '*Marion*.'

p. 334, l. 2 from foot, delete 'after 1469,' and insert 'contract dated at

Edinburgh 14 September 1469, when she was twelve years of age ; 1000 merks in tocher, one of the largest of the time (MS. *penes* Editor). They were certainly married before 23 April 1475, when they had a grant of lands in Midlothian from his grandfather, the first Lord Seton.'

p. 334, l. 2 from foot, after 'George,' insert 'second.'

p. 335, ll. 2 and 3, delete 'generally said to have been executed in his father's lifetime, 1490,' and insert 'before 5 March 1478-79, on which date he granted a discharge of part of her tocher to the Earl (Argyll Charter-Chest).'

p. 335, l. 5, 'On 14 September 1469 Helen is styled second daughter (*Harl. MSS.*, 4693, f. 9a, printed in the *Family of Seton*, ii. 845). She was living 23 January 1528-29 (*Complete Peerage*).'

p. 335, l. 6, for 'June' read 'September.'

p. 335, after l. 6 insert

'6. *Margaret*, married to Patrick Buchanan, younger of Buchanan, tocher 600 merks. The marriage-contract, dated at Stirling 22 June 1486, bears that my lord shall pay so much of this sum at Michaelmas "if he may gudlie gett it" (*Third Rep. Hist. MSS. Com.*, 390 ; Fraser's *Lennox Book*, ii. 127, 128 ; Argyll Charter-Chest).'

p. 335, ll. 7, 9, 13, and 16, for '6, 7, 8, 9,' read '7, 8, 9, 10.'

p. 335, l. 18, after 'Maclean,' add 'Either this Catherine or another daughter of the same name, and styled "second dochter," was contracted at Stirling, 6 February 1464-65, to James Haldane, eldest son and heir of John Haldane of Gleneagles, it being provided that if she died he should have any younger daughter of the Earl (Argyll Charter-Chest).'

p. 336, l. 7, after '1511,' insert 'He married, first, Jonet, daughter of James Stewart, Sheriff of Bute, from whom he was divorced (cf. vol. ii. of this work, 288).'

p. 336, l. 7, delete 'an only child,' and insert 'a son *John*, who, as son and heir of the deceased Archibald Campbell of Skipinche, had in 1542 (*Reg. Sec. Sig.*, xvi. f. 33) an order from the King under the Privy Seal for the restoration of his father's property. His superior alleged that he had no title to the lands because his father had not died at the faith and peace of the King inasmuch as being in ward in the Castle of Edinburgh he broke out of it and rendered null an order of the King for his enlargement. John married Marion Montgomery, daughter of Hugh Montgomery of Hazelhead, widow of Thomas Crawford of Auchinames and of William, second Lord Sempill (cf. vol. vii. of this work, 535). Archibald Campbell had also.'

p. 336, l. 28, for 'fourth' read 'fifth.'

p. 336, l. 32, after 'John' insert 'Stewart.'

p. 336, l. 33, after 'died,' insert 'before.'

p. 336, l. 35, after 'married,' insert 'before 10 November 1522 (when she is called Moir).'

p. 336, l. 35, delete 'of that Ilk,' and insert 'of Inveryne (*ex inform.* John Macgregor, W.S.).'

p. 337, delete ll. 10 and 11, and accompanying note, and insert 'This Earl, or possibly his father, had another daughter, married to Iain "Brayach" M'Iain of Ardnamurchan, with issue. His eventual heiress, Mariota M'Iain, in 1538 resigned her lands in favour of Archibald, fourth Earl of Argyll, and to this deed her seal, showing the Campbell arms of her mother impaled with those of Ardnamurchan, is appended (Argyll Charter-Chest).'

'He also had two other daughters, *Katherine* and *Elizabeth*, as on 27 March 1501 a marriage-contract was entered into at Edinburgh between George, Earl of Huntly, and Alexander, Lord Gordon, on the one part, and Archibald, Earl of Argyll, on the other, whereby Alexander's son and apparent heir George Gordon (whose existence has been previously unknown) was to marry which of the two best pleased him, whilst Colin, third Earl, was to marry either Janet or Margaret Gordon. He did marry the former, but George Gordon must have died young, and his projected marriage did not take place (Argyll Charter-Chest).'

p. 337, last line, delete 'towards the end of,' and insert '9 October (Chronicle of Fortingall).'

p. 338, l. 21, after 'first,' insert 'James Stewart, Sheriff of Bute, but her marriage must have been annulled (*Acts and Decreets*, vi. 474). She was married, secondly.'

p. 338, l. 24, 'after 'Glen,' delete 'secondly,' and insert 'He died in 1565, and she married, thirdly.'

p. 338, l. 26, after 'captivity' insert 'Her legitimacy is doubtful; she is called "base sister" to the Earl of Argyll (*State Papers, Ireland*, 296).'

p. 340. l. 9, after 'Maclean,' insert 'contract dated 12 March 15— -6, year illegible, but perhaps 1545-46; in it her father is styled Hector Maclean of Doward, and it appears she married the Earl to appease the great feud between her house and his (Argyll Charter-Chest).'

p. 340, l. 10, after 'her,' insert 'She is stated to have married, secondly, Callough O'Donell, Lord of Tyrconnel, and to have been taken prisoner with him by John O'Neill prior to 30 May 1561 (*Carew State Papers*, 1515-74, p. 314; *Calendar of State Papers, Ireland*, 172; cf. also *Irish Statutes*, i. 323, 324; *Carew Papers*, fifth series, 204, 209). To O'Neill she bore two sons (*Misc.* Maitland Club, pt. I.), and her kinsmen, the Macleans, endeavoured to get her released (*State Papers, Ireland*, 29 September 1562). After O'Neill's death she returned to Scotland, married John Stewart of Appin (writ in Reg. Ho., Edinburgh, No. 2352, where she is styled Katherine M'Lane, Countess of Argyll), and died not many years prior to 1595.'

p. 340, l. 13, after '1575,' insert 'The Earl had another natural son, *John*, who was Provost of the Collegiate Church of Kilmun. In a charter of 14 November 1566 the fifth Earl calls him his brother (Argyll Charter-Chest); a third natural son, *Archibald*, was the progenitor of the Glendaruel family.'

p. 342, l. 30, for '5 July,' read '1 July (*Eleventh Rep. Hist. MSS. Com.*,

Duke of Hamilton's MS., App. vi. 54), and after '1553,' insert 'bearing to be in fulfilment of another contract of 10 December 1538, when both parties must have been infants (Moray Writs).'

p. 343, l. 1, after 'dying,' insert '7 January 1587-88 (Edin. Tests., 26 March 1588).'

p. 343, l. 5, after 'Glencairn,' delete ' but had no issue by her,' and insert 'and had a son, who died at birth (30 June 1574, *Cal. of Scottish Papers*, v. 13).'

p. 343, l. 10, delete from '1. *John*, to end of sentence (see corrigenda on p. 340).'

p. 343, l. 12, for '2' read '1.'

p. 343, l. 20, after 'Earl,' insert 'He was aged fifteen in 1573, when he was a hostage in England. On 18 June 1592 he granted a precept at Stirling, in which he is styled Lord of Craignish, and his mother's name Beatrix Campbell is mentioned (Argyll Charter-Chest; *Acts and Decreets*, cxvii. 346).'

p. 343, ll. 21 and 24, for '3' and '4,' read '2' and '3.'

p. 343, l. 31, for 'a daughter,' read 'two daughters, *Jean* (styled sister's daughter of Colin, Earl of Argyll) and.'

p. 344, l. 6, for '5' read '4'; after 'will,' insert 'She was married, before 6 June 1590, to Iain Macfarlane, fiar of Arrochar, who then granted a discharge to the seventh Earl for the complete tocher payment of £500 (Argyll Charter-Chest).'

p. 345, l. 28, after 'age,' insert 'They had a previous contract 21 February 1547-48 (*Acta Dom. Conc. et Sess.*, xxvi. 35).'

p. 345, l. 28, after 'secondly,' insert 'between May 1571 and 26 February 1571-72 (*Complete Peerage*).'

p. 345, last line, after 'who,' insert 'chose curators 5 July 1592, the next-of-kin on father's side being John, Bishop of the Isles, and Archibald Campbell of Lochnell, and on mother's side George, Earl Marischal, and Robert, Lord Altrie (*Acts and Decreets*, cxxxvii. 349). He.'

p. 346, after l. 5 insert
'4. *Jean* (*Acts and Decreets*, lxxi. 95).'

p. 349, l. 4, after 'faith,' insert note, ' Alexander Craig wrote the following lines on the Earl becoming a Roman Catholic :—

    "Now Earl of Guile and Lord Forlorn then goes,
    Quitting the Prince to serve his foreign foes,
    No faith in plaids, no trust in Highland trews,
    Cameleon-like they change to many hues."
(*Staggering State*).'

p. 349, l. 14, after '1638,' add, 'Will dated 9 October, proved 29 November 1638 (Somerset House Wills, *ex inform.* Hon. Vicary Gibbs).'

p. 349, l. 15, delete 'before October 1594,' and insert '24 July 1592.'

p. 349, l. 24, for '1659,' read '1649.'

p. 349, l. 25, delete ' in 1611,' and insert ' Contract 24, 25, and 27 May 1611 (*Reg. of Deeds*, cci. 230).'

p. 349, l. 29, after 'first,' insert 'contract dated 1624 (*Reg. Mag. Sig.*, as in note).'

p. 349, l. 29, for 'Robert,' read 'John.'

p. 349, l. 32, for 'September,' read 'February (Edinburgh Marriage Reg.).'

p. 349, note 4, delete '*The Complete Peerage* gives the date of the marriage as 1628.'

p. 349, last line, insert bracket after '1617.'

p. 350, l. 8, after 'had,' insert 'by her, who died 12 January 1635.'

p. 350, l. 9, delete 'born 1611.'

p. 350, l. 9, after 'Chapel Royal,' insert '25 September 1610 (*Reg. of Chapel Royal*).'

p. 350, l. 11, the reference number [3] should be inserted after 'sponsors,' and deleted from the next line.

p. 350, note 6, delete '*Ibid.*', and insert 'Check-book *ut sup.*'

p. 350, ll. 15, 16, delete 'after 21 September 1644,' and insert 'in France about 15 September 1645 (*Complete Peerage*).'

p. 350, l. 17, delete 'and 9'; delete from 'and,' down to end of paragraph and relative notes, and insert 'born at Ashley House, Waltham, Surrey, 14 November 1611, died young (List of Children of seventh Earl by his second wife, from a document in his own handwriting).'

p. 350, after l. 22, insert

'9 and 10. *Frederick* and *Charles*, evidently the twins christened at Somerset House, 31 December 1616, for whom Queen Anne and Prince Charles stood sponsors (List., *ut sup.*). Charles died young. Frederick may have been the son who died 1636, having been " in warrs."

11. *Charles* (*secundus*), born at Stirling about 1618; died before 1636 (List, *ut sup.*).

12. *Eugene*, born in the winter of 1619 at Brussels; died before 1636.

13. *Charles* (*tertius*), born in St. Martin's Lane, London, about 1629, and died young before 1636.'

p. 350, l. 23, for '10' read '14.'

p. 350, l. 23, after '*Mary*,' insert 'born in Brussels about 1622 (List, *ut sup.*).'

p. 350, l. 25, for '11' read '15.'

p. 350, l. 28, after '1694,' insert 'as an Augustinian Canoness, under the name of Isabelle Claire d'Arguille. She is not mentioned in her father's list of his children.'

p. 350, l. 29, for '12' read '16.'

p. 350, l. 29, after 'Victoria,' insert 'born at Brussels 1627 (List, *ut sup.*). "A very fine lady," she.'

p. 350, l. 31, after 'sister,' insert 'She is mentioned as "dead lately" in a letter of 9 August 1694 (*Letters from James, Earl of Perth*, Camden Society, 40).'

p. 350, l. 32, for '13' read '17.'

p. 350, l. 32, after '*Barbara*,' insert 'born at Brussels about 1624.'

p. 350, l. 33, after 'Brussels,' insert 'afterwards in a nunnery at

Louvain, where she was known in religion as Barbara Meliora Campbell.'

p. 350, l. 33, after 'yearly,' insert 'She died before 9 August 1694 (Letter, *ut cit.*).'

p. 350, l. 34, for '14' read '18.'

p. 350, l. 34, delete '1619,' and insert 'at Fisher's Folly in S. Botolph's, Bishopsgate, and christened 6 December 1614.'

p. 350, after l. 37 insert—

'The following additional daughters are also mentioned in their father's list

19. *Elizabeth*, born at Brussels 1621.

20. *Constance*, born at Brussels about 1625 or 1626. Became a Benedictine nun as Anne Constance d'Arguille.

21. A daughter, born at Leith in Scotland, who died unbaptized, 1617.'

p. 351, after l. 3, insert 'The Earl had also a natural daughter Anna, married, first, as his second wife, to Sir Donald Campbell, Baronet, of Ardnamurchan, who died 1651 ; and, secondly, in or before 1652, to Alexander Campbell of Inverliver; both are named in a bond dated 1652 (Argyll Charter-Chest).'

p. 351, l. 10, after '1623,' insert 'He chose curators 27 March 1622, the next-of-kin on the father's side being Colin Campbell of Lundie, Alexander Campbell of Lochenzell, Colin Campbell of Kirktowchmachill, and Sir John Campbell of Calder, on mother's side William, Earl of Morton, and Sir Archibald Douglas of Killour (*Acts and Decreets*, ccliv. 270).'

p. 360, l. 20, delete 'who,' and insert 'eldest, not second son, was born at Roseneath, 14 December 1668, and (see a curious attestation to his having been baptized, a fact which was doubted, *Scottish Antiquary*, i. 13).'

p. 360, l. 23, after 'married,' insert 'as his second wife (contract 11 April 1694).'

p. 360, l. 25, after '1744,' insert 'leaving eight sons and seven daughters.'

p. 360, l. 29, after '*Jean*,' add 'married in 1700 to George Maxwell of Dalswinton, and had issue (*Decreets* (Mackenzie), 21 January 1747 ; Fraser's *Maxwells of Pollok*. i. 453).'

p. 361, l. 1, after 'marriage,' read 'Admitted advocate in 1704.'

p. 361, l. 7, after 'unmarried,' delete 'probably before 1660,' insert 'and died insane at Inveraray after 29 January 1712, at a great age. She is said to have fallen into a melancholy on account of King Charles II. having refused to marry her. She was kept at Dunoon Castle.'

p. 361, l. 17, delete 'before 19 October 1663,' and relative note, and insert 'at Edinburgh 1691, unmarried (*ex inform*. Niall D. Campbell, Esq.).'

p. 366, l. 2 from foot, after 'Earl,' insert 'was contracted in his youth, about 1641 or 1642, to Lady Ann Hamilton, daughter of James, first Duke of Hamilton, and afterwards Duchess, with a tocher of 100,000 merks; but the marriage did not take place (*Eleventh Rep. Hist. MSS. Com.*, App. vi. 55). He.'

p. 367, l. 1, delete 'May 1668,' and insert 'in 1706, aged eighty-five (Willcock's *Scots Earl*).'

p. 368 l. 3, after 'outrage,' insert 'Miss Wharton ultimately married Colonel Brierly, who commanded a regiment of horse in the service of William III. (*Patrician*, v. 276).'

p. 368, ll. 9 and 10, delete 'at least one son.'

p. 368, l. 10, after '*Charles*,' insert 'born 20 March 1703 (Canongate Reg.).'

p. 368, l. 11, after '1718,' insert '*John*, born 1 February 1705 (*Ibid.*).'

p. 368, l. 11, for 'two' read 'three.'

p. 368, l. 12 after '*Mary*,' insert 'born 25 October 1695.'

p. 368, l. 14, after 'Saltoun,' add 'and *Anna* (*secunda*), born 7 August 1700 (*Ibid.*).'

p. 368, l. 15, after '1657,' add 'Probably the Lady Mary Campbell, "daughter of Orgyel," buried in Greyfriars, Edinburgh, 12 January 1695 (Greyfriars Reg.).'

p. 368, after l. 21, insert

'8. *Margaret*, baptized 12 January 1692 (Canongate Reg.).'

p. 368, l. 28, after 'Argyll,' insert 'baptized 25 July 1658 (*Ibid.*).'

p. 370, l. 2, after '1703,' insert 'He left his estate of Charton, near North Shields, to his mistress, Mrs. Alison. The Duchess and her son disputed the settlement (see Maidment's *Scottish Elegiac Verses*, Edinburgh, 1842; also *Argyll Papers*, privately printed; and the privately printed part of Maidment's *Scottish Pasquils*).'

p. 370, l. 6, after 'married,' insert '12.'

p. 370, l. 14, after 'Anne,' insert 'born 12 January 1692 (Canongate Reg.).

p. 370, l. 21, delete paragraph, and insert

'4. *Margaret*, born 2 June 1690 (Canongate Reg.).'

5. *Katherine*, baptized 11 February 1697. Lady Katherine Campbell, daughter of John (*sic*), Earl of Argyll, was buried in Petersham, Surrey, 25 January 1699-1700 (*ex inform.* Keith W. Murray, Esq.).'

p. 371, l. 4, for 'Mackay' read 'Macky.'

p. 377, l. 1, after '*Caroline*,' insert 'born 7 November 1717.'

p. 377, l. 7, for 'Marquess of Townshend' read 'Marquess Townshend.'

p. 380, l. 26, 'after 'married,' insert 'Licence 19 January 1713.

p. 380, l. 26, delete 'the daughter of Mr.' and insert 'Anne, daughter of Major Walter.'

p. 381, l. 12, for 'Charles' read 'Archibald.'

p. 382, l. 6, for 'Philip' read 'Edward.'

p. 382, ll. 24 and 25, delete 'and had issue, and,' and insert 'who.'

p. 382, l. 25, after '1756,' add 'His widow died at Bath 3 December 1783.'

p. 382, l. 3 from foot, after 'issue,' add 'Jean raised an action of declarator of marriage in 1747 and got decree. A Margaret Cochrane, widow of Lewis Kennedy, Collector of Customs at Irvine, alleged marriage with Captain John at the seat of Lord Dundonald at Paisley, 3 July 1724; the claim, however, failed. Captain John and his wife had four children, the first, Elizabeth, being born 10 October 1726; the youngest, Jean, born 19 November 1729, was the only one alive at the time of raising the process (*Consistorial Processes*, Scot. Rec. Soc., No. 372).'

p. 382, l. 2 from foot, after '*Primrose*,' insert 'born 1710.'

p. 383, l. 2, after 'issue,' add 'She had a half-witted grandson who poisoned her porridge, but she did not eat it, and her cousin, Mrs. Elphinstone, took it instead and died, (*ex inform*. Lady Constance Russell).'

p. 384, last line, delete 'divorced.'

p. 385, l. 2, after '1760,' insert 'and from whom she obtained a judicial separation on account of cruelty.'

p. 385, l. 3, for '24 July' read '25 June.'

p. 385, l. 4, after '1807,' insert 'aged about seventy (Miss Berry's *Journal*, ii. 229; Lady Constance Russell's *Three Generations of Fascinating Women*). Miss Berry says she was burned to ashes in the only room in the house that was burned. It is supposed she took a fit (both her sisters died in fits) and fell with her head on the candle.'

p. 385, ll. 5 and 7, '*Mary* and *Jane* are both said to have been illegitimate (*ex inform*. John Ferrier, Esq.).'

p. 385, l. 14, after '1773,' insert 'but did not go out till 1775 (*ex inform*. L. Campbell Johnstone, Esq.).'

p. 385, l. 27, for '*Anne*' read '*Louisa* (*ex inform*. L. Campbell Johnston, Esq.).'

p. 386, l. 3, for 'George' read 'John.'

p. 386, l. 5, delete 'died without issue,' and insert 'was a spendthrift, and shot himself at the Bedford Arms, Covent Garden, 15 August.'

p. 386, l. 8, after 'fortune,' insert 'She died, 28 May 1828, at Upper Brook Street, London. Lady Caroline died 17 January 1803, aged eighty-two.'

p. 387, l. 15, for '3 March' read 'Saturday, 3 February (*Notes and Queries*, 10th ser. iv. 384).'

p. 387, l. 19, after 'she,' insert 'born 1733, at Hemingford Gray, co. Huntingdon.'

p. 387, l. 24, for '20' read '21' (Miss Berry's *Journal*, i. 269).'

p. 387, l. 31, after 'married,' insert 'without her parents' consent.'

p. 387, line 35, after '*Maria*,' add note, 'For an account of her under the title of A Bygone Beauty, see Lady Constance Russell's *Three Generations of Fascinating Women*. Her birth is there given as on 28 January 1775. There is a portrait of her by Tischbein at Swallowfield; another by Anna Tonelli, and a drawing of her and her husband by Edridge. She was also painted by Hoppner and by Alexander Blackley.'

p. 388, line 3, for '17 March' read '23 March,' and add note, Miss Berry (*Journal*, iii. 157), who was there, says the marriage took place at Lord Burghersh's house in Florence, he being the English minister there.'

p. 388, l. 26, after 'offspring,' add note, 'A natural daughter, Catherine Black Campbell, was born April 1806. She was engaged successively to the Duke of Newcastle and the Duke of Marlborough, but married neither, and died in obscurity and poverty in a lodging house in Brompton Row about 1862 (See Lady Constance Russell's *Three Generations of Fascinating Women*).'

p. 391, l. 1, for 'Assory' read 'Ascog.'

p. 391, l. 20, after '1895,' add 'Lady Colin Campbell died in London 2 November 1911.'

p. 391, line 28, after '1854,' add 'died at Edinburgh 6 July 1910.'

p. 392, l. 22, for 'President of the Council for India,' read 'Secretary of State for India.'

ARRAN

p. 397, l. 5, after 'Societie,' insert '"A lewd, fascinating woman." She died "miserablie" in September 1595 (*Wardlaw MS.*, Scot. Hist. Soc., p. 221).'

p. 397, last line, after '*Elizabeth*,' add 'married, contract 9 December 1602, to Duncan Bayne of Tulloch (*Reg. of Deeds*, clxxxvii. 35).'

p. 397, after last line, add

'5. *Marie* (*P. C. Reg.*, 2nd ser. iv. 403), married to Mr. John Finlayson of Killeith (*Reg. of Deeds*, cccvi. 293).'

p. 398, for 'Fife' read 'Galloway.'

ASTON OF FORFAR

p. 401, l. 1, for '1651,' insert '1615.'

p. 402, l. 12 from foot, after 'had,' insert 'issue' and remove ':—'

p. 403, l. 21, after '1763,' insert 'She died 11 August 1764.'

p. 404, l. 14 from foot, after 'died,' insert '24 August.'

p. 411, l. 29, after 'secondly,' insert 'apparently after 1680.'

p. 412, l. 16, after 'married,' insert 'about 1 October 1698 (*Complete Peerage*).'

p. 413, l. 22, for 'October,' read '9 November.'

CELTIC EARLS OF ATHOLL

p. 415, ll. 14 and 20, delete 'Norwegian,' and insert 'Icelandic

p. 416, l. 20, Same correction.

p. 419, l. 9 of notes, delete 'and successor.'

p. 422, l. 30, after 'house,' insert 'He was buried in the graveyard of the Franciscans at Haddington (*Chron. de Lanercost*).'

p. 423, l. 22, after 'Ferneleth,' insert note, 'In the original charter among the Cupar Abbey writs in possession of the Earl of Moray, the Countess's name is written Forueleth, which is the Gaelic Forbhflaith, "perfect princess" (*ex inform.*, W. J. Watson, LL.D., Rector, High School, Edinburgh). Another Forveleth, "filia Keraldi," occurs about 1240 (*Reg. Episc. Glasg.*, No. 177).'

p. 425, l. 13, for 'quarelled' read 'quarrelled.'

p. 425, l. 4 from foot, after 'Chilham,' delete 'who,' and insert 'the granddaughter of Richard Fitzroy. (See *corrigenda*, p. 168, line 2, *supra*.) She died 18 March 1292, and was buried, 24 March, in the church of Canterbury, near the altar of St. Edward (*Hist. Works*, *Gervase of Canterbury*, ii. 300). She.'

p. 429, l. 8, after 'manors,' insert 'On 16 November 1316 he had a pardon as David, Earl of Asceles (*Patent Rolls* [1313-17], 567).'

p. 429, l. 22, delete 'before,' and insert 'between 8 February and.'

p. 430, l. 18, after 'Atholl,' insert note, 'See *Archæologia Æliana*, 3rd ser., vol. iii.'

p. 433, last l., insert after or, 'but the quartering for Atholl in the more modern arms is given as Paly of six or and sable.'

CAMPBELL, EARL OF ATHOLL

p. 435, last line, after 'Atholl,' add 'Moray died 17 October 1346, and Joanna married, fourthly, dispensation dated 5 Id. November 1347, as his second wife, William, Earl of Sutherland (*See that title* and *Cal. of Papal Reg. Letters*, vol. iii.).'

p. 435, at end of note 1, add 'Cf. also another copy recorded in *Reg. of Deeds* (Durie's Div.), 103, 9 Aug. 1704.'

STEWART, EARL OF ATHOLL

p. 436, ll. 12, 13, 14, 15, and 16, delete from 'The' down to 'Crown,' and insert
'On 31 May 1367 King David II. granted a charter of the earldom to Robert's son, John Stewart of Kyle (afterwards King Robert III.), and Annabella, his wife, on the resignation of his father (*Exch. Rolls*, iv. p. clxx, where 3d is a misprint for 31st). He is called Earl of Atholl in a charter by Robert II. to Cupar Abbey (*Reg. Avenion.* ccix. 377). The Earldom remained in his hands.'

p. 437, l. 14, delete 'May 1409,' and insert '8 June 1404,' adding note—
'He is described on the last-mentioned date as Walter Stewart, Earl of Atholl and Caithness, in a safe-conduct by the English King (Rymer's *Fœdera*, viii. 361 ; *Cal. Doc. Scot.*, iv. No. 656).'

p. 438, l. 23, after 'known,' delete 'but,' and insert, 'though it must have been before 1 August 1404, when he had a dispensation to marry Margaret (or Elizabeth) Grahame, daughter of Sir William Grahame of Kincardine (cf. vol. vi. 218), though this marriage did not take place, and.'

p. 438, l. 24, for 'her' read 'his wife's.'

p. 442, l. 6, after 'Caithness' read 'She died 21 March 1518, and was buried with him (*Complete Peerage*).'

p. 442, l. 12, delete 'before 1482,' and insert 'contract dated 14 October 1474 (Menzies Charter-Chest ; cf. *Herald and Genealogist*, vi. 596).'

p. 442, l. 18, after 'consanguinity⁶,' add 'She was married again (contract

9 December 1529) to Ninian, third Lord Ross (vol. vi. 252; cf. *Acta Dominorum Concilii*, xli. f. 25).'

p. 443, l. 14, after 'Ruthven,' add 'and, possibly fifthly, James, son of (Gilbert?) Grey of Foulis, but the only authority for this is Sir Robert Gordon in his *Genealogy of the Earls of Sutherland*, 106.'

p. 443, l. 22, for 'Colin' read 'Kenneth.'

p. 443, l. 31, after 'first,' insert 'before December 1533 (*Fourth Rep. Hist. MSS. Com.*, 536).'

p. 443, l. 32, after 'Grizel,' delete 'daughter,' and insert 'granddaughter and senior heir of line (*ex inform*. Rev. John Ferguson of Aberdalgie; Rattray Writs in Dupplin Charter-Chest).'

p. 443, note 2, 'The note in the Sutherland Book here referred to is wrong. It does not refer to the deed mentioned in the text of that volume, and the authority there quoted should be the seventh, not the eighth, Report of the *Hist. MSS. Com*. In that Report (pp. 711 and 713) there are two retours showing that Janet Campbell was wife of John Stewart, second Earl of Atholl.'

p. 444, l. 4, for '1536' read '1556.'

p. 444, l. 13, after 'Redhall,' insert as note, 'The marriage must have taken place before January 1545-46. Cf. Letter by Countess of Atholl 14th January 1545-46 (Gen. Reg. Ho. See also *Comm. Decreets*, iii. 347).'

p. 445, l. 9, after 'Erskine,' insert 'She was living 15 August 1584 (*Complete Peerage*).'

p. 445, l. 15, after 'first,' insert 'contract 24 December 1567; for 'sixth' read 'fifth.'

p. 445, l. 24, delete 'about,' and insert 'in December.'

p. 445, l. 24, after '1581,' insert '(contract registered 18 January 1583).'

p. 446, l. 5, for 'James' read 'John.'

p. 446, l. 6, delete 'and had issue,' and insert 'She married, thirdly, James Stewart, eldest son of James, Master of Buchan, son of John, third Earl of Buchan. By her first husband she had issue.'

p. 446, l. 17, after 'Standenflat,' insert 'She died 19 July 1623.'

p. 446, l. 20, for 'first,' read 'second.'

p. 446, note 5, for '950' read '280.'

p. 447, l. 15, for 'IV.' read 'VI.'

p. 447, l. 20, after 'Leslie,' insert reference number [3] and semicolon.'

p. 447, l. 21, delete reference number [3].

p. 447, l. 23, for '1580' read '1582.'

MURRAY, DUKE OF ATHOLL

p. 454, l. 2 of notes, for '1284' read '1319-33.'

p. 462, l. 29, for '1562' read '1562-63.'

p. 462, l. 31, after 'him,' insert 'and was still alive on 17 December 1577' (James Harlaw's Protocol Book, Gen. Reg. Ho., f. 223).'

p. 462, l. 34, for '1596' read '1596-97.'

p. 462, last l., for '1565' read '1565-66.'

p. **463**, l. 6, after '1599,' add 'He married, contract 20 and 22 January 1600, Agnes, daughter of Robert Bruce of Blairhall (*Reg. of Deeds*, lxxxiv. 354).'

p. **466**, ll. 22 and 23, delete 'He was living 28 May 1618,' and insert 'He was buried in March 1621 (Canongate Reg.), having married Katherine Preston (*Reg. of Deeds*, cxlii. 126).'

p. **467**, l. 4, delete 'Sir.'

p. **467**, last l., after 'married,' insert 'first.'

p. **468**, l. 3, after 'London,' add 'She married, secondly, Col. Patrick Robertson of Sir Patrick Livingstone's Regiment of Dragoons before 24 February 1694 (*Reg. of Deeds*, Mackenzie, lxxiv., 29 June 1694).'

p. **468**, after line 8, insert

'ii. *John*, baptized 31 March 1633 (St. Andrews Reg.).

'iii. *Elizabeth*, married to Simon Fraser of Inverallochy, with issue a son, Simon, baptized 3 May 1639 (*Wardlaw MS.*, Scot. Hist. Soc., p. 512).'

p. **468**, l. 9, for 'ii.' read 'iv.'

p. **469**, l. 29, after 'issue,' insert 'besides a son James, baptized 5 July 1580 (Perth Reg.), but who must have died young.'

p. **469**, note 12, add to note, 'The Dunfermline Parish Register, 4 February 1584-85, gives her name as Margaret, not Catherine.'

p. **470**, l. 8, after 'son,' insert 'born at Dunfermline 14 February 1584-85 (Dunfermline Par. Reg.).'

p. **470**, l. 26, for '*Catherine*,' read '*Annabella* (*Inverness Sas., Secretary's Reg.*, i. 139)'

p. **470**, l. 28, after 'married,' insert 'contract 27 January and 9 February 1607 (*Reg. of Deeds*, ccvi. 340).'

p. **471**, l. 21, delete 'before 30 January 1628.'

p. **471**, l. 22, delete 'in the Chapel of Tullibardine,' and insert 'at St. Margaret's, Westminster, 30 July 1627.'

p. **472**, after line 3, insert

'2. *Mungo*, baptized 23 February 1617 (Canongate Reg.).'

p. **472**, l. 4, for '2' read '3.'

p. **480**, l. 4, after 'time,' insert note, 'For a quaint medical certificate see Fraser's *Melville Book*, ii. 227.'

p. **480**, l. 16, The date of the Duke's death is given as 12 November in Maidment's *Scottish Elegiac Verses*.

p. **480**, l. 21, According to the last-mentioned authority the Duchess died 9 January.

p. **480**, l. 30, *Scot. Eleg. Verses* gives 1 September as the date of Tullibardine's death at Mons.'

p. **487**, l. 11, for 'fourth' read 'third.'

p. **491**, l. 9 from foot, delete '10 November 1786.'

p. **493**, l. 5, after '1789,' delete 'and,' and insert 'Both Lord William and his wife were buried in St. George's Cemetery, Tyburn (*Notes and Queries*, 10th ser., xi. 217, quoting F. A. Crisp's *Visitations*, vol. xv.).'

p. **493**, l. 6, after '1827,' insert 'he.'

p. **494**, 1. 30, for '8' read '4.'

p. **495**, 1. 15, for 'EARL OF STRANGE' read 'EARL STRANGE.

p. **499**, 1. 24, for 'uncle' read 'granduncle.'

p. **500**, 1. 7 from foot, delete '*Stewart.*'

p. **501**, 1. 8, delete '*Stewart.*'

BADENOCH

p. **503**, delete pp. 503, 504, and down to 'Kilbride' on 1. 22 of p. 505, and insert

'The traditional origin of the Comyns given by Sir Robert Douglas and other writers, and followed in this article, seems open to serious question. All that can safely be said is probably this :—the first of the family known in Scotland was William the Chancellor. He had three nephews, sons of a brother whose name is uncertain :—

'1. *William*, killed *circâ* 1144.

'2. *Richard*, who acquired the castle and honour of Northallerton as part of the settlement of his uncle's claims to the Bishopric of Durham.

'3. *Walter.*

'This Richard and his wife Hextilda had certainly four sons, John, William, Odinell, and Simon (as in text), and probably a fifth son David, and from them the various Scots families of the name appear to be descended.'

p. **505**, after 1. 22, insert

'6. *Idonea*, married to Adam FitzGilbert, with issue a daughter *Christian* (*Reg. Hon. de Morton*, ii. 4; *Origines Parochiales*, i. 189).'

p. **507**, after 1. 20 insert

'4. *Alexander*, named in two charters of his brother John in 1278 (*Chart. of Inchaffray*, pp. 100, 101, 291). He was taken prisoner at Dunbar, and afterwards liberated on mainprise to serve King Edward beyond seas (*Cal. of Docs. Scot.*, ii. 177).

'5. *Robert*, also taken and liberated as above (*Ibid.*). Slain at Dumfries along with his nephew the Red Cumyn (*Ibid.*, ii. 1747)'

p. **508**, note 7, for 'lxvi.' read 'lvi.'

BALCARRES

p. **512**, 1. 9 from foot, for '23 February 1574' read '21 October 1572.'

p. **512**, 11. 3 and 2 from foot, delete 'succeeded to the earldom,' and insert 'was created Earl.'

p. **513**, after 1. 3, insert

'8. *Jonet* (natural daughter), married, first (contract 13 March 1562-63), to William, son of George Marshall of Auchnacree, and secondly, before 22 August 1594, to David Jameson (*Reg. of Deeds*, ccxxviii. 458).'

p. **513**, 1. 21, after 'dated,' insert '1 and 2 (*Reg. of Deeds*, xi. 384).'

p. 514, l. 6, for 'May' read 'March (*Reg. Mag. Sig.*, 19 March 1619).'

p. 515,, after l. 3, insert

'2. *Margaret*, daughter of David Lindsay of Edzell, was married to Sir James Keith of Benholm, contract 13, 21, and 22 February 1618 (*Reg. of Deeds*, cccxxxvi. 394).'

p. 517, last line, after '1639' add 'He married Margaret Elphinstone (Stirling Tests., 15 November 1625), without issue. She died in July 1625, within a year after her marriage, and names a brother Michael and a sister Marie in her will.'

p. 518, l. 11, after *Margaret*, insert 'second daughter (Moray Writs, vol. iv. No. 52.

p. 519, l. 1, delete 'before 31 January 1642,' and insert 'in March 1642.

p. 519, l. 17, delete '11 June,' and insert '10 January (Lamont's *Diary*).'

p. 519, l. 22, delete reference number [4], and insert it after 1643 on next line.

p. 520, l. 3 from foot, after '1689,' add 'She died in the Canongate, Edinburgh, and was buried at Balcarres in March 1698 (Funeral Entry, Lyon Office).'

p. 521, l. 2, delete 'in,' and insert '15 October.'

p. 521, l. 7, delete reference number [1], and insert it after Kilconquhar, on line 5.

p. 522, l. 6 from foot, after 'Wigtown,' insert 'She was divorced by him 7 December 1708 (*Consistorial Processes*, Scot. Record Soc., No. 162).'

p. 523, l. 4 from foot, delete 'who,' and insert 'She was forty years his junior, and rejected his offer at first, whereupon he took to his bed, and became so ill that his life was despaired of. He made his will, by which he left half his estate to Miss Dalrymple, and she, hearing of this, relented, and married him. She.'

p. 528, l. 3 from foot, after 'Hope,' insert, 'As a young woman, she was admired by Mr. Atkinson, a great army contractor, and a supporter of Pitt. He died, however, in 1785, leaving her a considerable portion of his fortune (Wraxall's *Posthumous Memoirs*, i. 120).'

p. 528, line 2 from foot, after '*Margaret*,' insert '*Janet*' (Kilconquhar Reg.

p. 529, l. 1, after 'banker,' insert 'son of George Fordyce, Provost of Aberdeen, who died at Hammersmith, 8 September 1789, aged sixty.'

p. 529, l. 4, after 'issue,' add, 'Burges was an old lover of Lady Margaret, but monetary difficulties prevented their union, and she married Fordyce, a wealthy but rather elderly person, whereupon her sister Ann wrote her well-known ballad of "Auld Robin Gray," "Jamie," it is said, being James Bland Burges. The latter married, first, Elizabeth, daughter of Edward, first Viscount Wentworth, 19 June 1777. She died 25 January 1779, and he married, secondly, Anne Montoline, daughter of Baron de St. Hyppolite. He survived her, and then, Lady Margaret's first husband being dead, he married his first love, as stated in the text. . . . Fordyce, her first husband, was a reckless speculator, and ruined many other people besides himself. His firm of Neall, James, Fordyce & Downe failed in June 1772.'

p. 529, l. 21, after 'sable,' insert 'all.'

BALFOUR OF BURLEIGH

p. 531, l. 25, after 'death,' add 'but it was previous to February 1499-1500 (*Acta Dom. Conc.*, ix. 101).'

p. 531, l. 27, after 'Treasurer,' insert 'He, or possibly his son Michael, also married, in 1476, Elizabeth, daughter of Douglas of Lochleven (*Harl. MS.*, 6433).'

p. 532, l. 20, delete 'probably other issue,' and insert 'at least another son, Robert (*Acta Dom. Conc. et Sess.*, i. 36).'

p. 532, l. 31, after 'Forrester,' insert '(who survived him, and was married, secondly, to James Pringle of the Tynnes) (*Acta Dom. Conc. et Sess.*, i. 36).'

p. 533, l. 22, after 'her,' insert '(who survived him, and was married, secondly, to Patrick Kinninmont of Craighall, contract 3 July 1579) (*Reg. of Deeds*, xvii. 263).'

p. 533, l. 24, for 'Michael' read 'Andrew (*Reg. of Deeds*, v. 515).'

p. 533, l. 25, after 'Montquhanny,' insert as note, 'From a writ dated 24 August 1568, it clearly appears that Andrew Balfour of Montquhanny was father of *Michael* (then deceased), *Gilbert* of Westray, *Sir James* of Pittendreich, *George*, Prior of Charterhouse, *John, Andrew, Robert,* and *David* Balfours (*Reg. Acts and Decreets*, xlii. f. 331).'

p. 536, l. 19, after 'secondly,' insert 'in the Old Kirk of Aberdeen, June 1604.'

p. 536, l. 22, after '1597; [8]' insert 'she also obtained a divorce from her second husband, Balfour, 24 March 1620 (*Edin. Com. Decreets*).'

p. 536, l. 23, for 'Blaney' read 'Blayney.'

p. 536, l. 24, after 'daughters,' add 'one of whom, *Anne*, married Archibald Hamilton of Ballygelly, etc., ancestor of the Hamiltons, Barons of Glenawley (*Gen. Reg. Sasines*, liv. f. 333; Burke's *Ext. Peerage*, 259).'

p. 537, l. 10, after '*David*,' insert 'baptized 1 September 1577. He was apparently named after David, eleventh Earl of Crawford. who was the first witness to the ceremony (Anstruther Wester Reg.). He was.'

p. 537, l. 20, after 'Collairnie,' add 'She was certainly granted the marriage of David Barclay of Collairnie, 13 August 1587 (*Reg. Sec. Sig.*, lvi. 2).'

p. 537, l. 21, delete this line and substitute 'Agnes Balfour, who married John Henderson of Fordell, is erroneously stated to be a daughter of Margaret Balfour, but she was a daughter of David Balfour of Balbuthie (*Reg. of Deeds*, lxiv. f. 406).'

p. 542, l. 7, after 'married,' insert 'contract 12 July 1591 (*Reg. of Deeds*, lxxxiv. 504).'

p. 542, l. 7, after 'of,' insert 'William.'

p. 542, l. 11, delete 'in,' and insert 'contract 30 August (*Reg. of Deeds*, ccxxii. 156).'

p. 542, l. 16, after 'Balfour, add 'being styled Sir Robert Balfour of Star during his father-in-law's lifetime (*Gen. Reg. Inhibs.*, v. 380).'

p. 544, note 3, add to note 'Charter to her as his future spouse, 22 February 1633 (*Gen. Reg. Sasines*, xxxvii. 275).'

p. 546, l. 4, after 'married,' insert 'contract 3 July 1680 (Fife Sheriff-Court Reg. of Deeds, 10 July 1680).'

p. 546, l. 8, after 'first,' insert 'contract 16 April 1684 (Gask Charters).'

p. 546, ll. 10, 11, 12, 13, delete from 'The' down to '1684.'

p. 546, l. 16, delete 'said to have been.'

p. 546, l. 16, after 'married,' insert 'contract 28 September 1688 (*Fife Sasines*, xv. 427).'

p. 547, l. 3, after '*Mary*,' insert 'baptized 7 July 1790 (Canongate Reg.).'

p. 547, l. 9, delete 'Miss Robertson,' and insert 'Janet Thomson (Inverkeithing Par. Reg., 17 November 1705), niece of Andrew Thomson, minister of Orwell.' *Note.*—Stenhouse and she were proclaimed at the latter place, 17 November 1705, and were married on 6 December.

p. 549, l. 27, after 'Laffrie,' insert 'or Lafriese (Edin. Mar. Reg.).'

p. 550, l. 8, after 'married,' insert '8 April 1669.'

p. 550, l. 2 from foot, delete '1670, or,' and insert 'after 4 October.'

p. 551, l. 22, for '1784' read '1684.'

p. 552, l. 7 from foot, for 'fifth' read 'fourth.'

p. 552, l. 2 from foot, after 'Margaret,' insert 'born 4 October 1716 (Edin. Reg.).'

p. 553, l. 22, after 'married,' insert '(proclaimed in the Canongate Church 12 October 1792).'

p. 553, l. 25, 'He was sometime a merchant in China.'

p. 553, l. 26, after 'married,' insert '13 February 1793.'

p. 553, l. 27, after 'Glasgow,' delete 'and,' and insert 'By her, who was born at Killearn, near Glasgow, 13 August 1768, and died at Edinburgh in December 1851, he.'

p. 553, l. 4 from foot, after '1817,' insert note 'For an amusing story of Laurence Dundas Bruce while a midshipman aboard the *Bellerophon* on the day that Napoleon surrendered see *Memoirs of an Aristocrat.* (by George Home), 218.'

p. 555, l. 14, for '7 August' read '16 July.'

p. 555, l. 20, after 'First,' insert 'on a rock.'

BALMERINO

p. 561, l. 21, after '1612,' insert note, 'The evidence for the first Lord's death on this date is precarious: Calderwood's date, about the end of May, is more probable. At all events he was dead by 2 June 1612 (*Gen. Reg. Inhibitions*, 2nd series, iii. 344).'

p. 562, l. 5, after 'first,' insert 'after 10 April 1589, when a testimonial was directed to Alva as to their having been proclaimed in Stirling on.'

p. 562, l. 9, for 'another son,' read 'issue.'

p. 562, ll. 10 and 11, delete 'and three daughters.'

p. 562, after line 11 insert,

'3. *Alexander*, baptized 6 May 1603 (Canongate Reg.). He must have died young.'

p. 562, ll. 12, 13, 14, for '3, 4, 5,' read '4, 5, 6.'

p. 562, after l. 15, insert 'Lord Balmerino had a natural son *Robert,* witness to a deed 4 June 1604 (*Reg. of Deeds,* cxix).'

p. 569, l. 7 from foot, delete '16,' and insert 'at Holyroodhouse, 15 (Canongate Reg.).'

p. 569, l. 3 from foot, insert

'1. *James,* born before 3 March 1673, to whom the third Lord Balmerino on that day disponed his books (Moray Writs, Box 40, No. 1124). This James must have died in infancy.' For '1.' read '2,' and on p. 570, for '2, 3, 4, 5,' read '3, 4, 5, 6.'

p. 569, l. 3 from foot, after 'eldest,' insert 'surviving.'

p. 570, l. 8, after '16 February 1692,' add note, 'This date is given by Wood but the marriage did not take place till after 30 April 1701, the date of the marriage contract (Earl of Moray's Writs), followed by a charter of same date made in contemplation of the marriage (cf. *Fife Sasines,* xx. f. 68).'

p. 570, after l. 12, insert 'One of these children was baptized at Leith 3 September 1674 (South Leith Kirk-Session Minutes).'

p. 570, l. 13, for '7 June' read '12 June (Edin. Mar. Reg.).'

p. 571, l. 4, after '5,' insert 'and was buried at Restalrig 9.'

p. 571, l. 7, after '1767,' insert 'She was buried at Restalrig 27 September (Restalrig Burial Reg.).'

p. 571, l. 8, for 'brother' read 'half-brother.'

p. 575, l. 5, after 'Tower,' insert 'The inscription on his coffin plate was "Arthurus dominus Balmerino decollatus 18 die Augusti 1746, ætatis sue 58" (*Historical Papers,* New Spalding Club, i. Plate xi.).'

p. 575, l. 15, after '1765,' insert 'aged fifty-seven, and was buried there.'

VOL. II.

BANFF

p. 8, ll. 18 and 19, delete 'when her eldest son George is mentioned.'

p. 9, l. 6, after 'thanked,' insert 'He was provided to the parsonage of Cruden by Pope Paul IV., 26 May 1555 (Slains Inventory).'

p. 13, l. 18, for 'Dempter' read 'Dempster.'

p. 15, l. 18, for 'Tilbertie' read 'Tibbertie.'

p. 15, l. 18, for 'Torfaulds' read 'Forfaulds.'

p. 15, ll. 18, 26 and 31, for 'Oatlaw' read 'Outlaw.'

p. 15, l. 29, for 'Monteoffer,' read 'Montcoffer,' and insert 'he.'

p. 18, l. 14, after 'married,' insert 'contract 25 June 1635 (Forglen Writs).'

p. 19, l. 17, after 'married,' insert 'contract 12 August and 2 September 1648 (Forglen Writs).'

p. 19, l. 18, after ' and,' insert 'by her, who died in March 1708.'

p. 21, l. 4, after 'annum,' add note, 'There was apparently an action of adherence by him against her in 1686 (*Edin. Consistorial Processes*, Scot. Record Soc., No. 40).'

p. 21, l. 6, after '*Anne*,' insert 'or *Anna*, married to James Law (Forglen Writs).'

p. 21, l. 10 from foot, delete 'and had by Helen Lauder (who,' and insert, 'having married, 11 January 1712, Helen, daughter of Sir John Lauder of Fountainhall. She.'

p. 21, l. 6 from foot, after '1742' insert 'having had by her first husband :—'

p. 22, l. 8, after 'London,' insert 'She died 31 January 1784, aged sixty-nine, and was buried at Cheam, Surrey.'

p. 22, l. 13, after 'Navy,' insert note, 'An account of his outfit for Navy in January 1732-33 including "a lac'd hat," six "fine cheque shirts," six nightcaps, "a fair wigg," a silver hilted sword, and a prospect glass, is given in *The Genealogist* for April 1909.'

p. 22, l. 29, after '1746,' insert 'He was buried, 10 May 1747, at St. Martin's-in-the-Fields.'

p. 22, note 1, for 'Brim's' read 'Burn's.'

BARGANY

p. 27, l. 19, after '1637,' delete 'By his wife,' and insert 'He married, first, Katherine, daughter of John Carnegie of that Ilk. She died 17 February 1595-96 (Edinburgh Tests.); and he married, secondly, in 1596 (Bargany MSS.).'

p. 27, l. 21, insert full stop instead of comma after 'family.'

p. 27, l. 21, for 'had' read 'left.'

p. 27, after line 24 insert

'4. *Alexander*, who was in Germany in 1635 (*Reg. of Deeds*, DXIII. 340).

5. *Margaret*, eldest daughter, married (contract 11 January 1615, tocher 11,000 merks), to John (afterwards Sir John) Hamilton of Bearcrofts, eldest son of Sir John Hamilton of Grange (*Reg. of Deeds*, ccxciv. 293).'

p. 27, l. 25, for '4' read '6.'

p. 27, l. 25, after 'married,' insert 'contract 5 and 7 March 1619, tocher 10,000 merks (*Reg. of Deeds*, ccxciv. 302).'

p. 27, l. 27, for '5' read '7'; after 'married,' insert 'in 1623 (Nisbet's *Heraldry*).'

p. 27, ll. 29, 30, for '6 and 7' read '8 and 9.'

p. 27, after l. 30, insert—

'10. *Jean*, married (contract 18 and 20 December 1632) to Thomas Hay of Park (Bargany MSS.).'

p. 28, l. 20, for 'Elliott' read 'Alyth.'

p. 28, l. 4 from foot, after 'married,' insert 'contract 1660 (Bargany MSS.).'

p. 28, l. 2 from foot, after 'Grizel,' insert 'died May 1678 (*Ibid.*).'

p. 29, l. 4, before 'December,' insert '28 (*Reg. of Deeds*, Durie, 29 January 1680).'

p. 31, l. 8, for 'in' read 'contract 23 August (*Edinburgh Sasines*, v. 188).'

p. 32, l. 5, after 'married,' insert 'as his first wife.'

p. 32, l. 17, after 'issue,' insert 'Some years after Sophie Johnston asserted that she was married to Lord Bargany, and was accused of having suborned witnesses to prove her case (*P. C. Decreta*, 16 December 1684).'

p. 32, l. 23, after 'first' insert 'about 1694 (Bargany MSS.).'

BARRET OF NEWBURGH

p. 35, l. 10, for '17 October 1627' read 'before 18 July 1618.'

p. 35, l. 15, after 'secondly' insert 'in August 1635 (*Cal. of State Papers*).'

p. 35, l. 20, after '1664, dying 22 July 1674 (*Families of Lennard and Barret*, 402).'

BELHAVEN

p. 40, l. 8 from foot, for 'Gairnie' read Gairnsay in Orkney.'

p. 40, after l. 5 from foot, insert

'4. *Elizabeth*, married as his third wife, to Alexander, first Viscount Kingston (*Haddington Inhibitions*, xviii. 412).'

p. 43, l. 16, after 'married,' insert '17 March 1653 (Edin. Mar. Reg.).'

p. 43, l. 25, after 'died,' insert '30 May (*Scottish Elegiac Verses*).'

p. 44, after l. 13, insert

'(6) *Rachel,* married to Sir William Weir of Blackwood. Baronet (Douglas's *Baronage*).'

p. 44, l. 18, delete notice of Daniel Hamilton, and insert '*Daniel,* appointed Clerk of the Admiralty Court 10 December 1702, and died *s.p.* before 20 November 1717, when his testament was recorded in Edinburgh. He did not marry Mary Hamilton, as stated in the text, and probably did not marry at all. Mary was the wife of another Daniel Hamilton, a writer in Edinburgh, brother of Gavin Hamilton, deputeclerk of the Court of Session 1687-1714, and laird of Inverdovat, co. Fife. They had issue six children. Mary died 2 December 1717, and Daniel about 20 August 1718 (*ex. inform.* W. H. C. Hamilton).'

p. 44, l. 25, after 'Edinburgh,' insert 'President of the College of Surgeons 1704-5 and 1710-11.'

p. 44, l. 25, after 'married,' insert 'in September 1700 (Edin. Mar. Reg.).'

p. 44, l. 25, delete 'died *s.p.m.*' and insert 'Testament recorded at Edinburgh 12 June 1713 (Edin. Tests.). He had a son *James* Hamilton of Swanston, who was served heir to his mother 9 April 1740.'

p. 44, l. 32, after '1661,' insert 'married 16 March 1682 to Hew Dalrymple, Advocate, ultimately Sir Hew Dalrymple of North Berwick, Lord President of the Court of Session (Edin. Mar. Reg.).'

p. 44, l. 7 from foot, after 'married,' insert 'as his second wife 25 August 1693 (Edin. Mar. Reg.).'

p. 46, l. 9 from foot, after 'married,' insert 'proclamation 17 January (Edin. Reg.), contract 5 February 1697 (*Edin. Sasines,* lxvii. 318).'

p. 46, l. 7 from foot, after 'and,' insert 'by her, who died 17 August 1707 and was buried at Stenton.'

p. 47, l. 7 from foot, for 'third of Wishaw' read 'first of Wishaw.'

p. 49, l. 6 from foot, for 'George' read 'James.'

p. 52, after last line insert

'7. *Euphemia,* married to Col. Alexander Baillie (see p. 51).'

p. 59, l. 10, after '1884,' insert 'married 29 March 1910 to William Michael Jamieson Martin, R.A.'

BELLENDEN

p. 64, after line 18, insert note, 'Adam Bothwell, Bishop of Orkney, writing to Napier of Merchiston in February 1660-61, seems to say that two sisters of Sir John Bellenden, the Justice-Clerk, were married through his influence with two Sinclairs (Napier's *Memoirs,* 68).'

p. 65, l. 9, after '1576,' insert 'aged fifty-six (*Foulis Account Book,* Scot-Hist. Soc., p. xliv).'

p. 65, l. 20, after 'Fordel,' add 'and of Nicol Cairncross, burgess of Edinburgh (*Acts and Decreets,* xlix. 168).'

p. 65, l. 23, after '*Mary,*' delete 'These both died young,' and insert 'who was her mother's executor before 8 July 1569 and she and her sister Catherine were both dead before 14 June 1571 (*Acts and Decreets,* xlix. f. 168).'

p. 65, l. 5 of notes, at the end of note 5 insert 'Katherine Bellenden is styled "spous to Robert Crag" in July 1541 (*Treasurer's Accounts*, vii. 463).'

p. 71, after note 11, add 'He appears to have been Treasurer by 30 February 1660-61. See original bond by Charles II. to him for £4000 (*penes* J. Mackenzie, Esq. Edinburgh).'

p. 72, l. 1, for '1602' read '1662.'

p. 73, l. 9, after '1707,' insert note, 'The following is a copy of the invitation to Lord Bellenden's funeral : "The honour of your presence to accompany the corps of my Lord Bellenden, my father, from his lodgings in Paterson's Land, near the Canongate foot, to his burial-place, the Abbey Church, upon Sunday the 3rd inst. at eight of the clock in the morning is earnestly desired by John Bellenden." Lady Constance Russell states that this was sent out in *November* 1706 (*Notes and Queries*, 10th series, vi. 54).'

p. 74, l. 11, after '*Mary*,' insert 'baptized at Edinburgh 4 May 1685 (Edin. Reg.).'

BLANTYRE

p. 84, l. 33, for 'William' read 'Alexander.'

p. 85, after l. 1, insert

'5. *Alexander* (*Reg. of Deeds*, ccclxvii. 393).

6. *Ludovic*, (*Ibid.*, 20 November 1622).'

p. 85, ll. 2 and 8, for '5' and '6' read '7' and '8.'

p. 86, l. 2, for 'Margaret' read 'Marie (*Gen. Reg. Sas.*).'

p. 86, l. 3, after 'Rowallan,' delete from 'sasine' to 'was,' and insert 'He granted a charter to her as his future wife on 24 September 1641, where she is designed Marie Muir, daughter of the late Sir William Muir of Rowallan, and Sara Brisbane, his spouse, and she had sasine 2 October 1641, but he died in that month. She married, secondly, in terms of disposition 14 May 1644, John Brisbane, younger of Bishoptoun, and is there designed relict of Walter, Lord Blantyre (*Gen. Reg. Sas.*, liv. 250). He was, etc.'

p. 86, l. 24, after '1690,' insert '"Grenok yr." writes to "the laird of Kelburne" 2 May 1676 about Lord Blantyre then apparently dying in Bute. Asks Kelburne to see him buried and secure the bed clothes and drugget. Complains of the neglect of many friends. He probably died of smallpox (*ex inform.* Col. the Hon. R. E. Boyle).'

p. 88, l. 21, after 'married,' insert 'in 1725 (Dunbar's *Social Life in Former Days*, 121).

p. 88, l. 4 from foot, after 'married,' add note 'He was reported in 1725 as about to be married to Lady Catherine Cochrane, afterwards Lady Galloway (*Ibid.*, 119).'

BORTHWICK

p. 95, l. 20, after 'him' add note, 'On 1 May 1411 a dispensation was issued for the marriage of William Borthwick and Beatrice Sinclair, but there is no clue as to which William Borthwick is meant (*Reg. Aven.*, 337,

f. 170). He had a daughter, Janet Borthwick, for whose marriage to Adam Hepburn, lord of Hailes, a Papal dispensation was granted on 2 November 1411 (*Reg. Aven.*, 339, f. 549).'

p. 99, note 7, add ' He was the son and heir of David Borthwick, burgess of Haddington (*Twelfth Rep. Hist. MSS. Com.*, App. viii. 112).'

p. 100, l. 3, after ' married,' insert ' first.'

p. 100, l. 4, after ' and,' insert ' secondly, in or before 1625, Helen Preston, widow of Henry Forrester of Corstorphine (cf. vol. iv. 90). He.'

p. 100, l. 18, after ' married,' delete ' Janet Lies,' and insert ' contract 25 January 1622, Janet, eldest daughter of William Leyis, merchant burgess of Edinburgh (*Reg. of Deeds*, cccxciii. 95).

p. 103, l. 28, after ' 1659,' insert ' chaplain of John, Lord Borthwick, 1667 (*Justiciary Records*, Scot. Hist. Soc., xlviii. 245, 251).'

p. 105, l. 11, add ' died 12 July 1907.'

p. 106, l. 12, for ' M. L. L.' read ' H. L. L.'

p. 107, l. 6, for ' Cairnsmuir ' read ' Cairnmuir.'

p. 107, after l. 18, insert—

' *e. Beatrice*, contracted, about September 1556, to John, son of William Lithgow of Drygrange (Protocol Book of Gilbert Grote, f. 20).'

p. 107, after l. 25 insert—

' 6. *Cristine*, named with her sister Catherine in a letter under the Privy Seal 21 May 1502 (*Reg. Sec. Sig.*, i. 832).'

p. 107, lines 26, 27, for ' 6, 7 ' read ' 7, 8.'

p. 108, l. 24, for ' 28 November 1528,' read 15 December 1530 (*Acta Dom. Conc. et Sess.*, iii. 152). His marriage with Mariot Seton was annulled by the Pope.'

p. 108, l. 25, for ' his widow ' read ' Mariot Seton.'

p. 108, l. 26, after ' Eglinton,' insert ' whom she survived, and married, thirdly, Alexander Graham of Wallaston (cf. vol. iii. p. 439).'

p. 109, l. 10, after ' married,' insert ' contract 28 May 1538 (*Acts and Decreets*, xliv. 159).'

p. 109, l. 24, for ' in March ' read ' 27 February.'

p. 110, l. 16, for ' in March ' read ' 28 March ' (Retour of his son, Canongate Court Book, 31 December 1573).'

p. 111, l. 3, after ' Castle ' add note, ' When, on 11 June 1567, certain of the nobility suddenly beset the castle and demanded the delivery of Bothwell, Lord Borthwick answered that he was fled to Dunbar (Birrel's *Diary*, 9).'

p. 112, l. 16, for ' in 1582 ' read ' contract 26 October 1582 (*Reg. of Deeds*, xx. pt. ii. 309).'

p. 113, l. 13, after ' William,' insert semicolon; delete ' and,' and insert ' he was of full age in July 1612 (*Reg. of Deeds*, cxcviii. 296), though.'

p. 114, l. 2 from foot, delete between ' 13 March 1674 and 27 November 1675,' and insert ' in November 1674 (cf. Service of John Dundas of Harvieston, 28 January 1674, Arniston Writs, p. 157).'

p. 116, l. 3, after '1772,' add 'and was buried there 9 September (St. Nicholas Burial Reg.).'

p. 119, l. 4, after 'Freeland,' add 'and died 13 June 1910.'

p. 119, l. 15, after 'Wigtown,' add 'He was elected a Representative Peer, 30 January 1906.'

p. 119, after l. 19, add 'Lord Borthwick died 4 October 1910, when the Peerage became dormant, if not extinct.'

MORAY AND RAMSAY, LORDS BOTHWELL

p. 128, after l. 5 from foot, insert—
    3. Possibly *Maurice* (Macfarlane's *Gen. Coll.*, ii. 505, quoting Kilravock MS.).'

p. 128, note 4, delete from 'Thomas' on line 5 from foot of notes to 'to *Scotiæ*' on line 2 from foot.

p. 133, line 24, for 'Fife' read 'Forfar.'

p. 134, last l., for 'in' read 'on.'

HEPBURNE, EARL OF BOTHWELL

p. 135, l. 19, after 'had,' insert 'with Marion Fourbuire or Fourbour, his spouse.'

p. 136, l. 1, after 'Berwickshire,' insert 'This charter was confirmed by David II. about 1343 (*Reg. Mag. Sig.*, vol. i., new ed., App. i. No. 117).'

p. 137, l. 19, for 'inherited his father's title of,' read 'was created (cf. p. 437).

p. 137, note 7, add at end of note '*Cal. Papal Letters*, iv. 222.'

p. 139, l. 2, after '1443-44.' insert 'On 2 November 1411 a Papal dispensation was issued for a marriage between Adam Hepburne and Janet Borthwick, daughter of Sir William Borthwick (*Reg. Avenionensia*, cccxxxix. f. 549).'

p. 141, l. 15, after 'chest,' add 'Annes (Agnes) Hepburne, by the contract cited, was affianced to Alexander Home, son and apparent heir of Sir Alexander Home of that Ilk, and on 2 January 1450-51 a Papal mandate was issued to grant a dispensation for the marriage of Alexander Home and Agnes Hepburne who had married, knowing themselves to be in the third and third degrees of affinity, and that her father was Alexander's godfather (*Reg. Vaticana*, ccccxvi. f. 122). This Alexander was son of the first and father of the second Lord Home.'

p. 142, l. 20, delete 'who is not known to have married,' and insert 'who married Margaret, sister of William Douglas of Whittingham; They appear in a contract 22 November 1521. It is added that an action of divorce by the said Margaret against the said John then depended (*ex inform.* W. Keith Murray from fragment of a record of the Court of the official of St. Andrews *penes* Lord Bolton).'

p. 143, note 2, after '94a,' insert 'see also Gilbert Grote's Protocol Book, f. 43b.'

p. 144, l. 15, after 'Galloway,' delete '7,' and insert 'on 15 January 1509-10.7'

p. 144, after l. 31, insert—

'(5) *Jean Hepburne*, married, as second wife, to William, Master of Ruthven (cf. vol. iv. 259), (MS. at Newhailes; Wood's Douglas's *Peerage*, i. 661).'

p. 144, note 7, after '205' add 'Earlston Charters, *penes* E. Rainsford Murray.'

p. 145, l. 16, after '1544-45,' add 'and may have been his wife.'

p. 147, l. 26, after '1506-7,' insert 'The bulls of the Priory of St. Andrews were delivered to him 26 May 1483 (Roman Transcripts, Public Record Office).'

p. 147, ll. 33 and 34, delete 'within a few months thereafter,' and insert '15 January 1525-26 (*Black Book of Taymouth*).'

p. 148, l. 6, after '1451,' insert 'in terms of a Papal dispensation granted 6 July 1448 (*Reg. Vat.*, Dxxii. fol. 56).'

p. 148, l. 22, delete '(afterwards created Lord Home).'

p. 149, l. 31, after 'married,' insert 'first, before 1511, to Sir William Preston of that Ilk (New Hailes Muniments; *Reg. Mag. Sig.*, 13 February 1510-11); and secondly.'

p. 149, l. 32, delete 'He,' and insert 'The latter.'

p. 150, last two lines, delete the whole sentence. See note above, page 141.

p. 156, l. 4 from foot, for '1523' read '1523-24.'

p. 156, note 9, after '50,' insert 'contract in Wigtoun Charter-chest, (Scot. Rec. Soc., p. 44.)'

p. 158, l. 6 from foot, after '1544.' insert note, 'He appears to have been taken prisoner in September 1544 (cf. *Treasurer's Accounts*, viii. 315).'

p. 159, l. 21, for 'first,' read 'third (cf. vol. vii. 571).'

p. 160, l. 8 from foot, for '28 December 1561,' read '11 January 1561-62 (*Cal. of Scot. Papers*, i. 190),' and delete note 8.

p. 165, l. 16, after 'married,' insert '24 February (Canongate Reg.).'

p. 166, l. 25, after '1567,' insert reference number 7.

STEWART, EARL OF BOTHWELL

p. 168, l. 19, for '4 January,' read '11 January (*Cal. of Scot. Papers*, i. 190).'

p. 169, l. 29, after 'Hamilton,' insert 'described in 1643 as "indweller in Canongate" (Treasury Precepts, H. M. Reg. Ho., 27 Feb. 1643).'

p. 169, l. 30, after 'Ferguslie,' add 'and secondly, before November 1638, to John Hamilton, brother-german to the late James Hamilton of Peill (son of James Hamilton of Corshill) (*Reg. of Deeds*, Dxvi. f. 354).'

p. 171, l. 4 from foot, after 'Coldingham,' insert 'styled in 1615 of Springkell (*Reg. of Deeds*, cclxx. 141).'

p. 171, last line, after 'Home,' delete 'and,' and insert 'daughter of Sir

Alexander, and sister of Sir George Home of Manderston (*Gen. Reg. Inhibitions*, 26 September 1621). They.'

p. 172, l. 6, after '1679,' insert comma, and add, 'but this is a mistake, as he must have died before 1658, when Francis Stewart, presumably his son, was charged to enter heir to John Stewart of Coldingham, his grandfather (*Gen. Reg. Inhibs.*, 8 July 1675). It must have been this younger Francis who fought at Bothwell Brig. His commission as Lieutenant of Dragoons is dated 27 September 1678, as Captain, 24 July 1679 (Dalton's *Scots Army*, 106). Captain Francis Stewart's testament was confirmed 20 February 1684 : he must have died before 17 March 1683, when Sir Patrick Home, his executor, petitioned the Privy Council for possession of his effects (*P. C. Decreta*).'

p. 172, l. 16, after 'Margaret,' insert 'eldest daughter.'

p. 172, l. 16, after 'married,' insert 'contract August 1621 (cf. vol. ii. 517, note 6).'

p. 172, after l. 25 insert

'9. *Christian*, married to Edward Withrington of Kirkington (*Gen. Reg. Inhibitions*, 7 November 1635).'

p. 173, l. 11, after '*Robert*,' insert 'He was in 1656 charged to enter heir to his father and elder brother. He died before 8 July 1675 (*Gen. Reg. Inhibitions*).'

BREADALBANE

p. 174, l. 19, after 'Ardgowan,' insert 'He must therefore have been born after February 1522-23, about which time the marriage took place.'

p. 177, l. 6 from foot, after 'Clandonoquhy,' add note, 'Further research shows that she was apparently not married to Sir John. John, Bishop of the Isles, had a dispensation for illegitimacy in connection with his provision to the Bishopric (*Vatican Index*). On 26 March 1466 Pope Paul II. dealt with the petition of Sir Colin Campbell, then ambassador from James III. to the Holy See, on behalf of John Campbell, scholar, of Lismore diocese, of baronial race on both sides, born of said Colin, a married man, and an unmarried woman, then in his seventh year, for dispensation to hold two canonries : which the Pope granted when he should reach his ninth year (Reg. of Petitions to the Pope, DLXXXV. 206). This may well have been the future bishop (*ex inform.* J. Maitland Thomson, LL.D).'

p. 177, line 2 from foot, after 'Merchiston,' insert 'who died before 10 July 1552 (St. Giles' Charters, 115).'

p. 180, l. 17, after 'Merchiston,' add 'She was married, secondly, to Robert Fairlie of Braid (*Acts and Decreets*, iii. 50).'

p. 182, l. 24, after 'married,' insert 'probably about October 1559, when she was infeft in certain lands in virtue of their marriage-contract (Lawers Inventory).'

p. 182, l. 26, after '*Margaret*,' insert 'adopted in 1561 by Patrick M'Athair (*Black Book of Taymouth*, 205), and afterwards.'

p. 182, l. 28, delete 'before 15 June 1551,' and insert '28 January 1550-51.'

p. 182, note 10, after '10,' insert '*Black Book of Taymouth*.'

p. 182, note 12, delete '*Reg. Mag. Sig.*,' and insert '*Acta Dom. Conc. et Sess.*, xxvii. 36.'

p. 183, l. 2, delete 'on 16 January 1610,' and insert 'by 25 February 1607.'

p. 183, l. 3, after 'son,' delete comma, and insert 'chose curators. (*Acts and Decreets*, ccxxvi. 46).'

p. 183, l. 4, after '*Colin*,' insert 'his son,' after 'him,' delete full stop, and insert '16 January 1610.'

p. 183, l. 12, after 'issue ⁶,' insert 'before 20 August 1622, when his brother Archibald had a precept of clare constat in certain lands in Lismore as his brother and nearest heir.'

p. 183, l. 26, for '1589,' read '1587 (*Reg. of Deeds*, xxx. 164).'

p. 184, l. 11, after '1575,' insert 'On 26 November 1578 on the narrative that "our cusenge Duncane Campbell fiar of Glenurquhay for his serves and gudwill borne touertis us is to be put at be his father," the Earl of Argyll granted an undertaking to protect him against his father (*Black Book of Taymouth*, 221).'

p. 186, l. 6, after '1614,' insert reference '(*Reg. of Deeds*, cclxxxi. 381).'

p. 187, note 14, after '*Deeds*,' insert 'lxv. 239.'

p. 188, l. 1, delete 'had been.'

p. 188, l. 2, after 'married,' insert 'contract 19 November 1625, Margaret, eldest daughter of Colin Campbell of Aberuchill (*Reg. of Deeds*, ccclxxxiii. 154).'

p. 188, l. 6, delete 'and others,' and insert

    (3) *Patrick.*

    (4) *James.*

    (5) *Elizabeth*, styled youngest lawful daughter. She had come of age before 4 March 1662, and is mentioned along with Patrick, James and John as "oyes of Elizabeth Sinclair," in February 1654 (*Stirlingshire Sasines*).'

p. 188, l. 17, after 'married,' insert 'contract 3 and 7 April 1628 (*Reg. of Deeds*, cccclv. 326).

p. 189, l. 26, after 'and,' insert 'by her who died 24 December 1667, aged eighty-four (Auchlyne Family Bible).'

p. 189, l. 3 from foot, after 'married,' insert 'contract 10 and 11 March 1641 (*Reg. Mag. Sig.*, 20 June 1642.)'

p. 189, note 10, add to note, 'the Auchlyne Family Bible gives the date of his death as 16 November 1658, at the age of eighty.

p. 190, l. 18, after 'married,' insert 'as her first husband.'

p. 190, l. 23, after '1772,' insert reference '*Scots Mag.*, 1772, p. 226.'

p. 190, l. 25, after 'Stonefield,' insert 'She died 16 April 1813 (*Lairds and Lands of Loch Tayside*, p. 12).'

p. 190, l. 34, after 'married,' insert 'John, second son of Andrew,' and after 'Gartartan,' add ' A marriage contract of date 18 June 1719 states she was then his spouse.'

p. 191, l. 9 from foot, after 'issue,' insert 'besides five daughters.'

p. 191, l. 8 from foot, after 'died,' delete 'without issue,' and insert '10 May 1713 (Auchlyne Family Bible).'

p. 191, l. 4 from foot, after 'Regiment,' insert 'was wounded at the battle of Fontenoy.'

p. 192, l. 9, delete ——, and insert 'Duncan.'

p. 192, l. 10, after 'Macpherson,' insert 'in Cult or in Glenorchy (*Court of Sess. Minute-Book*, ii. 106, 107).'

p. 192, l. 12, after 'Hellsglen,' insert 'with issue a son *Archibald*.'

p. 192, l. 2 from foot, after 'Lochdochart,' insert '(They gave in their names for marriage 8 November 1800. [Killin Parish Register]).'

p. 193, l. 4, after 'Campbell,' insert 'born 2, and baptized 10 October 1801 (Callander Par. Reg.).'

p. 198, l. 9, after '1794,' insert 'ensign 96th Regiment of Foot,' and after 'unmarried,' insert 'on 5 March 1813, in Jersey, aged 18 (*Scots Mag.*).'

p. 198, l. 13, delete 'exchanged into 42nd Regiment.'

p. 198, l. 14, delete from 'for,' down to 'Regiment,' in line 17, and insert 'he served as an officer in the 60th, 91st, and 9th North British Militia Regiments, and became captain in the 21st Royal North British Fusiliers, 12 June 1806.'

p. 198, l. 8 from foot, after '1720,' insert 'was a subaltern in the 43rd Regiment in 1745 (Brown's *Hist. of the Highlands*, iv. 150).'

p. 199, l. 22, after 1730.[12],' insert 'besides the before-named nine sons Colin had five daughters, Susanna, born 28 June 1717, Mary, 3 August 1727, Christian, 6 December 1728, Lucie, 26 February 1730, and Jean, 13 September 1731 (Glenfalloch Family Bible).'

p. 199, l. 27, after 'issue,' insert note, 'These daughters are mentioned in Court of Session Minute-Book (ii. 9), where they are mistakenly said to be the daughters of Archibald, son of William.'

p. 199, l. 6 from foot, delete 'between 1648 and 1651,' and insert 'in 1648 or 1649.'

p. 199, l. 2 from foot, after 'Lochdochart,' insert 'of which he had sasine, 28 March 1650 (*Part. Reg. of Sasines, Perthshire*, i. 40). He died 8 November 1699 aged seventy-two (Auchlyne Family Bible).'

p. 200, l. 3, after 'issue,' insert

'(1) *John*, who had sasine of Loragen and Lochdochart (Sheriff Court Books, Perth).

    i. *William*, his son, had sasine of these lands 16 January 1743; Crown charter 12 March 1744 (*Part. Reg. of Sasines, Perth*, xxiii. 230-231; *Reg. Mag. Sig.* lib. xcviii. 140).

        (i) *Charles*, his eldest son, had also sasine of the above lands, 1763. Late in life he married a second wife, Catherine Buchanan, by whom he had a son:—

            a. *Charles Archibald*, M.D., Montreal, baptized 30 September 1814 (Perth

Par. Reg.). He married Marjorie M'Gillivray of Salrevors, Canada, with issue *James, Charles,* and *Robert* (marriage, births, and baptisms, registered in Perth, 1861-62).

(a) *James,* of Montreal, married Louise V. Phillips of Chicago, U.S.A., and has issue, *Marion, Rosyln,* and *Norman* (marriage, births, and baptisms recorded in St. James' Parish Church, Chicago, 1878-86.'

p. 200, l. 6, after ' He died' delete ' in,' and insert ' 24 February.'

p. 200, l. 6, after ' she died,' delete ' in 1698,' and insert '17 January 1693, aged fifty-three (*Ibid.*).'

p. 200, l. 8, after 'married,' insert 'contract 26 October 1626 (*Reg. of Deeds,* DX. 234).'

p. 200. l. 17, delete ' before 5 July 1625,' and insert 'contract 8 June 1624 (*Reg. of Deeds,* cccci. 407).'

p. 200, l. 3 from foot, after ' 1637,' insert ' She died in March 1660, leaving issue (Dunblane Tests.).'

p. 201, l. 12, delete ' in,' and insert ' 24.'

p. 201, l. 12, after ' 1686,' insert 'aged seventy-nine (Auchlyne Family Bible).'

p. 201, l. 27, after 'Tulloch,' insert ' He was alive 18 April 1692.'

p. 202, l. 1, for ' Robert,' read ' Gilbert' (*Perth Sasines,* iii. 272 and other evidence).'

p. 202, after l. 9 insert

'15. *Elizabeth,* married, contract dated at Ardchattan 16 April 1701, to John Darroch, minister of the parish of Craignish,' and add one to subsequent numbers of children.

p. 202, l. 18, after 'Company,' insert ' In the *Gen. Reg. of Inhibs.,* 20 November 1679, William is named before Colin, so he may have been older.'

p. 202, l. 26, after ' had,' insert note, ' In the Register mentioned above the order of children by third wife is given thus :—Charles, Susanna, Mary, Jean, Sophia, Grisel and Anna.'

p. 202, l. 3 from foot, after 'married,' insert 'as his third wife, probably on 10 October 1697 (Killin Par. Reg.).'

p. 207, l. 4 from foot of notes, after 'sister,' insert ' She is designed " only lawful daughter to the deceast John, Earle of Brodalbine" (Canongate Reg. of Marriages).'

p. 207, l. 7 from foot, for ' Abbey' read ' Palace (*Scots Mag.*).'

p. 210, l. 7 from foot, after 'Berwick,' add note, ' David Gavin, or perhaps his father, made a large fortune as a tailor in Holland : he married, first, a Miss Hearsey, whose father lived in Middleburg, Zeeland.'

p. 210, last line, after ' married,' insert ' as his second wife.'

p. 211, l. 3 from foot, after '1677,' add 'He left about £300,000 personalty divided between the issue of his two sisters.'

p. 213, l. 16, delete 'Assistant' and 'Deputy.'

p. 213, l. 11 from foot, after 'Watch,' insert 'A.D.C. to the King.'

p. 213, l. 7 from foot, delete 'who.'

p. 213, l. 6 from foot, delete 'was an extra lady-in-waiting to H.R.H. the Duchess of Albany.'

p. 214, l. 12, after '2nd,' insert 'argent.'

BRECHIN

p. 221, l. 1, for 'lenient' read 'venial.'

p. 223, l. 16, after 'Seton,' delete from 'Neither' to 'identified,' and insert 'She was the wife of Sir William Seton of that Ilk. Her son, Alexander, became Lord of Gordon. (*See title* Huntly).'

p. 223, last line, after '1369[8],' add 'He had, 27 June 1358, a dispensation to marry Elizabeth Ramsay, daughter of William Ramsay, Earl of Fife, but it does not appear that the marriage took place (*Papal Petitions*, i. 331).'

BUCCLEUCH

p. 228, l. 19, after 'Angus,' insert 'who married, secondly, before October 1488, George, second Earl of Rothes. (*See that title*.)'

p. 228, note 3, for 'i. 74' read 'ii. 74.'

p. 228, note 5, for '*Ibid*' read '*Scotts of Buccleuch*, ii. 71.

p. 231, ll. 6 and 7, delete 'shortly before 19 May 1552,' and insert 'between 20 August 1550, when he signed a deed as curator of a son of his stepmother, Janet Beátoun, by a former husband (*Scotts of Buccleuch*, ii. 199), and 9 February 1551-52, when his widow had married again (see vol. iii. 503 ; *Reg. Mag. Sig.*, 9 February 1551-52).'

p. 231, l. 3 from foot, before 'contract,' insert 'post-nuptial.'

p. 236, l. 4, after 'failing,' insert 'the eldest heir-female of his body, whom failing' (it was thus, of course, that his daughter Mary succeeded).

p. 239, l. 14, after 'state,' insert 'She was very crooked, and had one leg shorter than the other' (from an accident at dancing at the Court of Charles II. v. *Pepys's Diary*). 'She was the last lady in Scotland who had as pages, young gentlemen of good birth, who learned their breeding in attending on persons of quality (Sir Walter Scott's letters to R. Chambers, privately printed, 1904).'

p. 239, l. 14, delete 'there,' and insert 'at Dalkeith.'

p. 239, l. 15, delete 'at Dalkeith,' and insert 'there.'

p. 243, l. 7, after 'died,' insert 'of inoculation for smallpox' (Fraser's *Melville Book*, ii. 265).'

p. 243, l. 9 from foot, after 'issue,' insert 'The Duchess gives her £20,000, the Duke £10,000, and they settle £15,000 more (Horace Walpole to Miss Berry, 17 October 1790).'

p. 247, l. 8 from foot, for ' third ' read ' first.'

BUCHAN

p. 251, l. 23, after '1182,' add note, 'Magnus, "son of Earl Colbeyn," is a witness to two charters by W. Comyn, Earl of Buchan (*Antiq. Aberdeen and Banff*, ii. 427, 428).'

p. 252, note 2, delete ' may have been,' and insert ' was,' adding after ' Fergus ' '(see *Antiq. Aberdeen and Banff*, ii. 427, 428).'

p. 256, l. 17, for '*Emma*,' read '*Agnes* (*see title* Strathearn).'

p. 256, l. 23, delete ' ——,' and insert ' Margaret,' and after ' Soulis ' insert ' the Competitor (*Cal. Doc. Scot.*, ii. No. 870).'

p. 262, after ' note 3,' add ' cf. vol. vii. 159.'

p. 266, l. 14, for '1 March 1466 ' read ' 27 March 1459.'

p. 266, note 1, delete note, and insert ' *Acta Dom. Conc.*, xvi. 264.'

p. 267, ll. 22 and 23, for ' probably in 1498-99,' read ' in 1499 (*Acts and Decreets*, xxvii. 366).'

p. 267, l. 24, for ' only one ' read ' a.'

p. 267, after l. 25, insert ' He is also said to have had a daughter married to Alexander Abernethy, fourth Lord Saltoun (*Frasers of Philorth*, ii. 50; see also vol. vii. of this work, p. 409), and another, *Marion*, contracted in 1505 to Sir Thomas Ogilvy (*Acts and Decreets*, xvi. 233).'

p. 267, l. 7 from foot, after ' Bothwell,' insert ' another, *Elizabeth*, married Mungo Home of Ersiltoun (cf. vol. iv. 469).'

p. 268, l. 23, delete ' in,' and insert ' 5 April (Dun *obits*).'

p. 268, l. 3 from foot, for ' 1551,' read ' 1561,' and add ' He was alive on 13 February 1560-61, when he entered into a contract with a John Mortimer as to certain lands (Protocol Book of Duncan Gray, f. 19).'

p. 269, l. 1, after ' first,' delete from ' Mary ' down to ' Kennedy ' on l. 3, and insert ' Elizabeth Stewart, natural daughter of James, Earl of Moray (see vol. vi. 312 ; the Earl of Moray's testament there quoted makes no mention of any legitimate issue). On 12 September 1546 there was an agreement between John, Master of Buchan, and Elizabeth Stewart his putative spouse, whereby she obliged herself to furnish proof that before their marriage she had cohabited with a gentleman who was in the fourth degree of kinship with the Master, so that they might be divorced ; for which (she having never received maintenance, meat, or clothing of him to this day) she was to be paid 100 merks, with a gown and kirtle with suitable trimming (Moray Writs, box ii. No. 34). After the Master's death an action of bastardy against Christian, his daughter, was raised before the Commissary-general of Aberdeen, on the ground that Elizabeth Stewart, the Master's wife, having survived him, his daughter, by Margaret Ogilvy, must have been born in adultery (*Ibid.*, box ii. Nos. 17 and 20). But in 1549 James, Master of Buchan, renounced the process of bastardy, and consented that Christian should be served heir to her father, also that James, Commendator of the Priory of St. Andrews, should, after the decease of the Earl and of Christian, enjoy the earldom of Buchan, and might, if he so pleased, have Christian to wife. All which the Master ratified by a notarial instrument, dated 3 August 1550 (*Ibid.*, box ii. No. 35).'

p. 269, ll. 5 and 6, delete 'two years at least,' and insert 'and married secondly, after 16 December 1549, George Barclay of that Ilk (*Acts and Decreets*, xx. 436; *Reg. Mag. Sig.*, 27 June 1551).'

p. 269, l. 15, after '1618,' add 'He married Mary, daughter of William Ruthven, first Earl of Gowrie, and relict of John Stewart, fifth Earl of Atholl, and of John Stewart, sixth Lord Innermeath, afterwards Earl of Atholl (see vol. i. 446, 447).'

p. 269, l. 18, after 'Denmark,' add note, 'Adrian Damaan was a Professor in the University of Leyden, and was in 1594 agent for the States General at the Scottish Court.'

p. 269, after l. 19 insert

'3. *Eleanor*, said to have been married to Dempster of Muiresk (Douglas's *Peerage*, 95; Dempster's *Hist.*, sec. ii. 173).'

'The Earl had also a natural son, *Robert*, who, on 12 January 1558-59 had a tack from his father of part of the lands of Nevay, Forfarshire (Protocol Book of Duncan Gray, fol. 18b.).'

p. 269, l. 21, for '1551,' read '1561.'

p. 269, l. 8 from foot, after 'was married,' insert '6 October 1652 (*Harl. MSS.*, 6437).'

p. 270, l. 14, after 'married,' insert 'contract 22 and 28 February 1590-91 (*Reg. of Deeds*. xxxvi. 336), proclamation of banns 4 July 1591 (Aberdeen Reg.).'

p. 271, ll. 3, 4 and 5, delete 'about 1580. He succeeded to his father in 1586,' and insert 'perhaps in or about November 1565, at which time his mother is said to have been "travelland with child" (*P. C. Reg.*, i. 396).'

p. 271, l. 11, delete 'Margaret, second,' and insert 'in 1598 Anne, eldest (*Harl. MSS.*, 6442).'

p. 271, l. 18, after married,' insert 'contract 2 December 1608.'

p. 271, ll. 18 and 19, delete 'probably about 1608 and had by him an only child.'

p. 271, l. 20, delete 'who.'

p. 271, l. 21, after 'married,' insert '18 June 1615 (*Reg. of Deeds*, cccxxxvi. 299).'

p. 272, l. 18, delete 'in 1628,' and insert 'at Holyrood, and was buried at Auchterhouse 20 August 1628 (Funeral entry, Lyon Office).'

p. 272, after l. 28, insert

'5. *Anna* (*Gen. Reg. Sasines*, xxxix. 350).'

p. 272, l. 9 from foot, for '5' read '6.'

p. 272, l. 5 from foot, after '1638-39,' insert 'Crawfurd states that they had a daughter *Dorothy* married to —— Walker, co. Middlesex (*Peerage*, 48), and several other children who died young.'

p. 273, l. 12, after 'married,' insert 'after 11 April 1655, when she is described as his future wife (*Banff Sasines*, vii. 125).'

p. 273, after l. 22, insert

'2. *Margaret*, married to William Gray of Innereichty (*Forfar Sasines*, vi. 264).'

p. 273, ll. 23, 26, 27 for '2, 3, 4' read '3, 4, 5.'

p. 273, l. 23, for 'Margaret' read '*Mary* or *Marjory* (*Aberdeen Sasines*, vi. 286, xii. 533).'

p. 273, l. 27, after 'married,' insert '3 January 1684 (Edinburgh Reg.)'

p. 274, l. 1, for '5' read '6.' After 'Halkerton,' insert 'Sheriff Clerk of Angus: she married, secondly, Alexander Carnegie, second son of Sir John Carnegie of Balnamoon (Macfarlane's *Gen. Coll.*, ii. 181).'

p. 274, l. 8, for 'the soldiers of William III.' read 'the Master of Forbes (Edinburgh Letters of 13 July in *London Gazette*, 17-21 July 1690).'

p. 274, l. 9, delete 'unmarried,' and insert 'having married at the Chapel in Duke's Place, St. James's, London, 4 September 1683, Marjorie Foulis, widow of William, eighth Earl of Morton (certificate of marriage and other papers, Misc. Documents H. M. Register House). She was dead before 1690 (Edinburgh Tests., 19 February 1690).'

p. 275, line 4 from foot, delete 'in 1745' and insert '14, and was buried at Hampstead, 17 October 1745.'

p. 275, l. 3 from foot, for 'in' read '11 February.'

p. 275, last line, delete ——, and insert ' Anne.'

p. 276, l. 24, after 'born,' insert '7 December (Edin, Reg.),' after 'married' insert '11 July 1726 (Edinburgh Mar. Reg.).'

p. 276, l. 5 from foot, after '1739,' insert 'in Lady Huntingdon's Chapel at Bath.'

p. 276, l. 3 from foot, after 'Bart,' insert note, 'There was a Scotch Countess of Buchan who is carrying a pure, rosy, vulgar face to Heaven (Horace Walpole's *Letters*, 10 October 1766).'

p. 277, l. 6 from foot, after 'Buck,' delete 'who,' and insert 'against whom he unsuccessfully raised an action of divorce 1820. She.'

p. 279, l. 16, delete 'Bart.'

BURNTISLAND

p. 282, l. 23, after 'London,' insert note, 'He satisfied for fornication committed with one . . . Weymes at the Chapel of the Weymes in Fife, Mr. Harie Weilkie, minister of the Weymes did receave him in the Church of the Weymes. This cheild was gotten by him before he went into England with the armie. He went backe to London again March 1654 (Lamont's *Diary*).'

p. 283, l. 9 from foot, after '1705,' insert note, 'Her body was taken from Roystoun to Burntisland at 12 at night with a great many flambeaux: thence to Easter Wemyes where she was buried in the beginning of June (?) (*Edinburgh Courant*).'

BUTE

p. 292, l. 20, for 'Mary' read 'Agnes.' *Note.*—'In 1552 she is described as sometime spouse to James Stewart, Sheriff of Bute, now to James M'Donald of Donyveig and Glens (*Acts and Decreets*, vi. 474). Her marriage with the Sheriff of Bute must therefore have been annulled. See vol. i. 338, where she is said (following Gregory) to have been daughter of Colin, third Earl of Argyll.'

p. 293, l. 14, for 'Mary' read 'Jean (*Reg. Sec. Sig.*, lv. 35).'

p. 293, l. 19, delete 'before 15 September 1595,' and insert 'contract 11 June 1593 (*Reg. of Deeds*, cxxix. 126).'

p. 295, l. 4 from foot, after 'married,' insert 'contract 9 March 1631 (*Reg. of Deeds*, Dxxviii. 262).'

p. 297, l. 7, after 'had,' insert 'by her, who survived him and was on 1 August 1672 the wife of Robert M'Neill of Illandrow (*Reg. of Deeds*, Durie, 14 Feb. 1673).'

p. 297, note 4, after '*Peerage*,' insert '; Edinburgh Mar. Reg.'

p. 299, l. 23, delete 'marriage,' and insert 'first wife, who was buried 16 July 1696 (Greyfriars Reg.).'

p. 303, l. 12, after 'he,' insert 'died 1 March 1818, having.'

p. 304, l. 9 from foot, after '1822,' insert note, 'His wife gave him by mistake a lotion which had been ordered for a footman's leg, which poisoned him (Mrs. Warenne Blake's *Memoirs of a Vanished Generation*, 108).'

p. 305, l. 14, delete reference number '1.'

p. 305, l. 15, for reference '2' read '1.'

p. 305, l. 29, after 'Rothesay,' insert '2.'

p. 309, l. 24, for 'Phillipps' read Phillippo.'

p. 312, l. 12, after '3rd,' insert 'argent.'

CAITHNESS

p. 323, l. 5 from foot, after 'Blaknes [5],' add 'He married —— daughter and heiress of Duncan Cairns of Cairns and acquired the lands of Cairns and Whitburn (*History of the Family of Cairns*, by H. C. Lawlor, Killyfaddy, Belfast, 2 and Table at p. 16).'

p. 333, l. 25, delete 'sometime between the date of the charter and 29 March 1482 (*see below*)' and insert 'between Martinmas 1479 and Whitsunday 1480 (*Exch. Rolls*, viii. 48).'

p. 334, after l. 14, insert
'3. *Elizabeth* called also *Marjory*, married to Andrew, Master of Rothes, who died before January 1477-78; she died about 1508.'

p. 334, l. 20, for '3' read '4' and add one to each number thereafter.

p. 334, l. 32, after 'Atholl,' insert 'and died 21 March 1518.'

p. 337, l. 14, for 'Mary, daughter of Sir William,' read 'Margaret, daughter of Sir Gilbert (*Acta Dom. Conc.*, xxiii. 101).'

p. 338, after l. 19, insert
'3. *Archibald* (*Acta Dom. Conc. et Sess.*, xxii. 41).'

p. **338**, l. 20, for ' 3 ' read ' 4.'

p. **338**, l. 27, after '*David*,' insert 'also *Matthew* (*Reg. Mag. Sig.*, 19 May 1585).'

p. **340**, l. 7, after 'who,' insert 'was born in 1513, as he was twenty years of age or thereby on 8 November 1563 (Gilbert Grote's Protocol Book, 96). He.'

p. **340**, ll. 14 and 15, for 'about 1577-78' read 'in September 1575 (Edin. Tests.).'

p. **340**, l. 26, after 'married,' insert 'first.'

p. **340**, l. 28, delete 'by whom,' and insert 'and secondly, contract 6 October 1621, Grisel, daughter of Mr. Robert Crichton of Eliok, widow of Thomas Dunbar, Dean of Moray (*Reg. of Deeds*, cccxvii. 141 ; *Elgin Sasines*, 163, 164). She survived him, and is designed his widow 7 March 1633 (*Inverness Sasines*, 11 April 1633).'

p. **340**, l. 5 from foot, after 'first,' insert 'before 2 September 1626, when Sir James, being about to go abroad on military service, granted a factory in her favour (*Reg. of Deeds*, cccxci. 62).'

p. **340**, l. 4 from foot, after '1633),' insert 'daughter of Sir Walter Dundas of that Ilk and widow of Sir William Sharp of Ballindoch (*Reg. of Deeds*, cclxxxix. 97).'

p. **341**, l. 3 from foot, after 'issue,' add 'He married, 5 January 1764, Catherine, daughter of John Rose in Keiss, parish of Wick. She raised an action of declarator of the marriage in 1783 and divorced him in 1786 (*Consistorial Processes, etc.*, Scot. Rec. Soc., Nos. 791, 842).'

p. **342**, l. 11, after '1582,' insert 'married, contract 10 December 1587, to Sir John Home of Cowdenknowes (cf. vol. iv. 474 ; *Reg. of Deeds*, xxvi. 271).'

p. **342**, l. 12, after 'issue,' insert 'having been, it is said, slain by his elder brother John, who bruised him to death with his fetters during his imprisonment in Girnigo (Catherine Sinclair's *Shetland and the Shetlanders*, 35).'

p. **342**, l. 13, delete 'but leaving,' and insert 'He had.'

p. **342**, l. 20, after 'age,' add 'in 1572 (cf. vol. viii. 334). She was married, secondly, to Alexander Innes of that Ilk, after 10 September 1574, and died before 25 November 1575 (*Reg. of Deeds*, xvi. 369).'

p. **342**, l. 22, after 'secondly,' insert 'contract 10 April 1580 (*Reg. of Deeds*, xlvii. 24).'

p. **342**, ll. 25 and 26, delete entire sentence.

p. **342**, l. 27, for '9' read '8.'

p. **342**, l. 27, for 'about 1574,' read 'contract 20 and 21 September 1581.'

p. **342**, ll. 28 and 29, delete 'She was living 15 June 1598,' and insert 'She married, secondly, contract 1588, Alexander Gordon of Strathaven, and died 6 November 1619 (cf. vol. iii. 571).'

p. **342**, after line 29, insert

'9. *Jonet*, married, contract 20 October 1573, to William Sutherland younger of Dunbeath (*Reg. of Deeds*, xiii. 115).'

p. **343**, l. 13, delete '10 December 1606,' and insert '29 December 1615 (*Reg. Mag. Sig.*, 6 June 1616).'

p. 343, l. 25, delete 'in,' and insert 'contract 21 May (cf. vol. iii. 34).

p. 344, l. 3, delete 'between May 1633 and October 1634,' and insert 'contract 17 and 25 December 1633 (*Reg. of Deeds*, cccclxxxi. 445).'

p. 348, l. 25, after 'her,' insert 'who survived him and was alive in 1684 (*Gen. Reg. Sasines*, 25 September 1684).'

p. 350, after l. 11 from foot, insert

      '8. *Jean*, baptized 10 April 1764 (Dunnet Par. Reg.).'

p. 351, l. 9 from foot, delete 'before 1583,' and insert ' contract 13 December 1578 (cf. *Reg. Mag. Sig.*, 16 February 1578-79 ; *Reg. of Deeds*, xvii. 3),' and add note, 'There was an abortive proposal that he should marry Jean Gordon, sister to the Earl of Sutherland (see vol. viii. 343, note 1).'

p. 358, l. 6 from foot, after 'Baronet,' insert 'to whom he was served heir-male general 7 January 1890.'

CALLANDER

p. 362, line 4 from foot, after 'Helena,' insert 'the latter of whom was married to John Stirling of Herbertshire (*Reg. of Deeds*, lxxxiii. 222; *Linlithgow Inhibs.*, x. 227).'

p. 363, l. 7, for 'third' read 'second (*Maitland Club Misc.*, iv. pt. i. p. 202; Hamilton Papers, *Eleventh Rep. Hist. MSS. Com.*, App. vi. 59).'

CARDROSS

p. 365, ll. 22 and 23, delete 'shortly after 14 December 1625,' and insert 'on 18 April 1626 (contract 8 December 1625) (*Reg. of Deeds*, cccxcvi. 202 ; Canongate Reg.).'

p. 365, l. 24, after 'issue,' add 'along with a daughter *Mary*, baptized 22 April 1628 (Canongate Reg.), married to John Buchanan of that Ilk after 21 October 1654, when she had a charter as his future wife (*Gen. Reg. Sasines*, viii. 325).'

p. 365, l. 2 from foot, for '18' read '10.'

p. 366, l. 3, after '1671,' insert 'and was buried in Holyrood Church, 25 July 1671 (Canongate Reg.).'

p. 366, l. 8, after 'Kincardine,' delete 'and had issue,' and insert 'She survived him, and there was a warrant to bury her in Holyrood Church 28 December 1696 (*P. C. Acta*).'

p. 366, l. 13, after 'marriage,' insert 'along with two twins, William and David, who were baptized 9 March 1662 (Canongate Reg.), but who must have died young :—'

p. 366, ll. 16 and 17, delete '5 October 1700 (a date erroneously given in the *Services of Heirs*),' and insert 'in April 1697, and was buried in Holyrood (*P. C. Acta*).'

p. 367, l. 21, after 'undergone,' add 'and was buried at Holyrood.'

p. 367, l. 28, after 'married,' insert contract 14 August 1721 (*Perth Sasines*, xviii. 186).'

CARLYLE

p. 375, l. 27, after 'recorded,' insert 'but there is some reason to suppose that she may have been a daughter of Robert or Adam Crosby who lived at Corby, Cumberland. She was lady of Ormesby previously referred to (*ex inform.* by C. H. Herries Crosbie).'

p. 382, last line of note 9, add 'Edward Carlyle of Limekilns was, in 1596-97, a brother of Herbert Carlyle of Brydekirk (*P. C. Reg.*, v. 743).'

p. 386, after line 25, insert

'7. *Elizabeth*, contracted in 1492 to Robert Herries, son and apparent heir of George Herries of Terrauchty (*Acta Dom. Conc.*, 296).'

p. 389, last line, delete 'whose daughter Grizel he married, and.'

p. 390, l. 4, after 'wife,' insert Grizel, a sister of Edward Maxwell of Hills (*Drumlanrig Writs*).'

CARNWATH

p. 405, l. 16, after 'tombstone,' insert 'in Abercorn Church.'

p. 405, l. 19, after 'Carnwath,' add 'It is stated that he left a son (the General) and a daughter, married to William Drummond of Riccarton. His wife was Janet, daughter (Crawfurd says a natural daughter) of Edward, first Lord Bruce of Kinloss (cf. vol. iii. 477).'

p. 406, l. 10, delete '13 August 1607, when his son was still apparent of that Ilk,' and insert '2 January 1609 (*Reg. of Deeds*, cci. 317).'

p. 408, l. 2, after '1632,' insert 'He was alive 11 July 1635 (*Reg. Mag Sig.*) but died before July 1636 (*Lanark Sasines*, iii. 542).'

p. 408, l. 2, delete from 'In June' down to 'his body' on line 8, and insert same after 'Carnwath' on last line of p. 411. Note 'The information refers to the second Lord Dalzell, who, and not his father, was the first Earl of Carnwath.'

p. 408, l. 8, delete 'Died 1639.'

p. 408, l. 9, for 'Sir' read 'Mr.'

p. 408, l. 12, for 'second' read 'first.'

p. 409, l. 2, delete 'before 1625,' and insert 'contract 8 July 1624 (*Reg. of Deeds*, ccccxvi. 240).'

p. 409, l. 16, after '1685,[6]' insert 'He was captain of a company of Foot in the Earl of Mar's Regiment (*Warrant Book for Scotland*, iv.).'

p. 409, l. 20, delete 'between 13 May 1685 and 29 April 1686,' and insert '2 September 1685 (*Notes and Queries*, 10th ser., viii. 402).'

p. 409, l. 22, delete 'Miss Sandilands of the family of Torphichen,' and insert 'Catherine, daughter of Sir James Sandilands of St. Monans (Discharge for tocher 20 June 1644; *Reg. of Deeds*, dlvii. 70; cf. vol. i. 78, 79).'

p. 409, note 14, add to note 'see also *Privy Council Acta*, 19 January and

3 August 1697, when he was cited as a Jacobite. He is said to have married —— Graham and left issue (cf. vol. v. 129).'

p. 410, after l. 7, insert

'*b. Robert*, born and baptized 1 June 1704 (Canongate Reg.).'

p. 410, ll. 8 and 10, for '*b, c* and *d*' read '*c, d* and *e.*'

p. 410, l. 12, for '1652' read '1662.'

p. 410, l. 22, after '1685,' insert 'He had a commission, dated at Whitehall 12 December 1679, as captain of the company of Foot formerly commanded by Sir Robert Dalzell, his father, in the Earl of Mar's Regiment (*Warrant Book for Scotland*, iv.). In 1686 Sir John appears in the list of that Regiment (*Notes and Queries*, 10th ser., viii. 445).'

p. 410, l. 31, for 'sixth' read 'fifth.'

p. 410, l. 4 from foot, for 'seven' read 'seventeen.'

p. 410, l. 3 from foot, after '1734,' insert 'He left very shortly and became a soldier (*Scots Colleges*, New Spalding Club, i. 201).'

p. 410, l. 2 from foot, for '(*b*)' read '*c.*' Mary was daughter, not granddaughter of the second Baronet.

p. 411, l. 1, after 'son,' insert 'He was in a Scots Danish Company raised for service in Germany (*Reg. of Deeds*, cccc. 217).'

p. 411, l. 14, after '*William*,' insert 'of Chisholm (*Reg. of Deeds*, Dx. 167).'

p. 411, l. 18, after 'merks,' insert 'He married (contract 2 and 5 July 1629) Margaret, daughter of John Stirling of Glorat (*Ibid.*, Dlxxxiii. 58).'

p. 411, l. 25, delete 'Earl of Carnwath,' and insert 'Lord Dalzell.'

p. 411, note 10, after 'cccxxxvi.' insert '127.'

p. 412, l. 1, after 'Holyrood,' insert 'He succeeded his father as Lord Dalzell and, as appears from his son's marriage-contract on 21 July 1537 (*Reg. of Deeds*, cxxvi. 69) it was he (and not his father as generally supposed) who was on 21 April 1639 created at York EARL OF CARNWATH, BARON DALZELL AND LIBERTON, with remainder to heirs-male of his body.'

p. 412, l. 10, after 'day,' insert note 'Baillie calls him "that monster of profanitie" (*Letters*, ii. 78).'

p. 413, ll. 10 and 15, for 'third' read 'second.'

p. 413, l. 15, after 'Carnwath,' insert 'had, as son of Sir Robert Dalzell on 15 September 1633 a licence to pass beyond seas (*Genealogist*, April 1909). He.'

p. 413, note 5, after 'Dxxx.', insert '151.'

p. 414, l. 9, for 'merks' read 'pounds Scots.' *Note.*—The *Carnegie Book ut cit.* erroneously says merks as in the text.

p. 414, ll. 15 and 24, for 'fourth' read 'third.'

p. 414, l. 17, for 'fifth' read 'fourth.'

p. 414, l. 5 from foot, for '1684' read 'January 1682, by a charter confirmed 15 February 1684 (*Reg. Mag. Sig.*), the Earl being then described as deceased.'

p. 414, l. 5 from foot, for '1688' read '1683.'

p. 414, l. 5 from foot, after 'married,' insert '10 December 1676 (Pencaitland Reg.).'

p. **414**, ll. 3 and 4 from foot, delete 'who died January 1713, and by whom,' and insert ' By her, who died 15 January 1698 (Funeral entry, Lyon Office), and was buried at Holyrood.'

p. **414**, last line, delete 'first.'

p. **414**, note 16, last line, for ' 23 ' read ' 229, 230.'

p. **415**, l. 1, delete from 'and ' to end of paragraph and relative note.

p. **415**, l. 4, for ' fifth ' read ' fourth.'

p. **415**, l. 5, after ' 1659,' insert ' captain of a company in the Guards 1686 ; lieutenant-colonel, 1691.'

p. **415**, l. 18, for ' sixth ' read ' fifth.'

p. **417**, ll. 8 and 6 from foot, for 'seventh ' read ' sixth.'

p. **418**, l. 11, for ' eighth ' read ' seventh.'

p. **418**, l. 12, for ' tenth ' read ' ninth.'

p. **418**, l. 17, for ' eleventh ' read ' tenth.'

p. **419**, l. 5, for ' eighth ' read ' seventh.'

p. **419**, l. 9, for ' Blackford ' read ' Becford.'

p. **419**, ll. 14 and 15, for ' ninth ' read ' eighth.'

p. **419**, l. 18, for ' tenth ' read ' ninth.'

p. **419**, l. 23, for ' eleventh ' read ' tenth.'

p. **420**, l. 1, for ' twelfth ' read ' eleventh.'

p. **420**, l. 3, after ' 1892,' insert ' He died suddenly on his way to the House of Lords in Great Smith Street, Westminster, 8 March 1910.'

CARRICK

p. **426**, l. 15, after ' Margaret,' insert ' or Isabel,' and add note, ' Neil, Earl of Carrick, and Isabel, Countess of Carrick, granted a charter to the Abbey of Saddell in Cantyre (*Reg. Mag. Sig.*, 1 January 1507-8).'

p. **431**, l. 32, for ' third ' read ' first.'

p. **431**, l. 32, for ' Hereford ' read ' Hertford.'

p. **431**, l. 34, for ' 1284 ' read ' 1264 (*Cal. Doc. Scot.*, i. No. 2356).'

p. **432**, note 3, for ' 369 ' read ' 373.'

p. **435**, note 4, for ' 375 ' read ' 379.'

p. **437**, l. 6, for ' 1373 ' read ' 1370 (*Reg. Mag. Sig.*, vol. i., No. 356, new edition).'

p. **439**, l. 2, delete ' 28 April 1398.'

p. **442**, l. 1, delete from ' 1639 ' down to ' Carrick ' on line 4, and relative note, and insert ' 22 June 1643 and 3 March 1646, the date of the grant of his wife's administration.'

p. **442**, l. 12, for ' John ' read ' Matthew (see grant of administration above cited).'

p. **442**, l. 16, after ' and,' add ' another *Jean*, married, contract 23 July 1622, to John Campbell, son of Patrick Campbell of Balsalloch (*Gen. Reg. Sasines*, xvii. 116).'

p. **442**, l. 19, after ' 1639,' add ' He married Barbara Bannatyne (*Edinburgh Burgh Reg. of Deeds*, 9 July 1661).'

p. **442**, after l. 19, insert ' There was another son (presumably natural), *Adam*, mentioned 1627 (*Reg. of Deeds*, ccccxi. 48).'

CASSILLIS

p. 445, note 6, l. 3 from foot, for 'Kenredy' read 'Kennedy.'

p. 448, l. 4 from foot, for 'daughter' read 'half-sister.'

p. 448, last line, for '1405' read '1409.'

p. 448, note 3, for ' p. 440' read ' p. 444.'

p. 449, l. 19, for 'fourth' read 'fifth.'

p. 449, transpose notes 8 and 9; for 'clxxi.' in present note 8 read 'clxxiv.'; for '129, 130' in present note 9 read '159, 160.'

p. 451, l. 17, delete 'a fleur-de-lys,' and insert 'three fleurs-de-lys.'

p. 454, l. 3 from foot, delete 'who it is said had no issue,' and insert 'Gilbert, third Earl, was infeft as his heir November 1532 (Culzean Charters, No. 316).'

p. 458, l. 24, for ' 23 ' read ' 3.'

p. 458, note 8, delete note, and insert ' *Reg. Sec. Sig.*, No. 1754.'

p. 459, l. 14, after 'part,' insert 'They had, however, a daughter, Janet Gordon, described in 1515 as Sir Alexander's daughter and heir (see vol. v. 103, 104).'

p. 462, l. 22, for '1 May 1547,' read '18 March, 1546-47.'

p. 462, l. 29, for 'January' read 'February.'

p. 465, l. 9, for ' following ' read ' same (*Reg. Sec. Sig.*, i. 3878).'

p. 465, note 5, for ' *Trials*, 7' read ' *Trials*, i. 242*.'

p. 467, last line, delete ' a daughter,' and insert ' *Marion.*'

p. 467, last line, after 'Bomby,' insert 'She married secondly, before 1562, William Campbell, younger of Skeldon (*Acts and Decreets*, xxiv. 245).'

p. 470, at end of note 7 add ' He was Treasurer on 30 January 1553-54 (Cartulary of Holyrood, 290).'

p. 471, l. 18, delete from ' ane particular manne ' to end of sentence, and insert 'ane werry wyse manne, and veil beluiffit of all.³'

p. 471, note 3, after ' *Kennedyis*,' insert ' The character of "ane particular manne,' etc., belongs to the fourth, not the third Earl.'

p. 473, ll. 6 and 7 from foot, delete 'a boy of eight years old.'

p. 473, l. 6 from foot, transfer reference number ' 7 ' to after ' Arran' on line 4 from foot.

p. 474, end of note 3, insert ' He must have died before 11 July 1604 (cf. *Acta Parl. Scot.*, iv. 268 and 271).'

p. 475, after l. 6, insert

    '(3) *Jean*, described in 1665 as sister of John, Lord Cassillis, married to William Stewart of Carragan, co. Tyrone. His will 9 April 1665 (*ex inform.* J. Stewart Kennedy).'

p. 475, l. 7, delete ' was only eight years old when he succeeded his father, who,' and insert ' was probably born between Martinmas 1574 and April 1575, as on 14 August 1589 he chose curators (*Acts and Decreets*, cxxi. 144); and on 2 April 1596 he had sasine of many lands which had been in the superior's hands for nineteen years by reason of ward (*Exch. Rolls*, xxiii. 377). His father.'

p. 475, ll. 14 and 15, delete ' the following year.'

p. 477, after l. 22, insert 'He was contracted to Jean Cunningham, daughter of James, seventh Earl of Glencairn, who deceased 23 November 1597 "in her virginitie" (M. I. at Kilmaurs).'

p. 477, l. 31, after 'wealthy,' insert 'ane very unmeet match for she was past bairns bearing. . . . The King and Court mockit the same marriage, and made sonnets in their contempt, and specially his Majesty took his pastime of that sport (*Chronicles of the Kings of Scots*).'

p. 482, l. 17, after 'daughter,' insert 'Mr. Thomas Kennedy, son of the deceased Sir John Kennedy of Culzean and Lady Elizabeth Kennedy, daughter of the deceased John, Earl of Cassillis, were proclaimed with a view to marriage 10 September 1699, but "stopt by her order under hand 24 September 1699" (Edin. Mar. Reg.; cf. p. 490).'

p. 482, l. 23, for '1666' read '1668.'

p. 484, l. 13, for '20' read '26 (*Reg. Sec. Sig. Latin Reg.* iv. pt. ii. 182; *Gen. Reg. Sas.*, xxi. 129).'

p. 484, l. 15, after '1697-98,' insert 'post-nuptial contract 9 November 1698 (*Reg. of Deeds*, Dalrymple, 3 July 1710).'

p. 484, l. 30, delete 'She died 10 March 1734-35,' and insert 'She is called daughter of Sir Thomas Hutcheson, Knight, by his wife, a daughter of Sir Thomas Boteler, Knight, in her Funeral entry, Lyon office. She died at Barnton 10, and was buried at Holyrood, 16 March 1734. She is called Jean in the Holyrood Register.'

p. 485, l. 1, after 'married,' insert '26 (Canongate Reg.).'

p. 485, l. 19, for '7 March' read '8 August.'

p. 485, l. 22, for '1739' read '1738 (cf. vol. viii. 362; the *Gentleman's Mag.* gives the marriage as in October 1738).'

p. 487, l. 4, after 'wife,' insert 'contract 4 April and 15 May 1605.'

p. 487, l. 5, after 'Rowallan,' insert 'She died in January 1622 (Glasgow Tests.): in her testament she leaves Agnes Mure her "oye" certain sums of money which had been left by another Agnes Mure styled sister of the legatee in case of her decease before her marriage. Agnes was evidently the daughter of the William Mure, junior, mentioned in the charter of 20 June 1616 referred to in note 2.'

p. 488, l. 10, after '1629,' add 'He married, contract 15 February 1617, Margaret, daughter of Hew Kennedy of Garrihorn (*Reg. of Deeds*, ccccxlv. 1).'

p. 488, l. 15, after 'first,' insert 'contract 11 October 1600 (*Reg. of Deeds*, lxxxiv. 216).'

p. 488, l. 5 from foot, after '1643,' insert 'He was knighted at Holyrood 12 July 1633 (Balfour's *Annals*, iv. 366).

p. 489, l. 17, after 'married,' delete 'to James,' and insert 'in 1650 to Gilbert (*Ayr Sasines*, viii. 342).'

p. 489, l. 19, after 'married,' insert 'contract 12 April 1648 (*Ayr Sasines*, viii. 164).'

p. 493, l. 6, after '488.),' add note, 'A claim to the title is mentioned in the *General Evening Post* of 1-3 January 1793. It was made by Samuel Paterson, junior, a clerk in the Sun Fire Office, eldest son of Samuel

Paterson, librarian to the Marquess of Lansdowne. The wife of the elder Samuel, Mrs. Hamilton Lewis Paterson, died 29 November 1790, and is said (Ayre's *London Sunday Gazette*, 19 December 1790) to have been "a granddaughter of the noble houses of Kennedy and Cochrane, a niece of the late all accomplished Susanna, Countess of Eglinton, and cousin-german to the present Earls of Cassillis and Eglinton" (*Notes and Queries*, 11th ser., ii. 325). She was probably a granddaughter of Lewis Kennedy and Magdalene Cochrane (see p. 491). The claim of her son was of course never pressed. Both Patersons, senior and junior, are noticed in the *Dict. Nat. Biog.*'

p. 497, l. 3 from foot, delete entire line and accompanying note and insert 'and in 1793 a troop of yeomanry in Carrick, from which the Ayrshire Yeomanry (Earl of Carrick's Own), took its rise.'

p. 498, l. 11 from foot, delete 'and has,' and insert 'He died 10th April 1905, leaving issue.'

p. 500, l. 10 from foot, for 'March' read 'May.'

CATHCART

p. 516, l. 19, for 'before his father' read '15 May 1602.'

p. 516, l. 26, for 'a' read 'two.'

p. 516, l. 27, for 'daughter' read 'daughters.'

p. 516, l. 27, after '*Margaret*,' insert 'and *Jean*, the latter of whom was married, first, to Thomas, brother of William Cathcart of Bardarroch, and secondly, before 1626, to Archibald, brother of David Dunbar of Enterkin (*Reg. of Deeds*, ccclxxxiii. 8).'

p. 518, note 10, for '1572' read '1672.'

p. 519, l. 26, for '31' read '21 (*Caledonian Mercury*, 22 March 1733).'

p. 520, l. 2, after 'Bart,' delete 'by whom she had a daughter,' and insert 'She had a decreet of separation and aliment 7 March 1750 (*Consistorial Processes*, etc., Scot. Rec. Soc., No. 391 ; cf. vol. iii. 457).'

p. 520, l. 26, after 'Ireland,' insert 'On her wedding ring at her fourth marriage she had engraved "If I survive, I will have five."'

p. 521, l. 8, for '31 May' read '30 April (O.S.) or 11 May (N.S.).'

p. 522, l. 10 from foot, after '1764,' insert 'Bred at Glasgow, "very much under the eye of the Principal" : graduated at Balliol College, Oxford, 1786.'

p. 522, l. 7 from foot, after '1802,' insert 'died 1841.'

p. 524, l. 6, for '1776' read '1796.'

p. 527, l. 7 from foot, for 'November' read 'December (*Patrician*, iii. 93).'

p. 530, l. 3 from foot, after 'Cambridge,' insert 'He died 30 October 1905.'

p. 531, l. 3, for 'and has,' read 'having had.'

p. 531, l. 6, after 'Scots Guards,' add 'He succeeded his father as fourth Earl, and died, unmarried, in London 2 September 1911, being succeeded, as fifth Earl, by his brother George.'

COLVILLE OF CULROSS

p. 542, after l. 11, insert—

'5. *Janet*, married Alexander *de jure* third Lord Boyd ; there was a dispensation for the marriage, legitimising the children already born, 23 November 1505 (cf. vol. v. 151).'

p. 543, l. 1, after 'Ersiltoun,' insert '(Dispensation about 29 November 1502).'

p. 543, l. 2, delete 'Crichton, widow of —— Campbell,' and insert 'daughter of Sir Robert Crichton of Sanquhar, and widow of William Douglas, third of Drumlanrig, and of James Campbell of West Loudoun' (cf. vol. vii. 116).

p. 543, l. 18, after 'Drumskeath,' add 'who was in 1522 parish clerk of Erskine (*Culzean Inventory*, No. 258).'

p. 543, note 1, after '31,' add 'Margaret Ker must have been divorced and married again, as on 16 February 1508-9, she was the wife of a Robert Rynde (*Acta Dom. Conc.*, xx. f. 136).'

p. 557, l. 18, after '1630,' add 'She married secondly, on 27 January 1622, Laurence, afterwards Sir Laurence Mercer of Aldie, and had issue (Mercer Pedigree in Lyon Office).'

p. 557, after l. 22, insert—

'(3) *Mary*, married to Duncan Campbell of Glenlyon (*Reg. of Deeds*, Dxxvi. 57).'

p. 557, l. 2 from foot, after 'marriage,' add 'She was married to John Moncrieff of Balcaskie, and had a charter as his future spouse 16 October 1626 (*Fife Sasines*, vi. 176).'

COLVILLE OF OCHILTREE

p. 571, l. 5, after '1596,' insert 'He married Katherine Douglas, who survived him and married, secondly, William Stewart of Egilshay.'

p. 572, l. 2, after '*Elizabeth*,' add 'married (contract 1 November 1592) to James Lindsay of Dowhill (*Reg. of Deeds*, xlv. 255).'

p. 572, l. 3, after '*Janet*,' insert 'married Robert Douglas.'

p. 572, l. 3 from foot, after '*William*,' insert 'He was minister of Cramond, 1635, and subsequently of Greyfriars, Trinity College, and the Tron Kirks, all in Edinburgh (see Scott's *Fasti, passim*): deposed 26 July 1649, for favouring the "engagement," but reponed 8 November 1654 (Mar and Kellie Papers, *Hist. MSS. Com. Rep.*, 206). He was.'

p. 573, l. 21, after 'secondly,' insert 'in the Kirk of Carnock, 25 February 1656 (Dumfermline Reg.).'

COUPAR

p. 577, l. 13, after '1666,' insert 'when she was very young and subject to great pressure (*Athenæum*, 26 June 1905).'

CRANSTOUN

p. 586, l. 20, after 'confirmed,' insert 'by that King about 1339, and.'

p. 586, l. 21, after '1441,' insert 'He had also a grant from David II. on 24 July 1370 of the lands of New Cranstoun on his own resignation, to be held blench instead of ward (original at Oxenfoord).'

p. 586, l. 23, after 'grants,' insert 'to him.'

p. 586, l. 26, delete 'these,' and insert 'grants by William of Seton of certain.'

p. 586, l. 29, delete 'by William of Seton; and of the,' and insert 'and another grant by Thomas, son of Duncan of Symondston, of that.'

p. 586, l. 31, delete 'by Thomas, son of Duncan of Symondston.'

p. 587, l. 6, after 'CRANYSTOUN,' insert 'had from Robert III. charters of Cranstoundaw and Whitehope 29 April, and of New Cranstoun 21 September 1396, both on his father's resignation (Oxenfoord Writs). He.'

p. 590, l. 1, after 'Hume,' insert '(Dispensation granted about June 1503).'

p. 590, l. 10, after 'Macgill,' insert 'daughter of Sir James Macgill of Rankeillor.'

p. 594. l. 5, after 'Riccarton,' insert 'She was buried in the Kirk of Currie, 5 September 1702 (Funeral entry, Lyon Office).

p. 594, l. 21, after 'Wauchope,' insert 'daughter of Adam Wauchope of Keckmure, and widow of Sir John Murray of Blackbarony (*Gen. Reg. Sasines,* vii. 89; cf. Douglas's *Baronage,* 71).'

p. 595, l. 15, after 'secondly,' insert, 'contract 7 April 1623 (*Reg. of Deeds,* ccccIxxxvii. 66).'

p. 596, last line, for 'second,' read 'fifth.'

p. 598, l. 7, after '1752,' insert note, 'There is a full account of the circumstances in the *Patrician,* vol. vi., and in the *Wonderful Magazine,* vol. i. 209. The latter says of him "His person was diminutive: he was so marked with the smallpox that his face was in seams and he squinted, but he possessed the faculty of small talk which is but too prevailing with many of the fair sex."'

p. 601, l. 7 from foot, for 'Forfarshire,' read 'Kincardineshire.'

VOL. III.

CRAWFORD

p. 8, l. 22, for 'Bene' read 'Beneyt.'

p. 11, l. 3 from foot, after '1369,' insert '(mandate for dispensation for this marriage dated 12 January 1365-66) (*Reg. Aven.*, clxiii. 176).'

p. 13, l. 23, after 'married,' insert '(mandate for dispensation of this marriage dated 18 May 1357) (*Reg. Aven.*, cxxxv. 386).'

p. 15, l. 22, after '1385,' delete 'a lady variously named Jean, Kathrina and.

p. 15, l. 24, after 'regis [10],' insert 'A dispensation for the marriage was issued 22 February 1374-75 (*Reg. Aven.*, cxcvii. 34).'

p. 16, l. 14, for 'Gasclune' read 'Glasclune.'

p. 18, l. 21, after 'married,' insert '(mandate for dispensation of this marriage, dated 26 February 1422-23) (*Cal. of Papal Letters*, vii. 260).'

p. 20, l. 6, after 'issue,' add 'He died before 10 May 1558, leaving *David, Jonet*, and *Christian*. His wife married, secondly, before that date, Abraham Crichton (*Acts and Decreets*, xvi. 301; xvii. 206).

p. 23, note 10, after 'Charters,' add 'The spouses had precept of sasine of lands in the barony of Alyth 10 June 1480 (Gray Inventory).'

p. 24, after l. 11, insert
'5. *Jonet*, mentioned in her mother's will (Edin. Tests).'

p. 25, l. 11, after 'David,' add 'He married Matilda, daughter of William Graham of Fintry (*Acts and Decreets*, xvii. 165).'

p. 26, after l. 3 from foot, insert
'The "Wicked Master" had also two sons, possibly illegitimate, *Alexander* and *Patrick* (*Acts and Decreets*, xix. 439; liii. 356).'

p. 27, l. 12, after 'afterwards,' insert 'before 10 April 1543.'

p. 27, l. 16, after 'first,' insert 'contract 28 May 1538 (*Acts and Decreets*, xliv. 129).'

p. 28, l. 16 delete 'Lord,' before Gray, and insert 'Patrick, Master of.'

p. 28, l. 16, after 'widow of,' insert 'Alexander Blair of Balthayock (Gray Inventory, 511) and of.'

p. 29, l. 12, for '1580' read '1582.'

p. 31, l. 5 from foot, after 'Crawford,' insert 'was baptized 8 March 1575-76 (Perth Reg.) and.'

p. 32, note 4, after '1618,' insert 'His wife, indeed, was suing for divorce in 1610 (*Gen. Reg. of Inhibitions*, i. 212).'

p. 32, note 5, for 'Haig' read 'Haigh.'

p. 33, l. 8 from foot, after 'Crawford,' add note 'He was probably older than Henry, as he is mentioned before him in a bond of provision by his father to his sons and daughters, dated 17 February 1616 (*Reg. of Deeds*, ccxci. 445).'

p. 33, l. 4 from foot, after '1631,' insert 'She was married (contract 22 December 1626 (*Reg. of Deeds*, ccclxxxvii. 434) to Robert Fletcher of Balmirmer.'

p. 33, after l. 4 from foot, insert

'10. *Annas*, probably second daughter, as she is mentioned after Margaret in the bond of provision above quoted.

11. *Lilias*, also mentioned in the bond.'

p. 35, l. 5 from foot, for '1613' read '1633.'

p. 36, l. 13, after 'Windsor Castle, insert note 'Lamont (*Diary*, August 1652) says he was imprisoned in the Tower. Lady Crawford went up from Leith by the ordinary coach to see him.'

p. 36, l. 5 from foot, after 'buried,' add 'in August 1640 (Hope's *Diary*, 113).'

p. 36, after last line insert

'6. *James*, baptized 12 January 1649 (Canongate Reg.).'

p. 37, ll. 1, 4, 7, 9 and 11, for '6, 7, 8, 9, 10' read '7, 8, 9, 10, 11.'

p. 37, l. 1, after ' Anna,' insert 'baptized 1 September 1631, and named after Anna, Marchioness of Hamilton (St. Andrews Reg.).'

p. 37, l. 1, after 'married,' insert 'at the Kirk of Holyroodhouse 11 April 1648 (Canongate Reg.).'

p. 37, l. 4, after 'married,' insert 'two days after her eldest sister (*Ibid.*).'

p. 37, l. 21, after 'government,' insert 'The Earl figures in Pitcairn's comedy of *The Assembly* as Lord Whigridden, a Presbyterian Peer, a rigid fool. See also Maidment's *Scottish Elegiac Verses.*'

p. 38, l. 1, after '*Thomas*,' insert 'born 12 January 1694 (Canongate Reg.).'

p. 40, l. 11, for 'Cupar' read 'Ceres.'

p. 40, l. 29, for '1769' read '1759.'

p. 43, l. 26, delete 'left,' and insert 'died 15 August 1825, leaving.'

p. 46, l. 30, for '1878' read '1873.'

p. 46, l. 4 from foot, after 'George' delete 'comma'; for 'Baron' read 'Barons.'

p. 51, l. 4, delete 'The arms anciently borne by the Lindsays were usually an Eagle,' and insert 'The Lindsays in ancient times seem to have borne an eagle as a device.'

CRICHTON

p. 57, l. 8, after 'Gilberton,' insert note 'Recent research has brought to light the fact that on 1 July 1364 a grant of dispensation for the marriage of William de Krechtoun and Margaret, daughter of the late Sir John Preston, Knight, was issued (*Regesta Vaticana*, ccli. f. 302). If this lady be the Margaret Crichton who obtained the charter of Gilberton it would seem that she must have been the mother of all the sons.'

p. 57, l. 25, after 'appears,' insert 'as the grantee of a bond on 1 March 1422. He is next mentioned.'

p. **64,** l. 20, after 'Wardlaw,' insert 'of Kilbaberton (*Acta Dom. Conc.*, ix. 37).'

p. **67,** l. 3 from foot, for 'at least one child,' read 'several children, including.'

p. **67,** l. 2 from foot, after 'Rothes' insert 'By Patrick Panter, presumably the Abbot of Cambuskenneth, and Secretary to King James IV., she had a son David Panter, who was legitimated 12 August 1513 (*Reg. Mag. Sig.*, 19 January 1539-40), and became Bishop of Ross (Dowden's *Bishops of Scotland*, 228).'

CROMARTIE

p. **71,** l. 7, after 'Macleod,' insert 'eldest daughter of Torquil Macleod of the Lewis (contract 6 May 1605).'

p. **71,** after l. 22, insert

'6. *Torquil*, described as brother of Mr. Alexander and Charles in a writ of 1636, after his death (*Reg. of Deeds*, DXLIX. 215).'

p. **71,** l. 24, after 'married,' insert 'contract 23 and 27 February 1633 (*Reg. of Deeds*, ccccxci. 40).'

p. **71,** ll. 23, 24, for '6 and 7,' read '7 and 8.'

p. **72,** l. 13, delete 'in,' and insert 'contract 25 July.'

p. **73,** after l. 6. insert

'5. *Torquil*, baptized 28 September 1647 (Kinghorn Reg.).'

p. **73,** l. 7, for '5' read '6.'

p. **73,** l. 7, after '*Kenneth*,' insert 'baptized 26 November 1648 (*Ibid.*).'

p. **73,** after l. 8, insert

'7. *Charles*, baptized 9 April 1650 (*Ibid.*).'

p. **73,** ll. 9, 11, 14, 16, 18, and 20, for '6, 7, 8, 9, 10, 11' read '8, 9, 10, 11, 12, 13.'

p. **73,** l. 18, after 'married,' insert 'contract 4 March 1670,'

p. **73,** l. 20, after 'married,' insert 'contract 19 August 1667.'

p. **75,** l. 29, after 'first,' delete 'in,' and insert 'contract 6 July 1654.'

p. **75,** l. 30, for 'Moy' read 'Mey.'

p. **76,** l. 6, after 'married,' insert 'first, Mary, sister of David Kinnear of that Ilk (*P. C. Decreta*, 4 December 1690); secondly.'

p. **76,** l. 6, after 'Campbell,' insert 'thirdly, contract 14 January 1726, Elizabeth Edwards, widow, first, of Charles Graydon, and, secondly, of Alexander Sutherland of Kinminitie (see *infra*, p. 204).'

p. **76,** l. 8 from foot, after 'married,' insert 'July 1674.'

p. **76,** l. 7 from foot, after 'issue,' insert 'She raised an action of divorce against her husband 21 August 1694 (*Consistorial Processes*, Scot. Rec. Soc., No. 65). She died aged seventy, and was buried 29 September 1726 (Canongate Reg.).'

p. **76,** l. 5 from foot, after 'issue,' insert 'Sir George and his two sons were drowned in Colston Water, near his own house, on Wednesday, 5 May 1703, "the lady who was in the coach with them was very miraculously preserved" (Turnbull's *Diary*, Scot. Hist. Soc. *Misc.*, i. 431).'

p. **77**, l. 3, for '11,' read '29 (*Wemyss Book*, i. 318).'

p. **77**, l. 5, for 'but,' read 'and.'

p. **77**, l. 6, delete 'no issue,' and insert 'a daughter Sophia, who died 15 August 1727, aged twenty-five (Canongate Reg.).'

p. **78**, l. 13, for 'May 1726' read 'at the age of nineteen, and was buried 7 June 1728 (Canongate Reg.).'

p. **81**, after l. 25, insert '9. *Amelia*,' and alter numeration of subsequent children accordingly.

p. **81**, l. 2 from foot, after 'Baronet,' insert 'full stop,' and delete 'and.' Insert 'She was divorced in 1791 for adultery with Robert Harrup, surgeon, Dumfries (*Consistorial Processes*, Scot. Rec. Soc., No. 963).'

p. **83**, l. 10, for '1597' read '1797.'

p. **83**, l. 4 from foot, for '11 March 1869' read '14 March 1895, aged ninety-nine.'

p. **86**, l. 4, after '1st,' insert 'or.'

DALHOUSIE

p. **88**, after l. 2 from foot, insert 'In light of more recent research the pedigree and statements given on pp. 89, 90 fall to be revised. The William Ramsay de Dalwolsy mentioned above was probably the father of :—

1. SIR WILLIAM, of whom below.

2. *Alexander*, who had from his brother, Sir William, a charter of the lands of Kernok, confirmed by David II. 11 November 1341 (note of Carnock charters communicated by Horatius Bonar, W.S.). About the same time he had from the same king a charter of the lands of Hawthornden, forfeited by Laurence Abernethy (*Reg. Mag. Sig.* i. new ed. App. 2, p. 563). He was, no doubt, the hero of the exploits recounted on p. 89 of text, and the victim of the Knight of Liddesdale's revenge. He was buried in Newbattle Church, see text p. 90, l. 29. He left a son Alexander, of whom below.

SIR WILLIAM RAMSAY was at Berwick in 1338 as in text; granted Carnock to his younger brother as above; and was on the assize who tried Malise, Earl of Strathearn for treason in 1344 (Roll of Parliament, printed in *Scottish Historical Review* for April 1912). He had from David II. a charter of the lands of Inverleith about 1346 (Robertson's *Index*, 36). He left issue :—

1. SIR PATRICK, of whom below.

2. *Sir William*, Sheriff of Lothian in 1357, when he is styled brother of Patrick (Reg. of Newbattle, 309). He had from David II. a grant of £20 sterling yearly, 9 September 1362 (*Reg. Mag. Sig.*, vol. i. new ed. No. 109), and another to him (as of Dalwolsy) and Agnes his wife of the lands of Nether Liberton on 24 October 1369 (*Ibid.*, No. 334). He is styled thus probably to distinguish him from his contemporary Sir William Ramsay of Culluthy; he is never styled *dominus* de Dalhousie. He and his wife sold Nether Liberton to Adam Forrester of Corstor-

phine, 10 April 1384; he styles himself in the charter "lord of Inverleith" (notes from Corstorphine Charters by Thomas Thomson, W.S.). On 6 June 1377 he had a safe-conduct from Edward III., being infirm of body and under the care of the prior of Bermondsey (*Rot. Scot.*, i. 982). He was alive in 1388-89 (*Exch. Rolls*, iii. 188, 693). He had a son David, who had from Robert II. a charter of Inverleith, on his father's resignation, 2 July 1384 (*Reg. Mag. Sig.*, vol. i. new ed. No. 791).

SIR PATRICK was lord of Dalwolsy before 1353 and in 1357 as in text. He styles Alexander his uncle at the latter date (see text). In 1367 (not 1357 as text) he resigned the barony of Dalwolsy in favour of his cousin Alexander (see below). Thereafter he is styled of Kerynton (Charter of 1369 quoted in text). His wife's name was Margaret (see text), and he had a son James, a substitute in the Dalwolsy charter of 1367 (see below).

ALEXANDER, son of Alexander Ramsay of Kernok, had from David II. a charter of the barony of Dalwolsy to himself and the heirs of his body, whom failing, to James, son of Sir Patrick Ramsay and the heirs of his body, whom failing, Sir Patrick's nearest heirs bearing his surname; on Sir Patrick's resignation, dated 15 June 1367 (Original charter belonging to the Earl of Dalhousie), Alexander's charter granting the Blindhalch to Newbattle Abbey, quoted in text, is undated, but must have been granted between 1369 and 1374. It does not appear whether the later lords of Dalhousie were descended from Alexander or from his cousin James.'

p. 92, l. 3, after 'issue,' insert '(besides a daughter Jonet, to whom her grandfather on 3 April 1456 granted a bond to pay her 500 merks Scots in the event of her brother Alexander dying without issue, in which case she would have succeeded to the estates but for the tailzie of the day before) (original in Dalhousie Charter-chest).'

p. 92, l. 19, after 'Elizabeth,' insert 'more correctly Isabel.'

p. 92, l. 20, after 'Angus,' delete 'and,' and insert 'who survived him and was married, secondly, to Thomas Livingstone (*Liber Sententiarum Officialis S. Andree infra Laudoniam*, fol. 55). By her Alexander.'

p. 92, l. 22, after '*Elizabeth*,' insert 'married to Sir Alexander Boswell of Balmuto (*ex inform.* Marquis de Ruvigny),'

p. 92, l. 8 from foot, after 'married,' insert 'first, Elene Home, whom he divorced (notarial instrument *penes* Fraser Trustees); secondly.'

p. 94, l. 2, after 'complainer,' insert 'He was a burgess of Edinburgh: he married Janet Wycht and had issue *William* and *Nicol* (*Edinburgh Burgh Reg. of Deeds*, vol. vi., 19 September 1595), and *John* (Reg. Ho. Charters, 24 September 1595).'

p. 94, l. 7, after 'Agnes Stewart,' insert 'Countess of Bothwell.'

p. 94, l. 18, for 'married to' read 'mothers of.'

p. 95, l. 8 from foot, after 'Berwick,' add 'She was certainly in 1598 the wife of Lawrence Howburn, styled "apparent of Tullibole" (*Reg. of Deeds*, lxxiii. 70).'

p. 95, l. 2 from foot, after '1570,' add 'He is also styled son of George Ramsay of Dalhousie in a writ of 29 July 1570 (Protocol Book of Gilbert Grote, f. 132), but nothing more is known of him.'

p. 95, delete last sentence on page, as the statement applies to the William Ramsay mentioned on pp. 93, 94.

p. 97, l. 18, after 'marriage,' insert 'of date 16 April 1593 (*Reg. of Deeds*, xlvi. 53).'

p. 99, l. 7, for 'and' read 'OF.'

p. 99, l. 2 from foot, after '*John*,' insert 'He married, in or before 1660, Marjorie Spence, and had by her at least one son,

      WILLIAM, afterwards sixth Earl of Dalhousie.'

p. 100, l. 27, delete 'He married,' and the whole of ll. 28, 29, 30.

p. 101, after l. 14, insert

      '4. *James*, mentioned in his brother Robert's testament.'

p. 101, l. 15, for '4' read '5.'

p. 101, after l. 15, insert

      '6. *Lydia*, mentioned with her brothers and sisters in Robert's testament.'

p. 101, l. 16, for '5' read '7.'

p. 101, l. 16, after 'first,' insert 'in 1665 (cf. vol. vi. 600).'

p. 101, l. 16, for 'tenth' read 'eleventh.'

p. 101, l. 17, after 'secondly,' insert 'contract 26 December 1684.'

p. 101, l. 19, for '6' read '8.'

p. 101, l. 21, for '7' read '9.'

p. 101, ll. 7 and 8 from foot, delete 'and, thirdly, to Samuel Collins, M.D.' (The statement to this effect in Wood's Douglas's *Peerage* is erroneous.)

p. 102, l. 21, delete 'Captain.'

p. 102, l. 22, delete 'full stop' and 'Captain Ramsay was the,' and insert comma.

p. 102, l. 23, for 'second' read 'first.'

p. 102, l. 23, after 'was,' insert 'baptized at Dundee 2 December 1660 (Dundee Par. Reg.); became.'

p. 103, l. 17, for '3rd' read '1st' (Hamilton's *Hist. of the Grenadier Guards*).'

p. 104, l. 4, after '1831,' insert 'He died 13 April 1852, having married, first, 1 December 1794, Patricia Heron, daughter of Gilbert Gordon of Halleaths, who died 11 May 1821, and, secondly, in 1822, Elizabeth, daughter of John William Barton. She survived him and married, secondly, 25 April 1856, Bonamy Mansell Power of Guernsey, and died at Paris 25 June 1867.'

p. 104, l. 15, for '1743' read '1793.'

p. 104, l. 22, for 'second' read 'served.'

p. 105, l. 10, delete 'full stop,' and insert 'comma, a daughter *Charlotte*, who married Marcus Slade, colonel 50th Regiment, and died at Hampton Court 23 February 1909, aged eighty-six.'

p. 105, l. 4 from foot, delete 'and was present at the battle of Waterloo.'

p. 106, l. 19, for '76th Foot' read '26th Foot.'

p. 107, l. 23, for '19 October' read '22 December (Cockpen Par. Reg.).'

p. 107, l. 26, for '1850' read '1853.'

p. 110, l. 3, for 'CREST' read 'CRESTS.'

p. 110, l. 4, after 'or,' for full stop put comma, and insert 'for *Ramsay* : a double-headed wyvern with wings erect, spouting fire before and behind, proper, for *Maule*.'

DINGWALL

p. 117, l. 20, after 'Knight,' insert 'On 21 June 1338 he had a grant from his (half?) sister Christian of the lands of Myles, East Lothian, to which she had succeeded as heir of her brother Laurence de Preston, and which Edward III. had treated as forfeited (Craigmillar Charters ; *Cal. of Docs. Scot.*, iii. 337, 385).'

p. 118, l. 2, after 'Edinburgh,' delete 'His son,' and insert 'He died before 1 July 1364. He had two sons and a daughter :—

1. SIMON, of whom after.

2. *William*, who had from Robert III. a charter of the lands of Wester Benyne *circâ* 1399 (*Reg. Mag. Sig.*, vol. i. new ed. p. 642, No. 1884). He as Knight and Lord of Benyne granted some subjects in Musselburgh to Andrew, son of his deceased brother-german, Sir Simon, 28 May 1420 (Craigmillar Charters).

3. *Margaret* (see *ante* corrigend., on vol. iii. p. 57, l. 8).'

p. 118, l. 16, after 'Robert III.,' insert 'He had from his father a charter of Loganraw and others in 1395 (*Ibid.*), which was witnessed by his brother Andrew and by a hitherto unknown brother, *John*.'

p. 118, l. 17, after 'Craigmillar,' insert 'He died 22 August 1421 (*Ibid.*).'

p. 118, l. 18, and l. 4 of footnotes, for '1421' read '1426.'

p. 119, l. 11, after 'right,' insert 'He had a grant, on 21 June 1497, from his cousin, Sir Simon Preston of that Ilk, of the lands of Loganraw and others (Craigmillar Charters).'

p. 119, l. 19, after 'day,' insert 'He had a precept of clare constat as heir of Archibald, his father, in Loganraw 12 October 1526 (*Ibid.*).'

p. 119, l. 4 from foot, after '1532,' insert 'and another as heir of his father in Loganraw 16 October 1531 (*Ibid.*).'

p. 124, ll. 5, 7 and 27, for 'Gray' read 'Grey.'

p. 124, l. 20, for 'Julien' read 'Julian.'

MAXWELL, EARL OF DIRLETON

p. 131, after l. 3, add

'3. *Jane*, married to —— Wharwood.

4. *Anne*, married, in or before 1642, as his third wife, to Sir Thomas Bowyer, first Baronet of Leythorne. Both these children are mentioned in their mother's will, dated 22 August 1657, and proved in C.P.C. 20 August 1660 (*ex inform.* G. E. Cokayne).'

DOUGLAS, EARL OF DOUGLAS

p. 140, l. 21, after '1305,' insert 'But before the end of that year she was married, secondly, to Sir William Bagot of the Hyde (*Collections for a*

History of Staffordshire by Major-General the Hon. George Wrottes-
ley: London, 1908; *Genealogist*, xxv. 140).'

p. 141, l. 8, for 'Aberdeenshire,' read 'Banffshire.'

p. 152, l. 2 from foot, for '1584' read '1384-85.'

DOUNE

p. 186, l. 6 from foot, for 'Whitsunday 1547' read 'Whitmonday 1544, three
years before the remission (*Reg. Sec. Sig.*, xxi. f. 40*b*, 4 September 1547).'

p. 187, l. 2, after 'Aichisoune,' delete full stop, and insert 'who had
previously been the wife of —— Fraser (by whom she had a daughter
Margaret, her executor), of John Logan (*Reg. of Deeds*, ii. 20), and of
William Berry, burgess of Edinburgh (Moray Writs, Box i. No. 57).'

p. 187, l. 7, after 'ward,' insert 'He died 2 September 1584. His wife
survived him and died 26 March 1585 (Edin. Tests.).'

p. 187, l. 11, after 'Buchlivie,' insert 'He died in August 1576 (*Edin.
Sasines*).'

p. 187, l. 13, after 'Aberdour,' insert '(who is styled in 1582 Elizabeth
Robertson or Downie (Moray Writs, Box i. No. 24), and who married,
secondly, before 18 October 1597, John Wemyss of Cutkillhill (*Ibid.*,
Box iv. No. 114).'

p. 187, l. 15, for '*Janet*' read '*Barbara* (*ex inform.* Niall Campbell, Esq.).'

p. 187, after l. 19, insert

    '(2) *John*, mentioned in his father's will. He died before 10 Novem-
ber 1595, leaving a widow, Esther Thomson (Moray Writs, Box iv.
No. 97).'

p. 187, l. 20, after '1619,' insert 'married (contract 7 April 1614), **Agnes,**
eldest daughter of William Shaw of Lethangie, with issue.'

p. 187, ll. 20 and 21, for '(2)' and '(3)' read '(3)' and '(4).'

p. 187, l. 2 from foot, for 'ii.' read 'i.'

p. 188, l. 5 from foot, after 'Revenues,' insert 'He and his wife had a
charter of the lordship of Doune, 6 January 1587-88, ratified to his
grandson, James, Earl of Moray, in 1592 (*Acta Parl. Scot.*, iii. 628;
Reg. Mag. Sig.). She was at Donibristle when it was burned on
7 February 1591-92, and she was so suffocated by the fire that she
died shortly after (Moray Writs, Box iv. No. 58).'

p. 188, note 11, after '258,' add 'His will, dated 5 May 1590, is among the
Moray Writs (Box i. No. 52).'

p. 189, after l. 24, insert, 'In a note of the names of Lady Doune's executors (Moray Writs, Box iv. No. 59) Alexander is named before John;
Archibald is not named, so was probably dead. The daughters mentioned are *Margaret, Jean* and *Agnes*.'

p. 189, l. 25, for 'iii.' read 'ii.'

DUFFUS

p. 194, l. 22, after 'issue,' insert 'She married, secondly, Sir Thomas
Lundie of Pratis.'

p. 194, l. 23, after 'Oliphant,' add 'and, thirdly, Sir William Keith of Inverugy (*Acta Dom. Concilii*, xxviii. f. 71 ; cf. ff. 181, 192).'

p. 195, after l. 19, insert

'5. *Muriel* Sutherland, wife of Alexander Seton of Meldrum, was, it is said, another daughter. She was also the wife of Andrew Fraser of Stanywood. (*See title* Fraser, vol. iii. 109 ; cf. *Reg. Mag. Sig.*, ii. No. 2507 ; *Thanage of Fermartyne*, 688).'

p. 202, l. 2, after ' him,' insert ' being styled domina de Duffus 13 October 1579 (*Reg. Mag. Sig.*, 6 December 1579), and.'

p. 202, l. 27, after 'Rearquhar,' add note ' William Sutherland of Rearquhar died before 10 March 1707. He left two daughters, *Christian* and *Margaret*. He is described as brother-german of Hugh Sutherland of Kinnauld (*Abbreviate of Adjudications*, vol. lvii. 10 March 1707).'

p. 204, l. 1, delete ' before 1604,' and insert ' contract 21 December 1604 (Bulloch's *House of Gordon*, 84 ; *Reg. Mag. Sig.*, 25 November 1608).'

p. 204, l. 25, delete ' was apparently twice married, his second wife being,' and insert 'styled of Mosstowie, married, first, Barbara Guthrie, daughter of Sir Henry Guthrie of Kingedward, widow of William Lindsay of Culsh (*Abbreviate of Adjudications*, lxvii. pt. ii. 775), and had issue ; secondly.'

p. 204, l. 32, after ' married,' insert '(contract dated 30 April 1715) (Durie *Decreets*, vol. 486).'

p. 204, l. 32, after 'Edwards,' insert 'of Monmouth, widow of Charles Graydon, Receiver-General of Customs in Scotland (by whom she had issue a son, *Charles*).'

p. 204, l. 33, after 'Grandvale,' add note 'On 4 October 1727 she assigned to Sir Kenneth, *inter alia*, her share of thirty-two shares of 100 guineas each assigned by Archibald, Earl of Argyll, on 28 March 1691, giving right to a share of all manner of money, gold, silver, jewels, treasure, etc., which at any time had been wrecked or at any time found near or about the island of Mull or elsewhere upon or adjoining to Argyllshire on the coast of Scotland (*Reg. of Deeds*, M'Ken. Office, 143, 19 January 1728. The writer is indebted to Mr. D. Murray Rose for directing attention to this fact, and other additions to this article).'

p. 209, l. 18, after ' thirdly,' insert '(contract dated 26 August 1654 ; tocher £8000 and any jewels left her by her grandmother) (Moray Writs).'

p. 209, after l. 29, insert ' On 3 April 1666 Lord Duffus writes that his youngest son was dead. Robin and Marie were unwell on 6 March 1666 (*ex inform.* John Macgregor, W.S.).'

p. 212, l. 1, after ' *Elizabeth*,' insert 'fourth daughter. She was in 1704 taught dancing by William Badhame, dancing master, Edinburgh, who received £50 for his tuition (Dunbar's *Social Life in Former Days*, 14). She was married (contract 21 November 1709) as daughter of James, Lord Duffus, and sister-german of William Sutherland of Roscommon, to Sir John Gordon of Embo (*Inverness Sasines*, vii. 47).'

p. 212, after l. 7, add

'11. *Isabel*, buried in Greyfriars, Edinburgh, 26 July 1694 (Greyfriars Reg.).

12. *Esther*, married to John Rose in Balvraid; they were infeft in the lands of Easter Balvraid 22 November 1711.'

p. 213, l. 3, after 'executors,' insert 'Married to Baron Otto Gustaff Wrede of the kingdom of Sweden (Summons, Sutherland *v.* Sutherland, 3 April 1778, in *Extinct Processes*, Sale of Skelbo (Dal.), 29 June 1787).'

p. 214, l. 9, after 'Army,' insert 'In 1771 he eloped (being then a Captain in the 26th Foot) with Lady Mary Hay, daughter of James, Earl of Erroll, and wife of Major-General John Scott of Balcomie, whom she had married in November of the previous year (*Consistorial Processes*, etc., Scot. Rec. Soc., No. 583).'

p. 215, l. 20, for 'surmounted' read 'surrounded.'

DUMBARTON

p. 217, l. 17, after 'issue,' insert 'besides two daughters.'

DUMFRIES

p. 221, l. 7 from foot, after 'Elgin,' insert 'On 8 May 1472 he had from George, Lord Haliburton, a charter of the lands of Rossie (now Rossieochil) (Rossie Charters). He was styled of Rossie, and died before 2 February 1502-3, leaving a son and heir *John* (*Reg. Mag. Sig.*, 3 March 1502-3), who died before March 1507-8, leaving a widow Katherine Ross (*Acta Dom. Conc.*, xix. 231), and a daughter *Margaret*, his heir, who married Andrew Stewart of Calzebrochan, and had issue (Rossie Charters).'

p. 224, l. 7, after 'craig,[2]' add as note 'Robert Crichton had probably another daughter. At least in a charter of 1509 Robert, second Lord Crichton describes Thomas Kilpatrick of Closeburn as his brother-in-law. A Margaret Sinclair, widow of the late Patrick Crichton of Petlandy, is described on 6 February 1523-24 as sister of the late Robert (second) Lord Crichton. She had a son *Robert* (*Acta Dom. Conc.*, vol. xxxiv. 84).'

p. 228, l. 5, after '1677,' insert 'and was then probably the eldest surviving son.'

p. 228, l. 6, after '*William*,' insert 'eldest son (*Reg. of Deeds*, Dlx. 108).'

p. 228, after l. 8, insert

'iii. *John*, second son, mentioned 1646 (*Ibid.*) and 22 May 1649 (*Reg. Mag. Sig.*).'

p. 228, ll. 9 and 12, for 'iii' and 'iv' read 'iv' and 'v.'

p. 228, note 6, for '*Dumfries Retours*' read '*Ayr Retours.*'

p. 231, l. 23, after '1612,' insert 'Robert Carlyle and James Irving were hanged in Fleet Street for their share of the crime on 24 June (Craik's *Romance of the Aristocracy*, iii. 344).'

p. **231,** l. 26, after 'issue,' insert 'It is stated that he had been divorced from his wife only two days before the murder was committed. She, however, came and stayed with him in prison (Craik, *ut supra,* 357). It is also said (Winwood, iii. 385) that she married in a few weeks after Crichton's execution, "one Sands of Buckinghamshire."'

p. **231,** l. 5 from foot, after 'lady,' add note 'A base courtesan in Paris (Spotswood).'

p. **231,** note 2, add 'Apparently £500 was offered for Crichton alive and £300 dead (Sloane, MS. 4173 f. 318, cited in Craik's *Romance, etc.,* iii. 342).

p. **234,** l. 11, delete 'in 1642 and 1643,' and insert 'on 19 December 1637 (*Reg. Mag. Sig.,* 16 January 1638).'

p. **235,** l. 21, after '1618,' add note, 'They were married by Mr. John Guthrie, minister of Perth on "ane Sunday after the afternoon's sermon" (*Chronicles of Perth*).'

p. **236,** l. 10, after 'Alexander' read 'afterwards.'

p. **236,** l. 10, after 'Eglinton,' insert 'He "ran away without any advice," and married her, the daughter of "a broken man," when he was sure of Lady Buccleuch's marriage, "the greatest match in Britain. This unexpected prank is worse to all his kin than his death would have been" (Baillie's *Letters,* iii. 366).'

p. **236,** l. 30, for 'French' read 'Freugh.'

p. **236,** l, 5 from foot, after '1803,' insert 'They had issue a son

i. *William,* Prebendary of Peterborough, who, by his wife Euphemia Gauden had issue :—

    (i) *John Crichton Stuart* of New Freugh, N.S.W. He married, first, in 1841, Helen Maria, daughter of R. A. Fitzgerald ; secondly, in 1864, Susan Mary, daughter of the Rev. Edward Hartigan, with issue by first wife :—
        a. William Sutherland, Rector of Owsden, Suffolk.'

p. **237,** l. 19, for '26 July' read '19 June (*Annual Reg.*).'

p. **238,** l. 11, for '*Vallange*' read '*Ross.*' (The name in the text is that given in the Lyon Register.)

DUNBAR, EARL OF DUNBAR

p. **252,** l. 27, for 'Bruce' read 'Brice.'

p. **273,** l. 24, delete whole line, and insert 'to have been a Seton but may have been the daughter of Alan de Wyntoun who married the heiress of Seton and seems to have taken her name (*ex inform.* Colonel the Hon. R. E. Boyle).'

p. **278,** l. 13, delete from 'probably' to 'Colluthie' inclusive with note 7, and insert after 'Wemyss' 'whose parentage is not known. She married, before 1566, a John Wemyss and was his wife in 1570 (*Acts and Decreets,* xxxix. 431 ; xlv. 289).'

HOME, EARL OF DUNBAR

p. 280, l. 2 from foot, delete from 'married' to end of sentence.

p. 282, l. 23, for 'a son' read 'four sons and five daughters.'

p. 282, l. 14 from foot, after 'sons,' add 'by his second wife, besides a daughter *Isobel* by his first (*Gen. Reg. Hornings*, 18 October 1676).'

p. 283, after l. 7, insert
'ii. *Patrick.*'

p. 283, l. 8, for 'ii' read 'iii.'

p. 283, after l. 15, insert
'iv. *Alexander.* v. *Margaret.* vi. *Jonet.* vii. *Anne.* viii. *Elspeth.* ix. *Helen.* (*Reg. of Deeds*, cccxliii. 318).'

p. 284, l. 16, after 'secondly,' insert 'contract 14 August 1610 (*Reg. of Deeds*, cccxi. 16).'

p. 284, l. 18, after 'Edinburgh,' insert 'and widow of Isaac Morison, bailie of Edinburgh (Laing Hist. MS. Bibl. Univ. Edin. Div. ii. No. 473). She obtained decree of Adherence against him 22 June 1620 (*Edin. Com. Decreets*).'

p. 285, after l. 32, insert
'viii. *Margaret*, married to John Stewart of Coldingham (*Gen. Reg. Inhibs.*, 26 September 1631; cf. vol. ii. 171).'

p. 286, l. 12, after '1628,' insert 'married Christian Cockburn.'

VISCOUNT OF DUNBAR

p. 298, l. 8, delete 'She was living at the date of her husband's will,' and insert 'She married, secondly, John Dalton of Swine, co. York (*Genealogist*, new ser., xxvii. 220).'

SCRYMGEOUR, EARL OF DUNDEE

p. 304, l. 25, after 'Baliol,' insert 'He died in 1306, being executed by order of King Edward I. (*Cal. Doc. Scot.*, ii. No. 1811). He married Tiphanie, daughter of David de Inchesirth (*Scrymgeour Invent.*, Scot. Rec. Soc., No. 782).'

p. 305, l. 2, after '*reddendo*,' insert 'for the lands.'

p. 305, l. 3, after 'spurs,' insert note, 'A Richard Scrymgeour is mentioned as Constable of Dundee in 1329 (Inventory *ut sup.*, No. 147).'

p. 306, after l. 7, insert
'2. *John* (secundus) of Henristoun, styled *scutifer* in 1459; married Janet Stag and had issue *John* and *James* (charter of 20 July 1431. *Lauderdale Charter Chest*).

3. *James*, mentioned in 1418 (*Lauderdale Writs*).

4. *David*, mentioned in 1452 and had a charter of Balmakewan (Inventory *ut sup.*, No. 857).'

p. 306, l. 8, for '2' read '5.'

p. 306, ll. 20, 21, delete 'He died between January 1459-60 and August 1463,' and insert 'He was still alive on 8 August 1466 (*Acta Parl. Scot.*, vii. 160), and the date of his death is not exactly known.'

p. 306, l. 24, after 'Marion,' insert 'de Abernethy.'

p. 306, after l. 28, insert
'4. *John* (by third wife) (*Lauderdale Writs*).'

p. 306, last line, delete 'He had succeeded his father before,' and insert 'On.'

p. 307, l. 1, delete 'when.'

p. 307, l. 11, after 'Glassary,' insert '(by second wife) (*Acta Dom. Conc.*, 118).'

p. 303, l. 7, delete '1503,' and insert '4 April 1504 (Fife Sheriff-Court Book, f. 40).'

p. 308, l. 14, delete '——,' and insert '4. *Giles* (Benholm Writs).'

p. 309, l. 4, delete 'before 17 December 1551,' and insert 'in February 1543-44 (*Acts and Decreets*, xlix. 38b).'

p. 309, l. 9, for '1583' read '1533.'

p. 309, l. 18, after 'Kirkton,' insert 'It appears that they contracted marriage without her father's consent (*Acta Dom. Conc. et Sessionis*, vi. f. 111b).'

p. 309, l. 22, for 'to' read 'of.'

p. 309, l. 10 from foot, after 'inserted,' insert note, 'Since the above was written, the House of Lords (*App. Cases*, 1910, p. 342), reversing the decision of the Court of Session, has found that the office of Standard Bearer belonged *jure sanguinis* to the male representative of the house of Scrymgeour. The descent of Mr. Henry Scrymgeour Wedderburn from David Scrymgeour of Sonahard was admitted. Who this David of Sonahard was has not been definitely proved, but there is a presumption that he may have been identical with that David of Balmakewan mentioned above (*corrig*, on p. 306, line 7). Meanwhile, unless and until an heir is found with undoubted nearer descent, the effect of the House of Lords' judgment is that Mr. Scrymgeour Wedderburn has, as representative of the House of Scrymgeour, acted as the Hereditary Standard Bearer of Scotland at the coronation of King George v.

p. 309, l. 3 from foot, after 'Scrimgeour,' insert 'by his second wife, Margaret Maitland.'

p. 311, l. 6, after 'married,' insert 'contract 1583 (Moray Writs, Box xv., No. 1800).'

p. 312, l. 11, after 'uncle,' insert 'comma.'

p. 313, after l. 15, insert
'4. *Elspeth*, married to John Campbell of Lundie, without issue (Moray Writs, box xv. No. 1574).'

p. 313, ll. 24, 25, for '13 March' read '15 November.'

p. 313, l. 28, for 'George' read 'Sir David.'

p. 314, l. 2, after '*Margaret*,' insert '(afterwards wife of James Alexander, son of the first Earl of Stirling).'

p. 314, l. 11, after 'married,' insert 'contract 2 and 30 July 1617 (*Reg. of Deeds*, cclxxxiv. 1497).'

p. 315, l. 6, for '1486' read '1686.'

p. 315, l. 7, after '1686-87,' insert 'She was buried at Holyrood in 1697 (Warrant of 24 February; *P. C. Acta*).'

p. 315, note 7, for 'Fordell' read 'Fardill.'

GRAHAM, VISCOUNT OF DUNDEE

p. 316, l. 11, after 'issue,' add
 '1. *David*, who had issue a son (*Douglas Book*, iii. 119).'

p. 316, l. 23, for 'Dudhope' read 'Glassary.'

p. 319, l. 14, delete 'after 3 June,' and insert 'contract 20 May (*Reg. of Deeds*, xlvii. 74).'

p. 321, l. 18, for '*circâ* 1616-17' read 'contract 13 March 1617 (*Reg. of Deeds*, ccclxxxvii. 384).'

p. 324, l. 21, after 'to,' insert 'Robert, son of (*Aberdeen and Kincardine Sasines*, 23 April 1665).'

p. 324, l. 22, delete 'was his second wife,⁹ and,' with relative note.

p. 324, l. 4 from foot, delete 'Sir.'

DUNDONALD

Since the present article was written, the *Inventory of the Writs of the Earldom of Dundonald* has been published by the Scottish Record Society, and the information therein contained makes some changes on the pedigree given in the text necessary.

p. 336, l. 10, after 'assessment of,' insert 'a.'

p. 336, l. 12, after '1603,' insert note, 'The "four merk land of Linclive" appears to have been part of Wester Cochrane, and is mentioned in a wadset of 2 April 1583 (*Dundonald Inventory*, No. 24). It is not clear that the John Cochrane living there in 1460 was John Cochrane of that Ilk. In 1522 there is mention of a John Cochrane and Margaret Morton, his spouse, as joint tenants of Lincliff (Paisley Rental Book).'

p. 336, l. 16, delete 'issue as far as recorded,' and insert on next line
 'ROBERT OF COCHRANE, who, on 5 March 1456-57, resigned the lands of Cochrane in favour of his son Allan (*Dundonald Inventory*, No. 2).'

p. 336, l. 17, insert 'Robert' after 'father.'

p. 336, l. 21, after 'Armiger,' insert 'He had a charter of the lands of Cochrane from King James II. on the resignation of his father Robert, as above stated (*Dundonald Inventory*, No. 2).'

p. 336, ll. 23, 24, 25, delete 'comma' after '1476,' and insert 'full stop'; delete 'and must have succeeded his father by 1480, as on 8 May of that year,' and insert 'On 8 May 1480.'

p. **336**, l. 10 of notes, after '1488,' delete remaining lines and insert 'Peter married Isobel Spreull (*Acta Dom. Conc.*, xxii. 61) and was succeeded by John Cochrane, though there is nothing to show that John was his son. John Cochrane had sasine of Nether (or Easter) Cochrane in 1505 (*Exchequer Rolls*, xii. 717), and as "John Cochrane of that Ilk" entered into a contract with Isobel Spreull, "relict of Peter Cochrane, now spouse of Patrick Dunyng, anent her terce of Pitfour and others" (*Acta Dom. Conc.*, xxii. 61). Easter Cochrane was sold in 1519 to Archbishop James Beaton by a licence granted under the Privy Seal in 1509 (*Reg. Sec. Sig.*, i. 1943), and John Cochrane, was thereafter styled "of Pitfour," and held the lands under the superiority of the Earl of Crawford, by whom he had been infeft 2 May 1510. He was succeeded by his son *Peter*, who is named in a charter under the Great Seal to George Rollok of Duncrub in 1572, and who was followed by his son David. *David* died 1598, leaving nine children, and his will was proved in Edinburgh 23 January 1598-99. His successor, *Francis Cochrane* of Pitfour, is named in a cause that came before the Privy Council 1605. He was seised in the lands of Pitfour 4 September 1607, and is the last of that line. The Cochranes of Easter Cochrane and of Pitfour may have been descended from a Roger or Robert Cochrane who had a charter of Pitfour and others from King David II. about 1360 (*Reg. Mag. Sig.*, vol. i., new ed., App. 2, 1356).'

p. **337**, delete ll. 10, 11 and 12, and insert 'He died *vitâ patris s.p.*'

p. **337**, l. 13, delete from 'Robert Cochrane' down to 'of that Ilk' on l. 5 from foot of p. 338 and accompanying notes, and insert as follows :—

'ROBERT COCHRANE of that Ilk must have succeeded about 1488, as in that year he had sasine of the lands of Cochrane by command of Matthew, Earl of Lennox (*Dundonald Inventory*, No. 4). He was alive 2 January 1516-17, when he gave sasine of the lands to his son John and his wife (*Ibid.*, No. 7).

JOHN COCHRANE of that Ilk was seised in the lands of Cochrane by Robert, his father, 10 January 1492 (*Ibid.*, No. 5) and had a charter of the same lands 13 January 1498 (*Ibid.*, No. 6). He married Elizabeth Semple, before 20 January 1486-87, when they had a charter of Corsefoord (*Ibid.*, No. 26).

JOHN COCHRANE of that Ilk, served heir to his grandfather in the lands of Wester Cochrane 8 May 1520 (*Ibid.*, No. 8), and married Marion Stewart, who was his widow 27 November 1540 (*Acts and Decreets*, xxxiv. 385), and who, in 1556, was the wife of John Gibson (*Ibid.*, xii. 248). He had issue JOHN, who succeeded him, *William*, who is mentioned with Marion Stewart, his mother, in a renunciation dated 1 April 1565 (*Inventory*, No. 22), and *David*, who occurs in a mortgage on the lands of Cochrane with his brother William, 28 May 1536 (*Laing Charters*, 409).

JOHN COCHRANE of that Ilk succeeded his father 12 May 1539 (*Inventory*, No. 11). He is stated by Crawfurd to have married Mary, daughter of Lindsay of Dunrod, of which marriage no evidence has been found. He certainly married Elizabeth Semple of Fulwood, and with her had a charter of the lands of Craigton, dated 5 April 1529 (*Ibid.*, No. 9). By her he had issue :—

    1. WILLIAM, who succeeded him.

    2. *Janet*, named in the will of Elizabeth Montgomery, her sister-in-law. She may have been the daughter who was married to —— Maxwell, and had a son, William, mentioned in the will of William Cochrane of that Ilk.'

p. 339, l. 9 from foot, for 'Alexander' read 'John.'

p. 340, second last line of notes, delete 'Charles Home Cochran of Ashkirk, Hawick, N.B., Captain R.N,' and insert 'Alexander Charles Purves Cochran, born September 1879, captain 40th Pathans.'

p. 340, add to end of note, 'The Cochranes of Rochsoles, which was acquired by Patrick Cochrane in 1579, are stated by Nisbet to be descended from Barbachlaw.'

p. 342, after l. 6, insert

    'ii. *Hugh*, who took the name of Peebles, and died after 1717. He is mentioned in the will of his half-sister Eupheme, proved in Glasgow, 1749. The estate of Mainshill passed to the Earl of Eglinton.'

p. 342, ll. 7, 8, 10 and 11, for 'ii, iii, iv, v,' read 'iii, iv, v, and vi.'

p. 342, l. 24, after 'relict of,' insert 'Col. Walter.'

p. 342, l. 26, after 'him,' insert 'Her will was proved in Edinburgh, 1677, by Walter Scott of St. Leonards and Harlawood, her son by her first marriage.'

p. 342, l. 28, after 'navy,' add 'Died in Ireland before 1661 (*Books of Protestant Owners, Ireland*).'

p. 345, l. 6, for 'the' read 'James.'

p. 345, l. 7, after 'Lennox' read 'and Esmé, his son.'

p. 346, l. 23, after 'married,' insert 'after 14 April 1633, when she is styled his future wife (*Reg. of Deeds*, DXXVI. 205), and.'

p. 349, l. 24, delete 'only.'

p. 350, l. 23, after '1766,' insert 'Married —— Turnbull (*Reg. of Deeds*, Mackenzie, 1766).'

p. 350, after l. 25, insert

    '(3) *Thomas*, baptized at Ochiltree, 1 September 1664.

    (4) *Charles*, baptized at Ochiltree, 2 August 1669.

    (5) *Eupheme*, baptized at Ochiltree, 24 June 1660.'

p. 350, l. 26, delete '(3),' and insert '(6).'

p. 350, l. 26, after 'married,' insert 'in London, 18 February 1686 (Mar. Licences, Faculty Office).'

p. 350, l. 26, after 'Berwick,' insert 'Her husband died 27 September 1691, aged twenty-nine. She survived till 21 March 1748, when she died, and was buried with her husband in Legerwood Churchyard (cf. Turnbull's *Diary*, Scot. Hist. Soc. *Misc.*, i. 328). Their daughter, *Elizabeth*, married the eighth Earl of Dundonald. The story of Grizel Cochrane's robbery of the postbags containing the warrant for her father's execution appears to be mythical.'

p. 350, after l. 26, insert

'3. *James*, for whose burial at Holyrood a warrant was granted 13 February 1694 (*P. C. Acta*).'

p. 350, l. 27, for ' 3 ' read ' 4.'

p. 351, l. 10, after ' Glen,' insert ' Lady Katherine Kennedy died in 1700, and was buried in Greyfriars Churchyard, Edinburgh, 15 February (Commissary Rec.). By her.'

p. 351, l. 26, for ' Smith ' read ' Smythe.'

p. 351, l. 27, after ' issue ' delete to end of sentence and insert ' Her grand-daughter, Catherine Smythe, became heiress of her grand-aunt, Christian Cochrane.'

p. 352, l. 2, after ' 1694,' add ' when William Cochrane of Kilmaronock succeeded to the estate of Polkellie.'

p. 352, l. 13, after ' married,' insert ' as his first wife, 28 April 1680 (Dundonald Par. Reg.).'

p. 354, l. 17, for ' 1689 ' read ' 1687 (Paisley Par. Reg.).'

p. 354, l. 18, for ' twelve ' read ' fourteen.'

p. 355, l. 19, after ' issue,' insert ' a *Pastoral* on their nuptials was written by Alexander Pennecuik and published at Edinburgh, 1723.'

p. 357, l. 22, for ' 1790,' read ' 1740.'

p. 358, l. 23, after ' Dundonald,' insert ' baptized at Ochiltree, 23 July 1691.'

p. 359, l. 13, for ' James,' read ' John.'

p. 360, after l. 2 from foot, insert

'15. *Catherine*, married William Wood, and died 4 October 1776, and was buried at Holyrood.'

p. 360, last line, for ' second ' read ' third.'

p. 363, l. 21, after ' fleet,' insert note, ' Napoleon called him " Le Loup des Mers." '

p. 368, l. 5, delete ' 27 March,' and insert ' 26 December.'

p. 368, l. 8, after ' ARMS,' insert '(recorded in Lyon Register).—1st and 4th.'

p. 368, l. 9, after ' azure,' insert ' for *Cochrane* : 2nd and 3rd, argent, on a saltire sable nine lozenges of the field, for *Blair*.'

DUNFERMLINE

p. 372, l. 5 from foot, after ' married,' insert ' in Holyrood Abbey Chapel, 5 June 1614 (Canongate Reg.).'

p. 373, l. 4, for ' 1621 ' read ' 1624 (cf. vol. viii. 449).'

p. 373, delete ll. 12 and 13.

p. 373, ll. 14, 15, for ' 1608 ' read ' towards the end of November 1615,' and for ' fourteen ' read ' six.'

p. 373, 1. 28, after 'army,' insert 'On 14 January 1637 he describes himself as now of the age of twenty-one years complete (*Reg. of Deeds*, DI. 177).'

p. 373, 1. 28, for '1607' read '1637.'

p. 374, 1. 12, after 'married,' insert 'contract 29 March, 2 April and 9 November 1632 (*Reg. of Deeds*, 14 May 1450).'

p. 374, 1. 14, after 'born,' insert '13 June (Dunfermline Reg).'

p. 374, 1. 19, delete 'in September 1670,' and insert 'contract 8 September 1670; tocher 20,000 merks (*Wigtown Inventory*, Scot. Rec. Soc., No. 349).'

p. 374, 1. 24, after 'Dunfermline,' add 'born 12 June 1642(DunfermlineReg.).'

p. 374, 1. 25, delete 'in 1675,' and insert 'between 23 August and 27 October 1677 (*Reg. Sec. Sig.*, 2nd ser., iii. f. 159; *Paper Register of Great Seal*, x. 11).'

p. 375, 1. 11, after 'married,' insert 'contract 6 July 1682 (*Reg. of Deeds*, Durie, 12 January 1608).'

DUNKELD

p. 381, 1. 14, after '*Mary*,' delete 'who' and insert 'baptized 5 February 1701 at St. Germain—Marie d'Este, titular Queen of Great Britain, being her godmother (*Reg. of St. Germain en Laye*, p. 70). She.'

p. 381, after 1. 15, insert 'Lord Dunkeld had a natural son *Claude* by Estelaine Pen, said to be a Scotswoman, baptized 2 June 1697 (*Ibid.*).'

DUNMORE

p. 384, 1. 4 from foot, for 'Mastyr' read 'Martyr.'

p. 385, 1. 26, delete 'unmarried.'

p. 385, 1. 28, after '1731,' insert 'Mary Halket, daughter of Sir Charles Halket of Pitfirran, raised an action of declarator of marriage, alleged to have taken place in 1708, against him, and got decreet 10 October 1717. They had a daughter *Catherine*, baptized at Dunfermline in January 1709 (*Consistorial Processes*, etc., No. 199). He appointed Mary Megott of St. Olave, Southwark (probably his mistress) his sole executrix. He gave a factory to "his beloved spouse" in 1709 (*Reg. of Deeds*, Mackenzie, 14 February 1711).'

p. 386, 1. 12, for 'Drummie' read 'Drimmie.'

DYSART

p. 398, 1. 3, after 'Oliphant,' insert 'He was, no doubt, that Alexander Murray, Canon of Inchaffray, who signs various feu charters of the lands of that Abbey, *e.g. Lib. Insule Missarum*, p. 120.'

p. 398, delete from 'He' on 1. 17 to 'issue' on 1. 23 and insert 'He married, first, Marion, daughter of Alexander Alexander of Menstrie (cf. vol. viii. 168), who died in January 1595 (Edin. Tests., 10 March 1597); secondly, Barbara, daughter of John Murray of Arbenie. She died

15 September 1600 (Edin. Tests.); and he married, thirdly, Agnes, daughter of Nairn of Strathord. By his first wife he had issue :—'

p. 398, l. 26, delete entire line, and insert ' in February 1643, leaving issue.'

p. 398, l. 28, after 'married,' insert 'his cousin Jean, daughter of Mr. Anthony Murray, parson in England' (*Funeral Escutcheons*, Lyon Office, Scot. Rec. Soc., 42).'

p. 398, after l. 5 from foot, insert

' By his second wife he had :—

 (6) *Mungo.*

 (7) *Margaret*, mentioned in her mother's will.

By his third wife he had :—

 (8) *Margaret (secunda).*

 (9) *Janet (Reg. of Deeds*, ccix. 165).'

p. 401, l. 1, for 'Murray' read 'Conall (Gask Writs, Bundle cxxxi. No. 13[2]).'

p. 401, after l. 27, insert

' 7. *Anthony*, parson of Utricton (or Urthrisholm) in Kent (*Genealogist*, xxviii. 23).'

p. 401, l. 27, after 'father,' insert 'styled servitor to the Countess of Nottingham; died before 23 September 1611 (*Reg. of Deeds*, cxcii. 269).'

p. 401, l. 28, for '7' read ' 8.'

p. 401, after l. 28, insert

' 9. *Janet*, baptized 15 January 1575 (Par. Reg. Perth), married to Archibald Napier (*Genealogist*, xxviii. 23).'

p. 402, l. 17, for 'probably died about 1651,' read 'died after 11 September 1653 (Birch's *Transcripts of Nicholas' Letters*).'

p. 402, l. 2 from foot, after '*Anne*,' insert 'who had, in consideration of her bounty towards officers and soldiers who were in straits in and about London and Westminster after the battle of Worcester, on 18 November 1676, a pension of £200 (*P. C. Eng. Reg.*, iii. 89).'

p. 402, note 4, after 'Elizabeth,' add 'He appears, however, in the Register of the Great Seal after 1643 merely as William Murray.'

p. 402, note 6, delete from 'but no authority is quoted' down to end of note, and insert 'and this latter statement is correct, *vide The Nicholas Papers.*'

p. 405, last line, delete 'before February 1708' and corresponding note 8, and insert ' about 1705 (*Sutherland Book*, i. 367).'

p. 405, last line, after 'first,' delete ' on Wednesday.'

p. 406, l. 1, for 'before 1 January 1677-78,' read '26 December 1677.'

p. 409, l. 5, 'In the epitaphs from the "Abbey of Kilhampton" (*a jeu d'esprit* published in 1780) it is stated that "the loveliness of her disposition was clouded with remorse and sorrow as having provoked the slander of a V(illain) who dared justify his insult with the sword, and though she survived the fatal issue, the remainder of her days was known only to solitude and marked with lamentation," evidently referring to the circumstances of her husband's death.'

p. 409, l. 20, for ' February' read ' March,' and after ' 1751,' insert ' baptized 25 April following at St. James's, Piccadilly.'

p. 410, l. 1, after '*Jane,* insert ' born 26 March and baptized 29 April 1750 at St. James's, Piccadilly.'

p. 411, l. 10, after ' 1789,' insert ' Horace Walpole wrote the following epitaph on her :—

> " Adieu, sweet shade, complete was thy career,
> Though lost too soon and premature thy bier :
> For each fair character endowed thy life
> Of daughter, sister, friend, relation, wife.
> Yet lest unaltered fortune should have seemed
> The source whence virtues so benignly beamed,
> Long mining illness proved thy equal soul,
> And patience like a martyr's, crowned the whole.
> Pain could not sour, whom blessings had not spoil'd,
> Nor death affright, whom not a vice had soil'd."
>
> *Journal* of Miss Berry, i. 190.'

p. 413, l. 21, after ' Munro,' insert ' 109 Princes Street, Edinburgh.'

p. 413, l. 22, after ' issue,' insert '*Lionel Alexander Arthur,* who married Louisa Margaret Hope. On 15 October 1912 his domicile was declared to be Scottish (*Chancery Division*).'

p. 414, l. 35, for ' 3 ' read ' 2.'

p. 420, l. 18, for ' with ' read ' between two.'

p. 420, l. 19, after ' expanded ' insert ' or.'

EGLINTON

p. 426, l. 3 from foot, after '*John,*' add note ' John MacHenry had on 14 August 1394 a dispensation to marry Margaret, daughter of Thomas de Kirkpatrick, Knight. He had a previous intercourse with Evota, daughter of —— " Meclelan " laic (*Regesta Vaticana,* cccvii. f. 567).'

p. 428, third line of note 5, after ' 1357,' insert ' (The dispensation for their marriage is dated 19 February 1362-63) (*Regesta Vaticana,* cclxi. f. 21).'

p. 432, l. 24, delete ' and it is doubtful if he survived his grandfather.'

p. 432, l. 31, after ' heir,' insert ' He appears to have died in 1468, as in the retour of his son Hugh as his heir in Bonington and Pilton (Coupar Writs in Moray Charter-chest, Div. 5, No. 87) these lands are said to have been in the hands of Katherine Kennedy for eighteen years by reason of conjunct fee, and thereafter for one year in non-entry.'

p. 437, l. 22, after ' Argyll,' insert ' He died before 29 August 1538, when his brother Neil was infeft as his heir in Milnestaneflat and other lands (*Acts and Decreets,* l. 387).'

p. 437, note 8, after ' 1523,' insert ' cf. *Reg. Sec. Sig.,* i., No. 3024, 31 July 1518.'

p. 442, l. 19, after ' married,' insert ' apparently on 19 May 1583 (*Bowes Correspondence,* Surtees Soc., 440).'

p. 443, l. 22, after ' death,' insert ' He was born about 1584 (*Edin. Comm. Decreets,* 11 March 1612). He chose curators 3 August 1598 (Fife Sheriff Court Books).'

p. **444,** l. 6 from foot, after 'grants,' insert 'On 3 March 1610 the Earl petitioned the Privy Council for a summons against Hew Campbell, Lord Loudoun and Jean Campbell, Duchess of Lennox, requiring them to produce the Countess, who had been carried off in June 1608 by emissaries of theirs to Loudoun House, where she was still detained a prisoner (*P. C. Reg.*, viii. 820).'

p. **446,** l. 17, after 'first,' insert 'contract 6 June 1612 (*Reg. of Deeds*, cciv. 161).'

p. **447,** ll. 3 and 4 from foot, delete 'widow of John Hamilton of Letham, but also described in her husband's testament as.' *Note.*—John Hamilton of Bardanoch never possessed Letham, which was purchased by his son William about 1716.'

p. **448,** l. 3 from foot, for 'tenth' read 'fifth.'

p. **450,** ll. 16, 17, for '24 January 1688' read '27 November 1686 (*Seafield Correspondence*, Scot. Hist. Soc., 34).'

p. **452,** l. 1, after '*Montgomerie*,' insert 'baptized 11 September 1680, (Canongate Reg.).'

p. **452,** l. 4 from foot, after 'unmarried,' insert 'she married, secondly in December 1682, Sir Patrick Ogilvie of Boyne, Lord Boyne (*Seafield Correspondence*, Scot. Hist. Soc., xiii.).'

p. **452,** note 3, for '*Memorials*, i. 93' read '*Memorials*, i. 95.'

p. **453,** l. 6 from foot, after '1678,' add note 'She is said to have died 5 December 1675, which is so far corroborated by a reference to her funeral in Glasgow weaver's accounts, 1675-76.'

p. **454,** l. 27, for 'before 15 June 1687' read 'in August 1686 (*Seafield Correspondence*, Scot. Hist. Soc., 34).'

p. **456,** l. 12 from foot, after 'unmarried,' insert 'The Glasgow Council accounts, under date 11 April 1696, refer to the expenses of the Magistrates for one night at Kilwinning when at the burial of *two* Masters of Montgomerie. It would appear, therefore, that one of his two immediate younger brothers died at the same time as he did.'

p. **457,** l. 9, after 'issue,' insert 'Her third daughter Catherine was seduced by a blackguard Sir John Houston of Houston, Bart. (see vol. ii. 520) (though his wife divorced him for impotency). She went on the town, and wrote her own memoirs, *The Amours and Adventures of Miss Katty M.* (cf. *Letters of C. K. Sharpe and Sir Walter Scott to Robert Chambers*, p. 34, privately printed, 1904).'

p. **457,** l. 8 from foot, after '14,' insert 'and was buried at Restalrig, 16.'

p. **457,** l. 3 from foot, delete 'in,' and insert '24 (Reg. of Old St. Paul's, Edinburgh; *Scottish Antiquary*, v. 14).'

p. **458,** l. 5, for 'about' read 'on (*Ibid.*).'

p. **460,** l. 17, after '1788,' read 'for adultery with the Duke of Hamilton (*Consistorial Processes, etc.*, Scot. Rec. Soc., No. 882).'

p. **460,** l. 18, for '1734' read 1794.'

p. **462,** l. 4 from foot, for 'the elder brother' read 'grandnephew.'

p. **463**, l. 4, delete 'daughter of Charles Newcomen, Clonahard, co. Long-ford,' and insert 'one of the eight illegitimate daughters of Thomas, second Viscount Newcomen, by Harriet Holland (*Scottish Historical Review*, v. 103).'

p. **464**, l. 2 from foot, for '25' read '24.'

ELGIN AND AILESBURY

p. **468**, l. 24, for 'consecration' read 'enthronement.'

p. **470**, l. 17, after 'Rosyth,' insert '(she afterwards married —— Auchmuty, and had a son Henry (*Acta Dom. Conc.*, xiv. 105).'

p. **474**, l. 6 from foot, for 'nephew' read 'son.'

p. **474**, ll. 4 and 5 from foot, delete 'afterwards second Lord Bruce of Kinloss.'

p. **474**, l. 4 from foot, after 'him,' insert 'William, married Margaret Cruickshank (*Records of Sheriff-Court of Aberdeen*, ii. 22), with issue a son, as above stated.'

p. **475**, l. 3, after 'Kinloss,' insert 'of which he was appointed Commendator, 26 July following (*Reg. Sec. Sig.*, xlix. 135).'

p. **475**, l. 5, delete 'the position of Commendator of Kinloss, with.'

p. **477**, l. 19, delete 'Sir.'

p. **479**, l. 17, for '1872' read '1672.'

p. **482**, l. 18, for 'Allan' read 'Allen.'

p. **482**, l. 28, after 'her,' insert note 'Horace Walpole's name for her was "one more game at cribbage" (Miss Berry's *Journal*, i. 412).'

p. **483**, l. 12, for '1 August 1642' read 29 July 1641.'

ELGIN AND KINCARDINE

p. **485**, l. 17, delete 'Margaret, daughter of Archibald Primrose of Burn-Brae,' and insert 'Euphame, daughter of David Primrose in Culross (cf. vol. vii. 216).'

p. **485**, after l. 25, insert

'4. *Christina*, or *Christian*, "eldest lawful daughter," married, first, to Robert, Master of Colville (vol. ii. 557), who died before December 1614; secondly, after 29 December 1617, when she had a sasine as his future wife (Protocol Book of James Primrose, H.M. Reg. Ho., f. 153), Laurence, afterwards Sir Laurence Mercer of Aldie, with issue.'

p. **485**, ll. 26 and 29, for '4' and '5' read '5' and '6.'

p. **485**, delete ll. 31 and 32, with accompanying note.

p. **486**, l. 7, for 'Robert' read 'John.'

p. **486**, l. 11, delete 'to Sir John Arnot of Fernie, Fife,' and insert 'contract 31 May 1664, to Sir James Nicolson, younger of Cockburnspath.'

p. **486**, after l. 15, insert

6. *Grisel*, married, before 3 January 1642, to Sir Robert Arnot, eldest son of Sir James Arnot of Fernie (Fife Sheriff-Court Deeds, 20 January 1713).'

p. **486**, note 1, for '1635' read '1638.'

p. 486, note 3, for '*Ibid*' read 'Wood's Douglas's *Peerage*, i. 518.'

p. 486, note 4, for '*Ibid*,' read '*Gen. Reg. of Sasines*, x. 102.'

p. 487, after l. 12, insert

'2. *Cornelius*, baptized 13 June 1663 (Culross Reg.); died young.

3 and 4. *Alexander* and *Cornelius* (*secundus*), twins, baptized 13
September 1664 (*Ibid.*); also died young.'

p. 487, ll. 13, 14 and 17, for '2, 3, 4' read '5, 6, 7.'

p. 487, after l. 18, insert

'8. *Lucy*, baptized 1 September 1669 (Canongate Reg.).'

p. 487, l. 19, for '5' read '9.'

p. 487, l. 21, for 'second' read 'fifth,' and after 'son,' insert 'baptized
5 June 1666 (Culross Reg.).'

p. 488, l. 20, after 'Allan,' insert 'It was probably he who became Rector
of Wath, co. York, in 1716, and died 27 May 1723, aged eighty-one (*ex
inform.* H. B. M'Call, Esq.).'

p. 488, l. 21, after '*Helen*,' insert 'baptized 30 November 1643.'

p. 488, l. 24, after '*Janet*,' insert 'baptized 18 January 1638.'

p. 488, after l. 27, insert

'5. *Margaret*, baptized 6 August 1639.'

p. 488, l. 28, for '5' read '6.'

p. 488, l. 28, after '*Rachel*,' insert 'baptized 24 October 1648 (Edin. Reg.).'

p. 492, l. 26, after '1816,' add 'He, who was born 1763, married, secondly,
Ann Henderson, heiress of Fordel.'

p. 496, after line 5, insert

'(4) *Richard Frederick David*, born 2 March 1894.'

p. 496, ll. 6, 7, 8, 9, for '(4), (5), (6), (7)' read '(5), (6), (7), (8).'

p. 496, l. 30, for '18' read '8.'

p. 496, l. 32, for '9' read '29.'

ELIBANK

p. 500, ll. 5 and 28, for '1485' read '1485-86.'

p. 501, l. 12, after 'Register,' insert 'He was Clerk of Council in 1509
(charter *penes* Rev. A. T. Grant).'

p. 502, l. 13, for '22 April 1507' read '31 January 1503-4 (Protocol Book of
J. Foular).'

p. 502, l. 14. after 'Hoppar,' insert 'daughter of Richard Hoppar, burgess
of Edinburgh (*Acta Dom. Conc.*, xxii. 93).'

p. 502, l. 19, for 'Archibald' read 'Alexander (*Ibid.*, xxxv. 103).'

p. 502, l. 21, after '*Margaret*,' insert 'first contracted to Henry Wardlaw of Torry, which contract he was personally called on to imple-
ment by Andrew Murray her brother, 22 March 1530-31 (Edin. Council
Records).'

p. 502, l. 25, for '1513' read '1513-14.'

p. 503, ll. 20 and 22, for '1551' read '1551-52.'

p. 503, l. 23, after 'lands,' insert 'The Governor Arran gave her on her
marriage a tocher of £133, 6s. 8d. (*Treas. Accounts*, x. 115).'

p. 504, l. 8, delete 'is said to have.'

p. 504, note 4, after ' 184,' add ' (*Reg. Sec. Sig.*, xliv. 17).'

p. 507, l. 4, after 'married,' insert 'contract 18 January 1628 (*Reg. of Deeds*, ccciii. 144).'

p. 507, l. 4, delete 'Skene, by whom,' and insert 'second daughter of John Skene of Halyards, Clerk of Session. By her.'

p. 509, l. 8 from foot, after 'secondly,' insert '13 February 1670 (Edin. Reg.).'

p. 509, l. 24, delete from 'lieutenant' down to 'captain 1685-88' on l. 26.

p. 510, l. 13, for '1638' read 'contract 24 March 1638 (*Reg. of Deeds*, DXVIII. 289).'

p. 516, ll. 16 and 17, delete 'Miss Collier,' and insert 'a daughter and co-heir of John Collier of Hastings, Sussex (who died 9 December 1760).'

p. 516, l. 17, for 'who' read 'She.'

p. 518, note 2, after ' son,' insert ' was, in 1776, a member of the Council of Revenue at Patna, Bengal. He is mentioned as a substitute next after his half-brother Patrick in the entail of Simprim after noted (see next paragraph). He.'

p. 519, l. 7, after 'Aberlady,' insert note 'Besides William Young mentioned in the preceding paragraph, Lord Elibank had four other natural sons, one of whom *Patrick* was five years old on 9 November 1776, when his father, with whom he was living at Ballincreiff, entailed on him the estate of Simprim (*Reg. of Entails*, xix. 339).'

p. 521, l. 8, for ' 1833 ' read ' at Edinburgh 6 January 1834.'

p. 523, l. 8, after '1871,' insert 'created, 3 July 1911, VISCOUNT ELIBANK OF ELIBANK, co. Selkirk, in the Peerage of the United Kingdom.'

p. 523, l. 19, Created BARON MURRAY OF ELIBANK, co. Selkirk, 13 August 1912.

p. 524, l. 20, after ' 1643,' insert ' Viscount Elibank of Elibank, co. Selkirk, 3 July 1911.'

ELPHINSTONE

p. 527, l. 11, delete 'The name of Sir William Elphinstone's wife is unknown, but,' and insert ' He married, *ante* 6 November 1421, Margaret Hepburne. On that date the spouses had a charter from James Douglas, Lord of Dalkeith (Moray Charters, Box ii. No. 22).'

p. 529, last line, for ' 1578 ' read ' 1518.'

p. 530, l. 10, for ' 1524 ' read ' 1504.'

p. 530, note 1, delete note and insert 'Original in Elphinstone Charterchest.'

p. 531, l. 7, for 'death' read 'baptism.'

p. 531, l. 15, after 'Forbes,' insert ' and died in 1518, her *obit* being celebrated on 10 September (Spalding Club *Misc.*, i. 74).'

p. 532, l. 26, for 'fourth' read 'fifth.'

p. 533, ll. 6 and 7, delete 'before 8 August 1590,' and insert ' 10 June 1589 (cf. vol. vii. 463).'

p. 533, l. 3 from foot, ' after ' married,' insert 'proclamation 15 April 1592 (Stirling Reg.).'

p. 534, l. 15, for 'Lundrassie' read 'Findrassie.'

p. 536, l. 17, after 'issue,' insert 'and, secondly, to James Stewart of Ryland (*Reg. of Deeds*, ccccxviii. 345).'

p. 536, note 8, add to note 'According to *Records of the Scots Colleges* (New Spalding Club), p. 190, he was Rector of the Scots College at Rome from 8 September 1622 to the beginning of January 1644.'

p. 538, l. 14, after 'married,' insert 'contract 27 October and 24 November 1613 (*Reg. of Deeds*, cccclxxxvii. 253).'

p. 538, l. 25, after '*Jean*,' insert 'contracted to Alexander Elphinstone of Dunlugus, 29 April 1644 (*Banff Sasines*, v. 185).'

p. 538, l. 30, after '*Anna*,' insert 'contracted to Thomas, eldest son of Walter Kinnaird of Cowbin 2 May 1653 (*Elgin Sasines*, iv. 130).'

p. 539, l. 22, after 'Quarrell,' add 'while a daughter Marion was married to George Norvell of Boghall, Advocate.'

p. 542, after l. 16, add

'*Jean Elphinstone*, married, 16 November 1673, to Robert Mylne, Provost of Linlithgow, created Baronet 1686, is said to have been a a daughter of Lord Elphinstone but nothing has been found to prove the statement (Edin. Mar. Reg.; *ex inform*. Rev. R. S. Mylne).'

p. 545, l. 15, after '1784,' add (see vol. i. p. 383 *Corrigenda*).'

p. 549, l. 4, for 'titles' read 'two baronies.'

p. 549, after l. 9, insert

'By his second wife the Viscount had also a daughter :—

 Georgiana Augusta Henrietta, married, first, 20 September 1831, to the Hon. Augustus John Villiers, second son of George, fifth Earl of Jersey. He died 1837, and she was married secondly, 10 May 1870, to Lord William Godolphin Osborne, and died 21 September 1892.'

p. 550, l. 28, for 'Torriedale' read 'Torrisdale.'

ERROLL

p. 559, l. 12, delete 'June 1306,' and relative note, and insert '3 September of that year, when his son Gilbert is styled Lord of Erroll (Coupar Charters *penes* Earl of Moray, Div. 4, No. 32).'

p. 562, l. 7, for '1416' read '3 July 1416 (*Reg. Vat.*, cccxxviii. 453).'

p. 562, after l. 14, insert

 '(3) *John*.'

p. 563, l. 2, for '1436' read '1437.'

p. 563, after l. 9, insert

 '3. *Nicholas*, who died before 1452, leaving three sons, *Gilbert, Nicholas* and *Alexander*, substitutes in the charter of 1452 (see *infra*).

 4. *Alexander* of Mouchale, also a substitute in that charter.'

p. 563, delete ll. 10 to 15. 'These were brothers, not uncles of the first Earl.'

p. 563, after l. 29, insert

 '2. *Walter*. He and the rest of the younger sons are substitutes in the undermentioned charter of 1452, and he is a witness with his brothers David and Thomas to a charter of confirmation by their nephew William, third Earl of Erroll, to Allan Kynard of that Ilk, 14 March 1470-71.'

p. 563, l. 7 from foot, for '2' read '3. Mr.'

p. 564, after l. 2, insert

'4. David, in 1470-71 Mr. David.

5. Nicholas.

6. Thomas, in 1470-71 Mr. Thomas.'

p. 564, l. 7, after 'resignation,' insert 'He was raised to the rank of a Lord of Parliament before 10 April 1450, on which date, as well as in the September following, he is styled Lord the Hay (Writs in Erroll Charter-chest; Acta. Parl. Scot., 6 July 1451, ii. 67, 69).'

p. 564, note 2, l. 4 from foot of notes, delete 'and no copy of them has been discovered,' and insert 'but transcripts have recently been discovered in H.M. Register House. The charter of the Lordship of Erroll contains a destination to the Earl and the heirs-male of his body, with remainder successively to Walter, Mr. Gilbert, David, Nicholas, and Thomas, the Earl's brothers, William Hay of Ury, his uncle, and Gilbert, Nicholas, and Alexander, sons of his uncle Nicholas, Alexander Hay of Dronlaw, Gilbert and John Hay, brothers of the last, Alexander of Mouchale, the Earl's uncle, Sir David Hay of Lochorwart, Edmund Hay of Tallou and the heirs-male of their bodies respectively.'

p. 565, l. 10, after '1471,' add 'After Huntly's death she married, secondly, Andrew, second Lord Gray, who died in 1514, and she was apparently alive in 1517 (Acta Dom. Conc., xxix. 38, 39).'

p. 567, l. 3 from foot, after 'Calder,' insert 'She is named as Countess of Erroll in an order of Court, dated 9 July 1532, at which date she was dead, and her sons Mr. Peter and James Sandilands of Cruvie were her executors (Acta Dom. Conc. et Sess., i. f. 58).'

p. 568, l. 6, after '1511,' add as note 'This conclusion is wrong. They were the same person (cf. vol. vii. 411).'

p. 568, l. 25, after 'Sutherland,' add note 'On 26 May 1541 the Countess got from the King six ells Paris black and four ells French black for "dule weed." On 12 May 1542 she got thirteen ells of red velvet to be a gown "agane hir marriage" (Treasurer's Accounts, vii. 449; viii. 77).'

p. 569, l. 2 from foot, after 'Essilmont,' insert 'dying in February 1608 (Slains Charters).'

p. 571, l. 14, after 'secondly,' insert 'at Aberdeen in June 1604.'

p. 571, l. 16, after 'Burleigh,' add 'She obtained decree of divorce against him, 24 March 1620 (Edin. Comm. Decreets).'

p. 572, l. 13, after 'Earl,' insert note 'In a note on the Scots nobility of 10 April 1589 Francis is said to be third son, the two elder being deaf and dumb (Grampian Club, Estimate of Scots Nobility, 56).'

p. 573, l. 5, after '1626,' insert 'and died in September 1657 (Dunblane Tests.), having.'

p. 573, l. 9, for 'before 1672' read 'in July 1670 (Dunblane Tests.).'

p. 574, l. 2, after 'married,' insert 'contract 23 July 1602 (Slains Charters).'

p. 574, l. 3, after 'Erroll,' insert 'was baptized 30 April 1564 (Erroll Reg.), and.'

p. 575, l. 6 from foot, after 'time,' insert 'He was afterwards warded within a certain distance of his own house; but in order to make arrangements with his creditors he got a licence, 9 November 1615, to "repair to Edinburgh and there to remain in some lodging, not kything onyway in daylicht upon the heich street" (*P. C. Reg.*, x. 405).'

p. 576, note 2, add to note 'There is, however, in the same Charter-chest another will of this Earl, dated 12 November 1630.'

p. 577, l. 14, after 'secondly,' insert 'before 20 May 1643 (*Reg. of Deeds*, DXLIX. 364).'

p. 577, l. 21, after '*Margaret*,' insert 'baptized 11 April 1611.'

p. 577, l. 25, delete 'baptized 11 April 1611.'

p. 577, l. 28, delete from 'which' down to end of sentence, and insert 'probably intended to secure consideration for her on her travels as she was an invalid and obliged to live abroad for her health. She was one of the three noble ladies whom Gilbert Blakhal served (see his *Brief Narration*, Spalding Club). She died unmarried.'

p. 577, l. 31, for 'in' read '8 September'; and for 'ten' read 'twelve.'

p. 578, l. 14, for '7 December 1636' read 'December 1637 (Spalding's *Memorials*, i. 84).'

p. 579, l. 27, for '1 October' read '21 October (Slains Charters).'

p. 579, l. 7 from foot, after '*s.p.*' insert 'after November 1693 (*Perth's Letters*, Camden Society, 15).

p. 580, l. 7, after 'Edinburgh,' insert 'He spent three years, 1712-15, travelling abroad. His accounts for his tour are in the Slains Charter-chest.'

p. 580, l. 22, after 'Dalgaty,' insert 'He predeceased his wife, dying in July 1745 (Slains Charters).'

p. 581, l. 17, for 'mother' read 'aunt.' See previous page.

p. 581, l. 5 from foot, after 'divorced,' insert 'in 1771, she having eloped with Captain James Sutherland of Duffus of the 26th Foot (*Consistorial Processes*, etc., Scot. Rec. Soc., No. 583).'

p. 583, last line, after '1812,' insert 'and was buried in Bath Abbey (M.I.), aged thirty-four.'

p. 587, l. 19, for '1315' read '1314.'

FAIRFAX

p. 606, l. 5, after '1900,' insert 'He made out his claim to the title before the House of Lords, 17 November 1908.'

p. 606, l. 9, for 'gules' read 'sable.'

FALKLAND

p. 610, l. 4, after ' 1633,' insert note 'He broke his leg while out shooting; it had to be amputated, and in the absence of the doctors hemorrhage set in. When medical assistance was procured nothing could be done, and he bled to death. Another account says he died from blood poisoning, the result of the amputation, after a week's illness (Marriott's *Life and Times of Lord Falkland*, 2nd ed., 72).'

p. 610, l. 8, after ' fifty-four,' add ' The effigies of her and her husband appear at the head and foot of the tomb of Lord Tanfield in the Parish Church of Burford, co. Oxford.'

p. 610, l. 15, after ' 1642,' add ' while pursuing the enemy at the head of a troop of Royalist Horse in an obscure village in Devonshire (Clarendon's *Life*; for notices of Lorenzo and his elder brother see Godfrey's *Social Life under the Stuarts*).'

p. 610, l. 28, after ' Scott,' insert 'He was buried 15 March 1656 (Funeral entry, Ulster's Office).'

p. 610, l. 6 from foot, after ' her,' insert ' who died 25, and was buried 27 July, 1658, her will as Dame Susan Cary, widow, relict of Patrick Cary, late of Dublin, being dated 25 July 1658, and proved that year (*ex inform.* G. D. Burtchaell, Esq., Athlone Pursuivant).'

p. 610, l. 4 from foot, delete ' born about 1656,' and insert ' baptized 25 April 1656 at St. John's, Dublin (Par. Reg., *ex inform.* G. D. Burtchaell, Esq., Athlone Pursuivant).'

p. 611, l. 2, after ' her,' insert ' who was buried in Westminster Abbey 11 April 1719 (cf. vol. iv. 382).'

p. 611, after l. 9, insert

'(3) *Susanna Patricia*, baptized at St. John's, Dublin, 2 April 1657.

(4) *Patricia*, mentioned along with her sister in her mother's will.'

p. 611, l. 5 from foot, after ' man,' insert note 'Aubray says "I have heard Dr. Ralph Bathurst say that when he was a boy my Lord Falkland lived at Coventry (where he had then a house) and that he would sit up very late at night in his study, and many times came to the library at the school there." His teacher was Philemon Holland, "the Translator-General" (Whibley's *Literary Portraits*, p. 149).'

p. 614, l. 6, after ' *Dorothy*,' insert 'born 3, and baptized 21 October, 1705, at St. Gregory's by St. Paul's, London.'

p. 614, l. 11, after ' 1804,' insert ' in the house of her uncle, Arthur Richard Dillon, sometime Archbishop of Narbonne, Somerset Street, Portman Square. Her relations with him gave rise to some scandal (*Notes and Queries*, 10th ser., viii. 102; see also *Memoirs of the Comtesse de Boigne*.)'

p. 614, l. 4 from foot, for ' 1799' read ' 1779,' and after ' Chapman,' add ' of Tarrant Gunville, Dorset, who was buried in Bath Abbey, 12 January 1798. They left issue.'

VOL. IV.

FIFE

p. 8, after l. 9, insert

'2. *Annabella*, married to Sir Hugh. . . . (Inv. of Titles, H.M. Reg. Ho., iii. 16).'

FINDLATER

p. 19, l. 3, after 'Ythane,' insert 'She was married, secondly, to Alexander Irvine of Drum, and died in 1532, her obit being celebrated 19 May (Spalding *Misc.*, i. 68).

p. 19, l. 22, after Aberdeen delete 'she,' and transfer the remainder of the paragraph to new line, and insert

'11. *Margaret*, who, etc.' as in text.

p. 19, l. 24, for '11' read '12.'

p. 20, l. 6, after 'Moray,' insert 'An Elizabeth Ogilvy, daughter of the Laird of Findlater, is said to have been the wife of Alexander Irvine of Drum, who fell at the battle of Pinkie 1547 (*The Irvines of Drum*, by Col. Forbes Leslie, 66, 168).

p. 26, l. 12 from foot, for '1615' read '1616.'

p. 29, l. 22, for 'ninth' read 'eighth.'

p. 29, note 5, after 'c̠xxxii.' add '229.'

p. 32, l. 2 from foot, after '*David*' add ' of Templehall. He died before 27 January 1575-76, having married, before 10 April 1556, Christina Galychtlie, heiress of Ebrux, who survived him. They had issue a son *Gilbert* (Protocol Book of Duncan Gray, f. 7b ; *Acts and Decreets*, lx. 453).'

p. 33, l. 4, after '1535' add 'He was alive 31 March 1558 (Protocol Book of Duncan Gray, f. 15).'

p. 34, note 7, for '1161' read 1611.'

p. 35, l. 14, for 'p. 30' read 'p. 29.'

p. 35, l. 17, delete 'Inchmartin.'

p. 35, l. 18, for 'was sold in that year' read 'had been sold in 1650.'

p. 35, l. 23, for '30 March 1658' read 'in May 1659 (*Seafield Correspondence*, Scot. Hist. Soc., ix.).'

p. 35, l. 27, for 'Innes' read 'Irvine.'

p. 36, l. 5, after 'She,' insert '(who died in August 1687) (*Seafield Correspondence*, Scot. Hist. Soc., 39).'

p. 36, l. 8, after 'married,' insert 'in October 1703 (Edin. Reg.).'

p. 36, l. 15, after 'were,' insert '(besides other children, who died young).'

p. **36**, l. 17, for 'June 1698' read 'May 1699 (*Seafield Correspondence,* Scot. Hist. Soc., 265).'

p. **36**, l. 7 from foot, after 'married,' insert 'first, Elizabeth, daughter of Sir James Baird of Auchmedden, and widow of Sir Alexander Abercrombie of Birkenbog.'

p. **37**, l. 5, for '(4)' read '4.' After l. 5 insert
'5. A son born before 19 April 1672 died young.'
'6. *Robert,* born February 1673 (*Seafield Correspondence,* Scot. Hist. Soc., p. xv.), a cornet of Dragoons, died before 19 October 1693 (*Ibid.,* 124).'
'7. A daughter, born before July 1666, died young.'

p. **37**, l. 6, for '(5)' read '8,' and after '*Mary,*' insert 'married, first, in 1698, to a son of George Leslie of Burdsbank, much to the annoyance of her family ; and, secondly, on 25 September 1704, to George, son of Alexander Barclay in Banff (*Seafield Correspondence,* Scot. Hist. Soc., 247, 248, 381).'

p. **37**, l. 7, for '(6)' read '9.'

p. **37**, l. 8, for '1698' read '1692 (*Ibid.*).' *Note.*—The above were children not of Col. Patrick but of the third Earl.

p. **38**, l. 3, for '1' read '21 (*Warrant Books,* xviii. 239).'

p. **38**, l. 9 from foot, for '6 May' read 'shortly after 12 May (*Seafield Correspondence,* Scot. Hist. Soc., 266).'

p. **38**, l. 8 from foot, after '*George,*' insert 'probably born about January 1695 (*Seafield Correspondence,* Scot. Hist. Soc., 157, 158).'

p. **40**, l. 14, after 'Atholl,' insert note, 'She was a very capable woman, who saved the estate from being sold, through excellent management. She built from her own funds the bridge sixty feet high and with a span of eighty-two feet, across the Burn of Deskford to Cullen House. As a mark of respect, her portrait was hung in the County Rooms at Aberdeen (C. Sinclair's *Shetland and the Shetlanders,* 279).'

p. **40**, l. 23, for '1729' read '1779.'

p. **40**, l. 28, after '1813,' insert note, 'She became blind during the last years of her life, and was very badly off. Caroline, Princess of Wales, writes to Lady Charlotte Bury saying that she has no more than £300 a year. The Duchess of Brunswick gave her £250 a year and an allowance for candles, coals, and the rent of a small lodging in Manchester or Baker Streets (*Diary of a Lady in Waiting,* ii. 392).'

FORBES

p. **44**, l. 1, after 'is,' insert 'said to be.'

p. **44**, ll. 6 and 7, delete these lines and insert 'but the document is injured at the place where the name occurs. The surname is certainly not de Forbes : it is del . . ., and probably del Ard.'

p. **54**, l. 4, for 'John' read 'James.'

p. **54**, l. 8 from foot, after '1565,' insert 'It is also stated (*History of the Family of Burnett of Leys,* New Spalding Club, p. 29; Macfarlane's *Gen. Coll.,* ii. 244) that she was ultimately married to Alexander or Arthur Forbes of Echt, who survived her.'

p. 54, after l. 7 from foot insert

'5. *Alexander*, who, with his brother William, was tried and acquitted for art and part in the slaughter of Alexander Seton of Meldrum 27 January 1527-28 (Forbes Charters).'

p. 54, ll. 6, 5, and 2 from foot, for '5, 6, 7' read '6, 7, 8.'

p. 54, l. 2 from foot, after 'Brux' insert 'She is also said to have married as his second wife, Alexander Burnett of Leys (*Acts and Decreets*, xxxix.; *Family of Burnett of Leys*, New Spalding Club, p. 25).'

p. 55, l. 2, after 'her,' insert 'who died 1518.'

p. 56, l. 22, after 'issue,' insert 'He was instituted to the parsonage and prebend of Forbes 26 February 1562-63 (Forbes Charters).'

p. 59, l. 2 from foot, after 'divorce,' insert 'On 22 July 1577 William Douglas of Glenbervy had a remission for adultery with Margaret Gordon, sister of umquhile George, Earl of Huntly (*Reg. Sec. Sig.* xliv. 87).'

p. 62, l. 5, after 'married' insert 'contract 22 and 23 January 1628 (*Reg. of Deeds*, cccclxxvii. 224).'

p. 62, l. 21, delete 'Sir.'

p. 62, after l. 29 insert

'4. *Robert*, youngest son, captain in the Scottish service in 1666 (Forbes Charters).'

p. 62, ll. 30, 31, and 35, for '4, 5, 6' read '5, 6, 7.'

p. 63, l. 12, after 1675, insert 'as his first wife.'

p. 63, l. 15, after 'secondly,' insert 'contract dated 26 March 1668.'

p. 64, l. 9, after '1730,' insert 'She was alive in 1766.'

p. 68, l. 18, delete 'Bart. of Nova Scotia.'

FORBES OF PITSLIGO

p. 72, l. 3, insert 'great' before 'grandfather.'

p. 74, l. 5 from foot, after 'daughter' add 'married, contract 3 November 1620, to Walter Ogilvy of Boyne (*Reg. of Deeds*, cccclxxxviii. 274).

p. 74, l. 3 from foot, delete line.

p. 74, l. 2 from foot, for '6' read '5.'

p. 75, l. 6 from foot, after 'first,' insert 'contract 4 and 5 February 1706, tocher 10,000 merks (*Reg. of Deeds*, Dalrymple, 4 January 1711).'

FORRESTER

p. 82, after l. 15 insert 'He apparently had another daughter, J—— whose arms impaled with those of her husband, William Napier of Wrightshouses, and bearing date 137– is over the gateway of St. Margaret's, North Queensferry. William Napier acquired part of Wrightshouses from Adam Forrester in 1390 (Robertson's *Index*, 137, No. 9).'

p. 84, after l. 27 insert

'3. *John* (*secundus*) mentioned in the charter of 1430-31 (see preceding paragraph).

p. 84, ll. 28 and 32, for '3 and 4' read '4 and 5.'

p. 85. ll. 18 and 19, delete 'whose name is unknown, but.'

p. 85, l. 20, after 'husband,' insert 'and indicate her to have been a member of the well-known Edinburgh burgess family of Wigmore (*Eccles. Architecture of Scot.*, Macgibbon and Ross, iii. 261).'

p. 85, l. 30, after 'witnesses' insert 'He was served heir to his grandfather in Longniddry 12 October 1451 (Wintoun Inventory, No. 77).

p. 85, l. 33, after 'before,' insert '16 March 1466-67, when his son was served heir to him, On [20, etc.]'

p. 85, l. 33, delete 'when.'

p. 86, l. 17, after 'Corstorphine,' insert 'was served heir to his father 16 March 1466-67 (Wintoun Inventory, No. 77), and.'

p. 87, l. 5, after 'Calder,' insert 'She died in March 1562 (Edin. Tests.).'

p. 88, l. 2 from foot, after 'Corstorphine,' insert 'had a precept of clare constat from George, Lord Seton, 26 June 1548, as heir of his father (Wintoun Inventory, No. 79). He.'

p. 89, l. 29, delete 'one daughter' and insert 'issue :—'

'1. *James*, who died in the lifetime of his father, leaving a natural son *James*, to whom, as his grandson, Sir James, on 28 April 1587, granted the lands of Nether Barnton, Langnudrie, and others (Charter *penes* Earl of Moray).'

p. 90, l. 28, after '8,' delete '——' and insert '*Katherine*, married, contract 1621, to Robert son of James Douglas, Commendator of Melrose (*Reg. of Deeds*, cccxii. 295).'

p. 92, l. 15, for 'in 1654' read 'before 10 August 1652 (*Gen. Reg. Inhibs.*).'

p. 92, l. 22, delete lines 22 and 23.   Helen, Lady Ross, was the daughter of Sir James Forrester of Torwoodhead (*see title* Ross).

p. 92, ll. 24, 27, 32, 36, for '3, 4, 5, 6,' read '2, 3, 4, 5.'

p. 92, note 1, after 'cxcviii.,' insert '333.'

p. 93, last line for 'Brawford' read 'Brainfoord.'

p. 94, l. 15, for 'Lilian' read 'Lilias.'

p. 94, after l. 17, insert

'2. *Margaret* (*P. C. Reg.*, 3rd ser., ii. 569, where there is a narrative of the conjugal relations of Lilias Forrester and her husband).'

p. 99, l. 24, after 'stars,' insert 'argent.'

FORTH

p. 101, l. 24, for '1566' read '1556.'

p. 102, l. 7, after '*Alexander*,' insert 'styled Captain Alexander, died before 1615, leaving a daughter Elizabeth (*Reg. of Deeds*, ccclv. 415).'

p. 102, l. 5 from foot, after '1655,' insert 'Sir Francis had a natural daughter, *Margaret*, married to James Henderson (*Gen. Reg. Inhibs.*, 16 November 1676).'

p. 103, after l. 18, insert

'(4) *James*, (5) *Elizabeth*, (6) *Christian* (*Gen. Reg. Inhibs.*, 5 November 1674).'

p. **105,** l. 15, after ' Church,' insert ' Sir Philip Warwick in his memoirs describes the Earl as "a Scot, an experienced commander, and a man of natural courage : purely a soldier, and of a most loyal heart, which his countrymen remembered, for they used both him and his widow with all extremity afterwards." The number of the wound marks which the Earl bore is said to have been greater than the number of battles in which he was engaged (*Memoirs of Ann, Lady Fanshawe*, 348 n.).'

p. **105,** l. 21, after ' wife,' insert ' She was godmother to Lady Fanshawe's daughter Anne, born in Jersey in 1646.

FRASER

p. **109,** l. 10, after ' 1505,' add ' He married, contract 28 October 1501, (*Aberdeen Burgh Sasines*), Muriel Sutherland, widow of Alexander Seton of Meldrum. She must have been his second wife.'

p. **109,** ll. 11 and 12, delete these lines and insert ' He left issue :—'

p. **109,** ll. 5 and 6 from foot, delete ' is not ascertained,' and insert ' was Stewart as appears from a charter to himself and his wife of the lands of Blayrneill, 30 September 1505 (*Aberdeen Burgh Sasines*).

p. **116,** after l. 6 from foot, insert
  ' 4. *James*, witness to a deed in 1648 (*Reg. of Deeds*, Dlxvi. 26), died *v.p.*, *s.p.*, and alter succeeding numbers of children accordingly.'

p. **118,** after line 22, insert ' Andrew, third Lord Fraser, had also a natural daughter *Marjory* (*Reg. of Deeds* (Durie), 16 March 1681).'

FRENDRAUGHT

p. **125,** l. 25, after ' 1599,' insert ' He married Isobel Chalmers, with issue a son *George*. He was alive in 1637 (*Reg. of Deeds*, Dxviii. 371).'

p. **126,** l. 19, after ' Craig,' insert ' She was alive 1664 (*P. C. Reg.*, 3rd ser. i. 501).'

p. **128,** l. 24, for ' 2 ' read ' 3.'

p. **129,** l. 5, after ' married,' insert ' contract 9 May 1642 (*Reg. of Deeds*, Dlii. 160).'

p. **134,** after l. 2, insert note
  ' The following are said to have been children of James Crichton of Auchingone.'
  William, born 16 April 1710.
  Elspet, born 10 December 1711.
  George, born 7 February . . .
  Janet, born 21 September 1719.
  Margaret, born 4 January 1723.
  Anna, born 21 May 1726.
  Alexander, born 3 May 1729.
  (*ex inform.* Douglas Crichton, Esq. Lincoln's Inn Fields).'

STEWART, EARL OF GALLOWAY

p. **149,** l. 4, after ' preserved,' add note ' Her Christian name was Isobel (*Patent Rolls*, Henry IV. for 1400).'

p. 150, ll. 5 and 6 from foot, delete 'is believed to have died about 1479,' and insert 'was alive 8 October 1485 (Protocol Book of James Young).'

p. 150, l. 3 from foot, delete ' is said to have.'

p. 150, last line, after 'Menteith,' insert 'She was alive 23 October 1495 (*Acta Dom. Conc.*, 401).'

p. 151, l. 26, for 'about 1479-80' read 'between 1485 and 1495.'

p. 151, l. 6 from foot, for 'about 1500' read 'in 1496.'

p. 152, l. 5, after 'Kirkmaho,' delete down to 'Fintalloch' on l. 16.'

p. 152, after l. 24, insert

'ALEXANDER STEWART, fourth of Garlies, succeeded his father in 1496, having sasine of these lands in that year (*Exch. Rolls*, x. 771). He died in 1500, having married Janet Gordon, who survived him and married, secondly, Sir William Keith of Inverugie (*Acta Dom. Conc.*, xvii. 176). He had issue :—

    1. ALEXANDER.

    2. *Walter*, ancestor of Barclye.   3. *Janet*.

    4. *Elizabeth* (*Acta Dom. Conc.*, xxii. 161).'

p. 152, l. 25, for 'fourth' read 'fifth.'

p. 153, ll. 2 and 3, delete 'was one son,' and insert 'were.'

    '1. ALEXANDER.

    2. *Thomas*, alive in 1584 (*Reg. Sec. Sig.*, li. 76).'

p. 153, l. 4, for 'fifth' read 'sixth.'

p. 155, l. 6, for 'fourth' read 'sixth.'

p. 155, l. 25, after 'families,' insert 'He died 10 August 1592, having married Margaret Stewart, with issue (Edin. Tests.).'

p. 155, l. 10 from foot, after 'Barbara,' as note, insert 'Barbara Gordon survived her husband and married again, before 2 September 1592, Alexander Agnew of Ardoch (Cal. of Charters, Reg. Ho. at date).'

p. 156, l. 23, for 'Mureford' read Penninghame (cf. vol. v. 108).'

p. 156, l. 26, for 'fourth' read 'sixth.'

p. 158, l. 7, delete 'she married, secondly, John Wallace of Dundonald.'

p. 158, after l. 9, insert

    '2. *Thomas*.   3. *William*.

    4. *James*, all mentioned in mutual bonds of caution (*P. C. Reg.*, v. 574). The last named was his mother's executor (*v. post*, p. 408).'

p. 158, ll. 10 and 11, for '2' and '3' read '5' and '6.'

p. 158, l. 18, for 'fifth' read 'seventh.'

p. 159, l. 3, delete 'before 10 October 1576,' and insert 'contract 21 April 1574 (*Reg. of Deeds*, xiv. 350).'

p. 159, l. 4, for 'William' read 'James.'

p. 159, l. 5, after 'Queensberry' insert 'who died 13 Aug. 159—, and was buried at Glasserton (*Fourth Rep. Hist. Monuments Com.* i.).'

p. 159, l. 11, delete entire entry.

p. 159, l. 14, for '3' read '2.'

p. 159, delete ll. 23, 24, 25.

p. 159, ll. 26, 27, 28, 29, for '4, 5, 6, 7' read '3, 4, 5, 6.'

p. 159, l. 7 from foot, for 'sixth' read 'eighth.'

p. 161, after l. 16, add

'4. *Janet* (probably illegitimate) appears in the Charity Rolls of 1694 and 1696.'

p. 163, l. 25, for '1761' read '1701.'

p. 163, l. 27, for '1761' read '1701.'

p. 165, l. 14, after 'January,' insert note 'The marriage took place on 7 January according to a contemporary account (*Red Book of Grandtully*, ii. 324).

p. 165, l. 20, for 'proved' read 'recorded (*Reg. of Deeds*, ccxlv. 286).'

GARNOCK

p. 174, l. 23, for '1681' read '1680 (Edin. Tests.).'

GLASGOW

p. 184, note 2, for 'Fordun' read 'Bower.'

p. 185, after l. 17, insert

Robert Boyl, layman of Glasgow diocese, had an indult to choose a confessor 6 June 1372 (*Reg. Aven.*, clxxxiii. 551).

p. 187, note 9, after '*Reg. Mag. Sig.*,' insert 'Edin. Tests., 26 February 1584–85.'

p. 189, l. 10 from foot, after '1583,' insert 'and was living 26 December 1584 (Kelburne Writs).'

p. 197, note 5, delete '189.'

p. 198, l. 24, delete '15 October 1673,[16]' and insert '1 March 1688 [16].'

p. 199, l. 21, delete 'in,' and insert '23 April.'

p. 199, l. 21, delete 'is said to have.'

p. 200, l. 16, after 'Mr. William,' insert 'who had.'

p. 200, l. 18, after 'afterwards,' insert 'bought on the death of Sir Alexander.'

p. 200, l. 2, from foot, delete 'had,' and insert 'died 30 June 1730, leaving (original letter at Kelburne).'

p. 203, l. 22, for 'elder' read 'eldest.'

p. 204, l. 13, after 'issue,' insert '(besides two sons, both named *David*, who died young (correspondence at Kelburne).'

p. 204, l. 4 from foot, for '1721' read '1720.'

p. 205, l. 3 from foot, after '1729,' insert 'and was buried at Rowallan (original letter at Kelburne).

p. 205, l. 2 from foot, for '29 March 1720 [17]' read '9 July 1724 [17].'

p. 205, note 17, delete note and substitute 'Correspondence at Kelburne.'

p. 209, l. 6, after '1865,' add 'He died at Twyssenden Manor, Goudhurst, Kent, 29 September, and was buried at Kilndoun 2 October 1909.

p. 209, l. 16, for 'St. Helen's' read 'Middleton, near Freshwater.'

p. 210, l. 39, for 'Alister' read 'Alastair.'

p. 210, l. 9 from foot, after '1886,' add 'married at the Cathedral, Christchurch, to Agar Williams of Wellington, New Zealand, and has issue.'

p. 211, l. 23, for 'is' read 'became.' After 'barrister-at-law,' add 'He died at Horsington House, Templecombe, 22, and was buried at Horsington 27 March, 1907.'

p. 211, l. 26, after 'and,' insert 'by her, who survived him, and died at Parkstone, Dorset, 2, and was buried at Horsington 6, February 1911.'

p. 211, l. 27, for 'has' read 'had.'

p. 213, l. 12, after 'Hagley,' add 'She died at Salisbury 7, and was buried beside her husband 9, January 1907.'

p. 213, l. 21, after 'and,' insert 'by her who died at Fleet, Hants, 14, and was buried there 17, November 1909.'

p. 213, l. 3 from foot, delete 'has' and insert 'by her, who died at Tokio, Japan, 10 May 1910, aged forty-six, had.'

p. 214, l. 27, after 'was,' insert 'born at Craig, 17 July 1766 (Kilmaurs Par. Reg.), and was.'

p. 215, l. 1, for '25 September' read '5 November (Canongate Reg.).'

p. 215, l. 3, after 'Bart.,' insert 'Rear.'

p. 215, after l. 9, insert
    '13, Grissell, died young.'

p. 216, l. 1, after '1791,' insert 'aged sixty-three.'

p. 216, l. 1, for 'Jane' read 'Jane Mary.' For '30' read '13'; after '1823,' add 'aged fifty-nine; buried at Renfrew (Coffin plate).'

p. 218, l. 3, after 'died,' insert 'at Edinburgh.'

p. 218, l. 4, after '1868,' insert 'aged seventy-one.'

p. 220, l. 19, after '1897,' insert 'Commander.'

p. 220, l. 22, after 'Surrey,' add 'and has issue:—
    (1) *David William Maurice*, born at Kelburne 24 July 1910.'

p. 220, l. 4 from foot, after '1906,' insert 'He married, 15 September 1908 at Holy Trinity Church, Sloane Street, Katherine Isabel Salvin, daughter of Edward Salvin Bowlby of Gilston Park, Herts, and Knoydart, Inverness, and has issue:—
    '(1) *Patrick John Salvin*, born at Melbourne, Victoria, 21 March 1910.'

GLENCAIRN

p. 226, l. 24, after 'brother,' insert 'On 16 March 1365-66 a Papal commission was granted to dispense in Nigel Cunningham's marriage with a lady named Joanna Douglas, of St. Andrews diocese, not otherwise designed, to whom he was related in the third degree of affinity (*Reg. Aven.*, clxiii. f. 217).'

p. 230, last line, after '1417,' add in note, 'See *Acta Dom. Concilii*, xix. f. 15, for charter by Robert, Duke of Albany (dated at Stirling 17 December 1415), confirming a charter of 23 November 1400, by William of Cunynghame, knight, Lord of Redhall, granting to his natural son, William, the lands of Bonaly and Wodehall in the barony of Redhall and sheriffdom of Edinburgh.'

p. 230, note 3, after '1639,' insert 'see also *Reg. Mag. Sig.*, vol. i. (new ed.), App. 2, No. 1952, and *Ibid.*, 21 Nov. 1450.'

p. 234, l. 8, for 'fifteenth' read 'fourteenth.'

p. 235, l. 15, delete 'he was succeeded by his son,' and insert 'He had issue:—

   '1. CUTHBERT, who succeeded.

   2. *Archibald* (Protocol Book of James Young 1 November 1497).'

p. 236, l. 8 from foot, for 1499' read 1509.'

p. 238, l. 1, delete 'soon after' and insert 'in.' Add to note 1 '*Acts and Decreets*, xxxviii. 227.'

p. 241, l. 17, after 'Craigie' add 'She had a tocher of £466, 13s. 4d. from the Earl of Arran the Governor, which was paid to her husband in November 1552 (*Treasurer's Accounts*, x. 130).'

p. 242, ll. 22, 23, for '18 October 1580' read '24 February 1579-80 (*Reg. Sec. Sig.* xlvi. 106).'

p. 242, note 14, after 'Lyon Office' add 'see also Fraser's note books No. vi. (Lyon Office MSS.) note of contract and discharge of tocher by Earl of Glencairn 26 July 1549.'

p. 243, l. 2, after 'name' add 'He died in July 1610, his executors being two daughters *Ann* and *Marion* (Glasgow Tests., 20 January 1613).'

p. 243, ll. 12, 13, delete after '15 August' and insert 'contract 24 April (*Reg. of Deeds*, xviii. pt. i. 8).'

p. 243, l. 20, after 'married,' insert 'contract 30 December 1577 (Hutton Coll. Adv. Lib., vii. 103).'

p. 244, l. 23, after '1574,' insert 'Margaret.'

p. 245, l. 7, after 'Lennox,' insert 'He was dead before 23 February 1629 (*Reg. of Deeds*, ccccxiv. 274).'

p. 245, l. 8, after 'married,' insert contract 28 January 1618 (*Reg. of Deeds*, cclxxxviii. 231).'

p. 245, l. 8, after 'daughter of' delete to end of paragraph, and insert 'Andrew Knox, Bishop of the Isles. By her, who survived him, he had a son *John*, mentioned above, who died *s.p.*, and three daughters. *Margaret* was married to Sir Alexander Cunningham of Robertland; *Anna* to Robert Wallace, Bishop of the Isles; and *Elizabeth* to William Wallace of Helenton, Advocate (*Retours, Ayr*, 327, 394, 421, 539; *Fasti Eccl. Scot.*, iii. 449; *Ayr Sasines*, viii. 179; Edin. Tests.).'

p. 246, l. 4. after 'Mary,' insert 'youngest daughter.'

p. 246, after l. 7, insert

   'By his second wife the Earl had a son

     '10. *James*, baptized 21 January 1612 (Canongate Reg.). He died young (*Acts and Decreets*, cclxxxi. 402).'

p. 246, l. 23, delete 'before 26 July 1614,' and insert 'about 1609.'

p. 247, l. 1, after 'married,' insert 'in Cornwall 1660.'

p. 247, l. 2, after 'Minto,' insert 'against whom she raised an action of divorce in 1668 (*Consistorial Processes, etc.*, Scot. Rec. Soc., No. 12).'

p. 247, l. 5, after 'secondly,' delete 'to,' and insert 'contract 29 May 1661 (*Perth Sasines*, i. 152) to John.'

p. 247, l. 7, after '*Jean*,' insert 'married to John Blair of that Ilk, with whom, as his future spouse, she had a charter of lands 5 August 1646 (*Reg. Mag. Sig.*).'

p. 247, l. 12, delete 'as,' and insert 'being buried in Holyrood Church in January 1661 (Canongate Reg.) and.'

p. 248, l. 2 from foot, for '25 July' read '27 January.'

p. 249, l. 16, for 'Colestoun' read 'Orbistoun.'

p. 249, l. 28, for 'third' read 'fifth.'

p. 250, l. 4 from foot, delete '2,' and insert 'proclamation 23 (Edin. Reg.).'

p. 251, l. 1, delete '20,' and insert 'proclamation 27 (Edin. Reg.) as his second wife.' (Cf. vol. v. 509.)

p. 251, l. 14, for '24' read '25.'

p. 251, l. 14, after 'June,' insert 'and was buried in Restalrig 30.'

p. 252, l. 24, for '1469' read '1463.'

GOWRIE

p. 257, note 4, for '33' read '83.'

p. 260, l. 15, after 'Ilk,' insert 'who died 7 December 1592 (Edin. Tests.).'

p. 260, l. 20, for 'about 1612' read 'contract 28 April 1621 (*Reg. of Deeds*, clxxx. 229).'

p. 260, l. 25, after '1600,' add 'He was a burgess of Perth, and married, contract 14 October 1593, Bessie Mathow (*Reg. of Deeds*, clxxx. 229).'

p. 260, l. 26, after 'conspiracy,' add 'He married, contract 15 February 1598-99, Agnes, daughter of Henry Adamson, merchant, Perth (*Reg. of Deeds*, cxlii. 168).'

p. 260, l. 27, delete after '*Jean*' to end of sentence, and insert 'married, contract 23 May 1587, Laurence Mercer of Clevage, eldest son of James Mercer of Newton (*Reg. of Deeds*, xxxiii. 286).'

p. 260, l. 28, after '*Barbara*,' delete to end of sentence, and insert 'married contract 1611, to Henry Rattray of Kincarrochy (*Reg. of Deeds*, clxxx. 235).'

p. 260, after l. 30, insert

'(7) *Beatrix*, named with her sisters Annas and Dorothy in her mother's testament.

(8) *Annas.*

(9) *Dorothy*, married to James Ruthven in Feu (*Perth Sasines, Secretary's Reg.*, vi. 411).

There was also a son *John* (perhaps illegitimate) named in his eldest brother's testament.'

p. 260, note 8, for '*Ibid.*' read 'Wood's Douglas's *Peerage*.'

p. 261, l. 24, after 'secondly,' insert 'contract 9 April.'

p. 261, l. 29, after 'Dowager,' insert 'She survived Lord Ruthven, and is said to have married, fifthly, James, son of Gilbert Gray of Foulis, but the only authority for this is Sir Robert Gordon's *Genealogy of the Earls of Sutherland.*'

p. 262, l. 9, after 'Ruthven,' insert 'born about 1560 (*Cal. of Scottish Papers*, i. No. 707).'

p. 262, l. 26, after '*Alexander*,' insert 'of Halieland.'

p. 262, l. 27, after 'He,' insert 'married Elizabeth Wemyss (*Reg. of Deeds*, clxxxi. 150), and.'

p. 264, l. 6, after ' Anna,' read ' and the father of Charles I.'

p. 266, l. 17, for ' George ' read ' Hugh.'

p. 266, l. 27, after '*Lilias*,' insert ' baptized 27 January 1568-69 (Perth Reg.).'

p. 266, l. 29, after '*Dorothea*,' insert ' baptized 30 April 1570 (*Ibid.*).'

p. 266, after l. 30, insert

'14. *Katherine*, baptized 28 February 1571-72 (*Ibid.*)   Died young.

p. 266, l. 31, for '14 ' read '15.'

p. 266, note 2, after ' 1595,' add ' *Reg. of Deeds*, xlvi. 444.'

GRAY

p. 272, l. 4, for 'May' read 'December.'

p. 274, l. 13 from foot, the words ' and grandson of Sir Patrick ' should be in brackets.

p. 276, l. 1, after ' Balnamoon,' insert reference '(*Registrum de Panmure*, i. xxix.).'

p. 276, l. 5 from foot, after ' completed,' insert ' till much later.'

p. 277, l. 3, after ' Lyle,' add 'He married again, after 1501, Elizabeth Hay, relict of George, second Earl of Huntly, the lady to whom he had been contracted (*Acta Dom. Conc.*, xxix. ff. 38, 39).'

p. 277, l. 13, after ' 1500,' insert ' She was then contracted to Walter Drummond, grandson of the first Lord Drummond, but the contract was discharged in January 1501-2 (*Acta Dom. Conc.*, xii. 39).'

p. 278, l. 5, for ' secondly' read ' thirdly,' and for ('? Alexander)' read ' William (cf. vol. vi. 34).'

p. 278, l. 6, for ' thirdly ' read ' secondly. *See title* Wemyss.'

p. 281, l. 8, for ' 1562 ' read ' 1558.'

p. 281, l. 8 from foot, after ' issue,' insert ' She survived him and was married, secondly, to William Rollock of Balbegie (cf. vol. v. 220).'

p. 282, l. 18, after ' Invergowrie,' insert ' as Patrick Gray, son of Patrick, Lord Gray, was, on 31 May 1567, instituted as perpetual vicar of the church of Rossie (Protocol Book of Duncan Gray, f. 41). He.'

p. 285, l. 2, delete ' before 18 August 1604,' and insert ' November 1603.'

p. 285, l. 6 from foot, delete ' in 1612,' and insert ' 4 September 1611 (*Synod of Fife*, Abbotsford Club, 36).'

p. 287, l. 27, delete ' said to be widow of Sir John Sydenham, Bart. of Brompton, and to be aged eighty,' and insert ' daughter of Sir Thomas Guldeford of Hemsted in Cranbrook, Kent. She had married, first, John Baker of Sissingburst, Kent; secondly, as his second wife, Sir John Sydenham, Knight, of Brimpton, Somerset, who died 1626. The following year she married, when she was about eighty, Lord Gray (cf. Pedigree of Sydenham in *Misc. Gen. et Her.*, 2nd ser., iii. 327; *Complete Baronetage*, i. *sub* Baker; *State Papers, Dom.*, 1628-29, 28, 447; *Notes and Queries*, 10th ser., xi. 54).'

p. 287, note 3, for '28' read '58.'

p. 288, l. 1, after 'married,' insert 'first, to Captain Archibald Douglas, who was killed by the Dutch at Chatham, 11 June 1667 (*ex inform.* Patrick Gray, Esq.), and, secondly.'

p. 291, l. 14, after 'Gray,' insert born 9 Feb. 1671 (Perth Bap. Reg.).'

p. 292, last line, for 'thirteenth' read 'twelfth.'

p. 293, ll. 1 and 2, for 'fourteenth' and 'fifteenth' read 'thirteenth' and 'fourteenth.'

VISCOUNT OF HADDINGTON

p. 299, l. 5 from foot, for '1831' read '1631.'

p. 299, note 6, for 'Adjournals' read 'Adjournal.'

p. 300, after l. 4, insert

'8. *James* or *Jacob*, a general-major in the Swedish service, married, before 1614, Isobel, daughter of James Spens, Count of Hoya, Swedish Ambassador to England. In 1647 he raised a regiment.

9. *Jane*, married to Robert More, who had letters of denization in September 1661 (*Forty-third Rep. of Deputy Keeper of Records*, App. 193).'

p. 300, l. 9, after '1605,' insert 'of these, George was infeft in the barony of Wyliecleugh in 1632 (*Gen. Reg. Sas.*, xxxiii. 89), and was dead *s.p.* before 1645 (*Reg. Mag. Sig.*, 22 June 1635 and 26 November 1647).'

p. 301, l. 8 from foot, for '1 June' read '11 June.'

EARL OF HADDINGTON

p. 306, l. 16, for 'Cosmus' read 'Cosmas.'

p. 307, l. 25, after 'Newbyres,' insert 'She was buried 23 November 1612 (Canongate Reg.).'

p. 308, l. 10, delete 'about 1604,' and insert 'contract 26 June 1602 (Oxenfoord Writs).'

p. 308, l. 12, for 'at least one daughter' read 'six daughters.'

p. 308, after l. 13, insert

'(1) *Elizabeth*, married (contract 8 September 1619) to Robert Hamilton of Bathgate (*Reg. Mag. Sig.*, 25 October 1620).

(2) *Agnes*, married, as in text.

(3) *Christian*, married (contract 21 February 1630) to Mr. John Scharp of Houstoun (*Reg. Mag. Sig.*, 28 July 1632).

(4) *Margaret*.

(5) *Jean*, married to Cornet John Home (*Reg. of Deeds*, Dliii. 140).

(6) *Rebecca*.'

p. 308, l. 14, delete from 'Probably' down to '1627' on l. 16.

p. 308, l. 19, for '30' read '20.'

p. 308, l. 20, for 'teacher of the St. Mary Magdalene School,' read 'Preceptor of the Magdalene Hospital.'

p. 309, l. 24, after 'thirdly,' insert 'contract 13 January 1649 (*Gen. Reg. of Inhibs.*, 6 September 1675).'

p. 309, after l. 25, insert

'6. *Marion*, eldest daughter, married, in 1582, to James Ross, merchant, Edinburgh (Protocol Book of A. Lawson, i. 81).'

p. 309, ll. 26, 29 and 31, for '6, 7, 8' read '7, 8, 9.'

p. 315, l. 22, for 'young' read 'in November 1619 (Canongate Reg.).'

p. 317, after l. 7, insert

'7. *Mary*, baptized 5 May 1629 (Canongate Reg.).'

p. 317, ll. 8, 9, for '7, 8' read '8, 9.'

p. 317, after l. 12, insert

The earl had also a son, presumably natural, Mr. Thomas of Parkley, who married, first, Helen Stewart, eldest daughter of William, second Lord Blantyre (cf. vol. ii. 85); secondly, Janet Foulis (*Edin. Sasines*, vii. 371, 437). He was keeper of the General Register of Sasines in 1657 (*Acts and Decreets* (Durie) 23 June 1677). Will dated 17 May 1668 (Edin. Tests.).

p. 317, l. 30, after 'romance,' insert 'She was an intimate friend of Ninon de l'Enclos, and was included in the *Portraits* written by Mlle. de Scudery.'

p. 318, l. 14, after 'married,' insert 'in the Kirk of Holyroodhouse 13 April 1648 (Canongate Reg.).'

p. 321, l. 4 from foot, for 'David' read 'James.'

p. 322, l. 15, for 'in or before 1720' read 'before 1719.'

p. 323, after l. 40, insert the names of the following children of Charles, Lord Binning, which have been accidentally omitted :—

'3. *Charles*, born 6 October 1725, died in infancy.

4. *John*, born 22 October 1726, died 1730.

5. *Charles*, born 3 October 1727; lieutenant 3rd Dragoon Guards 29 July 1751 ; captain 1st Dragoon Guards 12 March 1755 ; major 19 May 1762; retired with rank of lieut.-col. 1776; Governor of Blackness Castle 1792, till his death, which took place at Tynninghame 28 September 1806.

6. *Grisell*, married, at London 24 July 1745, Philip, second Earl Stanhope, and died at Ovenden, Kent, 28 December 1811, in her ninety-third year.

7. *Helen Mary*, born 8 October 1724, and died young.

8. *Rachel*, died, unmarried, at Mellerstain 20 October 1797.'

p. 324, l. 8, after 'secondly,' insert 'proclamation of banns 4 March 1786 (Canongate Reg.).'

p. 326, l. 25, for 'younger brother' read 'great uncle.'

p. 327, l. 11 from foot, for '1836' read '1863.'

p. 327, l. 10 from foot, after 'Baronet' place full stop; delete 'with' and insert 'She died 16 January 1908, and he died May 1910, leaving.'

HALIBURTON OF DIRLETON

p. 332, l. 20, delete from 'married' down to 'He' in line 23 and insert 'who (*Exch. Rolls*, ii. 175).'

p. 332, l. 24, delete from 'his' down to 'presently' on l. 26.

p. 332, l. 27, for 'Adam' read 'Alexander.'

p. 332, l. 9 from foot, for '1372' read '1377.'

p. 333, l. 9, for '1372' read '1377.'

p. 333, l. 11, after '1378-79,' insert 'He was alive 1388 (see below), and had a son *John*, his successor, and a daughter *Jean*, married to Henry St. Clair, first Earl of Orkney of the St. Clair line; in the charter of 1388 quoted below, Henry, Earl of Orkney is styled brother of Sir John Haliburton, which proves that Jean in the text is placed a generation too low.'

p. 333, l. 12, for 'nephew' read 'son.'

p. 333, l. 19, after '1397,' insert 'On 24 July 1388 he granted license to mortify the lands of Cameron to the Lady altar of Musselburgh; in this deed he styles himself Lord of Drylton, while his father witnesses it as Walter, Lord of that Ilk (Craigmillar Charters). This indicates that he must have married Christian Vaus, heiress of Dirleton, but he may have also married the Cameron heiress referred to in the text; unless Christian Vaus was also co-heiress of the Camerons through her mother. John certainly used a seal quartering the arms of both Cameron and Vaus in 1384 during his father's lifetime.'

p. 333, delete lines 3 and 4 from foot.

p. 334, l. 3 from foot, after 'of,' insert 'Sir.'

p. 334, l. 2 from foot, delete 'first Lord Haliburton' and insert 'There was a papal dispensation for his marriage 18 August 1427 (*Cal. of Papal Letters*, vii. 527).'

p. 335, l. 4, after '1439,' insert 'He married Johanna, daughter of John Congalton of that Ilk. She appears as his widow 1446-47 (*Munimenta de Melros*, 567).'

p. 335, l. 22, after 'Congalton,' insert 'second son of John Congalton (cf. vol. viii. 575 and authorities there cited).'

p. 335, after l. 25, insert

   '3. *Walter*.

     4. *John*. Both mentioned in a charter of 1464 (*Hutton Coll.*, Haddington, f. 16).'

p. 335, l. 3 from foot, for '1448' read '1458,' and after 'marriage,' insert '(already consummated).'

p. 335, note 12, for 'Vatican' read 'Lateran.'

p. 336, l. 27, for 'Sauchie' read 'Sauchieburn.'

p. 337, l. 10, for 'was dead before 10 February 1506-7' read 'died 6 December 1505 (*Exch. Rolls*, xii. 432).'

p. 337, l. 16, after 'Stevenston,' insert 'widow of Andrew Mowbray, burgess of Edinburgh (Robertson's *Parl. Records*, 500)'; and for 'secondly' read 'thirdly.'

HAMILTON

p. 341, l. 18, for 'Lambert' read 'Larbert.'

p. 346, l. 4 from foot, after '1402,' insert 'He was certainly dead before

1410, when his widow had a dispensation to marry William Douglas of Drumlanrig (*Reg. Aven.*, ccc. f. 641 ; cf. vol. vii. 114).'

p. **349**, l. 17, after 'Hamilton,' insert 'He had also another son *James* and a daughter *Eupham.*'

p. **353**, l. 10, after 'Crawford,' add 'The marriage was dissolved, and in 1503 she was the wife of John Forrester of Niddrie (*Acta Dom. Conc.*, xii. 166, 173).'

p. **354**, l. 26, after 'Albany,' insert 'and had by her a son *James.*'

p. **354**, l. 26, after 'and,' insert 'married, secondly, David Ross of Balnagown, who died 20 May 1527 (*Acta Dom. Conc.*, xxxvii. 189). She.'

p. **361**, l. 2 from foot, after 'Somerville,' insert *Grisel*, married (contract 28 June 1548), to Andrew, Lord Rothes, was also a daughter, but whether by this marriage is not known. A son *Cuthbert* is mentioned at the Scottish Court in 1544 (*Treasurer's Accounts*, viii. 357).'

p. **362**, l. 3, after 'Ilk,' insert 'She was alive in March 1557-58 (Protocol Book of John Robeson, f. 226, where her husband is called *William*).

p. **363**, l. 7, after 'Lothian,' insert 'He was Sheriff of Lanark in 1543 (*Treasurer's Accounts*, viii. 192).'

p. **363**, l. 12, after 'first,' insert 'in 1544 (she had a trousseau in March 1543-44 (*Treasurer's Accounts*, viii. 267).'

p. **363**, l. 19, after 'Lindsay,' insert 'He had a grant of the lands of Parkhill 1 September 1547 (*Reg. Sec. Sig.*), and is styled of Parkhill in 1550, when he had a royal grant (*Ibid.*, xxiv. 8).'

p. **363**, l. 6 from foot, after '*James*,' insert 'of Kinnell.'

p. **364**, ll. 2, 3, delete 'The name of his wife has not been ascertained.' and insert 'He married Janet Murray (Canongate Court Book), who died before 1 October 1572, and had (1) *William*; (2) *Paul*, captain of Arran, ancestor of the Hamiltons of Coats (*Reg. of Deeds*, ccccxcv. 264); (3) *Gavin* (*Acts and Decreets*, ccxxxiv. 86) mentioned in 1608.'

p. **364**, l. 10, for 'fifth' read 'fourth.'

p. **365**, l. 10, after '12,' insert 'and were married 15.'

p. **365**, l. 13, after '1563' add 'She was married, thirdly, to John Crawford in Shaw (*Acts and Decreets*, lii. 96, A.D. 1573).'

p. **365**, l. 18, for 'fifth' read 'fourth.'

p. **365**, i. 21, after 'Finnart' add 'She was still alive in 1557-58 (Protocol Book of J. Robeson, f. 220).'

p. **365**, at end of note 10 add 'A "half-sister of the Governor's" is in December 1547 said to be wife of John Wemyss(*Cal. Scot. Papers*, i. 48).'

p. **368**, l. 27, after '1572-73,' insert 'He received the Order of the Cockle (St. Michael) from the King of France, apparently as a kind of pledge for an advance of money, as in his will he directs it to be delivered again to the King, so that his son Claud might receive payment of the sums advanced (Edin. Tests.).'

p. **368**, l. 7 from foot, for '1579' read '6 December 1580, when an inquest found that she ought to be interdicted from administering her property, being, and having been for twenty-four years, excessively profuse (Moray Writs, box 15, No. 1209).'

p. 369, l. 6 from foot, delete 'apparently without issue.'

p. 369, l. 3 from foot, after 'Fife,' add 'He appears to have left issue, as in his father's will of 16 January 1574 his " tua bairns" are consigned to the care of his brother John. In view of the above-mentioned service they must either have died young or have been illegitimate.'

p. 369, last line, after 'older,' insert note, 'There was a "bairn" of the Lord Governor baptized 9 June 1546, who may have been Claud (*Treasurer's Accounts*, viii. 461).'

p. 370, l. 12, after 'lands,' insert note 'She was undoubtedly married to him. On 2 February 1545-46 she got an extensive trousseau "at her departure to the northland with the Earl of Huntlie" (*Treasurer's Accounts*, viii. 436), and her marriage is alluded to as an accomplished fact in 1548-49 (*Ibid.*, ix. 282). She had a tocher of 5000 merks, of which, however, only 2000 were actually paid as Huntly owed Arran 3000 (Cf. also Letter in H.M. Reg. Ho. (Corr. Mary of Guise), 11 February 1545-46).'

p. 370, l. 15, after 'contracted,' insert 'on 10 July 1546 to Gilbert Kennedy, son of Gilbert, Earl of Cassillis (*P. C. Reg.*, i. 42) and.'

p. 373, l. 19, after 'married,' insert 'first, about 1594, Catherine, daughter of John Carnegie of that Ilk (*Carnegie Book*, i. 50). She died before 24 May 1597. Testament confirmed 21 January 1602 (Edin. Tests.); secondly.'

p. 373, l. 22, for '*Margaret*' read '*Jean* (See *Chiefs of Colquhoun*, and Glasgow Tests., 13 September 1633).'

p. 377, l. 22, after 'Castle,' insert note 'At Pendennis "he has not changed a sheet for sixteen weeks time ; they took all from him when he was put into that hole and left him neither money nor clothes, linen, nor woollen, but what was on his back ; onlie they permitted his dog to go with him" (Dunbar's *Social Life in Former Days*, ii. 44).'

p. 380, l. 15, after 'him,' insert 'and married, secondly, 19 June 1655, Thomas Dalmahoy of the Priory of Guildford, and was buried 2 September 1659 (cf. vol. iii. 130).'

p. 380, l. 5 from foot, after 'thirdly,' insert 'in October 1703 (Edin. Reg.).'

p. 382, l. 27, delete 'an Irish lady, name unknown, who,' and insert 'Anne, daughter and co-heir of Charles, Lord Lucas of Shenfield, and widow of Edward, son of Patrick Cary, and grandson of Henry, first Viscount Falkland. She (cf. vol. iii. 610).'

p. 383, l. 6, after 'married,' insert '5 February 1687 (Canongate Reg.).'

p. 391, l. 13 from foot, after '*Catharine*,' insert 'born 31 October and baptized 17 November 1700, being named after her aunt, the Countess of Tullibardine (Canongate Reg.).'

p. 391, after l. 9 from foot, insert

'7. *Henrietta*, born 19 April 1704 (Canongate Reg.).'

p. 391, l. 8 from foot, for '7' read '8.'

p. 391, l. 8 from foot, after '*Susan*,' insert 'born 26 September 1706 (*Ibid.*).'

p. 393, l. 3, for '10' read '5 (Canongate Reg.).'

p. 395, l. 9, after '1846,' insert 'in a small house in White Lion Street, Pentonville. She was at one time in the household of Queen Caroline, upon whose death she retired into private life. A portion of her remaining days was embittered by the fact of a person having insinuated himself into her confidence and obtained many of her letters and papers; and having then daringly published, without her sanction, *A Secret History of the Court of England from the Accession of George III. to the death of George IV.*, under her name. The legal difficulties that ensued caused her much vexation, and obliged her to reside for a time in France (*The Patrician*, ii. 297).'

p. 396, l. 1, after '1863,' insert note 'While in Paris he slipped on a polished stair and got concussion of the brain. The Empress nursed him to the end with much devotion (Lord Lamington's *Days of the Dandies*).'

HERRIES

p. 398, l. 17, for 'Vandosine' read 'Vandosme.'

p. 404, l. 12, after 'David,' insert 'On the dismissal of a later curator, George Herries of Terraughtie, for certain crimes, "Andro Heris sone and apparend are to Herbert, Lord Heris," and "Thomas M'K[l]ellane of Bondby" were appointed in his place, 27 May 1500 (*Reg. Sec. Sig.*, i. 532, 684).'

p. 404, l. 7 from foot, after '*John*,' add 'He had a remission, along with his brother Mungo, for certain debts owing to the King 12 December 1508 (*Reg. Sec. Sig.*, i. 1778).'

p. 405, l. 13, delete 'but was in favour again before,' and insert 'for the slaughter of George Sinclair of Highfield but was pardoned before 12 December 1508 at the request of the Queen of France (*Reg. Sec. Sig.*, i. 1498, 1721, 1778, 1854). On.'

p. 405, l. 13, delete 'when.'

p. 406, at end of note 2, add 'In an inventory of writs in the Angus Charter-chest (drawn up in March 1588-89, *Acts and Decreets*, cxx. 23b) is a note of "Ane charter maid vnder the gret and previe seill to Jonet Douglas, dochter to Archibald, Erl of Angus of Tarrigillis and Kirk-gunzie, xxij of December 1ᵐ iiijᶜ lxxxxv yeiris.'

p. 407, after l. 11, insert

'2. *Andrew*, "brother to William, Lord Hereis," and others had a respite for arson and other crimes 26 May 1528 (*Reg. Sec. Sig.*, i. 3966).'

p. 407, l. 12, for '2' read '3.'

p. 407, l. 22, for '3' read '4.'

p. 409, l. 4, after 'Skirling,' insert 'contract 1 May 1552 (*Acts and Decreets*, vi. 267).'

p. 415, l. 15, after '*James*,' add 'It was probably he who married Ælitia Collins and had a son *Robert*, aged nineteen in 1647, and a daughter *Alice* living in 1665 (*Records of Scots Colleges, etc.*, New Spalding Club, i. 197; *Carlaverock Book*, i. 388).'

p. 415, l. 20, after 'married,' insert 'contract 31 October 1603 (*Reg. of Deeds*, clviii. 422).'

p. **416**, l. 24, delete entire paragraph after '*Frederick*,' and insert 'educated at Douai at the charges of Colonel Semple from 29 July 1629 to November 1632, when he went to Spain and entered the Society of Jesus. He was Rector of the Scots College at Madrid from 1656 till his death on 9 May 1659 (*Records of Scots Colleges*, New Spalding Club, 25, 195, 202).'

p. **416**, note 12, for '3 August 1642' read '13 August 1649.'

p. **417**, l. 3, for '23' read '16.'

p. **418**, l. 9 from foot, for 'young' read 'in 1836.'

p. **418**, l. 4 from foot, for '1901' read '1891.'

p. **423**, l. 25, after '1884,' insert 'He died 5 October 1908, when the barony of the United Kingdom became extinct and his Scottish honours descended to his eldest daughter.'

p. **423**, l. 7 from foot, after '1905,' insert 'and a son Bernard Marmaduke, Earl of Arundel and Surrey, born 30 May 1908.'

HOLYROODHOUSE

p. **433**, l. 26, after 'respectively,' add 'He had also a natural son *John*, apprenticed 4 March 1640 to Robert Chrystie, barber, Edinburgh (*Edin. Reg. of Apprentices*, Scot. Rec. Soc.).'

p. **435**, l. 2, for '1628' read '1623.'

p. **435**, l. 5 from foot, after 'married,' insert 'contract dated 22 and 24 September 1629 (*Reg. of Deeds*, cccclxi. 342).'

p. **435**, l. 3 from foot, for '1639' read '1629.'

p. **436**, l. 8, after 'issue,' add 'In 1678 she was the wife of Mr. William Gray (*Reg. of Deeds* (Durie), 17 May, 1680).'

p. **438**, l. 18, after 'Glencorse,' insert 'born 10 July 1736 (Canongate Reg.).'

p. **439**, l. 1, delete 'married, according to Home Drummond's MS., to John Menzies, surgeon in Perth. *Note.*—It was no doubt Mary who was married to a Menzies. Anne was buried at Holyrood as Miss Anne Bothwell.'

p. **439**, l. 5, after '*Mary*,' delete 'who' to 'named,' and insert 'married to Neil Menzies, son of James Menzies of Comrie, and had issue.'

HOME

p. **445**, l. 4 from foot. According to a genealogy *penes* Sir William Fraser's Trustees, dated 1664, this George was ancestor of the Homes of Spott.

p. **447**, l. 16, delete from 'He is said' down to '1436' on l. 28, and then take in from 'Sir Alexander' on p. 448, l. 5 from foot, onwards.

Note.—Recent investigation shows that previous writers on this pedigree, including Sir William Fraser in his Report (followed by the writer of this article), to the Historical MSS. Comm. (*Twelfth Report*,

App. pt. viii. 78-79), have been wrong in making the first Lord
Home a separate personage from Sir Alexander. The mistake arose
from the supposed necessity of finding a husband for Marion, heiress
of Landells, and not perceiving that she was really identical with
Marion Lauder. In view of this the following rearrangement and
alteration of the text falls to be made:

p. 447, l. 5 from foot, delete from 'They had issue' to end of page.

p. 448, l. 18, after 'in,' insert 'or before.'

p. 448, l. 22, delete from 'I. SIR ALEXANDER' down to 'father' on next
line. *Note.*—The information contained from the words 'a charter'
on line 23, to 'Crown' on l. 5 from foot of same page, apply to Alexander, eldest son of Lord Home. (See *infra.*)

p. 449, after l. 4 from foot, delete down to 'Hepburn' on p. 450, l. 2, and
insert

'Lord Home married, first, before 1424, Marion, daughter of John
Lauder and his wife, Katherine, daughter of William de Landells and
his wife Jonet. In 1425 she got sasine of the lands of Swynset, as heir
of her mother, Katherine, who must have succeeded to them through
her father, who, along with his wife, had a royal charter of these and
other lands 4 January 1390-91 (*Reg. Mag. Sig.*, vol. i. new ed. No. 813).
Sir Alexander and Marion were related in the fourth degree of consanguinity, etc., as on p. 447. They had issue :—

1. *Alexander*, who had a charter, etc., as on l. 23, p. 448, down to
   'Crown' on l. 5, from foot of same page. He died *v.p.* about
   1456.   He married, contract 2 February 1448 (*Scotts of
   Buccleuch*, ii. 39), Annes or Agnes, daughter of Sir Adam
   Hepburn of Hailes: they had a papal dispensation for the
   marriage, 2 January 1450-51, on the ground that they were
   within the third and third degrees of affinity (*Reg. Vat.*
   ccccxvi. 122). They had issue, as on p. 450, ll. 4-6.

2. *George*, who seems to have been originally destined for the
   Church: he had papal provision of canonries of Glasgow and
   Dunkeld 14 June 1447, and was in his fifteenth year in
   1450-51 (*Reg. Vat.*, ccccxvi. 124, 126). He had a confirmation
   charter, etc., as in text on p. 450.

3. *John*, Prior of Coldingham, as in text on p. 450.

4. *Sir Patrick*, of Fastcastle, as in text on p. 450.

5, 6, and 7. *Nicholas, Katherine,* and *Elyne,* as in text on p. 448.'

p. 451, l. 4, after 'married,' insert 'about January 1496-97 (cf. vol. vi. 357).'

p. 454, l. 5, from foot. According to the genealogy of 1664, there were
eight daughters in all.

p. 456, l. 27, after 'forth.),' insert 'They had a dispensation for their
marriage, which had been carried out *per verba de futuro,* they being
within the third and fourth degrees of affinity, 24 and 25 February
1513-14 (*Laing Charters,* No. 301).'

p. 460, l. 18, after '1589' add 'He had a natural son George, who in 1574
was in Sweden (*Edin. Burgh Reg. of Deeds,* 7 Aug, 1574).'

p. 462, l. 8 from foot, for 'before February 1582-83' read 'contract 4, 15, 24, and 25 February 1580-81 (*Reg. of Deeds*, xix. 180).'

p. 463, after l. 10, insert

'The existence of two other daughters in 1578 is mentioned in the retour of the Commendator of Jedburgh as tutor to his nephew in that year (see below).'

p. 463, l. 14, after 'Home,' insert 'was for some time a student at St. Leonard's College, St. Andrews (*Reg. of Deeds*, xix. 90). He.'

p. 465, l. 7 from foot, after 'married,' insert 'contract 18 October 1627 (*Reg. of Deeds*, cccclxxvii. 440).'

p. 465, l. 5 from foot, after 'married,' insert 'contract 23 August and 6 September 1632 (*Ibid.*, cccclxxvii. 447).'

p. 467, l. 10, for 'Jane' read 'Fane.'

p. 468, l. 22, after 'her,' insert 'who survived him and married, secondly, before 1503, Sir William Colville of Ochiltree (cf. vol. ii. 543).'

p. 470, l. 4, from foot after '1584,' insert 'In 1586 he is styled Chanter of Ross (*Reg. of Deeds*, xxiv. 409).'

p. 471, l. 3, after 'Graden, and another son *John*, styled servitor to Lord Newbattle, who was dead in 1595 (*Edin. Inhibs.*, vii. 141).'

p. 471, l. 24, after 'Blyndlie,' insert 'who survived him (*Reg. of Deeds*, cxxxvii.).'

p. 471, l. 25, delete 'He married, secondly,' and insert

'5. *William* (*secundus*) of Bellitaw (*Reg. of Deeds*, ci. 11 July 1604) married.'

p. 471, l. 28, after 'Mellerstain,' insert 'He apparently murdered his step-son, John Haitlie of Mellerstaines, at the Salt Tron in Edinburgh 3 January 1602 (Birrell's *Diary*, 57).'

p. 471, ll. 29, 35, for '5, 6' read '6, 7.'

p. 472, after l. 14, insert

'8. *Barbara*, married to Robert Cairncross of Colmeslie (*Reg. of Deeds*, ii. 87).'

p. 473, l. 17, delete 'or before 22' and relative note, and insert '16 (Edin. Tests.).'

p. 474, l. 4 from foot, after 'first,' insert 'contract 10 December 1587 (*Reg. of Deeds*, xxvi. 271).'

p. 478, l. 24, delete 'was living 13 April 1683,' and insert 'died in 1694. (Her son Charles had licence to attend her funeral, 26 June. *P. C. Acta*.)'

p. 478, after last line, insert

'6. *Anna* (*Privy Seal, English Reg.*, ii. 342).

7. *Margaret*, married, contract 21 July 1662 (*Reg. of Deeds*, Durie, 16, 17 June 1670), to Alexander Home of Ayton.'

The genealogy of 1664 gives five daughters, *Anna, Margaret, Isabel, Jean*, and *Elizabeth*, all living in 1664.

p. 479, l. 4, after '1671,' insert note, 'The Duke of Lauderdale's daughter Mary was offered to him as a wife, but she was so deformed he would not have her. From that time Lauderdale would pay no more attention to the claim of Home of Wedderburn for repayment of money lent to the King (*Hist. MSS. Com.*, Milne-Home MSS., 106).'

p. 479, l. 6, for ' Withyam ' read ' Withyham.'

p. 479, l. 19, after ' sustained,' insert ' In 1693 he was a prisoner in Edinburgh Castle, and on 22 June his Countess was allowed to remain there with him (*Privy Council Acta*). On 13 March 1694 he was liberated, and confined to his house of Hirsel and two miles about it on this side Tweed (*Ibid.*).'

p. 481, l. 5, after ' Jamaica,' insert ' He deserted her 24 February 1743 (*Chancery Roll*, Jamaica, 19 August 1752).'

p. 482, l. 24, for ' 1873 ' read ' 1875.'

p. 484, l. 4, after ' vert,' insert ' beaked gules.'

HOPETOUN

p. 486, l. 12, for ' 20 April 1579 ' read ' 4 August 1580.'

p. 486, l. 19, after ' *Katherine* ' add ' married to Mr. Richard Brown, minister of Tynron, and had issue a son, Mr. *Daniel* (*Fasti Ecclesiæ Scoticanæ*, by Hew Scott, D.D., i. 685; *P. C. Reg.*, 2nd ser., vii. 304).'

p. 486, after last line, insert

'4. *Elizabeth*, married to Patrick Rig, merchant, Edinburgh; she died 28 October 1578 (Edin. Tests.; Hope's *Diary*, 31).'

p. 487, l. 8, for ' 1591 ' read ' 1609.'

p. 489, l. 10 from foot, for ' fourteen ' read ' fifteen.'

p. 489, after l. 9, from foot, insert

'1. *George*, of St. Albans, Herts, who granted a power of attorney to his father's clerk to uplift certain moneys, 27 April 1633 (*Reg. of Deeds*, cccclxi. 481). If eldest son he must have predeceased his father.'

p. 489, l. 8 from foot *et seq.*, The numbers attached to the names of Sir Thomas Hope's children fall to be increased by one.

p. 491, l. 17, for ' was dead before 1655' read ' died in May 1653.'

p. 492, l. 15, for ' Magalen' read 'Magdalen.'

p. 493, l. 21, after ' 1682' insert note, 'The family tradition is that in the wreck of the *Royal Gloucester* Hope got a seat in a boat, but gave it up to the Duke of York, and was in consequence drowned. On this account Queen Anne gave his son a Peerage almost immediately after he came of age (*ex inform.* Miss Jessie Hope).'

p. 494, last line, after ' army,' insert ' died at Clifton 1861, having.'

p. 504, l. 6, after ' Sleat, insert ' by Louise Maria La Coast, illegitimate daughter of H.R.H. the Duke of Gloucester, by Lady Almeria Carpenter, daughter of the Earl of Tyrconnel.'

HUNTLY

p. 517, note 7, add ' There was a commission to grant dispensation for the marriage of Thomas Somerville and Elizabeth Gordon 2 Nov. 1411 (*Reg. Aven.*, cccix. 549).'

p. 518, l. 7 from foot, after ' brother,' insert note, ' She appears to have been heiress in part at least during her brother's life. Her ward and marriage are said to have been bestowed by Robert III. on Sir Walter Buchanan 2 February 1403-4 (*Harl. MSS.*, No. 4693).'

p. 529, l. 21, after 'Lindsay,' insert 'she married, secondly, some time after Huntly's death, Andrew, second Lord Gray, in violation of a contract between her and Huntly (*Acta Dom. Conc.*, xxix. 38, 39). She had originally been contracted to Gray half a century previous (cf. *ante*, p. 276).'

p. 531, l. 10, for 'John Crichton of Invernyte' read 'the son and heir of Thomas, second Lord Innermeath. (Original Bond at Slains.)'

p. 532, l. 19, for '20 October' read '14 October.'

p. 532, after l. 5 from foot, insert

'1. *George*. The existence of this son has been hitherto unknown; but by contract between his father and grandfather on the one part, and Archibald, second Earl of Argyll, on the other, dated 27 March 1501, he (styled son and apparent heir of his father) was to marry either Katherine or Elizabeth Campbell, daughters of the said Earl, whichever of the two best pleased him, while Colin Campbell (afterwards third Earl) was to marry either Janet or Margaret Gordon, his sisters. The Earl did marry Janet, but George must have died young, and the marriage did not take place (Argyll Charter-chest).'

p. 532, l. 4 from foot, for '1' read '2.'

p. 533, l. 22, for 'a son' read 'two sons.'

p. 533, l. 22, after '*George*,' insert 'and *John*, the latter of whom became Dean of Salisbury, and died 3 September 1619, in the seventy-fifth year of his age. He married Genevieve Petaw, daughter of Gideon Petaw, Lord of Mauld, in the Isle de France, who died at Gordonstoun 6 December 1643, in her eighty-third year; their only child, *Louise*, married, in 1613, Sir Robert Gordon of Gordonstoun, Bart.'

p. 533, l. 24, for '2' read '3.'

p. 533, l. 28, for '3' read '4.'

p. 533, l. 34, for '4' read '5.'

p. 533, l. 5 from foot, for '5' read '6.'

p. 533, l. 5 from foot, for '1503' read '1505' (Adv. Lib. MS. 32.2.4. vol. 4, p. 274).

p. 533, after l. 4 from foot, insert

'7. *Margaret* (*Acts and Decreets*, xx. 182).'

p. 536, l. 8, for 'daughter' read 'sister.' (The title of the marriage-contract given in the Spalding Club *Miscellany* is wrong.)

p. 536, l. 19, after '370,' insert note, 'There is no doubt that he married her, and she went north with him in 1545-46 (*Treasurer's Accts.*, viii. 436).'

p. 538, last line, after 'married,' insert 'first, shortly before 4 February 1577-78, Jane Leslie, "Lady Moyness" daughter of John Leslie of Parkhill and widow of Sir Alexander Dunbar of Cumnock (Moray Writs, Box xv. No. 850: cf. *Records of the Family of Leslie*, ii. 151; Douglas's *Baronage*, 120). She died in August 1579 (Edin. Tests.). He married, secondly.'

p. 539, l. 2, after 'widow of,' insert 'James Ochterlony younger of that Ilk (*Acts and Decreets*, xlix. 126; *Reg. of Deeds*, xxvi. 420) and of.'

p. 539, note 1, for '1584' read '1585.'

p. 540, last line, after 'football' add note 'The Protocol Book of John Mushet, Stirling, contains the following: "The xix of October 1576, George, Erle of Huntly, etc. etc., decessit vpone ane haistie maladie at x hours nycht or thairby I being present with him, his secretar and familiar servand."'

p. 547, headline, for 'Marquess of Gordon' read 'Marquess of Huntly.'

p. 547, l. 25, for '1641' read 'contract 28 and 31 October 1639 (*Reg. of Deeds*, DXXIV. 62).'

p. 547, l. 3 from foot, for 'in December 1650' read 'in childbed at Traquair June 1651 (Balfour's *Annals*, iv. 351).'

p. 549, l. 9, after 'Crouly,' insert 'She died at sea on her way to Scotland (Letter at Slains, 22 February 1715).'

p. 549, l. 17, after 'Huntly,' insert was born in 1649 (*Addl. MSS.*, 23, 122, f. 80); but in a letter to Lauderdale 4 July 1664 he says he is almost fourteen (*Notes and Queries*, 10th ser., x. 7).'

p. 549, l. 18, after 'boy,' insert 'he.'

p. 550, l. 7 from foot, for '1697' read '1696 (*Consistorial Processes etc.*, Scot Rec. Soc., No. 74).'

p. 551, l. 2, for 'James' read 'Robert.'

p. 551, after l. 9, insert

'1. *George*, born 1680, died young (Letter at Gordon Castle).'

p. 551, ll. 10, 11, for '1, 2' read '2, 3.'

p. 552, l. 16, for 'Inverary' read 'Inverury.'

p. 554, line 4, after 'wife,' insert note, 'Catherine Gordon had been sent by her father (who did not approve of the match, as he was already brother-in-law to his proposed son-in-law) to her grandfather the Duke of Atholl. She wrote to him "My dear Father, I beg to inform you that I was married this day to the Duke of Gordon. We propose in a few days to present ourselves at Haddo House when I have no doubt we shall receive your blessing (*The Gay Gordons*, by J. M. Bulloch, 92).'

p. 554, l. 12, for 'George' read 'Alexander.'

p. 554, l. 18, After 'Bunbury,' insert note, 'She was a daughter of the second Duke of Richmond: was born 14 February 1744, and married, 2 June 1762, Sir Thomas Charles Bunbury, Bart. He divorced her 17 May 1776, and she married, secondly, 27 August 1781, as his second wife, Col. the Hon. George Napier, son of the sixth Lord Napier, and died blind, but still beautiful, in 1826.'

p. 554, l. 6 from foot, delete '(died 1831)' and insert '(born 6 March 1782, died 2 September 1831).'

p. 557, l. 12, after 'Lennox,' insert 'they were married in her mother's dressing-room at Gordon Castle, and nobody knew of it except two women servants till three days later, when it was announced at a big dance party by the Marquess of Huntly (Bulloch's *Gay Gordons*, 92).

p. 557, l. 23, delete 'of.'

p. 559, l. 18, After 'ninety-one,' insert note, 'He danced till he was eighty or more (Mrs. Warenne Blake's, *Memoirs of a Vanished Generation*, 124).

p. 559, after l. 28, insert 'There was a son born 11 January 1796 who probably died young.'

p. 559, l. 5 from foot, after 'Munster,' insert 'and natural daughter of William IV., and widow of the Hon. John Kennedy Erskine, second son of the first Marquess of Ailsa.'

p. 560, l. 1, Bulloch gives 1806, so does Burke.

p. 560, l. 6, Bulloch gives 1902, so does Burke.

p. 560, l. 9, Bulloch gives 3 July, Burke as in text.

p. 561, l. 1, for '29' read '28.'

p. 561, l. 8, delete '(*heir presumptive*).'

p. 561, l. 11, after '1900,' insert 'He died at sea 14 June 1907.

p. 562, l. 2, for 'second' read 'third.'

p. 562, l. 21, after '2nd,' insert 'or.'

HYNDFORD

p. 565, last line, after 'issue,' insert 'before 1556, when his brother David is described as of Balmedie (*Reg. of Deeds*, i. 462).'

p. 566, l. 10, after 'John,' insert 'born about 1564.'

p. 566, l. 10, after 'minister,' insert 'of Newburn 1595.'

p. 566, l. 10, after 'Kilconquhar,' insert '1603. Died at Edinburgh 1622.'

p. 566, l. 10, for 'a son' read 'two sons.'

p. 566, l. 11, after '*Frederick*,' insert 'β. *William*.'

p. 566, l. 21, delete 'Sir.'

p. 566, l. 33, delete 'no' before 'issue.'

p. 566, l. 33, for 'before 1622' read '15 September 1621.'

p. 566, l. 37, delete 'leaving issue,' and insert 'having had issue by his first wife :—

   (*a*) *William*.

   (*b*) *Jean*.

   (*c*) *Katrine*.

all mentioned in their mother's will.

And by his second wife :—'

p. 567, l. 7, delete 'of Balvaird,' and insert 'Doctor of Medicine in Perth.'

p. 567, l. 12, delete 'before 1800,' and insert 'at Balmblae 15 January 1786' (*Scots Mag.*).'

p. 567, after line 21 insert

   (*e*) *William* (*P. C. Reg.*, 3rd ser., vol. iii. 585).'

p. 568, l. 13, after 'He,' insert 'died at Craigpotty, Perthshire, 7 September 1761, aged eighty-six (*Scots Mag.*), having.'

p. 568, l. 14, after 'had,' insert 'by her, who died 1731.'

p. 568, l. 18, after 'married,' insert '3 October 1725 (*Edin. Mar. Reg.*).'

p. 568, l. 23, after 'died,' insert 'at Pitcallan near Perth, 29 September 1783 (*Scots Mag.*).'

p. 573, l. 12 from foot, delete from 'was succeeded by,' down to 'dominus de Carmichael,' on l. 6 from foot.

Note.—Recent investigation renders it probable that the John Carmichael mentioned in the text was identical with the John mentioned on p. 563, and that the two Williams on p. 573 are the same person.

p. 575, after l. 19 insert

'3. *David*, described in 1505 as brother of the laird of Carmichael (*Acta Dom. Conc.*, xvii. 40).'

p. 575, ll. 20 and 21, delete 'in 1474 when,' and insert 'on 23 April 1465, when he acted along with his father as attorney for Gilbert, Lord Kennedy (*Culzean Inventory*). In 1474.'

p. 576, l. 23, delete 'he was succeeded by his,' and insert. 'Besides a daughter *Jean*, mentioned in 1554 (*Acts and Decreets*, viii. 450), he had an.'

p. 577, l. 15, for 'He died about 1585,' read 'He survived till after 11 August 1586 (*P. C. Reg.*, iv. 94).'

p. 578, after l. 6, add

'4. *Margaret*, married to Robert Wardlaw, fiar of Kilbaberton (*Acts and Decreets*, lxxix. 185).'

5. *Abigail*, married, contract 17 April and 4 May 1590, to Hugh Weir, younger of Clowburn (*Reg. Mag. Sig.*, 20 August 1617). She was a widow 9 March 1595-96 (*Reg. of Deeds*, lii. 108), which proves that she was a generation older than she is represented in the text (p. 580).'

p. 579, l. 2, after 'Carmichael,' insert 'On 2 December 1585 he was appointed the King's Master Stabler (*Reg. Sec. Sig.*, liii. 73).'

p. 579, last line, after 'married,' insert 'contract 5 September 1561 (*Reg. of Deeds*, iv. 373).'

p. 580, l. 1, delete 'Sir George Douglas of Pittendreich,' and insert 'James, fourth Earl of Morton (*Ibid.*).'

p. 580, l. 2, delete 'who survived him certainly to the year 1620,' and accompanying reference, and insert 'She died in 1625 (Edin. Tests.).'

p. 580, ll. 26 and 27, delete this entry. See above, p. 578.

p. 580, l. 28, for '5' read '4.'

p. 580, after l. 29 insert

'5. *Helen* (*Reg. of Deeds*, xxv. 11).'

p. 581, l. 22, delete 'before 12 June 1624' and accompanying reference and insert 'contract 25 March 1613 (*Reg. of Deeds*, ccxvi. 327).'

p. 581, after l. 27, insert 'Hugh had also a natural son, *John* (*P. C. Reg.*, 2nd ser. vi. 612).'

p. 582, after line 3, insert, 'He married Elizabeth, daughter of Sir Patrick Home of Polwarth (cf. vol. vi. 11).'

p. 582, l. 24, after 'issue,' insert '(besides a natural son, *John*). (*Gen. Reg. Inhibs.*, xxxii. 56).'

p. 582, last line, delete 'a son,' and insert 'three sons :—

1. WALTER.

2. *John*, who was alive in 1632, being then about eighty, and who had a son, *John* (*Reg. of Deeds*, ccccliv. 118), Commissary of Lanark, to whom Lord Carmichael was served heir 17 June 1656 (*Inq. Gen.*). He died 3 March 1656 (Lanark Tests.).

3. *Gavin*, died *ante* 16 May 1656 (Edin. Tests.), having had—

    (1) *Gavin*, died 1625, without issue (Edin. Tests.).

    (2) *Margaret* (*Ibid.*).

    (3) *Elizabeth*, married John Fleming, schoolmaster in Edinburgh (*Ibid.*).'

p. 583, l. 21, for '1608' read 'contract 11 September 1598 (*Reg. of Deeds*, lxvi. 235).'

p. 583, l. 6 from foot, after 'she,' insert 'married, secondly, after 6 April 1635, John Muir, elder of Annestoun and.'

p. 583, l. 5 from foot, delete 'and had a son, *John*,' and insert 'By her first husband she had three sons, *Walter*, *William*, and *John* (Lanark Tests., 2 July 1638).'

p. 587, l. 21, after 'He,' delete 'was dead before 4 November 1681,' and insert 'died December 1680 (Lanark Tests., 7 June 1681).'

p. 588, l. 9, for '*Agnes*' read '*Rachel* (*Reg. Mag. Sig.*, 16 July 1649).'

p. 588, l. 9, after 'married,' insert 'contract 17 June 1642 (*Reg. of Deeds*, DXXXiv. 113).'

p. 588, after l. 17, insert

    '10. *Marion* (*Gen. Reg. of Inhibs.*, 30 June 1669).'

p. 591, l. 8 from foot, for '18' read '9 (*Scots Mag.*).

p. 591, l. 6 from foot, for '2' read '21.'

p. 592, l. 18, for '1769' read '1789.'

p. 592, l. 25, for 'sixth' read 'fifth.'

p. 592, l. 27, for 'seventh' read 'sixth.'

p. 592, after l. 13 from foot, insert

    'vii. *Grace* (Lanark Tests., 16 January 1786).'

p. 593, l. 2, after '*Beatrix*,' add note, 'She is called Barbara in her funeral entry in the Lyon Office.'

p. 593, l. 2, after '1700,' insert 'as his first wife.'

p. 593, l. 4, after 'Admiralty,' insert semicolon, 'she died 1 August 1702.'

p. 594, l. 16, for 'second' read 'first.'

VOL. V.

INNERMEATH

p. 3, l. 23, for 'eighth' read 'first.'

p. 5, l. 17, after 'secondly,' insert 'in June 1573 (see *Decreet* cited in note 8).'

p. 6, l. 4 from foot, after 'Robert,' insert 'married Janet Leslie (*Reg. of Deeds*, cccciii. 84), perhaps daughter of Robert Leslie of Auldcraig (*Family of Leslie*, iii. 383).'

p. 7, l. 24, after 'secondly,' add 'contract 11 February 1608 (*Reg. of Deeds*, cxlviii. 212).'

IRVINE

p. 11, ll. 16, 17, delete from 'baptized',down to '1616,' and relative reference.

p. 22, l. 28, for 'John' read 'Colin.'

LORD OF THE ISLES

p. 39, l. 9, delete 'about 1337,' and insert 'Papal dispensation for the marriage 4 June 1337 (*Regesta Avenionensia*, li. f. 125).'

p. 39, l. 10, after 'her,' insert 'whom he subsequently divorced (*Proc. Soc. Antiq. Scot.*, viii. 276).'

p. 42, after last l., insert

'5. *Marion.* There was a commission from the Pope 13 February 1419-20 for her marriage with Celestine Campbell (*Cal. of Papal Letters*, vii. 151), but it does not seem to have taken place. She is stated to have married Alexander Sutherland (Douglas's *Peerage*).'

p. 42, note 3, for '*Avinionensis*' read '*Avenionensia.*'

p. 45, after l. 10, insert 'He had three natural sons, Hugh, Alexander and Donald, legitimated by the Pope 29 June 1445 (*Cal. Papal Letters*, ix. 523).'

p. 47, l. 17, after 'issue,' insert 'A Papal Bull in April 1478 exempted her from ordinary jurisdiction during the controversy between her and her husband (*Roman Transcripts*, Public Record Office).'

JEDBURGH

p. 54, last l. of notes, insert '9' before '*Reg. Mag. Sig.*'

p. 59, l. 4 from foot, delete 'She was alive in 1546' and relative note, and insert 'She married, secondly (contract January 1529-30), Sir Walter Scott of Branxholm, from whom she was divorced (cf. vol. ii. 230).'

p. 67, ll. 28, 29, for 'in March 1685-86' read '30 March 1586 (Spalding Club *Misc.*, ii. 58).'

p. 68, l. 7, after 'Scotland,' insert 'and previously the wife of Patrick, sixth Lord Gray, whom she had divorced (cf. vol. iv. 285).'

p. 68, l. 32, after 'married,' insert 'contract dated at Oxnamcraig 6 November 1587 (Blackbarony Writs).'

p. 68, l. 36, for '1587' read '1587-88.'

p. 68, note 8, add to note 'She was a daughter of her father's second wife, not of his first as indicated in the text.'

p. 70, l. 15, after 'married,' insert 'contract 4 December 1660 (*Reg. of Deeds*, Mack, 17 Oct. 1667).'

p. 72, last l., for '1591' read '19 February 1584-85 (*Reg. Sec. Sig.*, lii. 12).'

p. 75, l. 26, delete 'died in 1631,' and insert 'was still alive on 20 April 1633 (see *post*, p. 76, l. 22 *corr.*).'

p. 75, l. 26, after 'married,' insert 'first.'

p. 75, l. 29, after 'Ochiltree,' insert 'He married, secondly (contract dated 2 July 1621), Katherine M'Culloch, widow of William Houston of Cottreoch, by whom she had a son, *William*, to whom, on 8 July 1645, she assigned her rights under her marriage-contract with Lord Jedburgh. She died between that date and 1 July 1647 (*ex inform.* John MacGregor, Esq., W.S.).'

p. 75, l. 29, for 'they' read 'by his first wife he.'

p. 76, l. 14, after 'married,' insert 'contract 2 and 5 March 1614 (*Reg. of Deeds*, ccciii. 51).'

p. 76, l. 18, after 'Alison,' insert '(styled fifth daughter in a charter to her of 1 May 1627) (*Reg. Mag. Sig.*, 5 February 1628).'

p. 76, l. 18, after 'married,' insert 'contract 21 and 24 July 1620 (*Ibid.*).'

p. 76, l. 19, after '1648,' insert 'buried in Greyfriars, 24 April 1671.'

p. 76, l. 20, after '1648,' insert 'buried in Holyrood Church, 8 March 1664 (Canongate Reg.).'

p. 76, l. 21, after '1648,' insert 'buried in Greyfriars, 3 May 1663.'

p. 76, l. 22, delete 'married to —— M'Culloch, and,' and insert 'married, but whether for her first or second husband is not known, Nicholas Lewin, eldest son of Thomas Lewin of Warkworth, Northumberland, by whom she had a son Thomas of Amble, who married his cousin, Helen Rutherford. On 20 April 1633 a receipt was granted to Andrew, Lord Jedburgh, for 600 merks of her tocher. She (*ex inform.* T. E. Watson, Monmouth; cf. vol. vii. 379); (*Reg. Mag. Sig.*, 4 April 1649, Chancery Depositions, Record Office (Bridges), 171-4, 1685).'

p. 78, l. 32, for 'without issue' read 'without surviving issue. A daughter Mary was born at Redbraes 17 November 1656, and died 3 October 1658 (Family Bible at Marchmont).'

p. 79, second last l. of note, for 'field' read 'chevron.'

KELLIE

p. 81, l. 1, after 'second,' insert 'surviving.'

p. 81, l. 2, for 'fourth' read 'fifth.'

p. 85, l. 2 from foot, for 'ERSKINE' read 'DIRLTOUN.'

p. 86, l. 2, after 'first,' add '30 November 1587 (Stirling Reg.).'

p. 86, l. 5 from foot, for 'third' read 'second.'

p. 88, l. 19, after 'died,' delete '1734,' and insert 'at Edinburgh, 17 July 1735 (Edin. Tests., 16 June 1736).'

p. 89, note 2, for 'Canongate' read 'Carnbee.'

p. 92, l. 21, delete 'Sir.'

p. 92, l. 24, after 'there,' insert 'Agatha Gigli.'

p. 92, l. 25, after '*Charles*,' insert 'born at Rome 1739.'

p. 92, l. 26, after 'ultimately,' insert '(17 January 1803).'

p. 92, l. 26, after 'Paris,' insert '20.'

p. 93, l. 6, after 'married,' insert '24 April 1743.'

p. 93, l. 6, for 'Laverockland' read 'Laverocklaw.'

p. 96, l. 6 from foot, for 'ERSKINE' read 'DIRLTOUN.'

p. 97, after l. 5, add

'The Earl of Mar and Kellie recorded the following arms in the Lyon Office :—

Quarterly : 1st and 4th, argent, a pale sable, for *Erskine*; 2nd and 3rd, azure, a bend between six cross crosslets fitchée or, for *Mar*; over all an inescutcheon gules, charged with the Royal Crown of Scotland proper within a double tressure flory counterflory or, as a coat of augmentation for the Earldom of *Kellie*.

CRESTS.—1st, a dexter hand holding a skene dhu in pale argent, hilted and pommelled or, for *Erskine*; 2nd, a demi-lion rampant guardant gules, armed argent, for *Kellie*.

SUPPORTERS.—Two griffins gules, armed, beaked and winged or.

MOTTOES.—*Je pense plus*, for *Erskine*; *Decori decus addit avito* for *Kellie*.'

KENMURE

p. 99, l. 20, after 'David II.' insert as note, 'These three writs are recorded at length in *Reg. of Deeds* (Dalrymple's Office), vol. cxli., 3 March 1738.'

p. 100, l. 15, after '1403,' as note, 'Recorded in same register.'

p. 102, l. 3, after 'Borgue,' insert 'and also of Kirkconnell in the parish of Tongland.'

p. 104, l. 5 from foot, before 'in Crosherie,' insert 'of Mundork.'

p. 105, l. 14, after '1492,' insert 'She was married, secondly, to Patrick Sinclair of Spotts and Woodhouselee (*Acta Dom. Conc.*, xx. 195).'

p. 105, after l. 14, insert

'9. *Annabel*, contracted to Cuthbert, son and heir of Andrew M'Dowell of Spotts (*Acta Dom. Conc.*, xix. 103).'

p. 106, last l., for 'Sir William' read 'James.'

p. 108, l. 22, after 'Glendonwyn,' insert 'daughter of John Glendonwyn of Drumrash (Earlston MS. Lyon Office).'

p. **108**, l. 27, after 'married,' insert 'contract 24 August and 19 September 1622 (*Reg. of Deeds*, ccclviii. 49),'

p. **108**, after l. 5 from foot, insert

'(iii) *Marion*, styled eldest daughter, married (contract 9 July 1689) to Alexander Lennox of Callie (*Reg. of Deeds*, DXXIX. 65; DXlvii. 266).'

p. **109**, after l. 2, insert

'iv. *Elizabeth*, married, contract 4 January 1612, to Alexander Gordon of Airds (Earlston MS., Lyon Office).

v. *Jean*, married, contract 17 May 1622, to David Arnot of Chapel (*Reg. of Deeds*, cccxcviii. 432).'

p. **109**, l. 25, after '*James*,' insert 'probably the second son (*Acts and Decreets*, vi. 23).'

p. **109**, l. 25, after '1540,' insert 'In 1555 he is styled titular of Glenluce (*Reg. of Deeds*, i. 258). He died in April 1559 (*Acts and Decreets*, xxix. 78).'

p. **109**, note 8, add to note, 'One of these Janets (or a third sister of the same name) was contracted in 1533 to Archibald Mure of Torhousmure (*Acta Dom. Conc. et Sess.*, ii. 184).'

p. **110**, ll. 1, 2, delete 'or 1561.'

p. **110**, l. 5, after ' to,' insert 'William, son of.'

p. **110**, l. 6, after ' from,' insert ' the latter of.'

p. **111**, l. 21, after 'intestate,' add note, 'He executed a testament and codicil a few days before his death, confirmed 3 September and 10 October 1605 (*Kenmore Inventory*. The confirmation mentioned in the text was not till 3 February 1610.'

p. **112**, l. 5, for 'in' read '24 July.'

p. **112**, l. 18, after 'married,' insert ' contract October 1615 (*Reg. of Deeds*. cccvi. 254).'

p. **112**, after l. 8 from foot, insert

'(4) *William*.   (5) *Elizabeth*.'

p. **112**, l. 2 from foot, for 'Mary' read 'Margaret (*Kenmore Inventory*).'

p. **112**, note 6, for 'v. 226' read 'iv. 226.'

p. **116**, l. 22, delete '1 January 1597' and relative note, and insert '1 February 1597-98 (*Reg. of Deeds*, lxi. 201).

p. **116**, l. 24, delete 'whom,' and insert 'her (who divorced him for adultery 11 August 1608) (*Edin. Comm. Decreets*).'

p. **117**, l. 7, for 'two' read 'three.'

p. **117**, l. 8, after 'daughters,' insert '*Margaret*, alive in 1639 (*Reg. of Deeds*, DXX. 470).'

p. **120**, l. 17, after 'Kenmure,' insert 'baptized after his father's death, 10 December 1634 (Canongate Reg.),' and for 'who' read 'He.'

p. **121**, l. 14, after 'homes,' insert 'In March 1651 Lord Kenmure was under the discipline of the Church for *inter alia* fornication with Margaret Seytoune.'

p. **121**, note 1, for '*Unique Traditions*, 1833' read '*Lights and Shadows*, 1824, 249.'

p. 123, l. 4, for 'his heir' read 'the heir'; after 'line, insert 'of the first Viscount.'

p. 123, l. 27, for 'preceding' read 'first.'

p. 124, l, 10 from foot, for 'before 7 September 1698 intestate and' read '20 April 1698.'

p. 125. l. 20, after 'secondly,' insert 'contract 1 and 3 October 1693 (*Reg. of Deeds* (Mackenzie), 28th May 1733).'

p. 125, l. 11 from foot, after 'adjoining' insert note, 'By this contract it was provided that the heirs-male of the marriage should succeed, not only to all the lands but also to the title and dignities, the latter an obviously impossible provision. By his *mortis causa* settlement, however, the Viscount left Kenmure to his eldest son and successor, the other estates going to his younger sons. It was not without difficulty that this was ultimately carried out; and in 1727 Mr. John sold Greenlaw to his sister-in-law, Mary, Viscountess of Kenmure. (Observ. by W. Gordon of Culvennan, *ex inform.* Mrs Walker; *Answers on behalf of the Publick*, on Forfeited Estate Proceedings, 26 August 1719).'

p. 131, l. 5 from foot, for 'fourth' read 'only.'

KILMARNOCK

p. 137, l. 5 from foot, for 'in' read 'dated 20 September (*Muniments of Burgh of Irvine*, Ayrshire and Galloway Arch. Assoc. 1890, No. 1).'

p. 139, l. 2 from foot, for 'third' read 'second,' and for 'fourth' ad 'fifth.'

p. 141, l. 8. after '1451,' insert 'He is stated to have been ancestor in the direct line (*ergo* illegitimate) of Edward Boyd of Merton Hall, in Wigtown, who died 27 August 1846 (*Patrician*, ii. 193).'

p. 152, l. 21, for 'third' read 'fourth.'

p. 155, note 3, after '399,' insert 'Nisbet's *Heraldry*, App. ii. 276.'

p. 168, l, 7, after 'Conyngham,' insert 'of Auchenharvie, widow of Thomas Boyd of Pitcon (*Reg. of Deeds*, cxcviii. 241; cf. *Reg. Mag. Sig.*, 7 February 1587-88).'

p. 171, l. 10, for 'circâ 29' read '26 April and 11 (*Reg. of Deeds*, DXXIX. 244).'

p. 171, l. 17, for 'Ardross' read 'Harden.'

p. 171, l. 7 from foot, for '1626' read '1628.'

p. 172, l. 5, after '1639,' insert 'tocher 35,000 merks, which was not fully paid till after Boyd's death (*Wigtown Inventory*, Scot. Rec. Soc., No. 342).'

p. 174, l. 14, after '1737,' insert 'He married Katherine Van Beest, and had a son Malcolm, ensign in the Army, who married Mary Collins (Slains Writs).'

p. 175, l. 27, after 'Baronet,' insert note, 'Her paternity is confirmed by the registration of an agreement between Margaret, Marchioness of Lothian, Mrs. Helenor Boyd, widow of Mr, Thomas (*sic*) Boyd,

Advocate, brother-german of the deceased William, Earl of Kilmarnock, and Mrs. Isabel Brisbane *alias* Nicolson, three of the four daughters and heirs of line of the deceased Sir Thomas Nicolson of Kemnay (*Reg. of Deeds*, Durie, 4 July 1730; *ex inform*. Ernest Axon, Esq.)'

p. 179, l. 2, for 'Gulielmus' read 'Wilhelmus.'

p. 179, l. 3, for 'ætat' read 'ætatis.'

p. 179, l. 4, after '42' insert note, 'There is a *facsimile* of the coffin plate in *Historical Papers*, New Spalding Club, i. 339.'

p. 179, l. 7 from foot, after 'issue,' insert note, 'Charles must have married twice, as his widow was the stepmother of his son Major Charles (see will of the latter).'

p. 180, l. 8, after '1792,' insert 'His will is dated Falmouth, 10 July 1790 (Slains Writs). He evidently left neither widow nor legitimate issue, as his natural son Charles, born at Halifax, Nova Scotia, was his residuary legatee.'

KILSYTH

p. 185, l. 23, for 'three' read 'four.'

p. 186, last line, for 'three' read 'four.'

p. 187, l. 2, after '(secundus)' add

'4. *Patrick* (*Hist. MSS. Com. Report* on Edmondstone of Duntreath MS., p. 86).'

p. 188, l. 11, after '*John*,' insert 'who under the designation of John ●ingston in Falkirk, received from his nephew Sir William Livingston of Kilsyth, on 27 May 1580, an annualrent of 20 merks, to himself and Elizabeth Fleming, his spouse (*Hist. MSS. Com.* Edmondstone MSS. 102).

p. 188, after l. 11, insert

'7. *George*, who had a feu-charter of part of Falkirk, 14 February 1552-53 (Holyrood Chart, H.M. Reg. Ho., fol. 77).'

p. 188, ll. 12, 14, 15, for '7, 8, 9,' read '8, 9, 10.'

p. 188, l. 16, delete entire line. The Baillies did not acquire Jerviswood till the time of Charles II.

p. 189, l. 17, delete from 'died' down to '1595-96,' in l. 18, and insert 'been alive up ●●●ast to 26 January 1596-97, when his son and successor is still styled of Darnchester (Protocol Book of A. Ker, Linlithgow).

p. 189, last line of note 4, after 'period,' insert 'It has since been discovered that the true year of the writ in question is 1599 (Cf. *Reg. of Deeds*, lxix. f. 16).'

p. 190, l. 11 from foot, delete 'a son.'

p. 190, after l. 10 from foot, insert

'(2) *Lilias*, married (contract 2 November 1631) to John Hamilton younger of Kinglass (*Reg. of Deeds*, DXVIII. 232).'

p. 190, l. 6 from foot, for 'by whom,' read 'and by her, who married, secondly, in 1630, John Cornwall, younger of Bonhard (*Reg. of Deeds*, DVI. 346).'

p. 191, l. 10, after 'married,' insert 'contract 25 February 1647 (Oxenfoord Writs).'

KINGSTON

p. 196. ll. 8 and 9, delete from 'said' down to 'family,' and insert 'daughter of Sir Andrew Fletcher of Inverpeffer (*Gen. Reg. of Inhibitions*, 31 August 1670).'

p. 196, ll. 13, 14, delete 'is said to have,' and after 'Hamilton' insert reference '(*Haddington Inhibs.*, xviii. 412).'

KINNAIRD

p. 203, l. 5 from foot, after 'of' add as a note,
'In an old Inventory of Kinnaird writs, dated March 1630 (*Acts and Decreets*, ccccxxxiii. f. 231, etc.), there is an entry of "ane chartour grantit be Allan of Kynnaird to Michaell Scot of Balverie of the landis of Flacraig and Craighall, quhilkis wer callit of befoir Dunnoir and Kinbrichour.' No date is given, but it was apparently before 1328, the date of the next writ.

p. 204, l. 3, for '7' read '17.'

p. 204, l. 5, for 'Walter' read 'Robert.'

p. 204, note 1, delete last sentence of note, and insert 'It is now in the Dalhousie Charter-chest : it is granted to Richard de Kynnard and to Richard his son and the heirs of his body, with remainder successively to *Alan, Reginald, Hugh, William, Thomas*, and *David*, brothers of Richard the younger, and the heirs of their bodies respectively.'

p. 206, l. 1, for 'name' read 'surname.'

p. 206, l. 2, after 'but,' insert 'by her, whose Christian name was Margaret, (*Reg. Mag. Sig.*, 28 October 1486).'

p. 208, l. 15, for 'Bertram' read 'Betoun.'

p. 208, l. 27, for 'Partick' read 'Patrick.'

p. 209, l. 12, for 'John' read 'Andrew.'

p. 210, l. 8, after 'married,' delete 'in' and insert 'contract 29 September (*Reg. of Deeds*, 25 February 1687).'

p. 211, l. 15, for 'July' read 'January (*Edin. Comm. Decreets*).'

p. 211, l. 29, after 'her,' insert 'who was dead before 11 March 1735.'

p. 211, l. 4 from foot, delete 'and,' and insert 'daughter of George Gordon, Doctor of Medicine in Banff. They were married 3 November 1731 in Dundee. She raised an action of Declarator of Marriage 11 March 1735, by which time George Kinnaird was dead, and got decree (*Consistorial Processes*, etc., Scot. Rec. Soc. No. 293).'

p. 212, l. 30, delete 'before majority,' and insert '12 February 1779.'

p. 213, l. 8, delete 'in,' and insert '23 December.'

p. 213, l. 19, delete 'in,' and insert '1 December.'

p. 214, l. 9 from foot, after 'and,' insert 'by her, who died 20 March 1910, aged ninety-two.'

p. 214, last line, after 'Victoria,' insert 'He died 12 March 1910.'

p. 215, l. 18, delete 'an infant in 1846,' and insert '14 May 1846, aged two years.'

KINNOULL

p. 220, after line 10, insert
    '2. *Peter*, baptized 9 November 1555.'

p. 220, l. 11, delete line.

p. 220, l. 12, after '*Peter*,' insert '(*secundus*), baptized 23 April 1557.'

p. 220, l. 14, after '*William*,' insert 'baptized 5 July 1560.'

p. 220, after line 15, insert
    '5. GEORGE, baptized 4 December 1570, of whom afterwards.'

p. 220, l. 16, for '5,' read '6.'

p. 220, l. 16, after 'Janet,' insert 'baptized 19 November 1554.'

p. 220, after line 16, insert
    '7. *Margaret*, baptized 16 February 1558-59.'
    '8. *Isobel*, baptized 13 May 1564.'

p. 220, line 17, for '6' read '9.'

p. 220, l. 17, after '*Elizabeth*,' insert 'baptized 29 March 1566.'

p. 220, l. 25, for '7' read '10.'

p. 220, l. 25, after '*Katherine*' insert '(third daughter), baptized 24 December 1561.'

p. 220, after line 25, insert
    '11. *Marjory*, baptized 14 November 1568.' *Note.*—The baptisms of these children are from the Errol Register, which, though not contemporary, appears to be based on authentic materials.'

p. 220, l. 26, for 'second' read 'fifth.'

p. 224, after line 25, insert
    '3. *Archibald*, baptized 23 May 1635 (Perth Reg.),' and alter numbers of succeeding children accordingly.

p. 224, line 26, after '*James*,' insert 'who married, and had a daughter, Grizel, married, c. 1668, to Lieut.-Col. Alexander, eighth son of first Earl of Stirling.'

p. 225, l. 1, after '*Elizabeth*' insert 'baptized 28 May 1636 (Perth Reg.).'

p. 230, after line 28, insert
    'There was also a natural daughter, *Isobel*, mentioned in the testament of George Hay of Balhousie.'

p. 230, l. 31, delete 'of Carnock.'

p. 230, l. 31, after 'Advocate,' insert 'brother of Sir James Nicolson of Cockburnspath.'

p. 232, l. 9, for '11 December' read '31 December.'

p. 233, l. 9, for 'Miles' read 'Milnes.'

p. 239, l. 13, after 'gules,' insert 'surmounted by a scimitar in pale argent.'

KINTORE

p. 240, ll. 21, 22, for 'INVERUGIE' read 'INVERURIE.'

p. 241, l. 2 from foot, for '9' read '19.'

p. 243, l. 15, after '1504,' insert 'As Sir George Falconer aftermentioned had a charter of Lethens in 1506-7, it is not improbable that this Alexander is identical with the Alexander who was father of Sir George.'

p. 244, line 7 from foot, for '*Janet*' read '*Marjorie* (*Reg. Mag. Sig.*, 2 October 1557).'

p. 244, note 10, after 'Kilravock 72;' insert 'She is there called *Janet* in error.'

p. 245, after line 3, insert

' 5. *Isobel*, married to John Middleton of Kilhill (cf. vol. vi. 173).'

p. 245, l. 11, delete 'only' and 'Sir (cf. vol. i. 184).'

p. 246, after l. 13, insert

'4. *Marjorie*, married, shortly after 27 November 1598, to Angus Macintosh of Termett (*Reg. of Deeds*, cclxxii. 145; cf. also Moray Writs, box. iv. No. 143, where he is called Angus Williamson).'

p. 246, ll. 14 and 16, for '4 ' and '5' read '5' and '6.'

p. 247, l. 12, after 'married,' delete 'Margaret, daughter of Robert Graeme of Crigie,' and insert 'first, Marjory Irvine, who died before Easter 1661. Her executors brought an action against his daughter and executor, Lady Balmain, with reference to her share in Sir Alexander's estate in 1719 (Sheriff Court Books of Kincardineshire, *ex inform.* Dr. Macnaughton, Stonehaven). He married, secondly, Helen, daughter of John Grahame of Crigie.

p. 247, ll. 13 and 14, delete 'and had issue ALEXANDER, fourth Lord,' and insert 'He had one daughter, *Elizabeth*, married, contract 1678, to Sir Charles Ramsay of Balmain, Baronet, as above mentioned.'

p. 248, l. 14, after 'child,' insert 'probably *David*, referred to as son of John Falconer of the Cunzie House (Factory in his favour, by David Barclay, Kincardine Sheriff-Court Books, 25 October 1666).'

p. 249, after l. 12, insert

' 2. *Thomas* (*Acts and Decreets*, cccxci. 111, A.D. 1626).'

p. 249, l. 13, for '2' read '3.'

p. 249, l. 13, after '*Agnes*,' insert '(called *Grisel* in her Funeral entry in the Lyon Office).'

p. 249, l. 5 from foot, after 'married,' insert 'proclamation of banns 24 February 1766 (Edin. Mar. Reg.).'

p. 250, l. 6, delete from 'IV. ALEXANDER' down to end of paragraph. *Note.*—As David, Lord Falconer, who died in 1751, served heir to his cousin David, third (not fourth as in text) Lord in 1724, the existence of an Alexander, fourth Lord, seems impossible. His name occurs in Wood's Douglas's *Peerage*, but he is not mentioned in the first edition by Sir Robert Douglas, and Sir Alexander of Glenfarquhar, of whom he is alleged to have been a son, died in 1717, his executor being his daughter (and probably only child) Elizabeth, wife of Sir Charles Ramsay of Balmain.

p. 250, l. 11, for 'V.' read 'IV.' for 'fifth' read 'fourth.'

p. 250, l. 14, for 'fourth' read 'third.'

p. 250, l. 20, for 'sixth' read 'fifth.'

p. 250, l. 21, for 'seventh' read 'sixth.'

p. 251, l. 2, after 'married,' insert 'proclamation of banns 16 December 1750 (Edin. Mar. Reg).'

p. 251, l. 12 for 'VI.' and 'sixth' read 'V.' and 'fifth.'

p. 251, l. 25, for 'VII.' and 'seventh' read 'VI.' and 'sixth.'

p. 251, line 30, for 'eighth' read 'seventh.'

p. 251, line 33, for 'VIII.' and 'eighth,' read 'VII.' and 'seventh.'

p. 252, l. 15, for 'IX.' and 'ninth' read 'VIII.' and 'eighth.'

p. 252, l. 20, after '1826,' insert 'aged fifty-six.'

p. 252, l. 31, for 'X.' read 'IX.'

p. 253, l. 32, for 'tenth' read 'ninth.'

p. 253, l. 7 from foot, for 'XI.' read 'X.'

p. 253, l. 6 from foot, for 'eleventh' read 'tenth.'

p. 254, l. 17, for 'XII.' read 'XI.'

p. 254, l. 18, for 'twelfth' read 'eleventh.'

p. 255, l. 2, for 'Inverugie' read 'Inverurie,'

KIRKCUDBRIGHT

p. 268, l. 15, after 'married,' insert 'contract 28 July 1640 (*Reg. of Deeds*, DXXXI. 45).'

p. 270, after l. 22, insert

'6. *Elizabeth*, married in 1589 to John, eldest son of John Herries of Maidenpaup, great-grandson of Herbert, first Lord Herries (Herries Peerage Case, Min. of Evidence, 119, No. 74).'

LAUDERDALE

p. 285, l. 21, for 'Lonchquerwart' read 'Louchquerwart.'

p. 291, l. 17, for 'fourth' read 'second.'

p. 298, l. 15, after 'married,' insert 'contract 30 May 1555 (*Acts and Decreets*, xix. 11).'

p. 298, l. 8 from foot, for 'Frances' read 'Francis.'

p. 301, l. 14, after 'Fleming,' insert 'daughter of James, fourth Lord Fleming (*Wigtown Inventory*, Scot. Rec. Soc., No. 569).'

p. 301, l. 20, for '23' read '22.'

p. 301, l. 8 from foot, for 'Novembris quintilis' read 'nonas quintilis (misquoted in *Family of Seton*, i. 220).'

p. 306, after l. 9, insert

'2. *Isobel*, baptized 3 September 1635 (Canongate Reg.). She must have died young.'

p. 306, l. 6 from foot for 'fell' read 'were assumed to fall.'

p. 307, l. 1, delete from 'And' down to 'Birkhill' on l. 4, and insert 'But in subsequent proceedings with regard to the office of Standard Bearer, the House of Lords, reversing the Court of Session, held on 7 April 1910 that the office had not been effectually acquired by Lord Halton (1910, *Sess. Cases, H.L.*, p. 35).'

p. 308, l. 29, after 'Earl,' add 'He joined James VII. and died 12 September 1691, at St. Germain-en-Laye (*Reg. of St. Germain*, i. 98, 158).

p. 309, l. 9, for '1705' read '1706, recorded 29 March 1706.'

p. 309, ll. 21 to 24. *Note.—Isobel* and *Mary* were sisters, not daughters of William Maitland. They should in consequence be numbered 7 and 8, and the notices should be in large type.

p. 311, l. 8 from foot, after 'her' insert '(who was born on or before 6 May 1692 (*Seafield Cor.*, Scot. Hist. Soc., 82, 83), and died at Bath, 24 September 1778).'

p. 312, l. 36, for '1883' read '1833.'

p. 317, l. 9, delete 'in,' and insert 'proclamation of banns 1 April (Edin. Mar. Reg.).'

p. 319, l. 24, after 'Lords,' insert note, '"One of those active, bustling spirits who will rather engage in perils and even mischiefs, than remain in a state of torpid tranquillity" (Lady Holland's *Journal*, i. 101).'

p. 319, l. 27, after 'Office,' insert note,
'A nice little painted doll, a cipher as to intellect . . . amiable and obedient (*Memoirs of a Highland Lady*, 293).'

p. 319, l. 5 from foot, after 'Torbreck,' insert note, 'She eloped with him ; "poor, silly and not wealthy" (*Ibid.*).'

p. 321, l. 26, after 'in the,' insert '8th and (*Army Lists*).'

p. 321, l. 27, for '1874' read '1869 (*Ibid.*).'

p. 321, l. 8 from foot, delete 'and Hereditary Royal Standard Bearer for Scotland.'

THE CELTIC EARLS OF LENNOX

p. 330, note 3, l. 6 from foot of notes, delete from 'with Cristinus' down to 'witness' on l. 4 from foot.

p. 330, l. 3 from foot of notes, delete 'therefore a separate personage,' and insert 'as Cristinus Judex de Levenax and Gilchrist or Cristinus the son of Earl Alwin appear as witnesses to the same charter they must be distinct persons (*Cart. de Levenax*, 96).'

STEWART, DUKE OF LENNOX

p. 346, note 5, after '*Aubigny*,' insert 'by Lady Elizabeth Cust.'

p. 350, l. 8 from foot, after 'Halkhead,' insert 'They had a charter 15 November 1515 (*Reg. Sec. Sig.*, i. 2661). Chronologically it is more likely that she was a daughter of the second Earl.'

p. **352,** l. 13, after 'issue,' add 'She married, secondly, before March 1529-30, Ninian, third Lord Ross of Halkhead (*Acta Dom. Conc.*, xli. 25, 30).'

p. **352,** ll. 7 and 5 from foot, for 'Queulle' read 'Queuille (*ex inform.* Lady Elizabeth Cust).'

p. **353,** after l. 4, insert

'5. *Margaret*, mentioned A.D. 1542 (*Rec. Sec. Sig.*, xvi. 58).'

p. **353,** l. 14, for '1543' read '1544.'

p. **353,** l. 31, after 'killed,' insert 'by one James Cadell or Cawdor (John Scott's Protocol Book).'

p. **354,** l. 5, after 'sons,' insert note, 'Their first child *Henry* was born in February 1545 and died 28 November in same year. M.I. in Stepney Church (Craik's *Romance of the Aristocracy*, ii. 353).'

p. **354,** l. 6 from foot, after 'and,' insert 'by her who died at Sheffield Castle 21 January 1582 (*Ibid.*, ii. 355).'

p. **355,** l. 26, delete '29 March 1586,' and insert '29 August 1586 (Monday between two and three p.m.) (Protocol Book of John Scott, notes, corroborated by tombstone in St. Leonard's Chapel ; cf. Hay Fleming's *Reformation in Scotland*, 634).'

p. **356,** l. 22, after 'Balsac,' insert note, 'Katharine de Balsac was descended from the Viscomtes of Milan and also from the Scaligers of Verona (*ex inform.* Lady Elizabeth Cust).'

p. **357,** l. 5 from foot, delete 'in 1621,' and insert '16 June 1621, the Earl of Hertford, her former husband, having died 5 April previous (Craik's *Romance of the Aristocracy*, ii. 392 ; *Complete Peerage*, iv. 225).'

p. **358,** l. 8, after '1620,' add 'He married a lady named Margaret Hamilton, whom he treated very badly, as appears from the *Register of Privy Council*, 2nd ser., vol. i. *passim.*'

p. **358,** l. 26, delete '3. *Francis*, died young.' (There was no such son.)

p. **359,** l. 6, after 'secondly,' insert 'within three months of her husband's death.'

p. **359,** l. 14, after '1674,' add note, 'The statement in the text is incorrect It was Lady Katherine O'Brien, and not her daughter, who was allowed the Barony of Clifton. At the time of the decision of the House of Lords her daughter was only eight years old (*ex inform.* Lady Elizabeth Cust), but according to the *Complete Peerage* (ii. 277) she was born 29 January 1673, and was therefore then only one year old.'

p. **359,** l. 18, for 'Newton' read 'Leighton.'

LENNOX, DUKE OF LENNOX

p. **371,** l. 8, after '4th' insert 'quarterly, 1st and 4th.'

p. **371,** l. 10, after '2nd' insert 'counterquarter.'

p. **371,** l. 11, after '3rd,' insert 'counterquarter.'

LEVEN

p. **373,** l. 24, after 'tocher,' insert note, 'Andrew, Earl of Rothes, is said to have had an illegitimate son, Alexander, by Christina Scott in Strathkiness. It was baptized by a layman, John Downy, who got into great trouble on account of his action with the Kirk-Session of St. Andrews. It has been suggested that this child was the Earl of Leven. The date of the birth is not recorded, but the baptism was in 1586, rather late for the accuracy of the theory (cf. *Records of Kirk-Session of St. Andrews*, Scot. Hist. Soc., 563, 567-70, 572).'

p. 378, l. 30, after 'married,' insert 'contract 5 September 1639 (*Reg. of Deeds*, Dli. 55).'

p. 378, l. 3 from foot, for '*Margaret*' read '*Janet* (cf. vol. iv. 130). She was older than Anne.'

LINDORES

p. 382, l. 11, for 'Turnberry' read 'Lumbenny.'

p. 383, l. 12 from foot, for 'between 1606 and 1609' read 'between 22 May and 5 October 1608 (*Gen. Reg. Inhibs.*, 2 December 1608).'

p. 383, l. 2 from foot, delete from 'It' to end of sentence, and insert 'He appears to have married twice, his second wife being Catherine Basset. As his widow she was, 17 November 1676, granted a pension of £100 sterling (*Privy Seal, English Reg.*, iii. 126).'

p. 384, l. 4, delete 'Loch of Lindores,' and insert 'River Tay.'

p. 384, l. 9, after '*s.p.*', insert 'and was buried at Holyrood in May 1668 (Canongate Reg.).'

p. 384, after l. 10, insert

'6. *George*.

7. *Henry* (*Reg. Mag. Sig.*, 11 August 1614).'

p. 384, ll. 11, 13, 15, 18, 20, for '6, 7, 8, 9, 10' read '8, 9, 10, 11, 12.'

p. 384, l. 11, for '1622' read '1609 (*Reg. of Deeds*, clxii. 146, and cccxxvii. 488, correcting *Reg. Mag. Sig.*, 13 January 1625).'

p. 384, l. 14, for 'Moy' read 'Mey.'

p. 384, l. 15, for '*Jean*' read '*Anna* (*Reg. Mag. Sig.*, 20 August 1618).' *Note.*—She, or another sister of the same name, had previously been married to James Leslie, fiar of Otterstoun, who, in 1614, is styled the second lord's brother-in-law (*Reg. of Deeds*, ccxx. 295; *Reg. Mag. Sig.*, 11 August 1614).

p. 385, l. 10, after 'first,' insert 'contract 10 April 1673 (*Perth Sasines*, vii. 248).'

p. 385, l. 11, after 'Innernytie,' insert 'who died at Edinburgh, 22 February 1680 (*Red Book of Grandtully*, ii. 251).'

p. 385, note 2, after '*Annals*, iii. 423,' insert 'of his natural children four sons are known: *James*, a lieutenant in the Army; *Robert* and *Ludovic*, who went to Barbadoes; and *Francis*, who lived at Weems. A natural daughter, *Anna*, was married to Captain James Drummond, and, as his widow, figures on the Royal Charity Rolls from Whitsunday 1683 onwards.'

p. 386, l. 25, for '8 and 15 September 1603' read '28 April 1616.'

p. 386, l. 10 from foot, delete 'killed along with his father at Dundee, 1651,' and insert 'also a knight, and died between August 1676 and February 1677 (*Privy Seal, English Reg.*, iii. 130).'

p. 386, l. 9 from foot, for '1550 the' read '1650 Jonet.'

p. 386, l. 7 from foot, after '*s.p.*,' insert 'in March 1686 (St. Andrews Tests.), and a daughter Elizabeth, who was married to William Dick of Grange. (See below, No. 5, where she is erroneously entered as as a sister instead of a daughter of John).'

p. 386, l. 2 from foot, after '5' transfer entire entry to No. 1, Elizabeth being a daughter of John Leslie and Janet Hay.

p. 386, l. 2 from foot, after '5,' insert '*Anna*, married to Robert Kirkcaldy of Grange after 7 April 1637, when she was his "future spouse" (*Gen. Reg. Sas.*, xlvi. 156).'

p. 386, note 8, for '472' read '479.'

p. 387, after l. 8, insert

'7. *Margaret*, married (contract 17 September 1649) to John Grant of Ballindalloch (*Chiefs of Grant*, i. 520).'

p. 388, l. 14, after 'her,' insert 'who survived him, and was married, secondly, to Patrick Forbes (Fife Sheriff-Court Book, 23 May 1682).'

LINDSAY.

p. 394, l. 8, for 'John' read 'George, first.'

p. 394, note 4, for '157' read '167.'

p. 394, l. 12, delete 'Alexander,' and insert 'Robert, afterwards second (cf. vol. iv. 235).'

p. 398, l. 11, after '1563,' insert 'He was contracted to marry Marjory, daughter and heiress of George Lindsay, but the marriage did not take place (*Acta Dom. Conc.*, xxix. 108).'

p. 398, l. 13, after 'Moncur,' insert note, 'There was "stop" to the marriage intimated by her son Patrick on 10 January 1564-65, and parties were ordered by the Kirk Session of St. Andrews to compear on the 21st of that month, but there is no further record of the ultimate issue of the case.'

p. 398, note 6, for 'xxxii' read 'lxxxii.'

p. 404, l. 6, for 'under' read 'over.'

p. 404, l. 8, for 'under fourteen' read 'above twelve.'

LIVINGSTON, EARL OF LINLITHGOW

p. 426, l. 6, for 'Barnton' read 'Banton.'

p. 426, after l. 14, add

'6. *Sir Henry*, Preceptor of Torphichen (cf. *ante*, p. 184, and *Hist. MSS. Comm. Report* on Duntreath Papers, 83).

p. 429, l. 20, delete from 'This' to end of paragraph, and insert 'He had issue, a son,

(1) *Alexander* of Dunipace. He was a member of the Town

Council of Stirling in 1527-28. He married Alison Gourlay
(*Reg. Mag. Sig.*, 24 December 1521), and had issue :—

    i. *David* of Bantaskine, died *vitâ patris*, having married
        Elizabeth Shaw, with issue.

    ii. *Mr. Alexander* of Dunipace and Fildes. He married Eliza-
        beth, daughter of Sir Adam Hepburn of Craigs (cf. *ante*,
        vol. ii. 149 ; *Reg. Mag. Sig.*, 24 July 1525) with issue (*Lands
        and Lairds of Larbert and Dunipace Parishes*, by J. C.
        Gibson, 1908).'

p. 429, l. 24, delete 'Sir Robert Bruce of Airth' and accompanying note,
and insert 'James Hamilton of Cadzow (*Eleventh Rep. Hist. MSS.
Comm.*, App. vi. 14, 15 ; cf. vol. iv. 348).'

p. 433, ll. 22, 23, for 'is supposed to have been' read 'was (see next
entry).'

p. 434, l. 7, after 'Kilsyth,' insert 'On 28 May 1498 he had a precept of
clare constat as heir of his uncle James, Lord Livingstone, in the
lands of Catscleuch from George Sinclair of Herbertshire (*Wigtown
Charter-chest*, Scot. Rec. Soc., 719).'

p. 434, l. 11, after '1503,' insert 'He appears on 1 November 1472 to have
entered into an obligation to marry Elizabeth, daughter of Robert,
Lord Fleming (*Wigtown Charter-chest*, Scot. Rec. Soc., 44), but it is
doubtful if the marriage took place, though in a pedigree of 1625 in the
Livingstone Charter-chest it is stated that it did, and that William
was Elizabeth Fleming's son.'

p. 434, note 7, delete 'probably first wife of Patrick Hepburn, first Lord
Hailes.'

p. 435, l. 5, for 'Whitson' read 'Whitsome.'

p. 435, l. 8, after 'James,' insert 'He is said to have married and to have
had a son, Alexander, minister of Monyabrock, whose great-grandson,
Robert, born 13 December 1654, went to America, and was ancestor of
the Livingstones of Livingstone Manor.'

p. 435, l. 12, after '1553' add 'He appears on 16 October 1563 as Captain
of the Royal Castle of Kirkwall, and demanding restitution of certain
gear and writs formerly belonging to his deceased wife, Margaret
Strang (Protocol Book of Gilbert Grote, f. 94).'

p. 435, note 2, for 'iii.' read 'ii.'

p. 436, l. 22, after 'Queen,' add as a note, 'He was at St. Germains in
France, 25 July 1549 (*Reg. Mag. Sig.*, 20 April 1550), also in April 1550
(letter in H.M. Reg. Ho.).'

p. 436, l. 24, after '1551,' note, 'He was perhaps dead before 1 October
1550. (Cf. letter from his son to the Queen Regent in H. M. Reg. Ho.).'

p. 436, l. 13 from foot, after 'Janet Stewart,' insert 'perhaps a daughter of
Alexander, second Earl of Buchan (Pedigree (A.D. 1625) in Livingstone
Charter-chest).'

p. 439, note 4, after '389' add '*Cal. of State Papers*, v. 248.'

p. 442, l. 20, delete from 'Whether' to 'ascertained' in l. 22, and insert
'Lady Livingstone survived her husband, but appears to have been

murdered before 18 October 1597, when Alexander, Master of Elphinstone, is charged to produce a certain Maws Livingstone suspect of
the crime (*Ninth Rep. Hist. MSS. Comm.*, pt. ii. No. 59).'

p. **442**, ll. 30 and 31, delete ' believed to have been of the family of Innernytie,' and insert 'Crichton, probably a daughter of William Crichton
of Drumcrocemuir (*Part. Reg. of Sasines, Linlithgow and Bathgate*, i.
306).'

p. **442**, l. 4 from foot, for ' Mary' read ' Margaret.'

p. **442**, l. 3 from foot, for ' Bailie' read ' Baillie.'

p. **442**, l. 2 from foot, after ' Dundrennan,' add note, ' 6 *Reg. Mag. Sig.*,
21 February 1610.'

p. **442**, l. 2 from foot, after ' William.' insert 'also married a Margaret
Baillie (*P. C. Reg.*, ix. 19, 154), and had a son, also William, who.'

p. **447**, l. 17, after ' first,' insert 'contract 22 August 1648 (*ex inform.*
Ernest Axon, Esq.).'

p. **448**, l. 7, delete ' 23 November 1660,' and insert 'in September 1662,
when the regiment was raised.'

p. **448**, l. 7, insert 'lieutenant' before ' colonelship.'

p. **448**, l. 9, after ' Council,' insert 'He was promoted Colonel in July
1666 (Dalton's *The Scots Army*, 1661-88, pt. ii. 13, 15).'

LOTHIAN

p. **452**, l. 5, for ' second' read 'third (cf. vol. vii. 324).'

p. **452**, l. 7, for ' Jedburgh' read ' Roxburghe.'

p. **452**, l. 15, after ' Altonburn,' insert note, ' It is pointed out that
Brigadier-General Walter Ker of Littledean was allowed by the House
of Lords the character of heir-male and representative of the Kerrs of
Cessford, and that his line is not exhausted. But see vol. vii. 331.
(*ex inform.* William D. Kerr, Esq., Glasgow).'

p. **457**, l. 14, after ' *s.p.*', add 'having married Jean, daughter of James
Donaldson, Advocate, widow of William Eigge, merchant, Edinburgh.'

p. **458**, l. 4, after ' December,' insert ' 1614.'

p. **467**, after line 28, insert
        ' 1. *Robert*, died in infancy.'

p. **467**, l. 29, for ' 1' read ' 2.'

p. **467**, after line 29, insert
        ' 3. *Margaret.*'

p. **467**, l. 31, for ' 2' read ' 4.'

p. **467**, l. 33, for ' 3' read ' 5.'

p. **468**, after line 8, insert
        ' 6. *Robert.*'

p. **468**, l. 9, for ' 4' read ' 7.'

p. **468**, after l. 10, insert
        ' 8. *Henrietta Maria.*'

p. 468, l. 11, for '5' read '9.'

    delete ll. 20 and 21, and insert

    '10. *Anna.*

     11. *Katherine.*'

p. 468, l. 22, delete 'These two,' and insert 'Two.'

p. 475, l. 16, after 'unmarried,' insert 'in 1717.'

p. 480, l. 19, after 'first,' insert 'contract dated at Edinburgh and New-battle, 7 and 8 December 1711 : tocher £3000 stg. (*Reg. of Deeds,* Durie, cxxx., 4 February 1713).'

p. 480, l. 20, for 'Nicholson' read 'Nicolson.'

p. 483, l. 25, for 'July' read 'April.'

p. 487, l. 11, for '28 October 1587,' read '15 October 1591.'

p. 487, l. 21, for 'in' read 'on.'

p. 487, l. 23, delete 'and.'

p. 487, l. 23, for 'sable' read 'of the first.'

LOUDOUN

p. 499, l. 21, for 'fourth' read 'third.'

p. 504, l. 13, after 'Clathick,' insert 'married, first, 18 June 1590, Margaret Donaldson (Stirling Reg.). He must have married again as he.'

p. 507, l. 2 from foot, after 'and,' insert 'by her, who died before 22 February 1686 (*Seafield Correspondence,* Scot. Hist. Soc., 20).'

p. 508, l. 10, delete 'in 1714,' and insert '7 March 1707.'

p. 509, l. 7, for 'only' read 'third.'

p. 509, l. 8, delete 'born 4 February 1677,' and insert 'baptized 25 August 1684 (Kirkliston Reg.).'

p. 509, l. 9, for '1777' read '1779.'

p. 509, l. 10, delete 'aged one hundred.'

p. 509, l. 16, after 'married,' insert 'proclamation of banns, 4 August 1728 (Edin. Reg.).'

p. 511, l. 11, for 'Kilmarnock' read 'Rowallan.'

p. 512, l. 17, for 'Rawdon' read 'Hastings.'

LOVAT

p. 525, l. 24, after 'Margaret,' insert 'perhaps the Margaret Lady Mackay, wife of John Mackay of Strathnaver (*The Book of Mackay,* 85).'

p. 527, l. 17, after 'will,' insert 'She married (contract dated at Kirktoun of Ferneway, 26 March 1562), Allan M'Ranald of Leyis, and had issue. (Sheriff-Court Book of Inverness, at date; *The Clan Donald,* iii. 228).'

p. 529, l. 27, after '1581,' insert 'She married James Cuming of Altyre before November 1602, with a tocher of 5000 merks. (*Reg. of Deeds,* cxci. f. 233; charters quoted in *The Bruces and the Comyns,* 464, 465.).'

p. 529, l. 28, delete whole line and relative note.

p. 529, l. 29, for '6' read '5.'

p. 529, note 10, delete note and insert 'Edin. Tests., 21 December 1597.'

p. 534, l. 21, after 'married,' insert 'contract, 29 September 1679 (*Reg. of Deeds*, 25 February 1687).'

p. 534, l. 24, after 'married,' insert 'contract 29 April 1684.'

p. 534, l. 27, for 'Mackenzie,' read 'Macdonell.'

p. 540, l. 2, after 'married,' insert 'contract dated at various places, according as the different consenters signed, from 3 April to 9 July 1733 (*Forfeited Estates Papers*, Scot. Hist. Soc. 46).'

p. 540, l. 19, after 'married,' insert 'in August 1742 (*Inverness Gaelic Society's Transactions*, xix. 192 n.).'

p. 540, l. 26, after '1726,' insert, 'He was educated at the University of St. Andrews, under the care of Prof. Thomas Craigie, 1744-45.'

p. 543, l. 6 from foot, for '1645,' read '1648. (*Reg. Inhibitions, Inverness*, 2 series, vol. 2, f. 139).'

p. 544, after line 2, insert

'3. *William*, named in 1656 as uncle of Thomas [fourth] Laird of Strichen.

4. *George*, also so named.

5. *Walter*, also so named. He also appears as a witness on 5 August 1651. (*Aberdeen Sasines*, xv. f. 162; Book of Debts, H.M. Reg. Ho., 28 August 1656).

6. *Margaret*, married to John Forbes of Corsindae (*Aberdeen Sasines*, ix. ff. 4-7).'

p. 544, l. 4, for '1645' read '1648.'

p. 544, l. 8, after 'in,' insert 'or before August.'

p. 544, l. 7 from foot, for 'her' read 'his wives.'

p. 545, l. 23, after 'son, insert 'besides one daughter, *Isabella*, married (proclamation of banns, 27 May 1784), to Lieutenant Æneas Mackay, late of Rhenorea (Canongate Reg.).'

p. 547, l. 18, after 'Buckinghamshire,' insert 'died at Bournemouth, 17 August 1912.'

LYLE

p. 551, l. 3, for '1365' read '1366.'

p. 551, l. 8, for 'Buchanan' read 'Boquhan.'

p. 551, last line, delete 'his brother-in-law.'

p. 552, l. 24, for 'Magaretum' read 'Margaretam.'

p. 552, l. 4 from foot, for 'Andrew' read 'Alexander.'

p. 553, l. 16, for 'Lisle' read 'Lyle.'

p. 554, l. 18, delete 'There is no evidence for the statement that' and relative note.

p. 554, l. 19, after 'married,' insert 'first, Margaret.'

p. 554, l. 19, after 'Seton,' add note, 'Since the above was written evidence has been found of the marriage, and that Lord Lyle had by his first wife at least one son, *George* (cf. vol. viii. 578, and authority there quoted).'

p. 555, l. 20, after ' Dunrod,' insert ' She was married, secondly, to William Menzies of Roro (*Acta Dom. Conc.*, xliii. 103).'

p. 556, l. 11, for 'Fymont' read ' Finnart.'

p. 556, l. 16, for ' Buchanan' read ' Boquhan.'

p. 556, l. 30, after 'married,' insert 'contract 28 August 1549 (*Acta Dom. Conc. et Sess.*, xxvi. 90). She got £1000 tocher and gifts of sundry dresses from the Governor Arran (*Treasurer's Accounts*, ix. 335-336).'

p. 557, l. 21, for ' quidam certam summam pecunia' read ' quadam certa summa pecunie.'

ANCIENT EARLS OF MAR

p. 589, l. 4, after 'issue,' insert 'and was buried in the Greyfriars Church, Inverness, 26 July (*Cal. of Papal Letters*, viii. 601).'

p. 589, after line 6, insert 'The Earl had another natural son, David, canon of Ross and treasurer of Moray (*Cal. Papal Letters*, ix. 484, 530).'

ERSKINE, EARL OF MAR

p. 597, l. 28, after 'father,' insert 'In 1388 he was "guardian of the Temple in Scotland" (Brit. Mus., *MS. Harl.*, 6439).'

p. 608, l. 3, after ' before,' insert ' 15 July (cf. vol. iv. 448).'

p. 608, l. 4, for ' Alexander, first Lord Home' read ' Sir Alexander Home of that Ilk. For 'Sir Adam Hepburn of Hales' read ' Adam, Master of Hales (*Ibid.*).'

p. 621, ll. 9, 10, delete from 'The' down to ' but,' and insert ' She died 23 December 1587, and was buried at Alloa 9 January 1587-88 (Funeral letter, Moray Writs, box 3, No. 241).'

p. 621, l, 26, after 'Hague,' insert ' In 1630 he is styled Captain Alexander Erskine of Cambuskenneth (*Reg. of Deeds*, ccccxxxv. 284).'

p. 621, l. 34, after ' so,' add ' Tradition identifies him (and rightly) with " the faithless lover " of " Lady Ann Bothwell's Lament." He probably did marry the Croft lady (Mar and Kellie MS. Rep. 178 ; *Fourth Rep. Hist. MSS. Com.*, 527). He refers to his wife in a letter to his mother, and after his death his brother Arthur does the same. She survived, and probably died between 1640 and 1643. They had three or perhaps four children. Two sons—*Alexander*, who was at Scots Craig with his uncle Arthur in May 1643 and was then sent to the wars abroad, and *Thomas*, who was about ten in 1646, and was sent by his uncle Charles, who was then in London, to his wife in Edinburgh. A daughter was kept by some one in England who was anxious to get rid of her by sending her to her father's representatives.'

p. 622, l. 25, after ' married,' insert ' first.'

p. 622, l. 27, after ' issue,' insert ' secondly (contract 1638), to Patrick Maule, first Earl of Panmure.'

p. 622, note 3, for ' 1671' read ' 1677.'

p. 634, l. 19, for ' father' read ' grandfather.'

VOL. VI.

MARCHMONT

p. 5, l. 19, delete 'first,' and insert after 'wife,' 'Margaret Crichtoun.'

p. 6, l. 11, delete 'second,' and insert after 'wife,' 'Margaret Lauder.'

p. 10, l. 4, for 'He' read 'She.'

p. 11, l. 6 from foot, for 'Sir James' read 'Sir John.'

p. 12, l. 19 from foot. The following list of Sir Patrick's family is from an old Family Bible at Marchmont:—

'1. *John*, born at Bailincrieff 25 September 1638, died 26 April 1639.

2. *Patrick*, born at Redbraes 12 January 1641.

3. *Alexander*, born at Redbraes 29 June 1644, died at Moscow 1676.

4. *Julian*, born at Polwarth Mains 23 October 1639, died at Yester 20 October 1687.

5. *Christian*, born at Redbraes 20 January 1643, died 5 February 1666.

6. *Anne*, born at Redbraes 31 October 1646, died at Edinburgh in August 1690.'

p. 19, l. 25, for 'Pettis' read 'Perris.'

p. 19, l. 28, after '*Anne*,' insert 'born 29 July 1698.'

p. 19, l. 4 from foot, after 'married,' insert 'proclamation of banns 30 January 1743 (Edin. Reg.).'

MARISCHAL

p. 38, l. 7, for '1363' read '1363-64.'

p. 44, l. 18, for 'Glenarthill' read 'Glencuthil.'

p. 45, l. 7 from foot, for 'second' read 'fourth.'

p. 49, l. 16, for '1543' read '1543-44, both parties being very young.'

p. 49, l. 16, for 'sixth' read 'seventh.'

p. 50, l. 16, after 'secondly,' insert 'banns proclaimed in Dunottar church 13 January 1571-72 (Moray Writs, box 15, No. 344).'

p. 53, l. 23, after '1598,' add note, 'The traditional circumstances of her death are curious. Having heard of the slaughter of one William Lauder, a bailie of the burgh of Lauder, by her brother Lord Home, she 'did mightily rejoice thereat, and writ it for good newes to sundry of her friends in the country. But within less than twenty-four hours after, the lady took a swelling in her throat, both without and within, after a great laughter, and could not be cured till death seized upon her with great repentance.—Pat. Anderson's *Hist. of Scotland*, cited in Chambers' *Domestic Annals*, i. 300.'

p. 53, last l., and **p. 54**, l. 1, for ' before 19 March 1623,' read ' contract 13, 21, and 22 February 1618 (*Reg. of Deeds*, cccxxxvi. 394).'

p. 54, l. 1, delete 'Sir.'

p. 54, ll. 14, 15, delete from 'but' to '1587' inclusive.

p. 54, after l. 17, insert 'The Earl had a natural son *Gilbert*, legitimated 19 May 1587.[9] Another son *Robert*, probably also illegitimate, married, contract 14 March 1618, Helen, daughter of John Bruce of Graysfortrie (*Reg. of Deeds*, ccclxxxvii. 424).'

p. 59, note 3, after ' Hay's *Gen. Coll.*' delete ' ii. 266,' and insert ' iii. 267.'

p. 62, l. 13, after '*Mary*,' insert ' born 1695 (*Letters of James, Earl of Perth*, Camden Society, 78 *n.*).'

p. 62, l. 21, for '1714' read '1715.'

MELFORT

p. 66, l. 15, after 'Guards,' insert ' He was admitted a Privy Councillor 12 December 1678.'

p. 68, l. 2 from foot, after ' married,' insert ' contract 28 February 1700 (*Reg. of Deeds*, Dalrymple, 12 January 1709).'

p. 69, l. 13, for ' 1691 ' read ' 1675 (The 1691 publication was a reprint).'

p. 69, l. 29, after 'first,' insert ' in July 1788.'

p. 70, l. 3, for ' Royas ' read ' Rozas.'

p. 70, l. 3, delete ' Bozas of.'

p. 70, ll. 4 and 6, for ' Castel Bianco ' read ' Castel Blanco.'

p. 70, l. 7, after 'their,' insert ' grand.'

p. 70, l. 7, after ' daughters,' insert '*Margaret* married Don Joseph Iquaz de Vallabriga, a captain of Aragonese cavalry (*L'Art de Verifier les Dates*, fol. ed. 1821. Continuation, i. 325), and had a daughter.'

p. 70, l. 7, after ' Theresa,' insert ' who.'

p. 70, l. 8 from foot after ' Louis,' insert ' Jean Edward,' and for ' born ' read ' baptized.'

p. 71, before l. 1, insert

(4) '*Xavier*, baptism recorded at St. Germains 6 December 1713.'

p. 71, l. 1, for ' 4 ' read ' 5.'

p. 71, l. 5, for ' May ' read ' March.'

p. 72, l. 24, for ' subects ' read ' subjects.'

LEVEN AND MELVILLE

p. 92, after l. 23, insert

' vi. *Jean*, executrix dative to Robert, second Lord Melville, 1635 (Edin. Tests.).'

p. 94, l. 6 from foot, after ' married,' insert ' Esther Tailor, relict of David Drummond, gentleman pensioner to James VI. (*Reg. of Deeds*, Dlvii. 23).'

p. 94, after l. 2 from foot, insert

'(4) *Margaret*, married (contract 25 March 1634), as second wife, to Mr. Thomas Maitland, minister of Garvald (*Reg. of Deeds*, DXXVII. 127); secondly, after 1637, to Mr. John Dalzell, minister of Prestonkirk (*Reg. of Deeds*, Mack., 8 February 1666).'

p. 99, l. 20, after '*Christian*,' insert 'a natural daughter.' After 'married,' insert '(contract dated 11th October 1581 (Reg. Ho. Cal., 20 November 1583).'

p. 101, l. 9, for '1613' read '1601 (*P. C. Reg.*, vi. 214).'

p. 103, l. 14, after 'Meldrum,' insert 'She was perhaps the Margaret, brother's daughter of Robert Melville of Murdocairnie, widow of Robert Ramsay, merchant, mentioned in *Fife Inhibitions*, 27 July 1602.'

p. 110, l. 20, after '1681,' insert 'in consequence of which he assumed the name and arms of Leslie (*Family of Leslie*, iii. 366).'

p. 114, l. 24, for '10 March' read '21 March (Edin. Reg.).'

p. 123, l. 2, for '17 August' read '10 August.'

GRAHAM, EARL OF MENTEITH

p. 151, l. 9, delete 'a.'

p. 151, l. 9, after 'Herries,' insert 'daughter of William Herries of Hartwood, co. Dumfries, and granddaughter of Mr. Robert Herries, minister of Dryfesdale.'

p. 151, l. 14, for 'son' read 'daughter.'

p. 151, l. 15, for 'his' read 'her (*Services of Heirs*, 1710-19, p. 2).'

p. 151, l. 15, delete from 'but' to end of sentence, and insert 'married to Michael Malcolm of Balbeadie, co. Fife, and died February 1733.'

p. 152, l. 25, delete from 'It is' down to 'Graham' on line 27, and insert 'He died about 1557, having married, first, Isobel Graham, and, secondly, Margaret, daughter of —— Shaw of Knockhill. She survived him and was described as his widow on 4 July 1558 (Protocol Book of Gilbert Grote, 52).'

p. 153, l. 25, after 'certain,' add 'but he was living on 28 February 1665 (*P. C. Reg.*, 3rd ser., ii. 630).'

p. 154, l. 15, after 'Captain,' delete to end of paragraph, and insert 'Philip Wilkieson, Balnahinch, Ireland. The marriage took place at Balnahinch in August 1714. Her husband instituted a divorce against her on 16 December 1726 (*Consistorial Processes*, Scot. Rec. Soc., No. 240), They had issue.'

p. 158, l. 28, after 'Hill,' insert 'He died before October 1595. Hill was also known as Easter Aikenhead. Helen Kincaid survived him, having issue a daughter *Agnes* Hamilton, married, before October 1595, to Alexander Hamilton of Haggs (Reg. Ho. Cal., 31 October 1595).'

p. 159, l. 23, delete '6 February 1588-89,' and insert '31 October 1595 (Reg. Ho. Cal. at date).'

p. 160, l. 6, from foot, for 'John, Lord Seton' read 'George, fourth Lord Seton.'

MIDDLETON

p. 188, l. 14, delete 'in 1705 or 1706,' and insert 'at S. Sulpice, Paris, 25 June 1702 (*Reg. of St. Germain en Laye*, i. 13).'

MONTROSE

p. 197, l 10. from foot, for 'Swinburne' read 'Symundburne.'

p. 213, note 1. Add to end of note, 'The statement in Burke is questioned by representatives of the Grahames of Auchincloich who claim, or suggest, a descent from the Dalkeith or elder branch of the Grahams. It is possible that Nisbet is right in placing the ancestors of the Grahams of Morphie a generation further back in the Montrose pedigree.'

p. 215, l. 20, for 'Robert, Duke of Albany' read 'Robert III.'

p. 220, l. 2, for 'sons' read 'children.'

p. 223, l. 2, after 'Oliver' read 'Ogilvie.'

p. 223, l. 2, after 'son,' delete comma, and add 'by her second husband James, first Lord Ogilvie of Airlie.'

p. 223, l. 19, delete from '4. *Oliver*' to end of paragraph, and alter the remaining numbers of children from '5, 6, 7' to '4, 5, 6.'

p. 224, note 7, for 'Lord Erskine' read 'Lord Graham.'

p. 225, l. 15 after 'relict,' add 'of Andrew Mowbray, burgess of Edinburgh, and.'

p. 225, l. 26, for 'Bucklyvie' read 'Buchlyvie.'

p. 227, l. 16, for 'Mathew' read 'Matthew.'

p. 230, l. 9 from foot, after 'issue,' insert 'She married, secondly, as his second wife, Sir Harie Graham of Morphie, and died in August 1587 (Edin. Tests.).'

p. 236, l. 17, delete 'Sir.'

p. 237, l. 6 from foot, for '1595' read 'March 1597-98 (Perth Reg.).'

p. 238, l. 26, for 'two' read 'three.'

p. 238, l. 27, for 'third' read 'fourth.'

p. 238, l. 27, after 'Braco,' insert '*Patrick*.'

p. 239, l. 15, after 'issue,' insert note, 'There was an assignation by John Earl of Montrose, donator to the ward and marriage of Lord Fleming to the latter himself and that in contemplation of the marriage *then contracted* between him and Lilias, dated 7 February 1582-83 (*Wigtown Inventory*, Scot. Rec. Soc., No. 127).'

p. 253, l. 8 from foot, for 'amounts appear' read 'account referred to appears.'

p. 258, ll, 3 and 4 from foot, delete 'Lord Graham.'

p. 259, l. 3 from foot, after 'troop,' insert 'He was admitted of the Privy Council, 15 November 1678.'

p. 271, l. 9 from foot, after 'issue,' insert 'She and her sisters, Georgina and Caroline, are described as "fine, civil and cheerful-looking girls" (Miss Berry's *Journal*, ii. 391).'

p. 273, l. 6 from foot, after '1902' add 'and also at that on 22 June 1911.'

p. 274, after l. 8, insert

'(2) *Ronald Malise Hamilton*, born 20 September 1912.

(3) *Mary Helen Alma*, born 11 April 1909.'

DUNBAR, EARL OF MORAY

p. 301, l. 5 from foot, after '*James*,' delete remainder of sentence, and read, 'who, in or after 1397, was presented to the Precentorship of Moray, being then fourteen years old. He resigned it in or before 1404.'

STEWART, EARL OF MORAY

p. 311, l. 4 from foot, after '1544,' insert 'within eight days of being "schorne of the stane,"' (Moray Writs, box 15, No. 1736).'

p. 312, l. 3, for '1525' read '1524.'

p. 312, ll. 6, 7, 8, 9, delete from 'They' to 'issue,' and insert 'He left no legitimate issue.'

p. 312, l. 10, for '*John*,' read '*James*.'

p. 312, l. 15, after 'her,' insert 'She was married to John, Master of Buchan (see *ante, corrigenda* on vol. i. p. 269).'

STEWART, EARL OF MORAY

p. 314, l. 28, after 'Strathearn,' add note, 'In a resignation of John Lamb, burgess of Edinburgh, 21 July 1564, he is styled Earl of Moray, Lord Pettie, Brachlie and Stratheirn (Protocol Book of Gilbert Grote, H.M. Reg. Ho., 113, 114).'

p. 316, l. 25, for 'before November 1572,' read 'before 29 March 1571 (Moray Writs, box 15, No. 211).'

p. 316, l. 26, after 'posthumous,' insert 'born before 18 April 1570 (*Ibid.*, box 15, No. 352).'

p. 316, l. 28, for 'before January 1586-87,' read '3 August 1586, (*Ibid.*, No. 1694).'

p. 317, l. 20, after '1591-92,' insert note, '(*Acts and Decreets*, ccxxxv. 5).'

p. 318, l. 12, after '1591,' insert note '(*Acts and Decreets*, cccxxxv. 5).'

p. 318, l. 18, after 'London,' insert 'He was a Vice-Admiral in the English Navy: he died *s.p.*, and was buried at Westminster (MS. Account of the Family, *penes* Niall Campbell, Esq.).'

p. 319, l. 17, after 'Dunrobin,' insert 'He was retoured heir of his mother in the earldom, 22 July 1602, but the precept of clare constat was not issued till 7 May 1604, when the lands are said to have been twelve years in ward (*Responde Book*).'

p. 320, ll. 6 and 7, delete 'to which he had succeeded on the death of his cousin James, the second holder of that title,' and insert 'which he acquired from the Earl of Morton, who had apprised the lands from Lord St. Colme (cf. vol. vii. 395).'

p. 320, l. 22, after 'Edinburgh,' insert 'in 1638 (MS. Account of the Family *penes* Niall Campbell, Esq.).'

p. 320, l. 23, for '*Margaret,*' read '*Mary.*'

p. 320, l. 23, delete 'about 24,' and insert 'contract 4.'

p. 321, l. 2, after 'buried,' insert 'at Dyke.'

p. 321, l. 17, after 'wife,' insert 'who died after 9 March (the date of her will), and before May 1683 (Moray Writs, box 5, No. 328).'

p. 321, l. 19, after 'unmarried,' insert 'in the twelfth year of his age (MS. History *ut sup*).'

p. 321, l. 19, delete from '14 June' to end of sentence, and insert '1 June 1647, the date of receipt for the price of his coffin (Moray Writs, box 5, No. 971).'

p. 321, l. 23, after 'unmarried,' add, 'and was buried in the Session-House of South Leith, 30 January 1692 (South Leith Kirk Session Minutes).'

p. 321, l. 27, delete 'had,' and insert 'dying 2 February 1688 left.'

p. 321, l. 28, after 'Charles,' insert 'born 16 December 1676.'

p. 321, l. 28, after 'first,' insert 'proclamation of banns 13 February 1697 (Canongate Reg.).'

p. 321, l. 29, after 'secondly,' insert 'proclamation of banns 24 August 1700 (*Ibid*).'

p. 321, l. 30, for 'Dalziel,' read 'Dalzell,' and insert 'who died 10 November 1708.'

p. 321, l. 32, after '1650,' insert '(contract 29 March 1650, tocher £36,000), (Moray Writs).'

p. 321, l. 33, after '1668,' insert note, 'It is stated by Mr. Willcock in *A Scots Earl*, that she survived to the end of 1706, when she died at the age of eighty-five.'

p. 321, l. 34, delete 'after March 1653,' and insert 'contract 26 August 1654 (Moray Writs).'

p. 321, last line, delete 'in,' and insert 'contract 28 January.'

p. 322, l. 25, after 'Revolution,' insert note, 'On his periodical visits to London as Secretary of State he used to take so much gold for his general expenses and a packet of fifty gold pieces for cards, etc. The family tradition is that he died, not at Donibristle, as stated in the text, but on his way to London, and that all his things were bundled into a box, where they remained untouched till quite recently. Whatever the facts may be, it is certain that the family have in their possession fifty new gold pieces of the period (*ex inform.* Earl of Moray).'

p. 322, second last line, for '1700,' read '1701' (Moray Writs).

p. 322, last line, after 'married,' insert 'before 31 January 1663 (Moray Writs).'

p. 323, l. 2, for '20 July 1702,' read 'in 1682.'

p. 323, l. 2, after 'issue,' insert 'besides seven children, who died *vitâ patris*, and unmarried.'

p. 323, l. 3, after 'Doune,' insert 'born at Darnaway 1658.'

p. 323, l. 3, after '*v.p.*' insert '12 December.'

p. 323, l. 2 from foot, after 'Moray,' insert 'born 4 September 167[4] at Darnaway' (MS. Account, *ut sup.*).'

p. 324, l. 5, after 'first,' insert 'in the beginning of September 1698.'

p. 324, l. 8, after 'no,' insert 'surviving.'

p. 324, l. 8, delete 'about 1702,' and insert 'contract 26 and 30 July 1700 (Moray Writs).'

p. 324, l. 26, delete 'unmarried.'

p. 324, l. 28, after 'age,' insert 'In a letter to his brother the Earl, dated from Murrich Hof, near Breda, 17 January 1764, he says "It has pleased God to afflict me . . . by taking from me on 15th inst. my dearest wife" (Moray Writs, *ex inform.* John Macgregor, Esq., W.S.). He had decree of declarator of marriage against Sybella Barbour, daughter of the deceased John Barbour, bailie of Inverness, 19 December 1732. She at the same time raised a counter action of freedom, etc. (*Consistorial Processes*, etc., Scot. Rec. Soc., No. 281).'

p. 324, l. 7 from foot, after 'Eglintoun,' insert note, 'The marriage was considered irregular, and the parties were fined for not declaring the names of the celebrant and witnesses (Moray Writs).'

p. 325, after l. 6, insert
     '6. *Hugh*, born about 1721 (*ex inform.* John Macgregor, Esq., W.S.).'

p. 325, l. 7, for '6' read '7.'

p. 325, l. 9, for '7' read '8.'

p. 325, l. 13, delete 'about,' and insert 'at his father's place, Frankfield, co. Perth, 13 May.'

p. 326, l. 1, for 'Saltarton' read 'Salterton.'

p. 328, l. 20, for 'Plowden' read 'Pounden,' and delete 'M.D.'

MORDINGTOUN

p. 332, l. 10 from foot, for 'Sir William' read 'Sir James.'

p. 333, l. 15, for 'Sir William' read 'Sir James.'

p. 334, l. 4, for 'the' read 'then.'

p. 336, l. 2, for 'in,' read 'on.'

DOUGLAS, EARL OF MORTON

p. 353, ll. 5 and 6 from foot, for 'Gifford' read 'Giffard.'

p. 358, after l. 20, insert
     '2. *Mr. William*, parson of Kilbucho, styled in 1543 brother-german and heir of tailzie of the third Earl (*Harl. MS.*, 6435; *Acts and Decreets*, i. 305).'

p. 358, ll. 21, 26, 29, for '2, 3, 4' read '3, 4, 5.'

p. 358, after l. 6 from foot, insert
     '6. *Helen* (*Acta Dom. Conc.*, xxxix. 48).'

p. 361, l. 18, after 'before,' delete to end of sentence with relative note, and insert 'before 17 September 1549 (*Acta Dom. Conc. et Sess.*, xxvii. 149), and possibly before December 1548 (*Treasurer's Accounts*, ix. 261).'

p. 361, l. 4 from foot, after 'Beatrice,' insert 'retoured co-heir of her father, 26 May 1551 (original retour in Advocates' Library).'

p. 363, l. 22, delete 'thrown into prison,' and insert 'was warded in Edinburgh Castle, Monday, 2 January 1580-81. Ten days after he was conveyed to Dumbarton where he remained till 27 May 1581, when he was brought back to Edinburgh (Notes in Protocol Book of John Scott. H.M. Reg. Ho.).'

p. 364, after l. 10, insert
'The Earl had also a natural daughter, *Jane,* married (contract 24 June 1579) to John Cumming of Earnside (*Reg. of Deeds,* xxi. 467).'

p. 366, l. 10, for '1488' read '1448.'

p. 368, after l. 3, insert
'4. Probably *Elizabeth,* married to Michael Balfour of Burleigh (cf. *Corrig.,* vol. i. p. 531).'

p. 372, l. 20, after '1624,' insert 'and who married (contract 15 February 1621) Katherine, daughter of Henry Forrester of Corstorphine (*Reg. of Deeds,* cccxii. 295).'

p. 372, l. 21, delete comma after 'Jean.'

p. 373, l. 12, delete 'in,' and insert 'contract 10 December (H.M. Reg. Ho. Cal.).'

p. 374, l. 4, for 'Hume' read 'Home.'

p. 378, l. 9 from foot, after 'Grandison,' insert 'She was governess to King Charles i.'s daughter, the Princess Henrietta, and after the surrender of Exeter she carried off the princess secretly to France while the King was at Newcastle (Clarendon's *Hist.,* x. 115). It is said she walked to Dover with the child on her back, attired as a beggar (*ex inform.* Hon. James Home).'

p. 379, l. 8 from foot, delete 'in 1681,' and insert 'about 1 November 1681 when a payment on account of sums due to him by the Treasury was made to his uncle, "his condition being such that without reddy money he cannot be handsomely interr'd as becomes a person of his quality" (*Treasury Papers (Royal Warrants*), H.M. Reg. Ho., 1 November 1681).'

p. 379, l. 8 from foot, after 'married,' insert 'first.'

p. 379, after l. 3 from foot, insert 'The Earl married, secondly, Marjory Foulis, who survived him, and married, secondly, William (Erskine), Earl of Buchan; dying before 1690 (Misc. Docs., H.M. Reg. Ho., and Edin. Tests., 19 February 1690; cf. *corr.,* vol. ii. 274).'

p. 382, l. 9 from foot, after 'Mary,' insert 'born 20 March 1737 (Canongate Reg.).'

MAXWELL, EARL OF MORTON

p. 389, l. 8 from foot, after '3rd,' insert 'Argent.'

NAIRN

p. 393, after l. 21, insert
'6. *Catherine,* eldest daughter, married, first, after 9 November 1639,

when she had a charter as his future wife, to Walter Stewart, son and apparent heir of Mr. John Stewart of Cluny (*Perth Sasines*, ix. 256): secondly, about 1653, James Ogilvy of Muirtoun, afterwards of Cluny (Cortachy Writs).'

p. 393, ll. 22, 23, for '6, 7,' read '7, 8.'

p. 399, ll. 27, 28, delete 'two daughters, of whom only the elder married,' and insert

'1. EMILY JANE, of whom after.

2. *Clementina Marie Hortense*, died, unmarried, 25 January 1836.

3. *Georgiana Gabrielle*, married, 2 Feb. 1871, the Marquis de Lavalette, and died 16 July 1907, *s.p.*

4. *Adelaide Elizabeth Josephine*, died, unmarried, 1841.

5. *Sarah Sophia Laura*, died, unmarried, 10 July 1853.'

p. 401, l. 14. The comma after 'azure' should be deleted and placed after 'base.'

NAPIER

p. 408, after l. 10 from foot, insert

'4. *William*, burgess of Edinburgh, who died before 1491, leaving a son and heir, *John* (Proctocol Book of James Young, 20 April 1491).'

p. 408, ll. 9 and 5 from foot, for '4. 5.' read '5. 6.'

p. 413, l. 26, for 'Torrie' read 'Towie.'

p. 413, l. 10 from foot, after '1601,' insert 'Another daughter, *Bessie*, was married, contract 6 Feb. 1617, to Archibald Campbell of Glencarradale (Protocol Book of John Hay, iv. 47).'

p. 417, l. 11, for 'of Pitcullo' read 'Balfour.'

p. 420, l. 22, after '1616,⁶' insert 'married, contract 3 Dec. 1633, to Mr. William Cunningham of Broomhill (*Reg. of Deeds*, DXV. 298).

p. 421, l. 2, delete 'By his wife, Anne Dunkeson,' and insert 'He married, contract 18 December 1634, Anna, daughter of Roger Duncanson of Easter Gellets, burgess of Edinburgh, and his wife, Margaret Douglas (*Gen. Reg. Sas.*, xlix. 412, xxxvii. 363). By her.'

p. 422, after l. 3, insert

'13. *Barbara*, baptized 23 October 1606 (St. Cuthbert's Reg. Edin.).'

p. 430, after l. 26, insert

'2. *Susanna*, married, contract 10 February 1609, to Walter Scott, younger of Whitslaid (*Reg. of Deeds*, clxxxi. 71).'

3. *Elizabeth* (perhaps by second wife), married, contract 13 and 14 August 1622, to Walter, grandson and heir of Walter Chisholm of that Ilk (*Ibid.*, cccxxix. 124).'

p. 434, l. 2, after 'her,' insert 'who had been divorced by her first husband, Sir Thomas C. Bunbury, Bart. (cf. vol. iv. 554).'

p. 434, l. 3, after 'had,' insert 'besides other three children (*Complete Baronetage*, iv. 118 n.).'

NEWARK

p. 442, after l. 11, insert

'2. *James*, a colonel in the Army, who died in the East Indies.

3. *Charles*, died young (*Family of Leslie*, ii. 203; the order is taken from *Fife Sasines*, vii. 61, and *Gen. Reg. Inhibs.*, 5 July 1671. The same records show that Helen and Anne were the youngest daughters).'

p. 442, ll. 12, 13, for '2, 3' read '8, 9.'

p. 442, ll. 20, 21, for 'in or before 1676' read 'contract 22 and 26 April 1675 (*Reg. of Deeds*, Mackenzie, 31 March 1682; *Privy Seal, English Reg.* iv. 8).'

NEWBURGH

p. 448, l. 18, after 'Livingston,' insert 'He died between 1 September and 31 October 1563, survived by his second wife, Elizabeth Douglas, (Protocol Book of Thomas Johnson, Linlithgow Town Clerk's Office).'

p. 448, after l. 4 from foot, insert

'7. *James*, a witness, 21 April 1565 (Protocol Book *ut sup.*).'

8. *Jonet*, who was the widow of Ninian Altoun, 21 September 1578.'

p. 450, l. 9 from foot, after 'Charles I.,' add note, 'As to his identification see *Reg. of Deeds*, ccccxxv. 154, and ccccxxix. 314).'

p. 450, l. 6 from foot, for 'James I.' read 'James VI.'

p. 450, note 14, for 'but actually' read 'and hers. He must have been at least forty-five, for he is a witness 2 February 1601 (Protocol Book of Andrew Ker, Linlithgow), so must have been born not later than 1587.'

p. 456, l. 10, for 'December,' read 'September' (cf. vol. ii. 300).'

p. 456, l. 15 from foot, for 'Chénecourt' read 'Chénencourt.'

p. 458, l. 24, for 'Hermora' read 'Hermosa.'

p. 458, l. 26, for 'Triorifi' read 'Trionfi.'

p. 458, l. 30, for 'Fredericao' read 'Frederico.'

p. 459, l. 20, for 'Marco' read 'Mario.'

NITHSDALE

p. 475, l. 3 from foot, after 'Seton,' insert 'Lord of that Ilk.'

p. 481, l. 23, for '1593' read '31 January 1593-94 (Edin. Tests.).'

p. 483, l. 2 from foot, after 'Craigie,[6]' insert 'secondly, to William Stewart, younger of Dunduff (*Gen. Reg. of Inhibs.*, xxvii. 40).'

p. 484, l. 10, after 'descended,[2]' insert 'He married (contract 5 October 1623) Marion, youngest daughter of Homer Maxwell of Speddoch (*Reg. of Deeds*, ccccii. 300).'

p. 486, l. 3 from foot, after '*Jean*,' insert 'married (contract 13 February 1634) to John, eldest son of Robert M'Brair of Almagill (*Reg. of Deeds*, DVI. 51; *Dumfries Sasines*, 19 February 1640).'

p. 487, l. 8 from foot, after '1656,' insert 'and was dead before 3 March 1663 (*P. C. Reg.*, 3d series, i. 347).'

p. 487, l. 5 from foot, after 'Elizabeth,' insert 'widow of George Glendoning, younger of Parton (Writ *penes* Sir William Fraser's Trustees), and.'

NORTHESK

p. 496, l. 22, delete ' of Thornton,' and insert 'of Lower Tooting or Mincing Lane, London.'

p. 499, l. 18, after 'first,' insert 'contract 9 August 1671 (*Reg. of Deeds,* Durie, 28 August 1675).'

p. 503, l. 20, after 'issue,' insert 'There was a declarator of marriage raised against him in 1770 by Christian, daughter of Captain Alexander Cameron of Dungannon (*Edinburgh Consistorial Processes,* Scot. Rec. Soc., No. 567). She claimed to have been married to him at Fort William on 27 January 1767.'

p. 503, line 6 from foot, for 'Francis' read 'Frances.'

p. 508, line 12, for 'regaurdent' read 'reguardant.'

OCHILTREE

p. 512, note 3, add to end of note, 'See also Pitcairn's *Criminal Trials,* i. *335, for an account of his death by drowning in the Water of Calder.'

p. 514, l. 13, for '1586' read '7 May 1585 (*Reg. of Deeds,* xxiii. 423).'

p. 514, ll. 14 and 15, for 'whose testament was recorded 14 February 1601' read 'She died 12 December 1599 (Edin. Tests.).'

p. 514, l. 21, after '1620,' insert 'He became a minister in Ireland, and died before 13 April 1654, having married Esther Wallace, with issue (Castlewig Charter-chest).'

p. 514, l. 22, for '(4) *James*' read '(4) *Janet.*'

p. 514, l. 22, after '*Helen,*' insert

　'(7) *Janet,* married to Andrew M'Dowell of Lefnoll (*Reg. of Deeds,* cccxlviii. 305).'

p. 514, after l. 22, insert

　'6. *Thomas* (*Gen. Reg. of Inhibs.,* 2nd ser., iii. 104).'

p. 514, ll. 23, 25, 32 for '6, 7, 8' read '7, 8, 9.'

p. 514, l. 2 from foot, after 'father,' insert 'after 29 December 1577, the date of his will (Protocol Book of William Stewart, Junior, f. 150, Edinburgh City Chambers), and.'

p. 517, l. 10, for '1594' read '1604 (cf. vol. i. 449; *Reg. of Deeds,* cxvii. 209).'

p. 517, after l. 21. insert

　'6. *Anna,* mentioned 1610 (*Reg. of Deeds,* cciii. 372).'

p. 518, l. 6, for '1639' read '1631.'

p. 518, l. 18, for '£14' read '£4' (*Reg. Sec. Sig.*, ii. 495).'

p. 518, l. 26, for 'William' read 'Major William (*Reg. of Deeds*, DLIX. 220).'

p. 518, l. 31, after '*Doratie*,' insert ' She, or another daughter, was married in or before 1644 to John Livingston of Hayning (*Reg. of Deeds*, DLIX. 117).'

p. 519, l. 2, after 'brother,' add ' She died at Edinburgh 8 February 1697, "absolutely destitute of all means whereby to be interred" (*Treasury Papers (Contingent Expenses)* 9 February 1697, H. M. Reg. Ho.).'

p. 519, l. 12, delete '12,' and insert ' in.'

p. 519, l. 13, delete ' next day,' and insert ' 13 of that month.'

p. 519, l. 14, after ' Holyroodhouse,' insert note, ' His mother, Lady Ochiltree, had a grant from the Treasury on 12 February 1675 of 500 merks "for defraying the charge and expense of the funerall of the late Lord Ochiltree hir sone " (*Treasury Papers (Royal Warrants)*, H. M. Reg. Ho.).'

OLIPHANT

p. 522, l. 4 of notes, for 'xii.' read 'xxii.'

p. 523, l. 5, for 'Oliferds' read 'Olifards.'

p. 523, l. 15, after 'sons' insert note, ' It is more likely that the three sons aftermentioned were the sons of William of Lilford, but that John, Hugh and Stephen, were descendants of Hugh of Stokes. The Northamptonshire lands seem to have passed to Walter, son of David, before 26 Hen. II. (1179-80) (Pipe Roll. Soc. xxix. 85).'

p. 536, note 10, l. 3 from foot of notes, after 'Gallery' insert 'See *Brit. Mus. Addl. MSS.*, 24276, f. 53.'

p. 539, after third line from foot, insert

' 6. *Elizabeth*, married to James Hering of Tullibole, younger of Glasclune (*Reg. Mag. Sig.*, 21 October 1501 ; Myln's *Vitæ Episc. Dunkelden.*, 37).'

p. 539, second line from foot, for ' 6' read ' 7.'

p. 549, note 13, delete ' probably.' The marriage-contract was dated 7 March 1617 (*Reg. of Deeds*, DXXXI. 30).'

p. 550, note 12, delete bracket after 2nd ed.

p. 554, after l. 6 insert

'2. *Isobel*, baptized 22 September 1622. At her baptism her father would not give confession of his faith (Perth Reg.),' and alter numbers of remaining children accordingly.

p. 560, delete l. 12.

p. 560, l. 13, before ' daughter,' insert ' a son and.'

p. 560, after l. 13, insert

' 1. *Joseph*, born at Mons 18-19 March 1684 ; died *v.p.* and *s.p.*'

p. 560, l. 14, before ' *Marie*,' insert '2,' and after ' Baptiste)⁶' insert ' born at Edinburgh in the Canongate 31 May 1687 (note by the ninth Lord Oliphant in an old book in the Gask Library).'

p. 560, l. 14, for ' who' read ' She.'

p. 562, note 10, add to note, 'and as early as 9 August 1751 (*Acts of P. C., Colonial Series*, iv. 130).'

SINCLAIR, EARL OF ORKNEY

pi. 565, l. 28, for ' 1357 ' read ' 1337.'

p. 567, l. 9 from foot, for '17 September 1358,' read 17 January 1356 (*ex inform.* Roland St. Clair, Esq.).'

p. 570, l. 2, for 'daughter' read 'grand-daughter.'

p. 570, l. 5 from foot, delete 'but see afterwards.'

p. 570, l. 4 from foot, delete 'first.'

p. 571, l. 1, for ' 1418 ' read ' 1422 (*Cal. of Papal Letters*, vii. 221).'

STEWART, EARL OF ORKNEY

p. 573, l. 24, after 'had' insert 'by her, who died September 1598, (*Edin. Comm. Decreets*, 14 March 1598-99).'

p. 574, l, 2, after ' 1635 ' insert, 'He married first, in or before 1603, Elizabeth Hamilton (*Edin. Burgh Reg. of Deeds*, 27 March 1604); secondly, in or before 1607, Margaret Lyon (*Reg. of Deeds*, ccxix. 16).'

p. 574, l. 9, delete ' 1639,' and insert ' 22 and 24 September 1629 (*Reg. of Deeds*, cccclxi. 342).'

p. 574, l. 12, after 'first,' add 'to Sir James Young of Seaton (*Reg. of Deeds*, ccccxxvii. 485); secondly.'

p. 574, l. 12, for ' Abekie ' read ' Arbikie.'

p. 574, l. 13, for 'secondly' read ' thirdly.'

p. 575, after l. 3 from foot, insert
' 11. *Jean.* 12. *Katherine*, both by Marjorie Sandilands (*Acts and Decreets*, clix. 299).'

p. 576, l. 3, after 'father,' insert 'He was of age by 25 June 1590 (*Reg. of Deeds*, xxxiv. 438).'

p. 576, l. 8 from foot, after 'forfeited,' insert note, ' There is a Bible which is said to have belonged to the Earl, printed in London 1595, in the possession of a person in South Ronaldshay (*Old Lore Misc. of Orkney*, etc., ii. 133, January 1909).'

HAMILTON, EARL OF ORKNEY

p. 582, l. 11 from foot, for 'Denby' read 'Danby.'

p. 583, l. 3 from foot, after 'proper,' insert 'on a chief argent three mullets gules.'

OXFUIRD

p. 588, l. 26, after 'married,' insert 'after 5 May 1542, when she was his affianced spouse (Andrew Brounhill's Protocol Book, Edin. City Chambers) and.'

p. 593, l. 20, for 'in the month of' read '13.'

p. 593, l. 21, for '1595' read '1595-96 (Court of Sess. Sederunt Book).'

p. 593, note 4, delete 'note,' and insert '*Reg. of Deeds*, ii. 374.'

p. 594, l. 6 from foot, after '1576,' insert 'was made Advocate-Depute to his father, 31 October 1585 (*Reg. Sec. Sig.*, liii. 59).'

p. 596, l. 21, for 'about' read 'contract.'

p. 598, l. 19, after 'dated,' insert '8 July (*Reg. of Deeds*, DXCIV. 332).'

p. 598, l. 24, *Note.*—The service referred to is by Robert M. to his brother *Patrick*, not David, and is dated 1656, not 1657.

p. 598, l. 2 from foot, after 'Galstoun,' insert 'She married, thirdly, some weeks before 6 January 1729, Henry Clark, "She might weall bee his granmother" (Letter from Lady Jean Mackenzie, relict of Sir Thomas Stewart, Lord Balcaskie, to her son Sir George Stewart of Grandtully, *Red Book of Grandtully*, ii. 324).'

p. 599, l. 7 from foot, after 'Army,' insert 'Ensign in Scots Foot Guards, 11 January 1700.'

VOL. VII.

PANMURE

p. 1, l. 1, for title and headlines of pages, for 'Maule, Earl Panmure' read 'Maule, Earl of Panmure.'

p. 4, l. 27, for 'name' read 'surname.'

p. 4, l. 28, after 'had,' insert 'probably by his wife Godit, with whom he granted the isle at the head of Hiliuespedberne to St. Cuthbert of Carram (orig. Charter in H.M. Reg. Ho.).'

p. 8, l. 14, delete '[Stonehaven].'

p. 18, l. 18, after 'married,' insert 'contract 7 December 1562 (*Reg. of Deeds*, xv. 301).'

p. 18, l. 22, after 'married,' insert 'first (contract 30 March 1593) (*Reg. of Deeds*, xliv. 399).'

p. 18, l. 22, after 'Carmylie,' insert 'secondly, to George Strachan (*Reg. Sec. Sig.*, lxxiv. 132).'

p. 21, ll. 21, 22, for 'after November 1640' read 'contract 20 August 1641 (*Gen. Reg. Sasines*, l. 125).'

p. 22, after l. 8, insert

'1. *Patrick*, baptized 29 September 1646 (Canongate Reg.). He must have died young'; and alter numbers of remaining children accordingly.

p. 22, l. 27, for 'Fifeshire' read 'Forfarshire.'

p. 24, l. 14, for 'Bonomy' read 'Bonamy.'

p. 24, l. 7, after 'NAVAR,' insert 'He was a *connoisseur* of the highest order in all culinary matters, and when he was in London attending Parliament used to stay at the Union Hotel near Trafalgar Square for the sake of the turtle soup for which it was famous. It is said that during his whole Parliamentary career he never opened his mouth except once, when he said "What a shame;" in 1815, when the mob attempted to break the windows of St. Stephen's Chapel during the discussion of the Corn Law Bill of that day (*Patrician*, iv. 522).'

p. 24, l. 6 from foot, for '6' read '26' (*Forfar Sasines*, vi. 389).'

p. 26, l. 12, after '1723,' insert 'of pleurisy, aged sixty-eight (Dunbar's *Social Life in Former Days*, i. 119).'

p. 27, l. 12, after '2nd,' insert 'argent.'

PERTH

p. 40, l. 12, after 'charter,' insert note, 'This charter is in the possession of the Earl of Kinnoull. It is dated 4 October 1486, and grants two-thirds of Ladecreif to Walter.'

p. 41, l. 11 from foot, for 'nephew' read 'brother.'

p. 41, l. 10 from foot, for 'Kinsale' read 'Kinnoul.'

p. 43, l. 9, delete 'is said to have.'

p. 43, l. 15, delete from 'Isobel' down to 'place' in line 17, and insert 'He gave a discharge of part of her tocher to her father 5 March 1478-79 (Argyll Charter-chest), and.'

p. 43, l. 8 from foot, after 'Innerpeffray,' insert 'He was contracted to Elizabeth, daughter of Andrew, second Lord Gray, which contract was discharged in January 1501-2 (*Acta Dom. Conc.*, xii. 39).'

p. 44, l. 20, after 'married,' insert 'Dispensation dated 20 January 1530-31 following on Papal mandate of 16 March 1529-30 (originals in possession of the Earl of Kinnoull).'

p. 45, l. 23, for 'fourth' read 'second.'

p. 46, l. 22, delete 'possibly on 20 October 1582,' and insert 'died at Stobhall in July 1579 (Inchaffray Papers *penes* Lord Kinnoull).'

p. 46, last l., for 'before 1592' read '23 December 1587 (Moray Writs, box 3, No. 241).'

p. 47, l. 3, after '*Catherine*' insert note, 'The Dunfermline Parish Register gives her name as *Margaret.*'

p. 47, l. 16, after 'career,' insert ' he had an exemption from hostings, etc., being "diseasit in his luggis," 1 August 1587 (*Reg. Sec. Sig.*, lv. 197).'

p. 47, after l. 27, insert

'3. *Elizabeth*, baptized 1 July 1565 (Canongate Reg.). She must have died young'; and alter numbers of remaining children accordingly.

p. 48, l. 9, after 'first,' insert '22 June 1602 (Edin. Reg.).'

p. 48, l. 11, after 'Muchalls, insert 'afterwards first Lord Fraser.'

p. 48, after l. 11, insert

'9. *Sibilla* (Edinburgh Tests.).

Lord Drummond had also a son *David*, but as he is not named in Lady Drummond's testament he was probably illegitimate.'

p. 48, l. 19, after 'record,' insert note, 'The date in text is corroborated by the *Fifth Rep. Hist. MSS. Comm.*, 644.'

p. 48, l. 26, for 'April' read 'November.'

p. 50, l. 20, delete 'previous to 1 February 1620, when,' and insert '(contract 10 March 1633) on 1 February 1634.'

p. 50, l. 23, for 'second' read 'first.'

p. 50, l. 26, for 'secondly' read 'as a third wife' (cf. vol. viii. 415).

p. 51, l. 3, after '1639,' insert 'contract 28 and 31 October 1639 (*Reg. of Deeds*, Dxxiv. 62).'

p. 52, l. 5 from foot, for '11' read '12 (*Cal. of Stuart Papers*, ii. 145).'

p. 53, l. 2, after 'secondly,' insert 'contract 5 October 1676 (*Perth Sasines*, vii. 44).'

p. 53, l. 26, for '*Teresa*' read '*Francesca Teresa*, baptized 9 March 1688 (Canongate Reg.)', and delete 'born in France.'

p. 53, l. 4 from foot, for '1692' read '1693.'

p. 53, l. 3 from foot, delete 'but,' and insert 'On 2 March 1696 he was a prisoner in Stirling Castle (*P. C. Acta*). He afterwards.'

p. 56, l. 20, delete 'the daughter and heiress of Fotheringham,' and insert 'Marjory Gray the heiress of (contract 26 November 1707) (*Perth Sasines*, xvi. 227).'

POLWARTH

p. 82, second line from foot, after '1690,' insert 'Died at Edinburgh 7 May 1749, having married Lieutenant Thomas Gordon, Royal Scots Fusiliers, of the family of Buthlaw (J. M. Bulloch in *Notes and Queries*, 11th ser., ix. 326).'

p. 87, l. 16, quotation mark should follow 'tryste,' not 'horse.'

PRIMROSE

p. 110, l. 23, for '1714' read 'March 1707-8 at St. Peter's upon Cornhill, London (cf. vol. viii. 154).'

QUEENSBERRY

p. 117, after l. 4, insert
'5. *Hugh* (Protocol Book of James Young, 26 October 1497, Edin. City Chambers).'

p. 117, ll. 5, 7, 12, for '5, 6, 7' read '6, 7, 8.'

p. 117, after l. 28, insert
'3. *James* (Protocol Book *ut sup.*, 29 March 1501).'

p. 117, l. 29, for '3' read '4.'

p. 119, l. 7, after 'death,' add note, 'According to the Sheriff Roll of 1544-45 he came of age in December 1521.'

p. 125, l. 23, for '8 July' read '21 June.'

p. 126, l. 25, after '1578,' insert 'He married, first, Marion, daughter of Edward Menzies of Castlehill. There is a contract of 27 September 1549 whereby he was to divorce her and marry Elizabeth M'Clellan, widow of Alexander M'Culloch of Cardines (*Acta Dom. Conc. et Sess.*, xxvi. 76).'

p. 128, after l. 7, insert
'7. *Margaret*, presumably also illegitimate, married to William, son of Herbert Maxwell in Cavens (contract 24 May 1549) (*Acts and Decreets*, iii. 188).'

p. 135, l. 10, after 'married,' insert 'contract 28 July 1640 (*Reg. of Deeds*, Dxxxi. 45).'

p. 136, l. 13, after 'secondly,' insert 'contract 26 March 1635 (*Reg. of Deeds*, Mackenzie, 6 November 1668).'

p. 140, after l. 17, insert
'4. *Margaret*, buried in Holyrood Church in March 1662 (Canongate Reg.).
5. *Henrietta*, baptized 3 January 1662 (*Ibid.*).'

p. 140, l. 18, for '4' read '6.'

p. 140, l. 19, after '1697,' insert ' and married the same day.'

p. 143, l. 13, after '*Jean*,' insert 'born at London 24 May 1701.'

p. 143, l. 19, after '*Anne*,' insert 'born at Edinburgh 12 February 1706 (*Peerage of England*, London, 1709).'

p. 143, l. 23, after 'father,' add 'having been born at Edinburgh, 24 November 1698 (*Political State of Great Britain*, 1711).'

p. 144, after l. 3 from foot, insert

'3. *Catherine*, born 21 November 1724; died 4 February 1725 (*Historical Register*).'

p. 146, l. 2, after 'original,' insert 'According to the *Privy Council Acta* the patent was stopped by the Council 30 April 1697, on the complaint of Viscount Teviot that the title Peebles had already been granted to him. But on 8 June following, a letter from the King (dated 24 May), was read, stating that it was his pleasure that the Earl should have the title Peebles, and that the Viscount's title was to be changed.'

p. 147, l. 5 from foot, after 'Queensberry,' insert 'He was infeft in Kelhead in virtue of a contract with his brother, the second Earl (*Reg. of Deeds*, DXXVI. 187).'

p. 148, l. 13, after 'Sophia,' insert 'He was baptized 9 March 1648, his mother being then dead (Canongate Reg.).'

p. 148, l. 15, after 'married,' insert 'contract 19 September 1676, Elizabeth, daughter of Thomas Ellis, merchant, Perth (*Reg. of Deeds*, Durie, 1 April 1679).'

p. 155, l. 5 from foot, after ' 4th,' insert ' argent.'

p. 155, last line, transfer ' for *Mar* ' to the previous line, after ' or.'

REAY

p. 166, l. 19, after 'divorced,' insert 'yet he was in 1606 charged to adhere to her (*Gen. Reg. Inhibitions*, xvii. 272).'

p. 166, l. 2 from foot, for '1618 ' read ' 1619 (she had a charter as his future wife on 29 July of the latter year) (*Inverness Sasines*, i. 159).'

p. 169, after l. 23, insert 'In 1652 there is mention of Dame Rachel Mackay, relict of Donald, Lord Reay, then wife of Captain Thomas Kakyne; and of Donald Mackay, her son by Lord Reay (*Gen. Reg. Inhibitions*, 20 November 1652).'

ROLLO

p. 187, l. 16, delete comma after ' James.'

p. 187, l. 20, after ' Banks,' insert note, ' He was apparently twice married, as there is a renunciation and grant of redemption by Mr. Thomas Rollock, advocate, and his spouse, Grizel Scott, of the lands of Castlerankine and others, in the barony of Herbertshire, 26 October 1605 *Wigtown Charter-Chest*, Scot. Rec. Soc., Nos. 697, 699).'

p. 191, l. 21, after ' Balbegy,' nsert 'died after 22 August 1621 and before

15 August 1622 (*Reg. of Deeds*, cccxxxix. 358 ; *Acts and Decreets*, ccclx. 278).'

p. 191, after l. 24, insert

    'ii. *Margaret*, married, contract 22 August 1621, to Richard Blyth, portioner of Craigie (*Reg. of Deeds*, cccxxxix. 358).

    iii. *Isobel* (*Acts and Decreets*, ccclx. 278).'

p. 191, l. 25, for 'ii.' read 'iv.'

p. 191, l. 25, after 'married,' insert 'contract 1 March 1633 (*Perth Sasines*, vi. 222).'

p. 203, l. 5, after 'sudenlie,' insert 'On 14 June 1696 she obtained decreet against him for aliment, he having deserted her and lived with another woman (*P. C. Decreta*).'

p. 207, l. 15 from foot, for 'Robinson' read 'Robertson.'

p. 207, l. 11 from foot, for 'Grey,' read 'Gray.'

ROSEBERY

p. 219, l. 23, for 'James' read 'John.'

p. 227, l. 7, delete comma after 'Stewart.'

p. 228, l. 12, after '1894-95,' insert 'By Patent, dated 3 July 1911, he was created Earl of Midlothian, Viscount Mentmore of Mentmore, Bucks, and Baron Epsom of Epsom, Surrey.'

p. 229, l. 1, after '1828,' insert semicolon, and add 'Earl of Midlothian, Viscount Mentmore of Mentmore, Bucks, and Baron Epsom of Epsom, Surrey.'

ANCIENT EARLS OF ROSS

p. 235, l. 3 from foot, for '1316' read '1315.'

ROSS, LORD ROSS

p. 250, after l. 11 insert

    '3. Perhaps *Elizabeth*, married to Thomas Sempill, Sheriff of Renfrew (see *post*, p. 530).'

p. 252, l. 12, after '10 May 1562,' insert 'contract dated 22 February 1561-62, at which date she had curators (*Wigtown Charter-Chest*, Scot. Rec. Soc., No. 327, where the date is erroneously given as 1571).'

p. 256, l. 18, after 'Baronet,' add 'She was his future wife 18 March 1688 (*Gen. Reg. Sasines*, xlvii. 145).'

p. 261, l. 11, for '10' read '21 (List of children by Lord Ross in Kelburne Family Bible).'

p. 261, l. 15, for '18 July 1687,' read '26 December 1688 (List *ut sup.*).'

p. 261, l. 17, for '1662' read '1692.'

p. 263, l. 4, delete '1502,' and insert 'some time before 31 May 1499.'

ROTHES

p. 306, l. 11, for 'Earl' read 'Marquess.'

p. 308, l. 7, for 'March' read 'May.'

p. 308, l. 7, for 'Shrub Hall' read 'Shrub Hill.'

p. 311, l. 4, after 'Caskieberrie,' insert '29 May 1680.'

ROXBURGHE

p. 323, l. 25, for 'August 1484' read '3 July 1483 (*Acta Dom. Audit.*, 111*).'

p. 325, ll. 1 and 2 from foot, delete 'He is said to have been the ancestor of the Kers of Greenhead,' and accompanying note (cf. vol. v. 52, 53).

p. 326, l. 9 from foot, for '1571' read '1471.'

p. 331, l. 6, after '1551,' insert 'His will was dated 16 July 1551. He had a curious interview with his eldest son Andrew concerning it (Protocol Book of Sir William Corbet, *Scot. Rec. Soc.* Nos. 63, 64).'

p. 332, l. 8, for '1493' read '1488.'

p. 332, note 3, for '*Ibid.*' read '*Acta Dom. Conc.*'

p. 334, after l. 25, insert

'4. *Robert*, a witness, 24 January 1535-36 (Protocol Book of Thomas Kene, Adv. Lib.).'

p. 334, ll. 26, 27, for '4, 5' read '5, 6.'

p. 338, ll. 19, 20, for 'is said to have been' read 'was.'

p. 338, l. 21, after 'Douglas' insert 'of Drumlanrig,' and for '19 February 1556' read '19 February 1556-57 (*Reg. of Deeds*, ii. 79).'

p. 339, ll. 14, 15, delete from 'It does' down to 'issue and.'

p. 339, l. 17, after '1573,' add 'He had a son and heir *Andrew*, infeft in an annualrent out of Morham, 12 December 1570 (orig. instrument in H. M. Reg. Ho.).'

p. 339, l. 18, after 'married,' insert 'contract 1 December 1558 (*Reg. of Deeds*, iii. 117).'

p. 341, after l. 20, insert

'5. *Jean*, married to George Towris of Inverleith : she was his future wife 2 August 1601 (*Edin. Sasines, Secretary's Reg.*, ii. 197).'

p. 344, ll. 29 and 30, delete 'the second, third, or fourth and youngest daughters of the said Harry, Lord Ker.'

p. 345, l. 14, for 'feuar' read 'flar.'

p. 346, l. 23, after 'first,' insert 'contract 12 and 14 October 1618 (*Reg. of Deeds*, cccxiii. 816)': and after 'Pitcur,' insert 'she was his widow in 1620 (*Ibid*).'

p. 347, l. 5, for 'step-brother' read 'half brother.'

p. 347, l. 6 from foot, after 'married,' insert 'at Glamis, 4 February 1638 (*Chronicle of Perth*, 35).'

p. 347, l. 5 from foot, after '1638,' insert reference, '*Reg. of Deeds*, DXli. 7.'

p. 348, line 4, after 'married,' insert 'contract 5 December 1660 (*Wigtown Charter-chest*, Scot. Rec. Soc., No. 348; *Reg. of Deeds*, Mack., 3 February 1663, where 1 December is given as the date).'

p. 348, after l. 17, insert

'The Earl had two natural daughters, *Margaret*, married, contract 30 November 1614, to John Mow, younger of that Ilk (*Gen. Reg. of Inhibs.*, 30 December 1616), and *Cecill*, who in 1636 was wife of John Ker of Gaitschaw (*Gen. Reg. of Sasines*, xlv. 24).'

p. 349, l. 12, for '8 May' read '6 May (*The Royal Navy*, by W. Laird Clowes, 1898, ii. 457).'

p. 355, l. 9. for 'He was dead before 1574' read 'He died in April 1565 (*Exch. Rolls.* xx. 443).'

p. 355, l. 30, delete 'and widow of John, eighth Lord Glamis.'

p. 356, note 3, for '356' read '536.

p. 357, l. 5, for 'eighty-five' read 'eighty-seven.'

p. 357, l. 11, for 'before' read 'after.'

RUTHERFORD

p. 366, l. 1, delete entire line and accompanying reference note.

p. 366, after line 13, insert

'WILLIAM OF RUTHERFORD, son and heir of the above. William was a minor on 6 November 1363, on which dateKing Edward III. granted to John Ker the custody of his lands till his majority, and his marriage (*Cal. Doc. Scot.*, iv. 89).'

p. 366, l. 18, delete 'was ambassador to England in 1398,' and note.

p. 366, l, 23, delete 'was Warden of the Marches in 1400, and,' and note.

p. 366, l. 7 from foot, for 'treaty' read 'truce.'

p. 373, after l. 26 insert

'*f. Janet*, married, first, George Thomson, maltman, Leith; secondly, 1632, Patrick Whitelaw of that Ilk.'

p. 379, l. 18, after '1648,' add 'She was buried in the Greyfriars, Edinburgh 24 April 1671.'

p. 380, after l. 10, insert

'Another daughter, *Lilias*, was married, contract 25 November 1677, to Mr. William Douglas of Plewland (*Reg. of Deeds*, Durie, 22 March 1681).'

p. 381, l. 12 from foot, for '1724' read '22 November 1720 (mourning ring *penes* Mr. Ernest Radcliffe Crump, *ex inform.* T. E. Watson, Esq.).'

p. 381, l. 6 from foot, after 'father,' add ' being buried 14 February 1710 (Elsdon Par. Reg.).'

RUTHVEN

p. 387, l. 8, after 'secondly,' insert '22 April 1673 (Canongate Reg.).'

p. 392, l. 10, for 'uncle' read 'granduncle.'

ST. COLME

p. 394, l. 16, for 'Moucastell' read 'Moncastell.'

p. 394, l. 24, after '1581,' insert 'He was again appointed Commendator thereof on his father's resignation 20 April 1587 (*Reg. Sec. Sig.*, lv. 53).'

p. **394**, l. 26, after ' Inchmahome,' insert ' in 1592 he appears as tutor-at-law of his nephew, James, Earl of Moray (*Reg. of Deeds*, xliii. 261).'

p. **395**, l. 6, after ' issue,' insert ' besides two daughters, *Anna* and *Jean* (*Gen. Reg. of Inhibs.* (6 September 1616).'

p. **395**, l. 15, after ' ascertained,' insert ' but it was before 17 August 1643 (Moray Writs, box v. No. 1019).'

p. **395**, note 2, after ' 1614,' insert ' The Canongate Register, however, states that he was buried at Holyrood 27 June 1612).'

SALTOUN (ABERNETHY)

p. **405**, l. 7 from foot, after ' son,' insert ' and possibly a daughter, *Marion*, styled daughter of Sir George Abernethy of St. Andrews diocese in a Papal mandate for a dispensation for her marriage with John, son of Sir Alexander Stewart of Glasgow diocese, they being in the fourth degree of consanguinity (*Reg. Aven.*, cxcvii. 33).' She may, however, have been a sister of Sir George.

p. **406**, note 5, for ' 351 ' read 96.'

p. **412**, l. 14, for ' 1586 ' read ' 1566.'

p. **412**, l. 18, for ' which ' read ' who.'

p. **414**, l. 8, for ' 21 September' read ' 13 July (Moray Writs, box iv, No. 480).'

p. **416**, for ' belted,' read belled.'

SALTOUN (FRASER)

p. **434**, l. 5, delete ' Sir.'

p. **440**, l. 21, for ' *Margaret* ' read ' *Anna*.'

p. **440**, l. 22, for ' 31 ' read ' 14,' and at end of sentence add, ' She died in July 1663 (Slains Charters).'

p. **449**, l. 8 from foot, for ' Cambria' read ' Cambrai.'

p. **452**, l. 20, for ' Essex' read ' Sussex.'

SEAFIELD

p. **463**, l. 2 from foot, after ' issue,' insert ' She obtained decreet of divorce against him for adultery 30 July 1576 (*Hist. Records Fam. of Leslie*, iii. 73), and was married, secondly, to William Cumming of Inverallochy (*Aberdeen Hornings*, 7 May 1584).'

p. **464**, l. 20, after ' 1584,' insert ' In 1582 she was suing for divorce from him (*Edin. Inhibitions*, i. 134).'

p. **465**, l. 10, after ' married,' insert ' first (contract 2 December 1596), Grizel, sister of Alexander Menzies of that Ilk (*Reg. of Deeds*, lxviii. 193); secondly.'

p. **475**, l. 18, after ' Lanark,' insert ' She was his future wife 27 June 1665 (*Gen. Reg. Sasines*, xii. 235).'

p. **493**, l. 9, after ' 1882,' insert ' married, 9 April 1912, to the Rev. William Rice, Rector of Sympson, Bucks.'

SEAFORTH

p. 501, l. 4 from foot, for '14' read '19.'

p. 502, l. 2 from foot, after '*Murdoch*,' insert 'of Melbost and Kernsarie, and of Inverewe. Married Catherine Mackenzie and had a son *John*, said to have been killed at Auldearn, and two daughters, *Marjory*, married to Alexander Mackenzie of Cliff, and *Barbara*, married to Thomas Graham of Drynie (*Reg. of Hornings and Inhibs., Inverness*, 2d series, ii. 193, 18 September 1649).'

p. 505, l. 6, for 'Margaret' read 'Isobel (Haddington Bap. Reg.).'

p. 509, l. 3, after 'Cromarty,' insert 'She had a charter as his future wife, 31 May 1655 (*Banff Sasines*, vii. 135).'

p. 509, l. 8 from foot, after '1674,' insert note, 'The date in the text is that given in Fraser's *Sutherland Book*, (i. 515), but in the *Reg. of Deeds*, Mackenzie (23 July 1709), it is stated to have been 8 September 1675.'

p. 510, l. 3, after 'Seaforth,' insert 'baptized 8 December 1661 (Kinghorn Reg.).'

p. 511, l. 17, after 'her,' insert 'Her fine complexion is said to have been ruined and to have become a lemon tint. Pope in his *Satires* mentions the incident in the line "poison from Deloraine." (See also Croker's *Lady Suffolk's Letters*).'

p. 511, last l., after 'unmarried,' add 'being drowned at Paris while skating, 8 December 1774 (*Lyon in Mourning*, Scot. Hist. Soc., iii. 348).'

p. 511, note 2, after '136,' add 'vi. 184.'

SELKIRK

p. 519, l. 6 from foot, after '1703,' insert 'Warrant to bury him in Holyrood Church, dated 23 June 1703 (*P. C. Acta*).'

SEMPILL

p. 530, ll. 4, 5, delete from 'and probably' down to 'apparent' and relative footnote 4.

p. 530, l. 17, for '1480' read '1470 (the former date is a misprint in the Commission Report).'

p. 535, l. 4, after 'On,' insert '28 August 1616 he was denounced rebel for frequenting the company of Mr. John Ogilvie, Jesuit (*Reg. of Hornings*, 12 February 1617), and on 13 May 1618 his escheat was granted to Mr. John Fentoun, comptroller-clerk to the King (*Rec. Sec. Sig.*). However, he seems quickly to have regained the royal favour, for on.'

p. 547, l. 5 from foot, for 'relieve' read 'rescue.'

p. 552, l. 12, for 'nephew' read 'cousin.'

p. 555, l. 2 from foot, delete 'and,' and insert 'was served heir to Francis, eighth Lord Sempill, 4 November 1684 (*Hist. MSS. Com., Report on Stuart Papers*, iv. 81; cf. *post*, p. 559). He.'

p. 558, l. 7, after 'him,' insert 'till February 1688 (*Seafield Correspondence*, Scot. Hist. Soc., 42).'

p. 558, after l. 22, insert 'On 11 February 1705 three shillings Scots were given by the kirk-session of Innerwick "to ane called a daughter of my Lord Semple, having a testimoniall from the Tolbooth Church in Edinburgh." She was probably illegitimate.'

p. 559, ll. 20, 21, delete from 'for' to 'was,' and insert 'for Robert Sempill (son of Dykehead; see *ante*, p. 555) says he was served heir to the estate and declared Lord Sempill, but by indirect means the heir-general kept this estate and assumed the title (*Hist. MSS. Com., Rep. on Stuart Papers*, iv. 81).'

p. 564, l. 33, for 'baronetcy' read 'barony.'

SINCLAIR

p. 571, after l. 4, insert

'5. *Marjory*, married to Sir Alexander M'Culloch of Mertoun. She is called 'oo' of George, first Earl of Rothes (*Acta Dom. Conc.*, xii. 97).'

p. 572, note 1, for 'xiii.' read 'xiv.'

p. 573, l. 21, for 'Mariota' read 'Agnes'; 'after 'Bruce,' insert 'She is styled "pretended" relict of William, Lord Sinclair, 14 January 1571-72 (*Acts and Decreets*, xlix. 4).'

p. 573, l. 6 from foot, after '1575,[9]' insert 'He married, secondly, contract 29 July 1578 (original instrument in H. M. Reg. Ho.), Beatrix, daughter of Sir William Sinclair of Roslin.'

p. 574, l. 26, after 'thirty-six,' insert 'He was contracted, 21 March 1564-65, to Marion, eldest daughter of William Maitland, younger of Lethington (*Acts and Decreets*, xxxi. 391).'

p. 574, l. 28, for 'fourth' read 'fifth.'

p. 574, l. 6 from foot, after '*Catherine*,' insert 'married to Sir George Hamilton of Blackburn (*Reg. Mag. Sig.*, 21 April 1618).'

p. 574, l. 2 from foot, after 'married,' insert 'first, Catherine Nisbet (*Reg. of Deeds*, xxxvi. 109), secondly, contract 20 June 1600 (*Ibid.* ccxix. 486).'

p. 574, l. 2 from foot, for 'James' read 'Sir John.'

p. 575, l. 2, after 'Williamston,' insert 'and thirdly, John Rolland (Douglas's *Baronage*, 311).'

p. 575, l. 25, after '*Jane*,' insert 'married to George Seton of Parbroath (*Fife Inhibitions*, 6 June 1608).'

p. 580, l. 14, after 'married,' insert 'first,' and after 'Wedderburn,' insert 'and secondly, to George Ker of Samuelston (*Acta Dom. Conc.*, ix. 95).'

p. 580, l. 6 from foot, after 'Kimmerghame,' insert 'He was probably the father of

1. JOHN, who succeeded.
2. *William*, and
3. *Patrick*, both mentioned in the will of their brother John.'

p. **581**, l. 10, for '1514,' read '1514-15,' and add, 'in his will of 21 August 1513, when he was *iturus ad guerram Anglie*, he mentions, without naming, two daughters not forisfamiliated.'

p. **582**, l. 26, for 'before 12 January 1565-66,' read 'in 1563 (*Acts and Decreets*, xxxiv. 80).'

p. **582**, l. 7 from foot, after 'executors,' insert 'She was dead in May 1569 (*Acts and Decreets*, xliv. 24), and apparently before 7 March 1568-69, when her son was seised in lands which she had held in conjunct fee (*Exch. Rolls*, xx. 394).'

p. **583**, l. 11, after 'after,' insert, 'He came of age in 1566, and was seised of the estates 7 May 1567 (*Exch. Rolls*, xix. 561), except the lands which his mother had in conjunct-fee, of which he was not seised till 7 March 1568-69 (*Ibid.* xx. 394).'

p. **585**, l. 16, after 'married,' insert 'first, 13 March 1705, Margaret, daughter of John Home of Ninewells (Canongate Reg.), and secondly,'

p. **585**, l. 17, for 'Thomas' read 'Andrew (*Genealogist*, iii. 112).'

p. **587**, l. 24, before 'ultimately,' insert 'whose descendants.'

p. **587**, l. 24, for 'the heir' read 'heirs.'

p. **588**, l. 26, for 'L'Orient' read 'Lorient.'

p. **589**, note 3, for 'fraternal' read 'paternal.'

p. **592**, l. 10, for 'January' read 'July.'

VOL. VIII.

Editorial Note, l. 12, for 'second' read 'third.'

SOMERVILLE

p. 9, l. 15, after '*Mary*,' insert 'erroneously.'

p. 9, l. 17, after '1427,' add, 'but except the *Memorie* there is no authority for this statement (cf. *infra*, pp. 424, 425).'

p. 17, note 10, delete '10 July to 10 August 1546, 19 March 1546-47,' and insert 'i. 24, 65.'

p. 19, note 15, for 'xi.' read 'xv.'

p. 24, l. 20, for 'in January' read 'between 10 February and 20 April (*Reg. of Deeds*, xli. 172, 268).'

p. 24, l. 3 from foot, for '*Robert*,' read '*Helen*,' and insert note, 'These illegitimate children were not the children of Lord Somerville, but of his eldest son William.'

p. 26, l. 22, for 'first' read 'seventh.'

p. 26, note 5, for '*Ibid.*' read '*Memorie*, ii.'

p. 28, l. 7, for 'granduncle' read 'kinsman.'

p. 32, l. 1, for 'Foot Guards' read 'in Scotland.'

p. 32, l. 15, after 'married,' insert 'contract 23 March 1695 (*Edin. Sas.*, lvi. 340).'

p. 34, note 4, after 'Heirs,' add, 'Gilbert, however, was not the brother of the twelfth Lord's *atavus*, but of his *abavus*, or great-great-grandfather.'

SOUTHESK

p. 57, note 2, for '363' read '313.'

p. 66, l. 16, for 'Lindsay' read 'Hamilton.'

p. 66, l. 31, after 'secondly,' insert '(contract 6 June 1643) (Inv. of Writs of Drumry at Crawford Priory).'

p. 67, l. 7, for 'in' read '14 October,' and for 'Inchbrayock' read 'Inchbrock.'

p. 67, l. 20, after '1654,' insert '(contract 12 December 1654, tocher 18,000 merks).'

p. 68, l. 5, after 'contract,' insert '30.'

p. 80, l. 3 from foot, delete from 'In 1747,' down to end of sentence.
  Note.—The statement made in the *History of the Carnegies* cannot be true, as Sir John died in 1729.

p. 90, l. 13, after 'year,' insert 'was.'

SPYNIE

p. 108, l. 2, after 'Earl,' insert 'of.'

p. 113, l. 15, after 'Cavalry,' insert 'Died 16 May 1911.'

STAIR

p. 124, l. 5, after 'Cousland,' insert (*vide* p. 121).'

p. 126, l. 11, after 'her,' insert 'who died shortly before 20 March 1708 (*Seafield Corr.*, Scot. Hist. Soc., 465).'

p. 131, l. 8, for 'Montgomery' read 'Montgomerie.'

p. 131, line 5 from foot, after 'of,' insert 'General.'

p. 132, l. 31, for 'grandfather' read 'brother Hew, 26 July 1746.'

p. 133, l. 3, after 'and,' insert 'Ensign.'

p. 133, l. 5, delete 'lieut.-colonel Scots Fusilier Guards,' and insert 'captain and lieut.-colonel 1 April 1795.'

p. 133, l. 12, transpose reference no. 8 to after 'there.'

p. 135, l. 7, after 'Elphinstone,' insert '-Dalrymple.'

p. 137, l. 5 from foot, after 'Douglas,' insert 'of St. Christopher's (cf. p. 131).'

p. 147, ll. 19, 20, delete from 'in the lifetime' to end of sentence, and insert 'in March 1682 from a fall from his horse (*ex inform.* Capt. J. Hope, St. Mary's Isle).'

p. 147, note 8, for 'large' read 'Large.'

p. 149, l. 20, for 'James' read 'John.'

p. 153, l. 16, for '1714' read '1743.'

p. 155, l. 14, after 'surviving,' insert 'son of William.'

p. 161, l. 7, after '1886,' insert 'married 14 January 1913 to Lieut. J. G. Ingham, R.N.'

p. 163, l. 6 from foot, for 'eighth' read 'third.'

p. 163, l. 6 from foot, after 'Winton' read 'of the creation of 1859.'

STIRLING

p. 169, l. 7 from foot, insert '*Note.*—From the dates it seems doubtful that these children, *William* and *John*, were sons of William of Menstrie, though it is so stated in the Apprentice Register.'

p. 170, l. 14, for 'Dubbiehead, co. Stirling,' read 'Dubheads, co. Perth (*Retours, Perth*, 473).'

p. 173, l. 26, for 'in' read 'on.'

p. 176, l. 4 from foot, for '1523' read '1623.'

p. 177, l. 23, after 'married,' insert '28.'

p. 177, l. 24, delete 'Lord Sandilands afterwards.'

p. 185, l. 15, for 'gules' read 'azure.'

STORMONT

p. 190, l. 15, after '1598,' insert note, 'The date in text is given in the Appendix to Lamont's *Diary* as having been copied from a journal of Moncrieff of Carnbee. But the procuratory of resignation following on the marriage-contract is dated 25 January 1598-99 (Adv. Lib. MS., 34.6.24, p. 249). And they were still only future spouses 24 April 1599 (*Reg. Mag. Sig.*).'

p. 190, after l. 17 insert

'4. *Christian* (*Fife Sasines*, x. 286).'

p. 198, l. 18, for ' before 30 July 1613 ' read ' six months before 7 September 1597 (*Fife Sheriff Court Books*).'

p. 198, l. 8 from foot, for ' before 1614 ' read ' before 7 September 1597, when her brother David was served heir to her (*Fife Sheriff Court Books*).'

p. 200, l. 5, before 'Drumcairn,' insert ' of.'

p. 214, l. 15, after 'gules.' insert 'three.'

p. 214, l. 16, after 'patée,' insert ' argent.'

STRATHALLAN

p. 217, l. 6 from foot, after '1625,' insert 'She was buried in Holyrood Church 15 July 1668 (Canongate Register).'

p. 218, l. 26, after 'time,' insert 'In 1658 he appears to have been incarcerated in the Edinburgh Tolbooth at the instance of his mother, but she agreed to his liberation 3 January 1659 (*Book of Old Edinburgh Club*, iv. 130).'

p. 221, note 6, for '*Ibid.*' read '*Genealogical Memoir of the House of Drummond*, Edinburgh, 1808.'

p. 222, l. 20, delete '(often called Elizabeth).'

p. 222, l. 21, after '1669,' for comma put full stop, and delete remainder of sentence.

p. 222, after l. 22, insert

'3. *Elizabeth* married, contract 20 September 1683, to Thomas, seventh Earl of Kinnoul (cf. vol. v. 231, *corrig.*).'

p. 222, ll. 23, 24, for 'born 18, baptized 27' read 'baptized 3.'

p. 222, l. 9 from foot, after 'married,' insert 'before 14 January 1688 (*Seafield Corr.*, Scot. Hist. Soc., 40).'

p. 223, note 6, delete note.

p. 226, l. 13 from foot, for 'W. P. Brigstocke' read 'William Brigstock, M.P., of Birdcombe Court, co. Somerset.'

p. 229, ll. 5, 6, for 'died young' read 'fifth Viscount of Strathallan.'

p. 229, l. 7, delete entry.

p. 229, ll. 8, 9, 19, 21, 22, for '3, 4, 5, 6, 7' read '2, 3, 4, 5, 6.'

p. 229, l. 8, after '*Charles*' insert '*Edward Louis Casimir John Silvester Mary.*'

p. 229, l. 8, for '19' read '23.'

p. 229, l. 22, for '13' read '12.'

p. 232, l. 15 from foot, for '5' read '7,' and after 'London' insert 'born 7 February 1730.'

p. 233, after l. 15 insert

' 8. *Margaret*, born 24 April 1714.

9. *Anne*, born 3 June 1715.

10. *Katherine*, born 7 August 1716.

11. *Mary*, born 23 September 1717.

12. *Clementina Maria*, born 29 March 1721.

13. *Amelia Anne Sophia*, born 27 October 1727.

(All these mentioned in *The Oliphants of Gask*, 113.)'

p. 233, l. 25, after 'Abergeldie,' insert 'for the romantic story of their marriage, see *The Oliphants of Gask*, 113.'

p. 233, after l. 26, insert

'1 and 2. Twins, a boy and a girl, born before 6 August 1751, "in the ninth month," which seems to imply that the marriage took place in November 1750 (*The Oliphants of Gask*, 228).' And alter the numbers of children accordingly.

p. 233, l. 9 from foot, after 'advocate' insert 'She died 1821.'

p. 233, l. 7 from foot, after *Elizabeth*, insert 'died unmarried 1831 (*The Oliphants of Gask*, 228).'

p. 236, l. 10, for 'Graham' read 'Graeme.'

p. 236, l. 11 from foot, after 'issue,' insert 'and died at Edinburgh 5 November 1912.'

p. 236, l. 7 from foot, for ' Francis' read ' Frances.'

ANCIENT EARLS OF STRATHEARN

p. 241, note 10, for ' *Ecelesia de Scion*' read ' *Ecclesiæ de Scone*.'

MORAY, EARL OF STRATHEARN

p. 256, l. 12, after 'Mary,' insert 'of.'

STEWART, EARLS OF STRATHEARN

p. 260, l. 23, after ' 1425,' insert 'mandate for dispensation dated 24 February 1422-23 (*Cal. of Papal Letters*, vii. 251).'

STRATHMORE

p. 277, l. 4, after 1492, insert reference no. ' 2.'

p. 280, after l. 25, insert

' 3. *Agnes* (*Acta Dom. Conc.*, xl. 120.'

p. 280, l. 26, for ' 3' read ' 5' (see footnote 8).

p. 296, l. 8, for 'Drumkibbo' read 'Drumkilbo.'

p. 304, l. 2 from foot, for ' 1706-24' read ' 1706-23.'

p. 308, l. 9, for ' Chaventon' read ' Charenton.'

p. 313, l. 14, for 'ever' read 'never.'

p. 315, l. 26, for ' Gordon-Rebow' read 'Gurden-Rebow.'

p. 316, l. 21, for 'Francis' read ' Frances.'

p. 316, l. 25, for ' 23' read ' 28.'

SUTHERLAND

p. 352, footnote 1, for 'Canongate' read 'Haddington. '

p. 364, l. 10 from foot, after 1888, insert 'married, 11 April 1912, Lady Eileen Gwladys Butler, elder daughter of the Earl of Lanesborough.'

LIVINGSTON, VISCOUNT TEVIOT

p. 369, l. 6 from foot, after 'sister,' insert ' She married, before 8 June 1449, John of Kynninmond of that Ilk (Macfarlane's *Gen. Coll.*, ii. 536).'

p. 372, ll. 22, 23, delete from 'is further said,' down to 'Somerville' and insert '(probably between the other two), Jean Somerville, who was mother of both his children (Birthbrief cited in footnote 11; *Reg. of Deeds*, ccclxiii. 157). The Birthbrief calls her Agnes, and states that she was a daughter of Lord Somerville, but she does not occur in the Somerville article. The Deed also mentions Marion Baillie, and implies that she was a daughter of Archibald Baillie of Auldston, and was previously married, contract 17 August 1575, to Robert Grahame of Westhall (*Reg. of Deeds*, xiv. 300).'

p. 374, l. 30, after 'sergeant-major,' delete from 'of' to '1665' on l. 32, and insert ' in Buccleuch's, Kirkpatrick's, and Drummond's Regiments, becoming lieutenant-colonel 11 June 1660 (*Scots Brigade in Holland*, Scot. Hist. Soc., i. *passim*).'

TORPHICHEN

p. 378, l. 9, after 'Lord,' insert ' of.'

p. 378, l. 19, delete from 'He was' down to 'David II.' on l. 21.

p. 378, l. 22, for 'in that year' read '1347.'

p. 385, l. 15, for 'she' read 'he.'

p. 389, l. 12, after '*Elizabeth*,' insert 'married in April 1644, as his third wife, to John Gibbeson, minister of Dalmeny (*Reg. of Deeds*, Dlvii. 115), and died the same year (Scott's *Fasti Eccl. Scot.*, i. 181). There was another daughter, *Anna*: she and Elizabeth were heirs portioners of their brothers (*Reg. of Deeds*, Dl. 102).'

p. 393, l. 6 from foot, for 'Viscount Canada' read 'Lord Alexander.'

p. 398, l. 5, for ' has ' read 'had issue.'

p. 398, l. 19, for ' gules' read 'or.'

TRAQUAIR

p. 399, after l. 4 from foot, insert

'4. *Margaret*, who had or claimed some right to the lands of Ormiston, in Peeblesshire (*Acta Dom. Conc. et Sess.*, iv. 114).'

p. 400, l. 5 from foot, after 'Knox,' insert ' who may have been the Lady Traquair who was buried in September 1623 (Canongate Reg.).'

TWEEDDALE

p. 417, l. 18, for ' Militis, Domini ' read ' Miles et Dominus.

p. 418, l, 2 from foot, delete ' of Locherworth.' *Note.*—It is uncertain whether the Sir Gilbert who swore fealty to Edward I. in 1296 was Sir Gilbert of Locherworth or his contemporary Sir Gilbert of Erroll.

p. 421, l. 10 from foot, delete ' 3 October 1357,' and insert '30 March 1389, but was dead before 29 August 1392 (*Laing Charters*, No. 379, (7) (8)). It is obviously he, and not his grandson William, who was Sheriff of Peebles in 1388 (*Exch. Rolls*, iii. 167).'

p. 422, i. 24, delete from ' shortly ' to ' widow,' on l. 26, and insert ' not later than 1397 as his son William witnesses a charter as William Hay of Locherworth in or before that year (*Laing Charters*, No. 379 (9)).'

p. 423, l. 15, delete from ' He ' down to ' and,' on l. 18, and insert ' He was knighted before.'

p. 424, l. 5, after ' William,' insert 'is said to have.'

p. 424, l. 7, for ' six ' read ' four.'

p. 424, l. 7, for ' he ' read ' to have.'

p. 424, l. 8, after ' rents,' insert ' But though he and others, the co-lords of Yester and patrons of the Kirk of Bothans, petitioned on 1 August 1420 for the erection of the Kirk into a College, it was not till 22 April 1421, by which time he was dead, that the petition was granted by the Bishop of St. Andrews (original at Yester).'

p. 424, l. 15, for 'August' read '12 April, when his widow took instruments upon the consent of the rector of Bothans to the foundation of the college (original at Yester).'

p. 424, l. 19, after 'Erroll,' insert note, ' It is doubtful whether this lady was a Hay at all. Her seal appended to her charter of mortification 23 February 1447-48 to the altar of the B.V.M. in the kirk of Bothans bears the arms of Hay of Yester impaling three stars or cinquefoils (original at Yester).'

p. 425, l. 3, for ' 1418' read ' 26 January 1418-19 (Yester Writs).'

p. 425, l. 7 from foot, delete from ' was still living 1451 ' down to ' Yester ' in l. 3 from foot, and insert ' died in 1463 (retour of his son 12 March 1466-67, Yester Writs).'

p. 425, last line, delete from ' If so,' down to '1517' on l. 2 of p. 426.

p. 426, l. 7, after ' daughter,' insert ' She married, secondly, before 2 April 1467, Patrick Dunbar of Bele, and was his widow in 1488 (Yester Writs; *Acta Dom. Aud.*, 114).'

p. 426, after l. 10, insert

    '5. *Mr. Hugh*, who appears as a witness, 1440-1447, to several charters of his brothers (Yester Writs).'

p. 426, l. 11, for ' 5 ' read ' 6.'

p. 426, l. 14, for '1425' read '3 December 1414 (original at Yester).

p. 426, ll. 16, 19, 33, for '6, 7, 8' read '7, 8, 9.'

p. 426, last line, delete from 'John,' down to 'Hunter,' on l. 7 of p. 427. *Note.*—John Hay of Oliver Castle in 1475 was son and heir of Sir David Hay of Yester, and afterwards first Lord Hay of Yester.'

p. 427, l. 14, for '1422' read '1432 (*Reg. Nig. de Aberbrothock*, No. 65).'

p. 427, l. 2 from foot, for 'the same year, and certainly before 6 April 1434' read 'in February 1433-34.'

p. 428, l. 5 from foot, for '1 March 1478-79' read '2 September 1478, when brieves of inquest were issued to his son (Yester Writs).'

p. 429, after l. 11, insert

'2. *William*, who is a witness, 1470-1482, to various deeds by his father and brother (Yester Writs).'

p. 429, l. 12, for '2' read '3.'

p. 429, l. 13, delete 'apparently.'

p. 429, after l. 18, insert

'4. *Robert*, who is a witness to an indenture and charter by his father in 1470 and 1474 (Yester Writs).'

p. 429, l. 19, for '3' read '5.'

p. 429, l. 19, delete 'married to Sir Niel Cuningham of Barns, co. Fife.'

p. 430, l. 12 from foot, for 'before 9 November 1508' read 'in September 1508 (Retour of second Lord, Yester Writs).'

p. 430, l. 8 from foot, after '1468,' insert 'dispensation dated 3 August 1469 (Yester Writs).'

p. 431, l. 6 from foot, after 'age,[5]' delete 'This son,' and insert 'from a comparison of dates, however, this story is probably untrue. Sir Thomas no doubt had a son,'

p. 431, l. 5 from foot, for '——' read 'Sir Thomas of Hoprew.'

p. 431, l. 5 from foot, delete 'must have been born in or about 1490,' and insert 'who may have been born about 1483, as he had a precept of sasine in 1504. If so, he cannot have been the son of Elizabeth Home, who was not born before 1477, and must have been the son of a former wife.'

p. 431, after last line, insert

'3. *William*, who had, on 9 October 1495, a charter from his father of the lands of Nether Menzeon, which had been resigned by another William Hay, styled "cousin" of the first Lord. Both these Williams witnessed the sasine of the Edinburgh and Haddington lands to John Hay, 7 October 1478 (Yester Writs).'

p. 432, l. 1, for '3' read '4.'

p. 432, l. 1, after 'Alexander],' insert 'of Olivercastle, of which he had a precept of infeftment in liferent from his father 21 February 1502-3 (Yester Writs); and.'

p. 432, l. 1, after 'Menzeon,' insert 'succeeded his brother William in the latter lands.'

p. 432, ll. 8, 11, for 'Lord John' read 'John Lord.'

p. 432, l. 15, after '1531,' insert, 'He was alive 30 May 1552 (*Liber Act. D. Off. S. And. infra Laud.*, f. 77). He married Euphemia Wauchope: they had a charter of Nether Menzeon from the second Lord 12 July 1512 (Yester Writs).'

p. 432, after l. 15, insert

'4. *Sir Nicholas*, prebendary of the College Kirk of Bothans, in which he founded a chaplainry at the altar of the Holy Cross 6 February 1488-89. He died in 1498 (Yester Writs).'

p. 432, ll. 16, 19, for '4, 5' read '5, 6.'

p. 433, last two lines, and p. 434, first two lines, delete these entries, George and William were brothers, not sons, of the second Lord (see *supra*).'

p. 434, l. 7, after '1521-22,' insert 'On 16 February 1538-39 he was presented to the Provostry of the College Kirk of Bothan, of which he had previously been a prebendary (Yester Writs). On 21 August 1542 he was appointed archpriest of the College Kirk of Dunbar (*Reg. Sec. Sig.*, xvi. 44).'

p. 434, after l. 11, insert

'5. *Mr. John* of Smithfield. On 2 April 1523 he witnessed a deed by his brother, the third Lord, and on 12 August 1539 the latter chose his brother, Mr. John Hay of Smithfield, to be his arbiter in a submission (Yester Writs). On 15 February 1542-43 he,' etc., as on p. 435, l. 20, down to end of page.

p. 434, ll. 12, 14, 16, 23, for '5, 6, 7, 8' read '6, 7, 8, 9.'

p. 435, l. 11, delete 'first.'

p. 435, l. 13, delete 'secondly —— daughter and sole heiress of John Dickson of Smithfield, co. Peebles. *Note*.--Smithfield was inherited by three heiresses, Christina, Mariota, and Elizabeth Dickson, who had a precept of sasine 6 May 1501 (*Exch. Rolls*, xi. 308, 309). Smithfield appears to have been acquired by John Hay, a brother, not a son, of the third lord (see *supra*).'

p. 435, delete ll. 17, 18, 19, and transfer remainder of entry to John Hay, son of the second Lord, as in *corrigendum* above.

p. 436, l. 1, for '3' read '2.'

p. 436, l. 2, after 'incorrect,' insert 'He succeeded his uncle Mr. Thomas Hay as archpriest of Dunbar (Crawfurd's MS. Baronage, f. 278, Adv. Lib.) and preceptor of S. Leonard's Hospital in 1547. He was tutor of Smithfield on 7 October 1550 (Renwick's *Peebles during Reign of Queen Mary*, 160).'

p. 436, l. 5, after 1555-56, insert 'He died between 30 January 1557-58 and 3 May 1558 when the Provostry of Bothans was vacant through his death (Yester Writs).'

p. 436, after l. 5, insert

'3. *John (secundus)*, on 15 February 1540-41 John Hay of Hoprew, Master of Yester, and John Hay, his brother-german, witnessed a resignation by William Hay of Tallo at Yester (Protocol Book of Alexander Symson, Haddington, vol. 1529-1544, f. 90 b.).'

p. 436, after l. 10, insert

'John, third Lord Hay, had also a natural daughter *Elizabeth,* who had letters of legitimation under the Great Seal 18 August 1558, when she is called natural daughter of the late John, Lord Hay of Yester, grandfather of William, then Lord Hay of Yester (*Reg. Mag. Sig.*) On 22 August 1558 she was, with consent of her cousin, Thomas Hay of Smithfield, contracted to Robert Lauder of Bass (*Reg. of Deeds,* iii. 231).'

p. 437, l. 7 from foot, for '———,' read '*James.* He must have been younger than his brother Thomas, as the latter is styled Master of Yester in 1560 (Ext. Peebles Records, pp. 267-8.). When the Provostry of Bothans was vacant on 4 July 1558 both these sons were under age, and were not presented to the benefice on that account (Yester Writs).'

p. 438, l. 9, delete this entry. Elizabeth was, as mentioned above, half-sister, not natural daughter, of the fourth Lord.

p. 442, l. 19, after '*Jean,*' insert 'is said to have.'

p. 442, l. 19, after 'Barra,' insert 'A Jean Hay was the wife of Mr. William Hay of Barra, commissary of Glasgow 1613-1618, and both are mentioned in the testament of Mr. David Hay, commissary-clerk of Glasgow, confirmed on 9 May 1616 (Glasgow Tests.).'

p. 442, line 24, delete '(date not given),' and substitute 'before 23 March 1640 (*Part. Reg. of Sas.,* Edinburgh, etc., xxviii. 373).'

p. 442, l. 10 from foot, for '1561,' read '1559. In 1589 he was said to be about thirty years old, and to have a son and heir of ten years old (*John Colville's Letters,* Bannatyne Club, 330).'

p. 444, l. 22, after 'and,' insert 'was.'

p. 446, l. 9, after 'ascertained,' insert 'but it was before 18 April 1648 (see below).'

p. 446, l. 11, for 'He' read 'She.'

p. 446, l. 14, after 'Linplum,' insert 'on the Committee of War for Haddingtonshire 18 April 1648 (*Acta Parl. Scot.,* vi. pt. ii. 32): his precept of clare constat as his father's heir dated 20 July 1648 (*Edin. Sas.,* xxxvi. 186).'

p. 446, note 1, for 'will' read 'testament-dative.'

p. 447, l. 21, for '1593' read '1595-96.'

p. 449, l. 1, for '1654' read '25 May 1653 (M. I., College Kirk of Bothans).'

p. 449, l. 9, for 'will was proved' read 'testament-dative was confirmed.'

p. 449, l. 12, for 'Montgomery' read 'Montgomerie.'

p. 449, l. 21, for 'as far as is known, only two sons' read 'issue.'

p. 449, after l. 22, insert

'2. *Charles* (M. I. of first Earl in College Kirk of Bothans).

3. *Alexander,* baptized 13 March 1644 (Kirk Session Records, Yester).

4. *James.* These three sons must have died *s.p.*'

p. 449, l. 23, for '2' read '5.'

p. 450, l. 25, delete 'niece and.'

p. **450,** l. 26, after ' line' insert ' daughter of William Hay of Newhall, and niece of George, who succeeded as seventh Marquess (cf. *post*, p. 460).'

p. **451,** after l. 30, insert

'6. *Margaret.*

7. *Grissel.*

8. *Anne.* (These three daughters mentioned in M. I. *ut supra.*)'

p. **454,** l. 1, after 'advice,' insert quotation mark.

p. **454,** l. 17, for 'near Edinburgh' read 'East Lothian.'

p. **456,** l. 10 from foot, for ' 8' read ' 6.'

p. **459,** l. 11, after ' secondly,' insert 'after May 1695,⁵' and delete ' (who was living May 1695⁵).'

p. **465,** note 4, for ' 463' read '460.'

p. **468,** l. 7, for 'Rendleshan' read 'Rendlesham.'

p. **468,** l. 15, for 'Francis' read ' Frances.'

p. **469,** l. 8, for 'became quarter-master general' read 'served in the quarter-master general's department.'

p. **472,** l. 20, 'for 'Viceroy' read 'Governor-General.'

p. **472,** after l. 2 from foot, insert

'He married, first, 18 February 1857, Helena Eleanora Augusta (lady of the bedchamber to the Princess of Wales), daughter of Count de Kielmansegge, Hanoverian minister at the Court of St. James's. She died 30 September 1871, and he married, secondly, 8 October 1873, Julia Charlotte Sophia, second daughter of Keith Stewart Mackenzie of Seaforth. She survived him, and married, secondly, 24 January 1887, the Right Hon. Sir John Rose Best, who died 24 August 1888; and thirdly, 8 February 1892, Major Sir William Evans Gordon.'

WEMYSS

p. **483,** l. 12, for ' 1429' read '1427.'

p. **483,** l. 13, for 'Elizabeth' read 'Margaret.'

p. **483,** l. 29, for 'John' read 'James.'

p. **490,** l. 25, after 'Henry,' insert 'Lord.'

p. **495,** l. 13, for 'Margaret' read 'Elizabeth.'

p. **499,** l. 1, after 'Tullibardine,' insert '(*see title* Atholl).'

p. **500,** l. 4 from foot, for '1639' read '1640 (Balfour's *Annals*, ii. 427, corroborated by a letter from Lord Wemyss, Wemyss Castle Writs).'

p. **503,** l. 15, after 'issue,' insert 'and was buried at Wemyss 6 May 1652 (Lamont's *Diary*, 18).'

p. **503,** l. 4 from foot, for '1717' read '1715.'

p. **509,** l. 7 from foot, after ' Castle,' insert reference no. '³.'

p. **509,** l. 6 from foot, delete reference no. '³.'

p. **514,** ll. 15 and 16, for 'Keek' read 'Keck.'

p. **516,** l. 4, for 'Balgonie' read 'Balgone.'

p. **517,** l. 14, after 'Major,' insert 'John.'

p. 517, l. 14, after 'Blackburn,' insert 'son of John Blackburn of Killearn, co. Stirling.'

p. 518, l. 6, for 'Yorks' read 'Yorke.'

WIGTOWN

p. 523, l. 4, after '*Marjory,*' insert 'born 1323-24, as she was foster-sister of King David II. ;' delete 'who.'

p. 524, l. 7 from foot, after 'arms,' insert 'He had a grant of the office of Sheriff of Peebles from David II. 8 September 1346 (copy at Yester, dated 31 December 1435).'

p. 524, l. 3 from foot, for 'cousin' read 'uncle.'

p. 529, l. 7 from foot, delete 'son of Alexander de Seton.'

p. 530, l. 20, insert 'i.' before '*John.*'

p. 530, l. 31, insert '(i)' before '*James.*'

p. 530, l. 36, insert '(ii)' before '*William.*'

p. 531, l. 12 from foot, after 'Albany,' insert 'Governor of Scotland.'

p. 532, l. 3 from foot, for 'David, Lord Hay of Yester,' read 'Sir David Hay of Yester.'

p. 534, l. 6, delete 'married to.'

p. 534, ll. 7, 8, delete 'son to Alexander, Lord Livingstone, who.'

p. 534, l. 9, after 'her,' insert 'but there is no evidence that this marriage was ever completed.'

p. 537, note 9, after '*Deeds,*' insert 'iii.'

p. 547, l. 25, after '1597,' insert 'He married Helen, daughter of Alexander Bruce of Cultmalindy, and widow of Robert Moray, younger of Abercairnie (Perthshire Sheriff Court Reg. of Deeds, 2 July 1659). She died May 1660 (Dunblane Tests).'

p. 547, note 11, for '10 March' read '9 October.'

p. 550, last line, after '*Helen,*' insert '9. *Margaret,* mentioned in the precept of 18 August 1669 (see p. 553).'

p. 550, transpose notes 13 and 14.

p. 551, l. 19, after 'afternamed,' insert '(except Jean).'

p. 551, l. 12 from foot, delete 'person or.'

p. 553, l. 4 from foot, for 'Earl of Panmure' read 'Earl Panmure.'

p. 555, l. 17, after 'claimed,' insert 'in his case before the House of Lords in 1762.'

p. 558, l. 3, for 'frases' read 'fraises.'

WINTON

p. 566, note 6, delete reference and substitute '*Acta. Parl. Scot.,* i. 474.'

p. 570, note 2, add at end of note, 'But if this theory is not correct, the later generations shown below were, of course, Setons in the female line only.'

p. 571, note 3, after '*Scotichronicon*,' insert '*Ibid.*'

p. 571, note 4, after '*Ibid.*' insert '*Orygynale Cronykil loc. cit.*'

p. 584, l. 8, for '1557' read '1557-58.'

p. 584, l. 9, for 'seventh' read 'sixth.'

p. 584, l. 12, after 'adherence,' insert 'and aliment.'

p. 584, l. 13, after 'him,' insert 'She got decree for aliment.'

p. 584, l. 13, after '1603,' insert 'and was buried in Seton Church (cf. p. 24).'

p. 595, l. 12, after '1673,' insert 'Christian, daughter of Lord Cranstoun, confessed to too great intimacy with him 22 May 1673 (South Leith Kirk Session Minutes).'

p. 598, l. 10, after 'attainder of,' insert 'George, fifth Earl of Winton, and.'

p. 601, l. 4, for 'fourth' read 'third'; and for '1688' read '1683.'

p. 602, l, 17, after 'Cockenzie,' insert 'He went abroad at the Revolution and remained abroad till 1695. "The Earl of Winton is come home after seven years absence, and is staying at Seton" (Letter at Slains 5 December 1695).'

p. 605, note 2, add to note, 'Doubtless identical with Magdalen M'Klear who, on 3 September 1723, made affidavit that she went to London about a fortnight after Lord Winton's committal to the Tower, and had frequent access to him during nine months thereafter (*i.e.* until his escape). She was then known as Mrs. Corsby, and in 1723 was Mrs. Jolly. She is believed to have had two children by Lord Winton, born several years before 1716, and named John Seton and Christian (Memorial for Commissioners of Forfeited Estates, respondents in appeal of Elizabeth Stevenson, Lady Pitcairn, 2 March 1724).'

p. 606, l. 15, for 'Getre' read 'Gelre.'

p. 606, l. 31, for 'venacular' read 'vernacular.'

INDEX

INDEX

A——, wife of Norman of Leslie, Constable of Inverurie, son of Malcolm, vii. 266.

Abbot, Charles, younger son of 1st lord Tenterden, ii. 307.
—— —— his wife Emily Frances Stuart, ii. 307.

Abdy of Albyns, Sir Thomas N., 1st bart., viii. 363.
—— Grace, wife of Albert Leveson-Gower, viii. 363.

Abel-Smith of Wilford, Henry, iv. 211.
—— —— Constance Helen, wife of Montgomerie Boyle, iv. 211.

Aberach Mackay, Ian, ancestor of the family of, vii. 160.
—— —— his wife * Mackintosh, vii. 160.
—— John, fourth chieftain, vii. 164.
—— —— his wife,* Mackay, vii. 164.

ABERCORN, HAMILTON, LORD OF, i. 46.

Abercorn, James Hamilton, eldest son of Claud, lord Paisley ; lord of, i. 46 ; iv. 372.
—— —— his wife, Marion Boyd, i. 46 ; v. 167.

ABERCORN, HAMILTON, EARL OF, i. 37-74.

Abercorn, Charles, fifth earl of, i. 51 bis.
—— —— his wife, Katharine Hamilton, i. 49, 51.
—— Claud, fourth earl of, i. 51.
—— George, third earl of, i. 49.
—— James, first earl of, i. 40, 46; ix. 3.
—— —— his wife, Marion Boyd, i. 47 ; v. 167.
—— James, second earl of, i. 47, 48 ; v. 358.
—— —— his wife, Katharine Clifton, i. 49; v. 358.
—— James, sixth earl of, i. 57, 58.
—— —— his wife, Elizabeth Reading, i. 59.
—— James, seventh earl of, i. 59, 62.
—— —— his wife, Anne Plumer, i. 62.
—— James, eighth earl of, i. 63, 64.
—— James, tenth earl of, i. 68.
—— —— his wife, Louisa Jane Russell, i. 70.
—— James, eleventh earl of, i. 72.
—— —— his wife, Mary Anna Curzon-Howe, i. 72.
—— John James, ninth earl of, i. 63, 64, 66.
—— —— his 1st wife, Katharine Copley, i. 66.
—— —— his 2nd wife, Cecil Hamilton, i. 64, 68.
—— —— his 3rd wife, Anne Jane Gore, i. 68.

* Name unknown.

ABERCORN, HAMILTON, MARQUESS OF, i. 66-74.

Abercorn, James, second marquess of, i. 67, 68.
—— —— his wife, Louisa Jane Russell, i. 70.
—— James, third marquess of, i. 72.
—— —— his wife, Mary Anna Curzon-Howe, i. 72.
—— John James, first marquess of, i. 66, 95.
—— —— his 1st wife, Katharine Copley, i. 66.
—— —— his 2nd wife, Cecil Hamilton, i. 64, 68.
—— —— his 3rd wife, Anne Jane Gore, i. 68.

ABERCORN, HAMILTON, DUKE OF, i. 69-74.

Abercorn, James, first duke of, i. 67 ; ii. 247.
—— —— his wife, Louisa Jane Russell, i. 70.
—— James, second duke of, i. 70, 72.
—— —— his wife, Mary Anna Curzon-Howe, i. 72.

ABERCROMBIE, SANDILANDS, LORD, i. 75-81.

Abercrombie, James, first lord, i. 79 ; vi. 442 ; ix. 4.
—— —— his 1st wife, Jean Lichtoun, i. 79 ; ix. 5.
—— —— his 2nd wife, Christian Fletcher, i. 80 ; ix. 5.
—— James, second lord, i. 81.

Abercromby, George Ralph (Abercromby), 3rd baron, iv. 219.

ABERCROMBY, LORD GLASFOORD, iv. 179-182.

Abercromby of Abercromby, Alexander, iii. 278.
—— —— his wife, Isabella Dishington, iii. 278.
—— Alexander, i. 77.
—— —— his wife, Euphemia Kinninmont, i. 77.
—— —— Sir Thomas, vii. 8.
—— of Achquhorties, David de, vii. 269.
—— —— his wife, Margaret Leslie, vii. 269.
—— of Afforsque, John, iv. 181.
—— of Balcormo, Robert, vi. 408.
—— of Birkenbog, Sir Alexander, 1st bart., iii. 204 ; ix. 90.
—— —— his 2nd wife, Jane Sutherland, iii. 204.
—— —— his 3rd wife, Elizabeth Baird, ix. 90.
—— —— Alexander, iv. 19.
—— —— his wife, Jonet Ogilvie, iv. 19.

* Name unknown.   * Name unknown

* Name unknown.

M

* Name unknown.

* Name unknown.　　　　　　* Name unknown.

* Name unknown.

Arbuthnott, Jean, wife of James Clephane, i. 293.
—— Jean, wife of 6th viscount Arbuthnott, i. 295, 313.
—— Jean, dau. of Andrew A. of Fiddes, i. 303.
—— Jean, wife of (1) Alex. Burnett; (2) Patrick Gordon, and (3) Sir William Douglas, i. 304.
—— Jean, wife of Samuel Straton, i. 306.
—— Jean, dau. of Romeo A., i. 307.
—— Jean, wife of William Galloway, i. 307.
—— Jean, wife of Alex. Gordon, i. 309.
—— Jean, dau. of John A. of Fordun, i. 309.
—— Jean, dau. of 2nd viscount of Arbuthnott, i. 310.
—— Jean, wife of capt. Crawford of Camlurg, i. 310.
—— Jean, wife of Alex. Cavendish, i. 315.
—— Jean Ogilvy, wife of Comr. Jas. Cheape, R.N., i. 316.
—— Jeannie, wife of Nicholas Dodd Beatson-Bell, i. 315.
—— Joan, wife of Jas. Clephane, i. 293.
—— John, physician to Queen Anne, i. 273, 280.
—— John, 3rd son of John A. of Legasland, i. 280.
—— John, son of Robert A. 'in Banff,' i. 281.
—— John, 2nd son of Alex. A. of Achtirforfar, i. 292.
—— John, son of Robt. A. of Findowrie, i. 295.
—— John, 2nd son of Robt. A. of Kirkbraehead, i. 307.
—— John, eldest son of Dr. A. of Arbuthnottshaugh, i. 308.
—— John, eldest son of Hugh Corsar A., i. 315.
—— John Campbell, C.I.E., i. 315.
—— —— his wife, Jeannie Sinclair Hamilton, i. 315.
—— John Ogilvy, i. 315.
—— John Pelly, i. 315.
—— John Robert, i. 315.
—— Josette, wife of (1) capt. Hughes, and (2) Gen. Sir De Lacy Evans, i. 307.
—— Josette Eliza Jane, wife of major Wollaston, i. 307.
—— Katharine, wife of * Gorthie of that Ilk, i. 280; ix. 15.
—— Katharine, wife of John Allardice, i. 281.
—— Katharine, wife of Alex. Grahame, tutor of Morphie, i. 282.
—— Katharine, wife of Alex. Burnett, i. 285.
—— Katharine, wife of Alex. Arbuthnott, i. 287.
—— Katharine, wife of (1) David Auchinleck, and (2) Gilbert Turing, i. 287.
—— Katharine, dau. of George A., i. 287.
* Name unknown.

Arbuthnott, Katharine, wife of James Thomson, i. 292.
—— Katharine, wife of Jas. Mortimer, i. 296.
—— Katharine, wife of Francis Melville, i. 299.
—— Katharine, wife of Chas. Stirling of Kippendavie, i. 306.
—— Katharine, wife of James Moir, i. 309.
—— Katharine, wife of (1) Robt. Gordon, and (2) David Riccart, i. 310.
—— Katharine, wife of rev. D. Lyell, i. 314.
—— Kathleen Georgina, wife of lt.-col. Rait of Anniston, i. 315.
—— Lindsay George, i. 315.
—— Louise Curzon, i. 315.
—— Magdalen, dau. of Robt. A. of Findowrie, i. 295.
—— Margaret, wife of Andrew Menzies, i. 279.
—— Margaret, wife of (1) Alex. Balbirnie, and (2) John Ogilvy, i. 280.
—— Margaret, wife of (1) Robt. A. of Caterline, and (2) Sir Geo. Ogilvy, i. 286, 292.
—— Margaret, wife of Andrew Sibbald of Kair, i. 291.
—— Margaret, wife of David Guthrie, i. 292.
—— Margaret, dau. of David A. of Findowrie, i. 294.
—— Margaret, dau. of Robt. A. of Findowrie, i. 295.
—— Margaret, wife of James Ogilvy, i. 295.
—— Margaret, wife of David Ogilvie of Powrie, i. 297; ix. 16.
—— Margaret, illeg. dau. of John A., Montrose, i. 304.
—— Margaret, wife of Alex. Carnegie of Pitarrow, i. 304; viii. 75.
—— Margaret, wife of Sir John Forbes of Monymusk, i. 306.
—— Margaret, wife of Jas. Napier, Montrose, i. 305.
—— Margaret, wife of T. L. Whittier, i. 307.
—— Margaret, wife of Sir T. Burnett, i. 308.
—— Margaret, wife of William Ross, i. 309.
—— Margaret, dau. of John A. of Fordoun, i. 309.
—— Margaret, dau. of 3rd viscount of Arbuthnott, i. 311.
—— Margaret, wife of Sir Alex. Dunbar of Northfield, i. 313.
—— Margaret, dau. of Donald S. A., i. 315.
—— Margaret, wife of W. J. Lumsden, i. 316.
—— Margaret, dau. of 9th viscount of Arbuthnott, i. 316.
—— Margaret Fanny, dau. of David A., i. 315.
—— Margaret Ogilvy, i. 315.
—— Margaret or Marjorie, wife of Sir William Monypenny, vi. 276.

* Name unknown.

*. Name unknown.

* Name unknown.

* Name unknown.

* Name unknown.

* Name unknown.

* Name unknown.

Berkeley, Richenda, wife of Robert, son of Wernebald, iv. 223.
—— Robert de, vi. 469.
—— —— his wife, Cecilia of Maccustoun, vi. 469.
—— Walter. viii. 319 n.
Berkshire, Henry Bowes (Howard), 4th earl of, vii. 103.
—— —— his wife, Katharine Graham, vii. 103.
—— Thomas (Howard), 3rd earl of, vii. 102.
Bern, father of Gamel, ii. 370.
Bernard of Airth, v. 329.
—— —— his wife, Helen, v. 329.
Berner of Saskendorff, John, iv. 105.
—— —— his wife, Anna Dyerlink, iv. 105.
—— Clara, wife of Patrick, earl of Forth and Brentford, iv. 105 ; ix. 93.
Bernham, David de, bishop of St. Andrews, ii. 217 ; viii. 476.
Berowald the Fleming, ii. 121.
Berrford, Johanna, variant of Joanna Beaufort, i. 450.
Berriedale, William, eldest son of 5th earl of Caithness ; styled lord, ii. 343.
—— —— his wife, Margaret or Mary Sinclair, ii. 343 ; vii. 574.
—— master of, John, eldest son of William, lord Berriedale, ii. 343.
—— —— his wife, Jean Mackenzie, ii. 344 ; vii. 507.
Bertie, Bridget, wife of 1st duke of Leeds, iii. 302.
—— Louisa, wife of Sir C. Stewart, ii. 304.
—— Mary Elizabeth, wife of Thomas Charles, viscount of Milsington, vii. 96.
—— Vere, 3rd son of 1st duke of Ancaster, ii. 304.
Bertolf of Leslie, vii. 264.
Bertram, Robert, sheriff of Northumberland, viii. 522.
BERVIE, ARBUTHNOTT, LORD OF, i. 305.
Bervie, James, first lord of, i. 305.
Berwick, James, FitzJames, duke of, i. 34.
—— —— his 1st wife, Honora Bourke, i. 34.
—— —— his 2nd wife, Anne Bulkeley, i. 34.
—— and Alba, dukes of, i. 34.
BERWICK, HOME, BARON HOME OF, iii. 287-289.
Berwick, Thomas, custumar of Edinburgh, v. 431.
Besingham, Henry de, v. 280 ; vi. 523 n.
Bessborough, John George (Ponsonby), 5th earl of, v. 368.
—— —— his wife, Caroline Amelia Gordon-Lennox, v. 368.
Best of Boxley, Mawdistley, iii. 603.
—— Dorothy, wife of 7th lord Fairfax, iii. 603.
Beth, alleged earl of Fife, iv. 2 n.
Bethell, Richard, son of 3rd lord Westbury, iii. 420.

Bethoc, wife of Crinan of Dunkeld, and dau. and heir of King Malcolm II., i. 3 ; iii. 240.
—— dau. of King Donald ' Bane,' and wife of Huctred or Godrith of Tynedale, i. 3, 417 ; vi. 288.
—— dau. of Malcolm, 2nd earl of Atholl, i. 418.
—— of Rowcastle, wife of Ranulf, son of Dunegal, vi. 288.
Bethune. See also Beaton.
—— of Bandon, Robert, v. 414.
—— of Blebo, John, viii. 496.
—— —— his wife, Margaret Wemyss, viii. 496.
Bevan of Fosbury House, Robert Cooper Lee, v. 254.
—— Gwendoline, wife of (1) Ion G. N. Keith-Falconer, and (2) major F. E. Bradshaw, v. 254.
Beverley, Algernon (Percy), 1st earl of, viii. 225.
BEVERLEY, DOUGLAS, MARQUESS OF, vii. 141-144.
Beverley, James, first marquess of, vii. 141.
Beverwaerth, Louis, lord of, i. 522.
—— —— his wife, Elizabeth of Horn, i. 522.
Beverwest, Amelia de, wife of Thomas (Butler), styled earl of Ossory, iii. 122.
Béza, Theodore, vi. 49 ; viii. 289.
Bezeley, Joseph, London, vii. 103.
—— —— his wife, Priscilla Billingsley, vii. 103.
Bickerton, Sir John de, viii. 420.
—— Richard de, viii. 420.
—— —— his wife, Lora de Cuningesburgh of Tullybody, viii. 420.
—— Sir Walter de, iv. 149.
—— —— his wife, Isobel, iv. 149 ; ix. 93.
Biddulph of Westcombe, Sir Theophilus William, bart., viii. 44.
—— —— his wife, Mary Agnes Somerville, viii. 44.
—— Caroline, wife of Edward Courtenay Leslie, vii. 310.
—— Thomas Tregenna, vii. 310.
Bidun, Amicia de, wife of Randolph de Limesi, iii. 3.
Biggar, Ada of, viii. 519.
—— Baldwin of, the King's sheriff, v. 488 ; viii. 519.
—— Marjory of, viii. 519.
—— Sir Nicholas of, viii. 519.
Bigod, Sir Hugh, chief justiciar of England, ix. 11.
—— Joan, wife of Sir Philip de Kyme, ix. 11.
—— Roger, earl of Norfolk, i. 5.
—— —— his wife, Isabella of Scotland, i. 5.
Billingsley, Case, Tottenham, vii. 103.
—— Priscilla, wife of (1) rev. Charles Graham, and (2) Joseph Bezeley, vii. 103.
Billyard, Elizabeth, wife of A. W. Hamilton, ii. 58.
—— W., Sydney, N.S.W., ii. 58.

* Name unknown.

* Name unknown.

* Name unknown.

* Name unknown.

Q

* Name unknown.

* Name unknown.

* Name unknown.

Campbell of Letters, Dorothy, dau. of Sir John C. of Lawers, v. 504.
— of Liston Hall, John, M.P., master in Chancery, i. 382.
—— his 1st wife, * Peter, i. 382.
—— his 2nd wife, * Hay, i. 382.
—— William, 4th son of John C. of Mamore, i. 382.
—— his 1st wife, * Barnard, i. 382.
—— his 2nd wife, Bridget Bacon, i. 382.
—— William Henry, i. 382.
— of Lochdochart, Alexander, 7th son of Sir Robert C. of Glenurchay, ii. 199; ix. 44.
—— his 1st wife, Julian Robertson, ii. 199.
—— his 2nd wife, Magdalene Menzies, ii. 200.
—— Charles, ii. 192; ix. 44.
—— his 2nd wife, Katharine Buchanan, ix. 44.
—— John, eldest son of Alex. C., ix. 44.
—— his wife, Susanna Campbell, ii. 99.
—— William, ix. 44.
— of Lochnell, Alexander, 3rd laird, ix. 23.
—— Alexander, 6th laird, ii. 202.
—— Archibald, ix. 21.
—— Sir Duncan, vii. 509.
—— his wife, Isabel Mackenzie, vii. 509.
—— John ' Gorm,' ancestor of the family of, i. 338.
—— his wife, Mary Campbell, i. 338.
—— Duncan, lieut.-general, vii. 447.
—— his wife, Eleanora Fraser, vii. 447.
— of Lochow, Sir Colin, 'Mor,' 1st laird, i. 319; vi. 534 n.
—— Sir Colin, keeper of Dunoon Castle, 3rd laird, i. 325.
—— his wife, Helena of Lennox, i. 325.
—— Sir Colin, ' Ionganlach,' 5th laird, i. 328, 330.
—— his alleged wife, Margaret Drummond, i. 328.
—— his wife, Mariota or Margaret Campbell, i. 324, 328.
—— Colin, 7th laird, i. 332.
—— his wife, Isabel Stewart of Lorne, i. 332; v. 3.
—— Sir Duncan, ' Na-Adh,' 6th laird, i. 330.
—— his 1st wife, Marcellina or Marjory Stewart, i. 149; ii. 331.
—— his 2nd wife, Margaret Stewart, i. 331.
—— Sir Gillespic or Archibald, ancestor of the family of, i. 319.
—— his alleged wife, Margaret Somerville, i. 319; viii. 3.
—— his alleged wife, Effrick of Carrick, i. 319.
* Name unknown.

Campbell of Lochow, Gillespic, Archibald, or Celestin, 4th laird, i. 318, 326, 330.
—— his alleged wife, * Menteith, i. 327; vi. 133 n.
—— his wife, Isabella Lamont, i. 327.
—— Gillespic, Archibald, or Celestin, the younger, i. 332.
—— his wife, Elizabeth Somerville, i. 332; viii. 12.
—— Sir Neil, 2nd laird, i. 320, 322; viii. 565.
—— his 1st wife, * Crawford, i. 324; ix. 18.
—— his 2nd wife, Mary Bruce, i. 323 : ii. 434.
— of Lochwinnoch, Colin, ancestor of the family of, i. 329.
— of Loragen, Charles, ix. 44.
—— John, ix. 44.
—— William, ix. 44.
— of Loudoun, Sir Andrew, 2nd laird, v. 491.
—— Sir Duncan, sheriff of Ayr, 1st laird, i. 321 : v. 490, 499.
—— his wife, Susanna Crauford of Loudoun, v. 490.
—— George, 3rd laird, v. 491, 494.
—— Sir George, 5th laird, ii. 401; v. 492.
—— Sir George, 6th laird, v. 492.
—— his wife, Elizabeth Stewart, v. 493.
—— George, 7th laird, v. 493.
—— his 1st wife, * Kennedy, v. 493.
—— his 2nd wife, Marion Auchinleck, v. 493.
—— Sir Hugh, 4th laird, v. 491.
—— Sir Hugh, 8th laird, v. 494.
—— his wife, Isobel Wallace, v. 494.
—— Sir Hugh, 9th laird, ii. 465, 470; v. 495.
—— his 1st wife, Elizabeth or Margaret Stewart, v. 351, 496.
—— his 2nd wife, Agnes Drummond, v. 496; vii. 47.
—— John, ancestor of the family of, ii. 178.
—— his 1st wife, Agnes Moncreiff, ii. 178.
—— his 2nd wife, Christian Ogilvie, ii. 142, 178.
—— Sir Hugh, 11th laird, v. 497.
—— his 1st wife, Margaret Gordon, v. 111, 498.
—— his 2nd wife, Elizabeth Ruthven, iv. 266; v. 114, 116, 498.
—— his 3rd wife, Margaret Home, v. 498.
—— Sir Matthew, 10th laird, v. 62, 496.
—— his wife, Isobel Drummond, v. 497.
* Name unknown.

Campbell, Alexander, officer in North British regiments, Kirktown of Strathfillan, ii. 198; ix. 44.
—— —— his wife, * Bowie, ii. 198.
—— Alexander, 9th son of Colin C., ii. 199.
—— Alexander, illeg. son of Sir Hugh C. of Loudoun, v. 496.
—— Andrew, 5th son of Sir John C. of Lawers, v. 504.
—— Alicia, wife of Allan Lauder of Hatton, i. 326.
—— Anne, wife of 2nd marquess of Huntly, i. 349.
—— Anne, wife of rev. Mr. Bulleyn, i. 350; ix. 23.
—— Anne, dau. of marquess of Argyll, i. 361; ix. 23.
—— Anne, wife of (1) 4th earl of Lauderdale, and (2) 7th earl of Moray, i. 368; v. 310; vi. 323.
—— Ann, dau. of James C. of Burnbank, i. 368; ix. 24.
—— Anne, wife of (1) 2nd earl of Bute, and (2) Alex. Fraser of Strichen, i. 370; ii. 300; v. 545; ix. 24.
—— Anne, wife of William, earl of Strafford, i. 377.
—— Anne, wife of Archibald Edmonstone, i. 382.
—— Anne (error for Louisa), wife of Alex. Johnstone, i. 385; ix. 25.
—— Anne, wife of Sir P. Ogilvy of Inchmartine, ii. 187; iv. 34.
—— Anne, wife of Sir K. Mackenzie of Grandvale, iii. 76.
—— Anne, dau. of Sir Archd. C. of Glencarradale, v. 504.
—— Ann, wife of 3rd lord Balmerino, v. 507.
—— Anna, wife of capt. Jas. Menzies of Comrie, i. 360.
—— Anna, wife of (1) Sir Donald Campbell of Ardnamurchan, and (2) Alex. Campbell of Inverliver, ii. 201; ix. 23.
—— Anna, wife of Robert MacNab of that Ilk, ii. 202; ix. 45 bis.
—— Annabella, wife of 2nd earl of Lothian, i. 349; v. 459, 460 bis; ix. 21.
—— Annabella, wife of (1) Alex. Napier of Merchiston, and (2) R. Fairlie of Braid, ii. 180; vi. 413; ix. 42.
—— Annabella, wife of (1) Thos. Boswell of Auchinleck, and (2) John Cunningham of Caprington, v. 495.
—— Annabella, wife of (1) D. Ker of Kersland, and (2) D. Dunbar of Enterkin, v. 497.
—— Annas, proposed wife of 5th earl of Cassillis, i. 346; ii. 477.
—— Annas, wife of John Campbell of Ardkinglas, ii. 183.

* Name unknown.

Campbell, Archibald, eldest son of Sir Duncan C. of Lochow, i. 331, 332; ix. 18.
—— —— his wife, Mariota of the Isles, ix. 18.
—— Archibald, 5th son of 1st lord Campbell, i. 332; ii. 174.
—— Archibald, captain of Skipness Castle, i. 336.
—— —— his 2nd wife, Janet Douglas, i. 336.
—— Archibald, bishop, son of Lord Neil C., i. 360; ix. 23.
—— Archibald, eldest son of 4th duke of Argyll, i. 384.
—— Archibald, 2nd son of 8th duke of Argyll, i. 390.
—— —— his wife, Janey Sevilla Callendar, i. 390.
—— Archibald, minister of Weem, i. 549.
—— —— his wife, Ann Stewart, i. 549.
—— Archibald, 4th son of Colin C. of Glenurchy, ii. 183.
—— —— his wife, Margaret Toshoch, ii. 183.
—— Archibald, son of John C. of Auchinryre, ii. 186.
—— Archibald, writer, lieut. 74th regt., ii. 195.
—— —— his wife, Jean Butter, ii. 195.
—— Archibald, 7th son of Colin C., ii. 198.
—— Archibald, in Succoth, 3rd son of Robert C., ii. 199; ix. 44.
—— Archibald, sergeant, Middlesex Militia, ii. 199.
—— Sir Archibald, iv. 289.
—— Archibald, his son, iv. 289.
—— —— his wife, Janet Gray, iv. 289.
—— Archibald, only son of Sir Archd. C. of Carradale, v. 504.
—— Archibald, son of Jas. C. of Hellsglen, ix. 44.
—— Sir Arthur, constable of Dunstaffnage, i. 321.
—— Augusta, wife of col. H. Clavering, i. 387; ix. 25.
—— Barbara (Meliora), dau. of 7th earl of Argyll, i. 350; ix. 22 bis, 23.
—— Beatrix, wife of Sir Wm. Hamilton of Manor Elieston, i. 42; v. 504; ix. 3.
—— Beatrix, wife of Sir John Campbell of Lawers, ii. 182; v. 503, 504; ix. 42.
—— Beatrix, dau. of Sir John C. of Glenorchy, ii. 202.
—— Beatrix, wife of Colin Campbell of Glenlyon, v. 504.
—— Beatrix, mother of Colin C. of Craignish, ix. 21.
—— Caroline, wife of (1) Francis, earl of Dalkeith, and (2) C. Townshend; baroness of Greenwich, i. 377; ii. 241; ix. 24.
—— Caroline, dau. of John C. of Liston Hall, i. 382.

* Name unknown.

* Name unknown.

Carnegie of Craig, David, viii. 67.
—— —— his wife, Katharine Wemyss, viii. 67, 501 ; ix. 159.
—— —— Sir John, 3rd son of 1st earl of Southesk, viii. 66.
—— —— his wife, Jane Scrymgeour, iii. 314 ; viii. 67.
—— of Craigo, David, dean of Brechin, viii. 55.
—— —— his wife, Helen Lindsay, viii. 55.
—— —— David, the younger, viii. 55.
—— —— his wife, * Stewart, viii. 55.
—— —— Elizabeth, viii. 55.
—— of Crechie, John viii. 57.
—— of Cruikston, David, vii. 14.
—— of Deischland, David, viii. 57.
—— —— John, viii. 57.
—— of Dunlappie, Sir John, vi. 491.
—— of Dunnichen, David, viii. 61.
—— —— John, viii. 57.
—— —— Sir Robert, vi. 494; viii. 58, 61.
—— —— his wife, Isobel Gray, iv. 286 ; viii. 61.
—— of Erlesfield, Sir John, viii. 58.
—— of Ethie, David, vi. 492.
—— —— Sir Robert, 1st laird, viii. 51.
—— of Fair Oak, John Jervis, vi. 505.
—— —— his 1st wife, Charlotte Stevenson, vi. 505.
—— —— his 2nd wife, Georgina Marjoribanks, vi. 505.
—— of Fethies, Sir Robert, viii. 51.
—— of Finavon, Barbara, wife of Sir Robert Douglas of Glenbervie, vi. 498.
—— —— James, 1st laird, vi. 497.
—— —— his wife, Anna Lundin, v. 303 ; vi. 498.
—— —— James, 2nd laird, vi. 498 ; viii. 295, 308.
—— —— his 1st wife, Margaret Bennet, vi. 498.
—— —— his 2nd wife, Violet Nasmith, vi. 498.
—— —— James, 3rd laird, vi. 498.
—— of Little Fithie, Sir James, viii. 89.
—— of Framedrum, Sir David, viii. 86.
—— of Fullerton, Sir David, viii. 86.
—— of Gartnafuaran, David, viii. 83.
—— —— James, viii. 83.
—— of Glenbuckie, David, viii. 83.
—— —— James, viii. 83.
—— of Glendye, Sir James, viii. 90.
—— of Idvy, Sir Robert, viii. 51.
—— of Inglismaldie, Sir John, vi. 494.
—— of Kinblethmont, Sir John, vi. 424.
—— —— John, vi. 495.
—— —— his wife, Jean Fothringham, vi. 495.
—— of Kinfauns, Alexander, vi. 499.
—— —— his 1st wife, Anna Blair, vi. 499 ; ix. 144.
—— —— his 2nd wife, Margaret Nairne, vi. 393, 499.

Carnegie of Kinfauns, Alexander, vi. 499.
—— —— his wife, Jean Carnegie, vi. 499.
—— —— Margaret, wife of John, lord Gray of Gray, vi. 498.
—— of Kinnaber, George, viii. 82.
—— —— his wife, Madeline Connel, viii. 82.
—— —— John, viii. 82.
—— —— his wife, Mary Fullerton, viii. 82.
—— of Kinnaird, David, 7th laird, iii. 278; viii. 53, 59.
—— —— his 1st wife, Elizabeth Ramsay of Leuchars and Colluthie, viii. 53, 60.
—— —— his 2nd wife, Euphame Wemyss, iii. 278 ; viii. 61, 491.
—— —— his 3rd wife, Janet Henrison, viii. 64.
—— —— Sir David, 8th laird, viii. 61, 64.
—— —— his wife, Margaret Lindsay, i. 514 ; viii. 66.
—— —— Duthac de, 1st laird, viii. 48.
—— —— his wife, Mariota of Kinnaird, viii. 48.
—— —— John, 3rd laird, viii. 50.
—— —— his wife, * Waus, viii. 51.
—— —— John, 4th laird, viii. 51.
—— —— his wife, Euphame Strachan, viii. 51.
—— —— Sir John, 6th laird, v. 205 ; viii. 56, 58, 60.
—— —— his 1st wife, Agnes Wood, viii. 58.
—— —— his 2nd wife, Margaret Keith, vi. 49 ; viii. 59.
—— —— Sir Robert, 5th laird, vi. 89, 493 ; viii. 51.
—— —— his wife, Margaret Guthrie, viii. 53.
—— —— Walter, 2nd laird, viii. 49.
—— —— his probable wife, * Lindsay, viii. 49.
—— of Kinnaldie, Sir John, vi. 494.
—— of Kinnoull, Anne, wife of Robt. Carnegie, vi. 495.
—— —— James, vi. 495.
—— —— his wife, Anne Ogilvy, vi. 495.
—— —— John, vi. 495.
—— —— his wife, Anne Auchinleck, vi. 495.
—— —— Robert, vi. 495.
—— —— his wife, Anne Carnegie, vi. 495.
—— of Leuchars, David, viii. 60.
—— —— his wife, Elizabeth Ramsay, viii. 53, 60.
—— —— Sir David, viii. 86.
—— —— Elizabeth, viii. 60.
—— —— Margaret, viii. 60.
—— of Leuchland, Robert, viii. 55.
—— —— his wife, Marjorie Wedderburn, viii. 56.
—— —— William, viii. 55.
—— of Lour, Patrick, 4th laird, vi. 499.
—— —— his wife, Margaret Bower, vi. 499.
—— —— Patrick, 5th laird, vi. 499.
—— —— his wife, Rachel Anne Forbes, vi. 499.

* Name unknown.   * Name unknown.

Carnegie, Margaret, wife of Sir C. Ramsay of Balmain, vi. 495.
—— Margaret, wife of John Fullarton of Fullarton, vi. 496; viii. 109.
—— Margaret, wife of (1) John Foulis, and (2) Charles Lewis, vi. 498.
—— Margaret, dau. of 3rd earl of Northesk, vi. 500.
—— Margaret, wife of Chas. Watson of Saughton, vi. 503.
—— Margaret, dau. of capt. J. Douglas C., vi. 507.
—— Margaret, wife of Patrick Falconer, viii. 54.
—— Margaret, legtd. dau. of Sir John C. of Kinnaird, viii. 59.
—— Margaret, wife of James Carnegie of Balnamoon, viii. 62, 76.
—— Margaret, dau. of Alexander C. of Balnamoon, viii. 62.
—— Margaret, wife of George Dunbar of Inchbrock, viii. 67.
—— Margaret, wife of Black of Haddo, viii. 76.
—— Margaret, wife of Henry Fletcher of Saltoun, viii. 78.
—— Margaret, dau. of Sir John C. of Pittarrow, viii. 83.
—— Margaret Mary Adeliza, vi. 506.
—— Marion, wife of Gilbert Gray of Bandirran, vi. 281; viii. 58.
—— Mariota Susan, viii. 91.
—— Marjory, wife of (1) William Halyburton, and (2) 1st viscount Arbuthnott, i. 305; viii. 67.
—— Marjorie, wife of (1) James Scott, and (2) John Prestoune, vi. 497.
—— Mary, dau. of 4th earl of Northesk, vi. 502.
—— Mary, wife of Walter Long of Preshaw, vi. 506.
—— Mary, wife of Strachan of Carmyle, viii. 57.
—— Mary, wife of (1) col. John Scott, and (2) * Forbes, viii. 83.
—— Mary, dau. of Sir James C. of Pittarrow, viii. 86.
—— Mary, wife of Thomas Henry Graham of Edmond Castle, viii. 88.
—— Mary Anne, wife of rev. Dr John Kemp, vi. 504.
—— Mary Anne, dau. of Sir David C. of Southesk, viii. 88.
—— Mary Elizabeth, viii. 92.
—— Mary Georgina, vi. 505.
—— Robert, 3rd son of 1st earl of Northesk, vi. 496.
—— Robert, 5th son of 2nd earl of Northesk, vi. 499.
—— Robert, parson of Kinnoull, viii. 54.
—— —— his wife, Elizabeth Wemyss, viii. 54, 491.

* Name unknown.

Carnegie, Robert, minister expectant, viii. 55.
—— Robert, 4th son of Sir Alexander C. of Pittarrow, viii. 75.
—— Robert, M.D., viii. 75.
—— Robert, 6th son of Sir David C. of Pittarrow, viii. 79.
—— Robert Francis, major Gordon Highlanders, viii. 91.
—— Stewart, wife of Wm. Fullarton of Fullarton, afterwards Lindsay of Spynie, vi. 496; viii. 111.
—— Susan Mary Anne, wife of David Carnegie of Stronvar, viii. 83 bis.
—— Swynfen Thomas, rear-admiral R.N., vi. 505.
—— —— his wife, Louisa Albertina Hope, vi. 506.
—— Sylvester, Arbroath, vi. 502.
—— Walter de, 2nd son of John de C. of Carnegie, viii. 47.
—— Walter, 2nd son of Walter C. of Kinnaird, viii. 50.
—— William, 2nd son of 3rd earl of Southesk, iii. 405; viii. 71.
—— William, 5th son of Sir David C. of Pittarrow, viii. 78.
Carnegie-Arbuthnott of Balnamoon, Anne, viii. 63.
—— —— Helen, viii. 63.
—— —— James, 6th laird, i. 295; viii. 62, 82.
—— —— his wife, Margaret Arbuthnott, i. 295; viii. 62.
—— —— James, 7th laird, viii. 62, 63.
—— —— James, 8th laird, viii. 63.
—— —— his wife, Anne Hunter, viii. 63.
—— —— Mary Anne Jemima, wife of Arthur Risden Capel, viii. 63.
—— Alexander, viii. 62.
—— Anne, viii. 62.
—— Charles, viii. 62.
—— Elizabeth, viii. 62.
—— Helen, wife of A. Knox of Keithock, viii. 63.
—— Jean, viii. 62.
—— John, viii. 62.
—— Margaret, viii. 62.
Carnegie-Knox, James, viii. 63 bis.
Carnoto, Thomas de, vii. 236.
CARNWATH, DALZELL, EARL OF, ii. 395-420.
Carnwath, Alexander, eldest son of 6th earl of Carnwath; titular earl of, ii. 416.
—— —— his wife, Elizabeth Jackson, ii. 416.
—— Arthur Alexander, ninth earl of, ii. 419; ix. 55.
—— Gavin, second earl of, ii. 413; viii. 25 n.; ix. 54 bis.
—— —— his 1st wife, Margaret Carnegy, ii. 414.
—— —— his 2nd wife, Margaret Erskine, ii. 414; v. 86.

Cathcart of Killochan, Robert, 2nd son of 2nd lord Cathcart, ii. 510.

—— —— his wife, Margaret Cathcart, ii. 510.

—— —— Robert, his son, ii. 511.

—— of Knockskaith, Hugh, 5th son of 2nd lord Cathcart, ii. 512.

—— —— his wife, Egidia Crawfurd, ii. 512.

—— of Pitcairlie, Robert, ii. 512.

—— of Trogwein or Trevor or Troweir, Alan, ii. 512.

—— —— Hugh, 3rd son of 1st lord Cathcart, ii. 509.

—— of Waterside, Alan, viii. 117.

—— Adelaide, wife of J. R. de Trafford, ii. 529.

—— Adolphus Frederick, lieut.-col., ii. 527.

—— —— his wife, Margaret Home, ii. 527.

—— Alan, eldest son of 1st lord Cathcart, ii. 509.

—— Allan, illeg. son of 3rd lord Cathcart, ii. 513.

—— Alan, illeg. son of Alan, master of Cathcart, ii. 516.

—— Alice, dau. of Sir George C., ii. 527.

—— Anne, dau. of Sir George C., ii. 527.

—— Archibald Hamilton, rector of Methby, ii. 522.

—— —— his wife, Frances Henrietta Fremantle, ii. 522.

—— Archibald Hamilton, 5th son of 3rd earl Cathcart, ii. 531 ; ix. 58 bis.

—— Archibald William, ii. 522.

—— Augusta Sophia, dau. of 1st earl Cathcart, ii. 527 ; ix. 58.

—— Augustus Ernest, King's Royal Rifle Corps, ii. 529.

—— Augustus Murray, lieut.-col. Grenadier Guards, ii. 529.

—— —— his wife, Jean Mary Orde-Powlett, ii. 529.

—— Cecilia, wife of John de Perthic, ii. 504.

—— Cecilia, wife of capt. E. T. Rose, ii. 531.

—— Charles, lieut. 79th regt., ii. 531.

—— Charles Allan, quarter-master-general to the Forces in India, M.P., ambassador to China, ii. 522.

—— Charlotte, dau. of Archibald H. C., ii. 523.

—— Charlotte Catherine, maid-of-honour, ii. 524.

—— Christian, wife of Alex. Hamilton of Brentwood, ii. 509.

—— Constance, wife of W. H. Ferrand, ii. 529.

—— David, 3rd son of 6th lord Cathcart, ii. 518.

—— Eleonora, wife of Sir John Houston, ii. 520.

—— Elizabeth, dau. of 8th lord Cathcart, ii. 520.

Cathcart, Elizabeth, wife of gen. Sir J. Douglas of Glenfinart, ii. 529.

—— Elizabeth Sarah, wife of major Robt. Stuart, ii. 523.

—— Emily, dau. of 3rd earl Cathcart, ii. 531.

—— Emily Sarah, Woman of the Bedchamber, ii. 527.

—— Eva, dau. of 3rd earl Cathcart, ii. 531.

—— Frances Louisa, ii. 522.

—— Frederica, wife of John Lodge, ii. 523.

—— Frederick, col., minister plenipotentiary, ii. 526.

—— —— his wife, Jane M'Adam of Craigengillan, ii. 526.

—— Frederick Adrian, York and Lancaster regt., ii. 529.

—— Sir George, K.C.B., adjutant-gen., ii. 526.

—— —— his wife, Georgina Greville, ii. 527.

—— George, lieut. 4th batt. Princess of Wales' Own, ii. 531.

—— George Greville, ii. 527.

—— Georgiana Mary, ii. 527.

—— Gilbert, 2nd son of 4th lord Cathcart, ii. 516 bis.

—— Helenor, wife of David Stewart, ii. 509.

—— Henrietta Louisa Frances, ii. 529.

—— Ida, wife of T. L. Hare, ii. 530.

—— Isobella Sophia, wife of Sir S. Crompton. ii. 523, 531.

—— James, 2nd son of 6th lord Cathcart, ii. 518.

—— James, major, 3rd son of 7th lord Cathcart, ii. 518.

—— Jane, wife of 4th duke of Atholl, i. 496 ; ii. 523.

—— Jane, dau. of Sir George C., ii. 527.

—— Jean, wife of John Shaw of Haily, ii. 512.

—— Jean, wife of (1) Thos. Cathcart, and (2) Archibald Dunbar, ix. 58.

—— John, illeg. son of 4th lord Cathcart, ii. 516.

—— Jonet, wife of John Crawfurd of Drongane, ii. 512.

—— Katharine Selina, wife of Robert Smith, ii. 523.

—— Leta Adine, ii. 529.

—— Louisa, wife of (1) David, 7th viscount Stormont, and (2) Robert Fulke Greville; countess of Mansfield, ii. 523 ; viii. 206, 209.

—— Louisa, dau. of 1st earl Cathcart, ii. 527.

—— Louisa, dau. of Sir George C. ii. 527.

—— Louisa Margaret, ii. 527.

—— Margaret or Marion, wife of Sir Wm. Sempill of Eliotstoun, ii. 509 ; vii. 530, 531.

—— Margaret, wife of John Hunter, ii. 512.

—— Margaret, illeg. dau. of 4th lord C., ii. 516.

—— Margaret, wife of Sir A. Whitefoord, ii. 518.

—— Margaret, dau. of 8th lord C., ii. 520.

* Name unknown.

Cochrane, Thomas, eldest son of 9th earl of Dundonald; captain R.N., styled lord, iii. 362; ix. 77.
—— Thomas Hesketh Douglas Blair, son of 12th earl of Dundonald; styled lord, iii. 367.
—— William, first lord, ii. 297; iii. 344.
—— —— his wife, Eupheme Scott, ii. 346.
—— William, elder son of 1st earl of Dundonald; styled lord, iii. 346, 350.
—— —— his wife, Katharine Kennedy, ii. 482; iii. 350.
COCHRANE OF PAISLEY AND OCHILTREE, COCHRANE, LORD, iii. 346-368.
Cochrane of Paisley and Ochiltree, William, first lord, iii. 346.
—— master of, John, eldest son of William, lord Cochrane, iii. 351.
COCHRANE, LORD COCHRANE OF DUNDONALD, iii. 344-368.
COCHRANE, LORD COCHRANE OF PAISLEY AND OCHILTREE, iii. 346-368.
COCHRANE, EARL OF DUNDONALD, iii. 334-368.
Cochrane of Ascog, Charles, iii. 335 n.
—— —— David, iii. 335 n.
—— —— Edward, iii. 335 n.
—— —— John, iii. 335 n.
—— —— Ninian, iii. 335 n.
—— of Ashkirk, Charles Home, captain R.N., iii. 340 n.
—— of Auchincreugh, Alexander, iii. 341.
—— —— his wife, Elizabeth Cochrane, iii. 339.
—— —— Alexander, colonel, iii. 341.
—— —— his wife, Agnes Richieson, iii. 341.
—— —— James, iii. 341.
—— —— his 1st wife, Marion Peebles, iii. 341.
—— —— his 2nd wife, Ursula Hamilton, iii. 342.
—— of Barbachlaw, Alexander, 4th laird, 2nd son of George C. of Barbachlaw, iii. 340 n.
—— —— Alexander, 8th laird, grandson of James C. of Barbachlaw, iii. 340 n.
—— —— Alexander, 9th laird, commissioner of supply, iii. 340 n.
—— —— his 1st wife, Helen Bruce, iii. 340 n.
—— —— his 2nd wife, Margaret Maule, iii. 340 n.; vii. 21.
—— —— Alexander, 10th laird, commissioner of supply, iii. 340 n.
—— —— Alexander, 11th laird, iii. 340 n.
—— —— George, 2nd laird, iii. 340.
—— —— Henry, 12th laird, iii. 340 n.
—— —— James, 5th laird, 3rd son of George C. of Barbachlaw, iii. 340 n.
—— —— James, 6th laird, legtd. son of Jas. C. of Barbachlaw, iii. 340 n.
—— —— James, 7th laird, commissioner to Parliament for Linlithgow, iii. 340 n.
—— —— his wife, Margaret Hamilton, iii. 340 n.

Cochrane of Barbachlaw, John, 1st laird, iii. 340 n.
—— —— Michael, 3rd laird, iii. 340 n.
—— of Bollinshaw or Bonshaw, Alexander, 4th son of William, lord Cochrane, ii. 491; iii. 352.
—— —— Alexander, his son, iii. 352.
—— of Cabbage Hall, Archibald, iii. 340 n.
—— —— John, iii. 340 n.
—— —— Thomas, bailie in Musselburgh, iii. 340 n.
—— of Cochrane, Alexander, 3rd son of Alexander Blair of Blair, iii. 339.
—— —— his wife, Elizabeth Cochrane, iii. 339.
—— —— Allan, son of Robert of C., iii. 336; ix. 74 ter.
—— —— Cosmo de, iii. 334.
—— —— Elizabeth, wife of A. Blair, iii. 339.
—— —— Goscelin or Glosmus de, iii. 334.
—— —— James, iii. 336.
—— —— John de, 1346, iii. 334.
—— —— John de, 1370, iii. 335 n.
—— —— John, iii. 336.
—— —— John, ix. 75.
—— —— his wife, Elizabeth Semple, ix. 75.
—— —— John, ix. 75.
—— —— his wife, Marion Stewart, ix. 75.
—— —— John, ix. 76.
—— —— his 1st wife, Mary Lindsay, ix. 76.
—— —— his 2nd wife, Elizabeth Semple, ix. 76.
—— —— Sir John, British Envoy to Denmark and Holland, iii. 341, 343.
—— —— his wife, Grace Butler, iii. 344.
—— —— Robert, 1368, v. 203.
—— —— Robert, son of William C. of Cochrane, iii. 335.
—— —— Robert, father of Allan C., ix. 74.
—— —— Robert, 2nd son of Allan C., iii. 336, 337; ix. 75.
—— —— Waldeve de, iii. 334.
—— —— William de, 1296, iii. 335.
—— —— William, son of Goslin of C., iii. 335.
—— —— his wife, Mary, ii. 397; iii. 335.
—— —— William, son of John C., iii. 338, 340 n. bis.
—— —— his wife, Elizabeth Montgomerie, iii. 339.
—— —— Sir William, 2nd son of Alexander and Elizabeth C. of Cochrane, iii. 341, 344.
—— —— his wife, Euphame Scott, iii. 346.
—— of Easter Cochrane, John, iii. 336 n., 338; ix. 75.
—— —— Michael, iii. 336 n.
—— —— his wife, Eupheme Erskine, iii. 336 n.
—— —— Peter, iii. 336 n.; ix. 75.
—— —— his wife, Isobel Spreull, ix. 75.
—— of Corsefoord, John, iii. 337.
—— —— his wife, Margaret Morton, iii. 338.

* Name unknown.

* Name unknown.

* Name unknown.

* Name unknown.

* Name unknown.

* Name unknown.

* Name unknown.

* Name unknown.

* Name unknown.

Damer, John, eldest son of Joseph, lord
Milton, i. 386; ix. 25 *bis*.
—— —— his wife, Anne Seymour Conway, i.
386.
Dana, Edward, in holy orders, v. 212.
—— —— his wife, Helen Kinnaird, v. 212.
Danby, Thomas (Osborne), 1st earl of, iii.
301.
Daniel, Elizabeth, wife of 3rd lord Cramond,
ii. 583.
—— James, Norwich, ii. 583.
Danielston of Danielston, Elizabeth, wife of
Sir R. Maxwell of Calderwood, iv. 230 *n*.
—— —— Sir John, viii. 522.
—— —— his wife, * Fleming, viii. 522.
—— —— Margaret, wife of Sir Wm. Cun-
ningham of Kilmaurs, iv. 229 *n*., 230.
—— —— Sir Robert, iv. 230.
—— of Inchcailloch, Sir John, viii. 523.
—— of Kilmaronock, Sir John, viii. 523.
—— Hew, vii. 35.
—— Robert, conservator of the privileges,
Middleburg, iii. 575; iv. 430.
—— Walter de, bishop of St. Andrews, v.
392.
D'Arces, Antoine, chevalier de la Bastie, ii.
6; iv. 356 *bis*.
D'Arcy, Caroline, wife of 4th marquess of
Lothian, v. 481.
Darcy, Katherine, wife of Gervase, lord
Clifton, i. 49.
Darell, Edward Tierney Gilchrist, v. 238.
—— Florence Mary, wife of 13th earl of
Kinnoull, v. 238.
Darlington, Henry (Vane), 1st earl of, iv.
494.
—— Katharine, illeg. dau. of King James
VII.; baroness of, i. 35.
DARNLEY, STEWART, LORD, v. 348-361.
Darnley, John, first lord, ii. 288; v. 348, 430.
—— —— his wife, Margaret Montgomerie,
v. 349.
—— Henry, eldest son of Matthew, 4th earl
of Lennox; styled lord, i. 22, 26, 155, 192;
ii. 459; iv. 157; v. 352, 354, 440; viii. 490.
—— —— his wife, Mary, Queen of Scots, i. 25;
v. 354.
DARNLEY, STEWART, LORD, ii. 168.
Darnley, Francis, second lord, ii. 170.
—— —— his wife, Margaret Douglas, ii. 170.
—— John, prior of Coldingham, first lord, i.
24; ii. 168.
—— —— his wife, Jean Hepburn, ii. 160, 169;
ix. 41 *bis*.
DARNLEY, STEWART, LORD, v. 355.
Darnley, Robert, lord, v. 355.
DARNLEY, STEWART, EARL OF, v. 356-362.
Darnley, Esmé, first earl of, v. 356.
DARNLEY, LENNOX, EARL OF, v. 363-371.
Darnley, Charles, illeg. son of King Charles
II.; earl of, i. 32; v. 363-371.
                    * Name unknown.

Darnley, John (Bligh), 1st earl of, v. 359.
—— —— his wife, Theodosia, baroness Clif-
ton, v. 359.
—— John (Bligh), 3rd earl of, iv. 170.
—— James, vii. 93 *n*.
—— Katharine, wife of (1) 3rd earl of Angle-
sey, and (2) 1st duke of Buckingham and
Normanby, i. 35; vii. 93 *n*.
Darroch, John, minister of Craignish, ix.
45.
—— —— his wife, Elizabeth Campbell, ix.
45.
Dashwood of Kirtlington, Sir James, 2nd
bart., i. 492; iv. 167.
—— Anne, wife of 7th earl of Galloway, iv.
167.
—— Anne Amelia, wife of (1) Charles
Murray, and (2) Geo. Warde, i. 492.
—— Charlotte Sophia, wife of (1) Charles
Andrew Bruce, and (2) Jas. Alexander, iii.
492.
—— Francis, v. 318.
—— —— his wife, Isabel Anne Maitland, v.
318.
—— George Astley Charles, vi. 271.
—— —— his wife, Harriet Anne Bateman-
Hanbury, vi. 271.
—— Thomas, H.E.I.C.S., i. 492; iii. 492.
D'AUBIGNY, STEWART, LORD, v. 356-362.
D'Aubigny, Esmé, first lord, v. 356.
Davenport of Ballynacourty, Thomas E., iii.
390.
—— Martha Frances Vincent, wife of col.
Alex. H. Murray, iii. 390.
David I., King of Scots, i. 2, 3; iii. 244; iv.
2 *n*., 3 *bis*.; viii. 240.
—— —— his wife, Matilda of Huntingdon,
i. 3.
David II., King of Scots, i. 8; iii. 145; iv.
398; vii. 238.
—— —— his 1st wife, Joan Plantagenet, i. 9;
iii. 145; iv. 141; ix. 1.
—— —— his 2nd wife, Margaret Drummond,
i. 9; ii. 262, 445; vi. 348; vii. 32.
—— earl of Huntingdon, i. 4.
—— —— his wife, Maud of Chester, i. 4.
—— son of David, earl of Huntingdon, i. 4 *n*.
—— younger son of King Alexander III., i. 6.
—— son of Morgund, 2nd earl of Mar, v.
570.
—— of Haliburton, son of Truite, iv. 330, 331.
—— of Inchesyreth, iii. 558.
—— Michael, possessor of the bell of St.
Medan, i. 113.
Davidson of Hedderwick, Thomas, ii. 110.
—— —— his wife, Isobel Borthwick, ii. 110.
—— of Marchcleuch, Robert, ii. 107.
—— —— his wife, Elizabeth Borthwick, ii.
107.
—— of Midmar, James, viii. 132.
—— —— Margaret, wife of James Dalrymple-
Elphinstone, viii. 132.

* Name unknown.   * Name unknown.

* Name unknown.

* Name unknown.

* Name unknown.

* Name unknown.

* Name unknown.

* Name unknown.

* Name unknown.

* Name unknown.

* Name unknown.

* Name unknown.

* Name unknown.   * Name unknown.

* Name unknown.

* Name unknown.

* Name unknown.

* Name unknown.

* Name unknown.

* Name unknown.

* Name unknown.

* Name unknown.

* Name unknown.

* Name unknown.

* Name unknown.

* Name unknown.

GREENWICH, CAMPBELL, BARONESS OF, i. 377.

Greenwich, Caroline, wife of (1) Francis, earl of Dalkeith, and (2) George, 1st marquess of Townshend; baroness of, i. 377; ii. 242.

GREENWICH, CAMPBELL, EARL OF, i. 371.

Greenwich, John, earl of, i. 370.

GREENWICH, CAMPBELL, DUKE OF, i. 374.

Greenwich, John, duke of, i. 370.

Gregory, bishop of Brechin, vii. 398.

— of Frendraught, John, minister of Drumoak, iv. 128, 130.

— Alexander, iv. 128.

— John, M.D., F.R.S., professor at Edinburgh, iv. 64.

— — his wife, Elizabeth Forbes, iv. 64.

Greig, Agnes, wife of 8th lord Rollo, vii. 208.

— William, Gayfield Place, Edinburgh, vii. 208.

Grelod or Grelauga, wife of Thorfinn Skull-splitter, ii. 314.

Gremislaw of Gremislaw, Christian de, wife of Sir John de Crichton, iii. 57, 60, 62.

Grenolias de Cournou, Louis, vi. 560.

— — his wife, Marie Jeanne Oliphant, vi. 560.

GRENVILLE, BARON KINLOSS, v. 199-201.

Grenville, Anne, wife of lt.-col. G. R. Hardaway, v. 200.

— Anne Eliza Mary, wife of W. H. P. Gore-Langton, v. 200.

— Caroline Jemima Elizabeth, dau. of 3rd duke of Buckingham and Chandos, v. 200.

Greswolde of Solihull, Marshall, in holy orders, iii. 411.

— — Mary, wife of David Lewis of Malvern Hall, iii. 411, 412.

Greville, Algernon William (Greville), 2nd baron, v. 238; vi. 273.

— — his wife, Beatrice Violet Graham, vi. 273.

— of Milcote, Sir Edward, v. 11.

— Algernon Frederick, Bath King of Arms, v. 369.

— Camilla Dagmar Violet, wife of capt. A. G. Hay, v. 238.

— Charles, viii. 362.

— Charlotte Mary, wife of 7th earl of Galloway, iv. 167.

— Frances Harriett, wife of 6th duke of Lennox, v. 369.

— Georgina, wife of Sir Geo. Cathcart, ii. 527.

— Harriet Katharine, wife of 1st earl of Ellesmere, viii. 362.

— Mary, wife of Sir Arthur Ingram, v. 11.

— Robert Fulke, ii. 524.

— — his wife, Louisa Cathcart, countess of Mansfield, ii. 523; viii. 206, 209.

Grey, Annabella, wife of Alexander, baron Hume of Berwick; countess de, vi. 23.

Grey, Jemima, wife of 2nd earl of Hardwicke; marchioness de, ii. 208; vi. 23.

— Thomas Philip (de Grey), earl de, iii. 124.

Grey of Groby, George Harry (Grey), lord, viii. 515.

— — his wife, Katharine Charteris, viii. 515.

Grey de Ruthyn, Barbara (Yelverton), wife of (1) 7th earl of Loudoun, and (2) Sir Hastings R. Yelverton; baroness, v. 514.

— Bertha Lelgarde (Hastings), wife of Augustus W. Clifton; baroness, v. 514.

Grey of Wilton, William (Grey), 14th lord, viii. 436.

Grey of Backworth, John, colonel, viii. 87.

— of Barnfield, Robert T. Moring, viii. 232.

— of Ballincor, James, iii. 415.

— of Lehena, Francis, iii. 415, 418.

— Amabel, wife of 3rd earl of Breadalbane, ii. 208.

— Caroline Eliza Moring, wife of rev. A. Drummond, viii. 232.

— Charles C., captain R.N., iv. 483.

— Diana, wife of Robert, 2nd earl of Elgin, iii. 478.

— Diana, wife of George Middleton of Seaton, vi. 178.

— Elizabeth Susan, wife of capt. John Renny-Strachan-Carnegie, viii. 87.

— John de, bishop of Norwich, iv. 140.

— Katharine Rebecca, wife of William, lord Huntingtower, iii. 415.

— Maria, wife of 12th earl of Home, iv. 483.

— Sir Robert de, ii. 396.

— Sarah, wife of F. T. Tollemache, iii. 415.

— William Booth, viii. 38.

— — his wife, Frances Somerville, viii. 38.

Grey-Egerton of Oulton Park, Sir Philip de Malpas, 10th bart., vii. 525.

— Cecely Louisa, wife of 6th earl of Selkirk, vii. 524.

'Greysteel,' Archibald Douglas of Kilspindie, called, i. 185.

— Alexander Seton, 6th earl of Eglinton, called, iii. 445.

Greystock, Ralph, 5th baron of, iii. 271.

Grier of Lag, see Grierson of Lag.

— Elizabeth, wife of Robt. Fergusson, ii. 410.

— Jean, dau. of Sir Wm. G. of Lag, iv. 587.

— Janet, wife of William King of Barra and Bourtie, iii. 589.

— Margaret, wife of Sir Jas. Carmichael of Bonnytoun, iv. 587.

Grierson of Bardannoch, William, lieut.-col., ii. 279.

— of Bargatton, John, v. 261.

— — his wife, Agnes Gordon, v. 261.

Haggerston of Haggerston, Sir Carnaby 3rd bart., iv. 418.
—— —— his wife, Elizabeth Middelton, iv. 418.
—— William, 2nd son of Sir Thomas H., iv. 418.
—— —— his wife, Anne Constable, iv. 418.
Haggerston-Constable of Everingham, William, iv. 418.
—— —— his wife, Winifred Maxwell of Terregles, iv. 418; vi. 490.
Haig of Bemersyde, James, 12th laird, ii. 228.
—— —— his wife, Margaret Scott, ii. 228.
—— —— John, 8th laird, v. 286.
—— —— his wife, Mary Maitland, v. 286.
—— —— Petrus de Haga or, 2nd laird, vii. 577.
—— —— his wife, Ada St. Clair, vii. 577.
—— —— William, 13th laird, iv. 469.
—— —— his wife, Isobel Home, iv. 469.
—— —— William, king's solicitor, 19th laird, i. 563.
—— —— Zerubbabel, 22nd laird, iv. 479.
—— Elizabeth or Janet, wife of James Home of Ayton, iv. 479.
HAILES, HEPBURN, LORD, ii. 135-167.
Hailes, Patrick, first lord, ii. 141.
—— —— his wife, Elyne Wallace, ii. 142.
—— Patrick, second lord, ii. 149, 151; iv. 452.
—— —— his 1st wife, Janet Douglas, ii. 152.
—— —— his 2nd wife, Margaret Gordon, ii. 152.
—— master of, Adam, eldest son of 1st lord Hailes, ii. 142, 148; iv. 448.
—— —— his wife, Elyne Home, ii. 148; iv. 447, 448; v. 608.
—— master of, Patrick, 2nd son of 1st earl of Bothwell; styled, ii. 153.
—— —— his 1st wife, Nicolas Home, ii. 153.
—— —— his 2nd wife, Katharine Fleming, ii. 153.
—— Sir David Dalrymple, senator of the College of Justice, lord, iv. 321.
Haines, Elizabeth, wife of rev. W. H. Aston, i. 404.
—— Nathan, D.D., i. 404.
Haining, Margaret Wallace, wife of * Ross; styled lady, v. 163; vi. 514.
Haitlie of Mellerstain, Henry, vi. 1.
—— —— his wife, Sibilla Home, vi. 1.
—— —— Henry, iv. 471 bis.
—— —— his contr. wife, Margaret Home, iv. 471.
—— —— his wife, Helen Edmestoun, iv. 471.
—— —— John, iv. 471.
—— —— John, son of Henry H., ix. 108.
—— Alexander, illeg. son of John H. of Mellerstain, iv. 471.
Halcro of Halcro, Harry or Hugh, vi. 574.
—— —— his wife, Barbara Stewart, vi. 574.
* Name unknown.

Halcro of Halcro, Hugh, i. 397.
—— —— his wife, Jean Stewart, i. 397.
Haldane of Ardonnen, James, v. 504.
—— of Gleneagles, George, iv. 243.
—— —— his wife, Jean Cunningham, iv. 243.
—— —— George, né Cockburn, viii. 233.
—— —— his wife, Margaret Drummond, viii. 233; ix. 162.
—— —— James, vi. 223.
—— —— his contr. wife, Katharine Campbell, ix. 19.
—— —— his wife, Christian Graham, vi. 223.
—— —— James, v. 609.
—— —— his wife, Margaret Erskine, v. 609.
—— —— James, i. 470, 514; iv. 115; v. 504.
—— —— his wife, Margaret Murray, i. 470.
—— —— Sir James, v. 532.
—— —— his wife, Margaret Fraser, v. 532.
—— —— John, v. 341; vi. 407.
—— —— his wife, Agnes Menteith, vi. 407.
—— —— [John], his wife, Marjory Lawson, ii. 99 n.
—— —— John, ii. 572.
—— —— Sir John, viii. 499.
—— —— his wife, Katharine Wemyss, viii. 499.
—— —— John, viii. 219.
—— —— his 1st wife, Mary Drummond, viii. 219.
—— —— Patrick, advocate, iv. 95; v. 312.
—— —— his wife, Margaret Forrester, iv. 95.
—— of Haldane, William, vii. 329.
—— Anna, wife of Andrew, 2nd lord Fraser, iv. 115 bis.
—— Beatrice, wife of R. Colville of Cleish, ii. 572.
—— George, governor of Jamaica, iv. 95.
—— Helen, wife of Sir D. Lindsay of Edzell, i. 514.
—— *, 2nd wife of Charles Barclay-Maitland of Towie, v. 312.
Hale of King's Walden, William, i. 62.
—— Mary, wife of col. Plumer of Blakesware, i. 62.
—— *, sergeant, viii. 460.
—— —— his wife, Dorothy Hayhurst, viii. 460.
Hales, Maria de, dau. of Kylvert, vii. 419.
HALIBURTON OF DIRLETON, HALIBURTON, LORD, iv. 330-338.
Haliburton of Dirleton, George, third lord, iii. 307; iv. 273, 336.
—— —— his wife, Mariota, iv. 336.
—— —— James, fourth lord, iv. 337.
—— —— Janet, wife of William, 2nd lord Ruthven; baroness, iv. 337.
—— —— John, first lord, iv. 335, 446.
—— —— his wife, Janet Seton, iv. 335; viii. 575.
* Name unknown.

Hamilton, William, third duke of, i. 205, 480; iii. 347; iv. 381; vii. 139.
—— —— his wife, Anne, *suo jure* duchess of Hamilton, iv. 381.
—— William Alexander Anthony Archibald, eleventh duke of, iv. 395; ix. 105.
—— —— his wife, princess Mary of Baden, iv. 396.
—— William Alexander Louis Stephen, twelfth duke of, iv. 396.
—— —— his wife, Mary Montagu, iv. 396.
Hamilton of Dalzell, John Glencairn Carter, first lord, vi. 120.
—— —— his wife, Emily Eleanor Leslie-Melville, vi. 120.
HAMILTON OF HAMELDON, HAMILTON, BARON, iv. 394.
Hamilton of Hameldon, Douglas, baron, i. 387, 388; iv. 393.
HAMILTON OF HAMILTON, HAMILTON, VISCOUNT, i. 65-74.
Hamilton of Hamilton, James, 8th earl of Abercorn, first viscount, i. 65.
—— —— James, eldest son of 1st marquess of Abercorn; styled viscount, i. 66.
—— —— his wife, Harriet Douglas, i. 67; vi. 383.
—— —— James, third viscount, i. 68.
—— —— John James, second viscount, i. 66.
Hamilton of Stackallan, Gustavus, 1st baron, i. 45.
—— —— his wife, Elizabeth Brooke, i. 45.
HAMILTON, BARON OF STRABANE, HAMILTON, LORD, i. 48-74.
Hamilton, James, first lord, i. 48.
HAMILTON OF STRABANE, HAMILTON, MARQUESS OF, i. 69.
Hamilton, James, first marquess of, i. 69.
—— James, second marquess of, i. 72.
—— James Albert Edward, eldest son of 2nd duke of Abercorn; styled marquess of, i. 72.
—— —— his wife, Rosaline Cecilia Caroline Bingham, i. 73.
HAMILTON OF WISHAW, HAMILTON, BARON, ii. 54.
Hamilton of Wishaw, Robert Montgomerie, first baron, ii. 54.
—— —— his wife, Hamilton Campbell, ii. 54.
HAMILTON OF HAMELDON, CAMPBELL, BARON, i. 387-393.
Hamilton of Hameldon, George William, first baron, i. 388.
HAMILTON OF HAMELDON, GUNNING, BARONESS, i. 387.
Hamilton of Hameldon, Elizabeth, wife of (1) James, 6th duke of Hamilton and Brandon, and (2) John, 5th duke of Argyll; baroness, i. 387.
HAMILTON, LORD OF ABERCORN, i. 46.
HAMILTON, EARL OF ABERCORN, i. 37-74.

HAMILTON, MARQUESS OF ABERCORN, i. 66-74.
HAMILTON, DUKE OF ABERCORN, i. 69-74.
HAMILTON, EARL OF ARRAN, iv. 355-377.
HAMILTON, EARL OF ARRAN AND CAMBRIDGE, iv. 377-383.
HAMILTON, EARL OF ARRAN, LANARK, AND CAMBRIDGE, iv. 383-397.
HAMILTON, EARL OF ANGUS, iv. 393-397.
HAMILTON, LORD AVON AND INNERDALE, iv. 377-397.
HAMILTON, LORD AVEN, POLMONT, MACHANSHYRE, AND INNERDALE, iv. 383-397.
HAMILTON, LORD BARGANY, ii. 27-33.
HAMILTON, LORD BELHAVEN, ii. 38-60.
HAMILTON, LORD BINNING, iv. 310-329.
HAMILTON, DUKE OF BRANDON, iv. 384-397.
HAMILTON, LORD BYRES AND BINNING, iv. 310.
HAMILTON, EARL OF CAMBRIDGE, iv. 374.
HAMILTON, DUKE OF CHATELHERAULT, iv. 367.
HAMILTON, MARQUESS OF CLYDESDALE, iv. 377-397.
HAMILTON, LORD DAER, vii. 516-525.
HAMILTON, BARON DECHMONT, vi. 573-584.
HAMILTON, MARQUESS OF DOUGLAS, iv. 396.
HAMILTON, BARON DUTTON, iv. 384-397.
HAMILTON, LORD EVAN, iv. 372-397.
HAMILTON, BARON OF HAMILTON, i. 46.
HAMILTON, LORD HAMILTON, iv. 349-397.
HAMILTON, VISCOUNT HAMILTON OF HAMILTON, i. 65-74.
HAMILTON, MARQUESS OF HAMILTON, iv. 372-380.
HAMILTON, DUKE OF HAMILTON, iv. 339-381.
HAMILTON, BARON HAMILTON OF HAMELDON, iv. 394.
HAMILTON, LORD HAMILTON, BARON OF STRABANE, i. 48-74.
HAMILTON, MARQUESS OF HAMILTON OF STRABANE, i. 69-74.
HAMILTON, BARON HAMILTON OF WISHAW, ii. 54.
HAMILTON, EARL OF HADDINGTON, iv. 303-329.
HAMILTON, LORD HILLHOUSE, vii. 361-363.
HAMILTON, LORD INNERDALE, iv. 374-381.
HAMILTON, BARON OF KILPATRICK, i. 46.
HAMILTON, VISCOUNT OF KIRKWALL, vi. 578-584.
HAMILTON, EARL OF LANARK, iv. 378-380.
HAMILTON, LORD MACHANESCHYRE, iv. 378-380.
HAMILTON, EARL OF MELROSE, iv. 310-311.
HAMILTON, LORD MELROS OF TYNNINGHAM, iv. 325-326.
HAMILTON, BARON OF MOUNTCASTELL, i. 46.
HAMILTON, BARON OF MOUNTCASTLE, i. 58-74.

* Name unknown.

* Name unknown.

* Name unknown.

* Name unknown.

* Name unknown.

* Name unknown.

* Name unknown.

* Name unknown.

* Name unknown.

*̤ Name unknown.

          * Name unknown.

* Name unknown.

* Name unknown.

* Name unknown.

* Name unknown.

* Name unknown.

* Name unknown.

* Name unknown.

* Name unknown.

* Name unknown.

Livingston(e of Dunipace, Alexander, v. 435; ix. 128.
—— his wife, Alison Gourlay, ix. 129.
—— Alexander, ii. 149; v. 437, 439; vi. 446, 447; ix. 129.
—— his wife, Elizabeth Hepburn, ii. 149; ix. 129.
—— John, iii. 534.
—— his wife, Margaret Elphinstone, iii. 534.
—— John, i. 298.
— of Dunloppie, Alan, viii. 372.
— of Edingham, Alexander, v. 492.
— of Falkirk, Henry, vi. 446.
—— his 2nd wife, Margaret Forrester, vi. 448.
—— James, v. 431.
— of Fennochthaucht and Middilthrid, William, v. 188.
— of Fildes, Alexander, v. 429; vi. 404; ix. 128.
—— Alexander, ix. 129.
— of Gairdoch, George, vi. 519.
—— William, vi. 518.
— of Gartsherrie, Sir William, iv. 471.
— of Over Garwalis, William, v. 187 n., 188.
— of Glassinwell, Edward, v. 185.
—— William, v. 185.
— of Glen, James, v. 431.
— of Glentirran, Sir Alexander, 1st bart., ii. 102, 363.
—— his wife, Mary Borthwick, ii. 102.
— of Gilmerton, James, viii. 370.
— of Gorgie, William, v. 422; viii. 368, 563.
—— Sir William, sheriff of Haddington, v. 423.
— of Graden, William, v. 184.
— of Haining, John, ix. 145.
—— his wife, * Stewart, ix. 145.
—— Thomas, 3rd son of 5th lord Livingston, v. 436, 437; vi. 446.
—— his 1st wife, Agnes Crawfurd of Haining, v. 437.
—— his 2nd wife, Elizabeth Forrester, v. 437.
—— Thomas, iii. 534.
—— his wife, Janet Henderson, iii. 534.
— of Inches, Alexander, v. 186 n.
—— James, v. 187 n.
— of Inchmawchane, Alexander, v. 185.
— of Jaw, James, v. 431.
— of Jerviswood, Hugh, viii. 372.
—— his wife, Bessie Wilkie, viii. 372.
—— James, 1st laird, viii. 370.
—— James, 2nd laird, viii. 370.
—— his 1st wife, * Lockhart, viii. 371.
—— his 2nd wife, * Hamilton, viii. 371.
—— James, 3rd laird, viii. 371.
—— his wife, Isobel Cunningham, viii. 371.

* Name unknown.

Livingston(e of Jerviswood, James, 4th laird, viii. 372.
—— his 1st wife, Grizel Carmichael, viii. 372.
—— his 2nd wife, Marion Baillie, viii. 372; ix. 163.
—— his 3rd wife, Agnes or Jean Somerville, viii. 372; ix. 163.
—— William, viii. 371.
—— his 1st wife, Janet Baird, viii. 371.
—— his 2nd wife, Janet Johnstone, i. 246; viii. 371.
—— William, vii. 133; viii. 372, 373.
—— his wife, Janet Douglas, vii. 133; viii. 373.
—— William, son of Hugh L., viii. 372.
—— his wife, Bethia Livingston, viii. 373.
— of West Kerse, William, v. 191.
— of Kilhill, James, vi. 175.
— of Kilsyth, Edward, 2nd laird, v. 185.
—— Sir James, 9th laird, v. 190, 191.
—— his wife, Euphame Cunningham, v. 192.
—— Sir William, ancestor of the family of, v. 183.
—— his wife, Christian of Callendar, v. 183, 424.
—— William, 1st laird, v. 184, 426.
—— his wife, Elizabeth Caldcotes, v. 184.
—— Sir William, 3rd laird, v. 185, 435.
—— his wife, Elizabeth Graham, v. 186; vi. 222.
—— William, 4th laird, v. 186, 187, 435.
—— his wife, Jonet Bruce, v. 187.
—— Sir William, 5th laird, iv. 470; v. 188; ix. 120 bis.
—— his wife, Christian Graham, v. 189; vi. 159.
—— Sir William, 6th laird, v. 189.
—— his 1st wife, Antoinette de Bord, v. 190.
—— his 2nd wife, Margaret Houston, v. 190.
—— William, 7th laird, v. 190, 191.
—— his wife, Margaret Ramsay, iii. 98; v. 191.
—— William, 8th laird, v. 191.
— of Kinnaird, Sir James, vi. 452.
—— his 1st wife, Katharine Howard, vi. 453.
—— his 2nd wife, Anne Poole, vi. 453.
—— Sir John, v. 205; vi. 446, 451.
—— his wife, Jane Sproxtoune, vi. 451.
—— Robert, alleged ancestor of the family of, v. 426; vi. 446.
— of Kippen, Sir Alexander, v. 429.
— of Kirkland, John, viii. 373.
— of Kittomure, Alexander, v. 492.
— of Lenturk, James, v. 429.
— of Lethbert, James, v. 431.

* Name unknown.

* Name unknown.]

* Name unknown.

* Name unknown.

* Name unknown.

* Name unknown.

* Name unknown.

* Name unknown.

* Name unknown.

* Name unknown.

Menteith of Pirehock, Christian, wife of (1) Sir Edward Keith of Sinton, and (2) Sir Robert Erskine of that Ilk, ii. 224 ; v. 580, 595, 599 ; vi. 33, 132.

— of Randyford, William, ii. 552.

— — his wife, Margaret Colville, ii. 552.

— of Roseneath, Alexander, vii. 34, 35.

— of Rusky, Agnes, wife of John Haldane of Gleneagles, v. 341 ; vi. 407.

— — Elizabeth, wife of John Napier of Merchiston, i. 335 ; v. 341 ; vi. 407, 408.

— — Sir John, 2nd son of Walter Stewart, earl of Menteith, i. 12 ; iii. 263 ; v. 335, 580, 581 ; vi. 132, 137.

— — Sir John, vi. 132.

— — his wife, Ellen of Mar, v. 579 ; vi. 132.

— — Sir John, vi. 132.

— — his wife, Katharine *, vi. 132.

— — Sir Murdac, i. 458 ; vi. 407.

— — his wife, Christian Murray, i. 458.

— — Patrick, vi. 407.

— — Robert, v. 341.

— — his wife, Margaret of Lennox, v. 341 ; vi. 407.

— — Walter, ancestor of the family of, vi. 132, 137.

— — Walter, his son, v. 595.

— of Strathgartney, Sir John, v. 579, 593.

— Alexander de, 4th son of Alexander, earl of Menteith, iv. 272 ; vi. 134 ; vii. 401.

— Alexander, vii. 217.

— — his wife, Agnes Primrose, vii. 217.

— Anna, wife of Sir Andrew Murray of Murrayshall, viii. 201.

— James, provost of Stirling, vi. 410.

— — his wife, Isabella Napier, vi. 410.

— Jean, wife of R. Graham of M'Keanston, vi. 155.

— John, sheriff of Clackmannan, i. 454 ; iii. 467 ; vii. 34.

— Jonet, wife of William Maitland of Lethington, v. 295.

— Katharine, wife of R. Graham in Shannochill, vi. 155.

— Katharine, wife of (1) Sir A. Murray of Balvaird, and (2) Sir G. Auchinleck of Balmanno, viii. 191.

— Margaret, wife of Sir Roger de Mortimer, iv. 272.

— Margaret, wife of Henry Graham, vi. 153.

— Maurice, *circa* 1293, 1309, vi. 134 *n.*

— Peter, 2nd son of Alexander, earl of Menteith, vi. 134.

— Robert, warden clerk of the Middle Marches, vii. 340.

— Sarah, wife of 1st lord Balmerinoch, i. 562 ; ix. 33.

— Walter, son of Walter M. of Kerse, v. 595.

* Name unknown.

Menteith, *, wife of Sir John Livingston of Callendar, v. 426.

— *, wife of Maurice Buchanan of Buchanan, vi. 133 *n.*

— *, alleged 1st wife of Archibald Campbell of Lochow, i. 327 ; vi. 133 *n.*

MENTMORE OF MENTMORE, PRIMROSE, VISCOUNT, ix. 152.

Mentmore of Mentmore, Archibald Philip, first viscount, ix. 152.

Menzies of Auldquhat, Gilbert. ix. 13.

— — his wife, Jean Menzies, ix. 13.

— of Balgownie, Francis, vi. 554.

— — his wife, Margaret Oliphant, vi. 554.

— of Boltoquhane, Adam, i. 512.

— — his wife, Margaret Lindsay, i. 512.

— of Carse, William, ii. 200.

— of Castlehill, Edward, ix. 150.

— — John, vii. 133.

— — his wife, Helen Douglas, vii. 133.

— of Chesthill, John Stewart, vii. 451.

— — his wife, Katharine Thurlow Fraser, vii. 451.

— of Comrie, James, tutor of Menzies, i. 360.

— — his wife, Anna Campbell, i. 360.

— of Culdares, James, 1st laird, v. 59.

— — his wife, Margaret Ker, v. 59.

— — James, col., ii. 191.

— of Culterallers, Alexander, iv. 591.

— of Dumblait, Patrick, vii. 411.

— of Durne, Thomas, provost of Aberdeen, ii. 13.

— — his wife, Margaret Ogilvy, ii. 5.

— — Thomas, ii. 5, 13.

— — his wife, Elizabeth Ogilvy, ii. 13.

— of Ferryhill, Patrick, vii. 411.

— of Findon, Gilbert, vii. 433.

— — Gilbert, provost of Aberdeen, vii. 437 *bis.*

— of Hangingshaw, John, ii. 390.

— of Kinmundy, Sir Paul, ii. 5.

— of Lashgoune, James, iv. 70.

— — his wife, * Forbes, iv. 70.

— of Menzies, Alexander de, i. 14.

— — his wife, Egidia Stewart, i. 14.

— — Alexander, ii. 185, 189 ; ix. 155.

— — his 1st wife, Margaret Campbell, ii. 187.

— — James, i. 444 ; v. 500.

— — his wife, Barbara Stewart, i. 444.

— — Sir John, v. 500.

— — Sir John, 4th bart., i. 497.

— — his wife, Charlotte Murray, i. 497.

— — Sir Neil, 6th bart., iii. 391.

— — Sir Robert, ii. 179.

— — Sir Robert, i. 337 ; iv. 533 ; v. 502.

— — his 1st wife, Christian Gordon, iv. 533 ; ix. 110.

— — his 2nd wife, Marion Campbell, i. 337.

* Name unknown.

Montgomerie, Montgomery, John, *perhaps* ancestor of the comtes de Montgomery, iii. 430.
—— John, nephew of Hugh, 2nd earl of Eglinton, iii. 436.
—— John, elder son of Sir Neil M. of Lainshaw, iii. 436.
—— —— his wife, Margaret Boyd, iii. 436; v. 155.
—— John, M.P., lieut.-col., governor of New York, iii. 452, 455; ix. 81.
—— —— his wife, Mary Carmichael, iii. 452.
—— John, major, 3rd son of 8th earl of Eglinton, iii. 454.
—— —— his wife, Jean Gibson, iii. 454.
—— Jonet, wife of Geo. Campbell of Cessnock, iii. 438.
—— Jonet, illeg. dau. of 1st earl of Eglinton, iii. 438.
—— Katharine, wife of George Montgomerie of Skelmorlie, iii. 438.
—— Katharine, illeg. dau. of col. Sir Alex. M., iii. 447.
—— Katharine, dau. of Hugh M. of Coilsfield, iii. 448.
—— Katharine, dau. of Alex. M. of Coilsfield, iii. 449.
—— Katharine, wife of 5th earl of Galloway, iii. 456; iv. 164.
—— Lilias, wife of John Hamilton of Sundrum, iii. 449.
—— Lilias, wife of (1) R. D. Macqueen, and (2) R. A. Oswald, iii. 462.
—— Margaret, wife of John Hamilton of Bargany, ii. 31; iii. 450; viii. 131.
—— Margaret, wife of (1) John, 1st earl of Tweeddale, and (2) William, 8th earl of Glencairn, iii. 450; iv. 248; viii. 449; ix. 98.
—— Margaret, wife of Sir Archibald Mure of Rowallan, iii. 425.
—— Margaret, wife of Alexander, 1st lord Home, iii. 433; iv. 451 *bis*.
—— Margaret, wife of John Stewart, lord Darnley, earl of Lennox, iii. 433; v. 348, 349.
—— Margaret, wife of William, 2nd lord Sempill, iii. 437; vii. 536.
—— Margaret, wife of Hugh Montgomerie of Stane, iii. 440.
—— Margaret, wife of Robert, 1st earl of Winton, iii. 442, 450; viii. 591; ix. 80.
—— Margaret, wife of (1) Hugh, 5th earl of Eglinton, and (2) Robert, 7th lord Boyd, iii. 444; v. 170; ix. 81.
—— Margaret, wife of John Chalmers of Gadgirth, iii. 447.
—— Margaret, wife of John Hamilton, Jamaica, iii. 448.
—— Margaret, wife of 2nd earl of Loudoun, iii. 452; v. 507; ix. 131.

Montgomerie, Montgomery, Margaret, dau. of 8th earl of Eglinton, iii. 454; ix. 81.
—— Margaret, wife of Sir Alexander Macdonald of Macdonald, iii. 457; ix. 81.
—— Margaret, wife of Robert Boyle of Figgidoch, iv. 188.
—— Margaret, alleged wife of Sir Archibald Hamilton of Innerwick, iv. 304.
—— Marjory, wife of William, master of Somerville, iii. 433; viii. 12.
—— Mary, wife of D. Kennedy of Kirkmichael, iii. 447.
—— Mary, wife of William Hamilton of Letham, iii. 448.
—— Mary, wife of Sir James Agnew, iii. 454.
—— Mary, wife of Sir David Cunningham of Milncraig, iii. 457.
—— Mary, dau. of Francis M. of Giffen, iii. 452.
—— Mary, wife of George, 4th earl of Winton, iii. 452; viii. 602.
—— Mary, wife of 1st lord Kirkcudbright, v. 267.
—— Matilda, wife of Colin Campbell of Ardkinglas, iii. 437.
—— Michael, legtd. son of Robert, bishop of Argyll, iii. 437.
—— Murthauch de, Homage Roll, iii. 425.
—— Nigel, *alias* Sir Neil M. of Lainshaw, iii. 436; iv. 191.
—— Philip de, son of Roger, earl of Shrewsbury, iii. 421.
—— Robert, archbishop of Glasgow, ii. 80.
—— Robert de, Normandy, iii. 421.
—— Robert, son of Roger, earl of Shrewsbury, iii. 421.
—— Robert, first to settle in Scotland, iii. 422.
—— Sir Robert, eldest son of Alan M., iii. 424, 425.
—— Robert, rector of Kirkmichael, bishop of Argyll, iii. 437; ix. 80.
—— Robert, legtd. son of Robert, bishop of Argyll, iii. 437.
—— Robert, major-general, gentleman of the bed-chamber to king Charles ii., iii. 450, 453; v. 228 *n.*
—— —— his wife, Elizabeth Livingstone, iii. 450; v. 192.
—— Robert, in Haltoun, ix. 8.
—— —— his wife, Euphame Guthrie, ix. 8.
—— Roger de, c. 1050; iii. 421.
—— Roger de, governor of Normandy, earl of Shrewsbury, iii. 421.
—— Roger de, son of Roger, earl of Shrewsbury, iii. 421.
—— Roger, lieut. R.N., 2nd son of 12th earl of Eglinton, iii. 462.
—— Seton Montolieu, lieut. Scots Fusilier Guards, iii. 463.
—— —— his wife, Nina Janet Williams, iii. 463.

Mora of Dalry, William de, v. 138.
Morant of Brockenhurst, John, iii. 584.
Moravia, *see* Moray.
MORAY, THE ANCIENT LORDS *or* EARLS OF,
  vi. 280-285.
Moray, Angus, earl of, vi. 285.
— Ed *or* Eth, earl of, iv. 2 *n.* ; vi. 284.
— — his wife, *, vi. 284.
— Finlay, earl of, vi. 281.
— — his wife, Donada, vi. 281.
— Gillecomgan, earl of, vi. 282.
— — his wife, Gruoch, vi. 282.
— Lulach, earl of, vi. 282, 283.
— Macbeth, earl of, iii. 240; iv. 1 ; vi. 282.
— — his wife, Gruoch, vi. 282, 283.
— Maelbrighde Mac Ruaidhri, earl of, vi.
  281, 282.
— Malcolm, earl of, vi. 282.
— Melsnechtai, earl of, vi. 284.
— Ruadri, earl of, vi. 281 *n.*
— Sigurd Eysteinsson, earl of, vi. 280.
— Thorfinn Sigurdsson, earl of, vi. 280,
  282.
— William Fitz Duncan, earl of, i. 3; iii.
  245.
MORAY, RANDOLPH, EARL OF, vi. 286-295.
Moray, John, third earl of, i. 431; iii. 89, 260;
  vi. 295.
— — his wife, Euphemia Ross, i. 134, 436;
  vi. 297; vii. 236.
— Thomas, first earl of, i. 169, 215; ii. 433;
  iii. 144, 260; iv. 270; vi. 291.
— — his wife, Isobel Stewart, i. 13; vi.
  294.
— Thomas, second earl of, [v. 583 *n.*; vi.
  295.
MORAY, BEAUMONT, EARL OF, vi. 295.
Moray, Henry (de Beaumont), constable of
  Scotland; styled earl of Buchan and, vi.
  295.
MORAY, PLANTAGENET, EARL OF, iii. 150.
Moray, Henry (Plantagenet), duke of Lancaster; earl of, iii. 150, 267.
MORAY, DUNBAR, EARL OF, vi. 298-307.
Moray, Elizabeth, Mary *or* Agnes, wife of
  (1) Archibald Douglas, earl of Moray, (2)
  George, master of Huntly, and (3) Sir
  John Colquhoun of Luss; countess of, iii.
  193; iv. 527; vi. 306, 308.
— James, fourth earl of, vi. 301, 304.
— — his wife, Katharine *or* Janet Seton,
  vi. 305.
— John, first earl of, iii. 260; vi. 298.
— — his wife, Marjorie Stewart, i. 16; vi.
  298, 301.
— Patrick (4th earl of Dunbar), styled earl
  of, ii. 136; iii. 266; vi. 295, 296.
— — his wife, Agnes Randolph, vi. 294.
— Thomas, second earl of, vi. 302.
— — his wife, Margaret *, i. 113; vi.
  303.

                 * Name unknown.

Moray, Thomas, third earl of, v. 522; vi. 303;
  vii. 242.
— — his wife (?), Isobel Innes, v. 521; vi.
  304.
MORAY, DOUGLAS, EARL OF, vi. 308-310.
Moray, Archibald, earl of, iii. 62, 63, 174, 178,
  193; v. 522; vi. 308.
— — his wife, Elizabeth Dunbar, iii. 193;
  iv. 527; vi. 306, 308.
MORAY, CRICHTON, EARL OF, iii. 63; vi. 309.
Moray, James, earl of, ii. 327; iii. 63; vi.
  309.
— — his wife, Janet Dunbar of Brawl, ii.
  327; iii. 62.
MORAY, STEWART, EARL OF, vi. 311-312.
Moray, David, 3rd son of king James II.;
  earl of, i. 20; vi. 311.
— James, illeg. son of king James IV.;
  earl of, i. 22; ii. 459; iv. 366; v. 103; vi.
  311; vii. 122.
— — his wife, Elizabeth *or* Isobel Campbell, i. 338; vi. 312; ix. 155.
MORAY, STEWART, EARL OF, vi. 313-330.
Moray, Alexander, fifth earl of, vi. 322; ix.
  139 *bis.*
— — his wife, Emilia Balfour, vi. 322;
  ix. 139 *bis.*
— Archibald George, thirteenth earl of,
  vi. 329.
— Charles, sixth earl of, vi. 323.
— — his wife, Anne Campbell, i. 368; vi.
  323.
— Edmund Archibald, fifteenth earl of, vi.
  327, 329.
— — his wife, Anna Mary Collinson, vi.
  329.
— Elizabeth, wife of James Stewart;
  countess of, iii. 189; vi. 316.
— Francis, seventh earl of, vi. 323; ix. 140.
— — his 1st wife, Elizabeth Murray, vi.
  324; viii. 202; ix. 140 *bis.*
— — his 2nd wife, Jean Elphinstone, i.
  570; vi. 324; ix. 140.
— Francis, ninth earl of, iv. 293; vi. 326.
— — his wife, Jean Gray, iv. 293; vi.
  326.
— Francis, tenth earl of, iv. 293; vi. 327.
— — his 1st wife, Lucy Scott, vi. 327.
— — his 2nd wife, Margaret J. Ainslie,
  vi. 327.
— Francis, eleventh earl of, vi. 328.
— Francis James, sixteenth earl of, vi.
  329.
— — his wife, Gertrude Floyer Smith,
  vi. 329.
— George, fourteenth earl of, iv. 293; vi.
  329.
— James, legtd. son of king James V.;
  Regent of Scotland; first earl of, i. 24, 26,
  183; ii. 269; vi. 312; vii. 284; ix. 138, 139 *bis.*
— — his wife, Agnes *or* Annas Keith, vi.
  50, 316.

* Name unknown.

* Name unknown.

* Name unknown.

* Name unknown.

* Name unknown.

Nisbet of Dirleton, William, ii. 44; viii. 460.
— — his wife, Mary Hamilton of Pencaitland and Biel, ii. 44.
— of Fern, Mariota, wife of John Lockhart, v. 496.
— of Manderston, Philip, iii. 282.
— of Mauldsley, Archibald, iv. 597.
— of Nisbet, Philip, iii. 282; vii. 370.
— — his wife, Helen Rutherfurd, vii. 370.
— — Sir Philip, iv. 476.
— of Nisbetfield, John, W.S., vii. 83.
— of Restalrig, James, ii. 409.
— Agnes, wife of Sir John Dalzell, ii. 409; ix. 53.
— Agnes, wife of Walter Scott of Whitefield, vii. 83.
— Alice Anne, wife of George Ramsay Maitland, v. 315.
— Elizabeth, wife of Wm. Hamilton, ii. 55.
— Elizabeth, wife of Geo. Carlyle, ii. 391.
— George, fencing-master, iv. 35.
— — his wife, Elizabeth Ogilvy, iv. 35.
— Janet, wife of James Ruthven of Ruthven, vii. 389.
— Jean, wife of 7th lord Banff, ii. 25.
— Jean, wife of Alexander, 6th earl of Kincardine, iii. 489 n.
— Jean, wife of (1) Sir Wm. Scott of Harden, and (2) Sir Wm. Scott of Thirlestane, vi. 431; vii. 78.
— Josiah, H.E.I.C.S., v. 315.
— Katherine, wife of (1) * Dickson of Belchester, and (2) Sir Henry Home of Herdrig, iv. 475.
— Katharine, wife of Patrick Sinclair of Balgriggie, ix. 157.
— Mary, wife of Jas. Hamilton, ii. 55.
— Thomas, 3rd son of Sir Philip N., iv. 475.
— Wilhelmina, wife of David, 6th earl of Leven and 5th earl of Melville, vi. 116.
Nisbet-Hamilton of Dirleton and Belhaven, Robert Adam Christopher, M.P., iii. 493.
— — his wife, Mary Bruce, iii. 493.
NISBITTS, KER, LORD KERR OF, v. 477-487.
Nisbitts, Robert, first lord Kerr of, 477.
NITH, DOUGLAS, VISCOUNT OF, vii. 138-156.
Nith, William, first viscount of, vii. 138.
NITHSDALE, MAXWELL, EARL OF, vi. 469-492.
Nithsdale, Elizabeth (Douglas), wife of (1) John, 8th lord Maxwell, (2) Alex. Stewart of Garlies, and (3) John Wallace; styled countess of, vi. 483.
— John, third earl of, iv. 416; v. 116; vi. 487.
— — his wife, Elizabeth Gordon, iv. 417; v. 116; vi. 487.
— Robert, first earl of, vi. 485.
— — his wife, Elizabeth Beaumont, vi. 485.

* Name unknown.

Nithsdale, Robert, second earl of, i. 228; iv. 416; vi. 487.
— Robert, fourth earl of, iv. 417; vi. 488.
— — his wife, Lucy Douglas, i. 206; vi. 488; ix. 13.
— William, fifth earl of, v. 131; vi. 488, 500.
— — his wife, Winifred Herbert, iv. 417; vi. 488.
— William, sixth earl of, v. 131; vi. 490.
— — his 1st wife, Katharine Stuart, vi. 490.
— — his 2nd wife, Anne Fox, vi. 490.
Niven of Monkredding, Thomas, iii. 439 n.
— Oswald, commander R.N., iv. 569.
— — his wife, Rose Gordon Carmichael, iv. 569.
Noble of Kinpunt and Eliston, Ralph, vi. 202.
— — Thomas, vi. 202.
— Agnes, wife of David de Graham of Dundaff, vi. 202.
— Margaret, wife of Wm. Sempill of Cathcart, vii. 534.
Noel, Alice, vii. 94.
— Bridget, wife of David, viscount of Milsington, vii. 93.
— Elizabeth, wife of Sir Jas. B. Burgess, ix. 31.
— Katharine Hamilton, wife of Sir James Carnegie of Southesk, viii. 94.
— William Frederick, colonel, iv. 386.
Noel-Edwards, Gerard, iv. 338.
— — his wife, Diana Middleton, baroness Barham, vi. 180.
Nonsuch, Barbara (Villiers), baroness, i. 31.
Norbury, Hector John (Graham-Toler), 3rd earl of, v. 419.
— — his wife, Stewart Lindsay Lindsay, v. 419.
Norcliffe of Langton, Fairfax, vii. 357.
— — Frances, wife of Sir John Wray, vii. 357.
— Sir Thomas, v. 10.
— — his wife, Dorothy Fairfax, v. 10.
Norfolk, Hugh le Bigod, earl of, vi. 288.
— Roger le Bigod, earl of, i. 5; vi. 288.
— — his wife, Isabella of Scotland, i. 5; vi. 288.
— Edward (Howard), 9th duke of, i. 412.
— Henry (Howard), 6th duke of, i. 55.
— Henry Charles (Howard), 13th duke of, ii. 311; viii. 362.
— — his wife, Charlotte Sophia Leveson Gower, viii. 362.
— Henry Fitzalan (Howard), 15th duke of, v. 516.
— — his 1st wife, Flora Paulyna Hetty Barbara Abney-Hastings, v. 516.
— — his 2nd wife, Gwendoline Mary Constable-Maxwell, iv. 423.
— Henry Granville (Fitzalan-Howard), 14th duke of, v. 485.

* Name unknown.

* Name unknown.

* Name unknown.

* Name unknown.

* Name unknown.

　　　　　　　　　　　　　　　* Name unknown.

* Name unknown.

* Name unknown.

* Name unknown.

* Name unknown.

* Name unknown.

* Name unknown.

* Name unknown.

Ruthven, James, illeg. son of 3rd lord Ruthven, iv. 262.

—— James, precentor of Dunkeld, iv. 262, 264.

—— James, 4th son of Sir John R. of Dunglass, ix. 92.

—— James, in Feu, ix. 98.

—— —— his wife, Dorothy Ruthven, ix. 98.

—— Jane, dau. of 6th lord Ruthven of Freeland, vii. 390.

—— Janet, wife of Adam Stewart, prior of Charterhouse, i. 25; iv. 101.

—— Janet, wife of 2nd lord Forrester of Corstorphine, iv. 93, 106.

—— Janet, wife of (1) John Crichton of Strathord, and (2) Laurence Mercer of Meiklour, iv. 261.

—— Janet, wife of Wade Toby Caulfield, vii. 389.

—— Janet Anne, dau. of 6th lord Ruthven of Freeland, vii. 390.

—— Jean, wife of 6th lord Ogilvy of Airlie, i. 122; iv. 266; ix. 8.

—— Jean, wife of Laurence Mercer of Clavedge, iv. 260; ix. 98.

—— Jean, wife of (1) Henry, 2nd lord Methven, and (2) Andrew, 5th earl of Rothes, iv. 262; vi. 169; vii. 294.

—— John, eldest son of Sir John R. of Dunglass, iv. 103.

—— John, captain R.N., commander of *Terpsichore*, vii. 389.

—— John, son of Alex. R. of Freeland, ix. 98.

—— Katharine, wife of Colin Campbell of Glenurchy, ii. 182; iv. 260; ix. 43.

—— Katharine, dau. of 1st earl of Gowrie, ix. 99.

—— Lilias, wife of David, 2nd lord Drummond, i. 469; iv. 260; vii. 46; ix. 149.

—— Lilias, illeg. dau. of general Archibald R. of Forteviot, iv. 262.

—— Lilias, dau. of 1st earl of Gowrie, iv. 266, 465; ix. 99.

—— Margaret, wife of John Murray of Trewin, i. 457.

—— Margaret, contracted to John Oliphant, and wife of (1) Alex. Stewart, earl of Buchan, (2) John Erskine, (3) Jas. Stewart of Ryland, and (4) Wm. Wood of Bonnytoun, ii. 267, 268; iv. 259; vi. 543; ix. 47.

—— Margaret, dau. of Wm. R. of Ballindean, iv. 101.

—— Margaret, dau. of Wm. R. of Ballindean and Gardyne, iv. 103.

—— Margaret, wife of Sir Alexander Seton, iv. 256; viii. 569.

—— Margaret, wife of Jas. Johnston of Elphinston, iv. 261.

—— Margaret, wife of 4th earl of Montrose, iv. 266; vi. 241; ix. 99.

Ruthven, Margaret, alleged wife of Sir Walter Drummond of Stobhall, vii. 40.

—— Margaret, wife of Jas. Henderson, ix. 92.

—— Maria, wife of Geo. Hay of Naughton, iv. 260; ix. 98.

—— Mariota, wife of (1) *, (2) Sir Patrick Edgar, and (3) Sir William of Home, iv. 255, 443.

—— Mary, wife of (1) John Stewart, 5th earl of Atholl, (2) John Stewart, earl of Atholl, lord Innermeath, and (3) James Stewart, i. 446, 447; iv. 266; ix. 28 *bis*, 48.

—— Mary, wife of Sir Robert Douglas of Ardit, iv. 103.

—— Mary, wife of (1) Sir A. Van Dyck, and (2) Sir Robert Pryse, iv. 265.

—— Patricia, dau. of 2nd lord Forrester of Corstorphine, iv. 94.

—— Patrick, son of Alexander, lord Ettrick, iv. 105.

—— Robert, grandson of 1st earl of Gowrie, iv. 265.

—— Sophia, wife of 2nd duke of Lennox, iv. 266; v. 357.

—— Stewart James, vii. 389.

—— William, 4th son of 2nd lord Ruthven, iv. 101, 260.

—— William, 4th son of 1st earl of Gowrie, iv. 264.

—— William, 2nd son of 5th lord Ruthven of Freeland, vii. 389.

—— Willielma, dau. of 6th lord Ruthven of Freeland, vii. 390.

—— Wortley-Montagu, dau. of 5th lord Ruthven of Freeland, vii. 389.

—— *, wife of Sir Patrick Edgar, iv. 255.

Rutland, Henry John Brinsley (Manners), 8th duke of, iii. 45.

—— —— his wife, Marion Margaret Violet Lindsay, iii. 45.

—— John (Manners), 1st duke of, iii. 479.

—— —— his wife, Diana Bruce, iii. 479.

—— John (Manners), 2nd duke of, iii. 412; vi. 268.

—— John Henry (Manners), 5th duke of, vii. 229.

—— John James Robert (Manners), 7th duke of, ii. 248; iii. 45.

Ryan of Derriweit Heights, Charles, ii. 247.

—— Ada Mary, wife of admiral C. T. Montagu-Douglas-Scott, ii. 246.

Ryder, Cyril John, capt. King's Royal Rifle Corps, iv. 389.

—— —— his wife, I. F. U. I. Douglas-Hamilton, iv. 389.

Ryklynton, Alexander de, iii. 90.

Rymer, Nicholas, rector of Newton Kyme, iii. 601.

Rynd of Broxmouth, James, viii. 277.

—— —— his wife, Margaret Lyon, viii. 277.

* Name unknown.

* Name unknown.

* Name unknown.

* Name unknown.

* Name unknown.

* Name unknown.

* Name unknown.

* Name unknown.

* Name unknown.

Stewart, Elizabeth, wife of 2nd earl of Argyll, i. 336 ; v. 350.
—— Elizabeth, wife of (1) Hugh, 5th lord Fraser of Lovat, (2) Robert (Stewart), earl of Lennox and March, and (3) James (Stewart), earl of Arran, i. 396, 445 ; v. 355, 528, 529 ; ix. 28.
—— Elizabeth, wife of Duncan Bayne of Tulloch, i. 397 ; vi. 513 ; ix. 26.
—— Elizabeth, wife of (1) John (Stewart), 3rd earl of Lennox, and (2) Ninian, 3rd lord Ross of Halkhead, i. 442 ; v. 352 ; vii. 252 ; ix. 27.
—— Elizabeth, wife of 2nd lord Gray, i. 442 ; iv. 276.
—— Elizabeth, wife of (1) Thos. Innes of Elrick, and (2) Alex. Robertson of Strowan, i. 442 ; iii. 569.
—— Elizabeth, wife of Robert Innes, i. 442.
—— Elizabeth, wife of Kenneth Mackenzie of Kintail, i. 443 ; vii. 500.
—— Elizabeth, wife of Mr. Walter Leslie, i. 448.
—— Elizabeth, wife of Sir John Maxwell, ii. 79.
—— Elizabeth, wife of capt. William Colquhoun, ii. 89.
—— Elizabeth, wife of Jas. Cranstoun, ii. 172.
—— Elizabeth, dau. of lord Stewart and Bothwell, ii. 173.
—— Elizabeth, wife of John, master of Buchan, ii. 269 ; vi. 312 ; ix. 47, 138.
—— Elizabeth, wife of A. Fraser of Muchalls, ii. 270.
—— Elizabeth, wife of John Stewart of Ambrismore, ii. 290.
—— Elizabeth, wife of N. Bannatyne of Kames, ii. 296.
—— Elizabeth, wife of Alex. Stewart of Auchinskeoch, ii. 297.
—— Elizabeth, wife of Francis I., duke of Brittany, ii. 326.
—— Elizabeth, wife of James Sinclair of Murchil, ii. 340 ; vi. 574.
—— Elizabeth, wife of Jas. Cranstoun, ii. 594.
—— Elizabeth, wife of Robert Crichton, iii. 187.
—— Elizabeth, wife of (1) Wm. Sutherland, and (2) Jas. Murray, iii. 199.
—— Elizabeth, wife of John Macdonald, Kintyre, iii. 447.
—— Elizabeth, wife of (1) John Bruce of Clackmannan, and (2) * Auchmuty, iii. 470 ; ix. 82.
—— Elizabeth, wife of 2nd lord Elibank, iii. 510 ; viii. 405.
—— Elizabeth, wife of John Fitzwalter or Hamilton, iv. 342.
—— Elizabeth, wife of (1) W. Maxwell, (2)
* Name unknown.

John Johnstone, and (3) Samuel Kirkpatrick, iv. 158, 415.
Stewart, Elizabeth, wife of (1) Mungo Home of Coldaneknollis, and (2) Patrick Sinclair, iv. 469 ; ix. 47.
—— Elizabeth, dau. of Robt. S. of Ravenstone, iv. 162.
—— Elizabeth, wife of John Hamilton of Ballencrieff, iv. 302.
—— Elizabeth, wife of Wm. Ochterlony of Kelly, v. 6.
—— Elizabeth, wife of David Gardin of that Ilk, v. 7.
—— Elizabeth, wife of Sir Alex. Gordon of Kenmure, v. 103, 104.
—— Elizabeth, wife of Sir John Colquhoun of Luss, v. 350.
—— Elizabeth, wife of Sir Hugh Campbell of Loudoun, v. 351, 496.
—— Elizabeth, dau. of 2nd duke of Lennox, v. 358.
—— Elizabeth, wife of Henry, earl of Arundel, v. 359.
—— Elizabeth, wife of Sir Geo. Campbell of Loudoun, v. 493.
—— Elizabeth, wife of Sir Robert Lyle of Duchal, v. 552.
—— Elizabeth, dau. of James, earl of Moray, vi. 312.
—— Elizabeth, wife of 8th lord Saltoun of Abernethy, vi. 318 ; vii. 414.
—— Elizabeth, wife of Alexander Grant of Grant, vi. 323 ; vii. 480.
—— Elizabeth, wife of 2nd lord Newark, vi. 443.
—— Elizabeth, legtd. dau. of 2nd lord Ochiltree, vi. 514.
—— Elizabeth, alleged wife of Sir Wm. Douglas of Drumlanrig, vii. 114.
—— Elizabeth, dau. of 2nd earl of Traquair, viii. 406.
—— Elizabeth, dau. of 4th earl of Traquair, viii. 407.
—— Elizabeth, dau. of Alex. S. of Garlies, ix. 94.
—— Elizabeth Euphemia, wife of Wm. Phillips Inge, iv. 169.
—— Ellen, wife of Sir David Baird, ii. 92.
—— Emilia, wife of (1) Alex. Fraser of Strichen, and (2) John, 19th earl of Crawford, iii. 38 ; v. 544 ; vi. 323.
—— Emily Octavia, wife of capt. F. A. J. Chichester, iv. 172.
—— Emma Georgiana, wife of 2nd lord Tollemache of Helmingham, iv. 172.
—— Euphemia, wife of Patrick, 6th earl of Dunbar, i. 12 ; iii. 256.
—— Euphemia, wife of Alex. Murray of Broughton, i. 221 ; iv. 164.
—— Euphemia, wife of (1) Patrick Graham of Dundaff, and (2) Sir Patrick Dunbar of Biel, iii. 260 ; viii. 260.

* Name unknown.

Stewart, Thomas, illeg. son of Sir Alex. S., earl of Mar, v. 588, 620.
—— his wife, Elizabeth Douglas, ii. 265; iii. 167; v. 589.
—— Thomas, 2nd son of Alex. S. of Garlies, ix. 94.
—— Thomas, 6th son of 2nd lord Ochiltree, ix. 144.
—— Walter, 'Bailloch,' 3rd son of 3rd High Steward, i. 12; vi. 130.
—— —— his wife, Mary, countess of Menteith, vi. 127.
—— Walter, 2nd son of king Robert II., i. 15; iv. 13.
—— —— his wife, Isabella, countess of Fife, iv. 13.
—— Walter, illeg. son of king Robert II., i. 17.
—— Walter, in Clunie, 3rd son of John, earl of Atholl, i. 448.
—— Walter, son of Sir Robt. S. of Minto, ii. 79.
—— Walter, prior of Blantyre, ii. 81; iv. 159.
—— Walter, M.D., son of 1st lord Blantyre, ii. 84.
—— Walter, master of Blantyre, son of 12th lord Blantyre, ii. 92.
—— Walter, illeg. son of 'the Wolf of Badenoch,' ii. 263.
—— Walter, 2nd son of 1st lord Ochiltree, vi. 512; ix. 144.
—— Walter, colonel, son of William S. of Mains, vi. 518.
—— —— his wife, Margaret (?) Stewart, vi. 518.
—— Walter, 4th son of James S. of Traquair, viii. 402.
—— Walter John, colonel, 4th son of 9th earl of Galloway, iv. 171.
—— Watte, Arran, 1505, iv. 356.
—— William, illeg. son of Thomas, earl of Angus, i. 170.
—— Sir William, alleged son of James, earl of Arran, i. 397.
—— William, bishop of Aberdeen, ii. 77; iv. 152.
—— William, lt.-gen., son of 10th lord Blantyre, ii. 91.
—— Sir William, K.C.M.G., C.B., son of 11th lord Blantyre, ii. 91.
—— —— his wife, Georgina Tremenheere, ii. 91.
—— William, 8th son of Ninian S. of Bute, ii. 291.
—— William, 2nd son of Henry S. of Buchlivie, iii. 187.
—— —— his wife, Agnes Shaw, ix. 68.
—— Sir William, iii. 447 n.
—— —— his wife, Elizabeth Hamilton, iii. 447 n.
—— William, 6th son of Sir Alex. S. of Darnley, iv. 145; v. 346, 347.

Stewart, William, 5th son of Sir Alex. S. of Garlies, iv. 156.
—— William, adjutant to the marquess of Montrose, iv. 159.
—— William, 5th son of 3rd earl of Galloway, iv. 163.
—— William, captain 12th Dragoons, M.P., iv. 164.
—— William, 3rd son of Richard, 3rd lord Innermeath, v. 5.
—— William, 3rd son of John, 4th lord Innermeath, v. 6.
—— William, 5th son of Sir John S. of Innermeath, v. 427.
—— William, 5th son of 2nd lord Avandale, vi. 511.
—— —— his wife, Isobel Ker, vi. 511.
—— William, Sweden, vi. 512.
—— William, son of Sir Wm. S. of Monkton, vii. 513.
—— William, in Ayr, vi. 515.
—— —— his wife, Marion M'Alexander, vi. 515.
—— William, 2nd son of 4th earl of Traquair, viii. 406.
—— William, 3rd son of Sir Alex. S. of Garlies, ix. 94.
—— William Molloy, viii. 226.
—— —— his wife, Ellen Urquhart, viii. 226.
—— Winifred, dau. of 4th earl of Traquair, viii. 407.
—— *, alleged 1st wife of Sir Gilleaspock Cambel of Lochow, i. 327.
—— *, wife of Wood of Balbegno, i. 444.
—— *, 2nd son of Sir John S. of Minto, ii.78.
—— *, alleged dau. of Sir John S. of Minto, and wife of * Crawford of Ferme, ii. 81.
—— *, 2nd son of Alexander S., earl of Buchan, ii. 268.
—— *, wife of Wm. Craigie of Gairsay, ii. 442.
—— *, wife of Sir Alexander de Lindsay, iii. 9, 11.
—— *, 1st wife of James Douglas of Balvany, iii. 174.
—— *, 2nd son of Sir Wm. S. of Jedworth, iv. 149.
—— *, contr. to Archibald, 6th earl of Angus, iv. 261; viii. 399; ix. 12.
—— *, illeg. dau. of king James V. and Elizabeth Beaton, iv. 462.
—— *, alleged wife of 1st lord Lindsay of the Byres, v. 3, 393.
—— *, alleged wife of Robert, 1st lord Erskine, v. 3, 604; ix. 115.
—— *, wife of Donald, lord of the Isles, v. 33; ix. 1.
—— *, alleged wife of John Melville of Raith, vi. 82.
—— *, wife of Alexander, 4th lord Saltoun of Abernethy, vii. 409; ix. 47.
* Name unknown.

* Name unknown.

Tredegar, Godfrey Charles (Morgan), 2nd baron, viii. 92.

Trefusis, Evelyn Anne, wife of Edward W. Douglas, vi. 385.

— Walter Randolph, col. Scots Guards, ii. 247.

—*— his wife, Mary Charlotte Scott, ii. 247.

Tremenheere, George Borlase, maj.-gen., ii. 91.

— Georgina, wife of Sir Wm. Stewart, ii. 91.

Tremouille, Charlotte de la, wife of 7th earl of Derby, i. 475; iii. 382.

— Louis Stanislas Kostka, prince de la, iii. 390.

— — his wife, Augusta Murray, iii. 390.

— Claude de la, duc de Thouars, i. 475; iii. 383.

— — his wife, Charlotte of Nassau, iii. 383.

Trentham, George (Leveson Gower), eldest son of Granville, lord Gower; styled viscount, viii. 360.

— — his wife, Elizabeth, countess of Sutherland, viii. 359.

Tresham, Mary, wife of 2nd earl of Cardigan, iii. 298.

— Sir Thomas, iii. 298.

Trevanion, Hugh Charles, viii. 312.

Trevelyan, Sir George, v. 267.

— — his wife, Mary Gage, v. 267.

Trevor, Arthur William (Hill-Trevor), 2nd lord, vii. 452.

— — his wife, A. M. E. Fraser, vii. 452.

— George Arthur, capt. Royal Sussex regt., ii. 499.

— — his wife, Susan Funnell, ii. 499.

Trionfi, Augustin,'marquis, vi. 458.

— — his wife, Elizabetta Bandini, vi. 458.

Tritton, Elizabeth, wife of lieut.-col. Jas. Sinclair, ii. 357.

— George, Westhill, Wandsworth, ii. 357.

Trotter of Ballindean, Robert Knox, col. 17th Lancers, vii. 209.

— — his wife, Mary Rollo, vii. 209.

— of Dreghorn, Archibald, v. 419.

— of Dyrham Park, John, ii. 57; v. 419.

— of Mortonhall, John, iv. 436.

— of Westville, Sir B. A. Coutts, bart., i. 92, 524.

— — his wife, Margaret Gordon, i. 92.

— Agnes Bruce, wife of 10th lord Rollo, vii. 209.

— Algernon R., capt. 2nd Life Guards, M.V.O., D.S.O., iii. 464.

— — his wife, Edith Mary Montgomerie, iii. 464.

— Anne, wife of lieut.-gen. Jas. Lindsay of Balcarres, i. 524.

— Coutts, wife of Sir H. Lindsay Bethune of Kilconquhar, v. 419.

Trotter, Edward, in Swinton Mylne Steill, iv. 298.

— — his wife, * Ramsay, iv. 298.

— James Stuart, lieut. R.N., v. 419.

— — his wife, Jane Coutts Lindsay, v. 419.

— Janet, wife of Alex. Bothwell of Glencorse, iv. 436.

— Martha, wife of C. F. Boyle, iv. 213.

— Martin, wife of W. J. Hamilton, ii. 57.

Troup of Craigie, William, iv. 270.

— Alison, wife of John Gray of Crichie, iv. 288.

— James, merchant, Edinburgh, iv. 288.

— John de, vi. 171.

Trubleville, Ralph de, vi. 527.

Truell, William Henry Augustus, Clonmannon, vi. 327.

—•— — his wife, Cornelia Stuart, vi. 327.

Truelock, George, archdeacon of Killala, iv. 571.

— Sarah Margaret, wife of David F. Carmichael, iv. 571.

Trumbull of Easthampstead Park, Sir William, viii. 182.

— — his 2nd wife, Judith Alexander, viii. 182.

Truro of Bowes, Sir Thomas Wilde, baron, iii. 392.

— — his 2nd wife, Augusta Emma D'Este, iii. 392.

Tucker, Ethel, wife of Archibald Lionel Lindsay, v. 420.

— William Austin, v. 420.

Tudor, Dorothy Susan, wife of major D. S. Carmichael-Smyth, iv. 571.

— Margaret, wife of (1) king James iv., (2) Archibald, 6th earl of Angus, and (3) Henry, 1st lord Methven, i. 21, 26, 27, 190, 192; iv. 261; v. 150, 353; vi. 166, 167; ix. 12.

— Mary, sister of king Henry viii., iii. 480.

— Mary, illeg. dau. of king Charles ii., wife of (1) Francis, earl of Derwentwater, (2) Henry Graham of Levens, and (3) James Rooke, i. 32; vii. 102.

— William, iv. 571.

Tufnell, Carlton, commander R.N., vii. 227.

— — his wife, Charlotte Henrietta Primrose, vii. 227.

— Frederick, rector of Sudbury, v. 96.

— — his wife, Frances Elizabeth Erskine, v. 96.

— Henry, M.P., vii. 227.

— — his wife, Anne Primrose, vii. 227.

Tufton of Hothfield, Sir John, 1st bart., iii. 297.

— — his 2nd wife, Christian Brown, iii. 297.

— Mary, wife of Henry, 1st viscount Dunbar, iii. 297.

* Name unknown.

Tughall, Robert, chamberlain of Berwick, vii. 317.

Tuite, Sir George, bart., iii. 362.

—— his wife, Janet Cochrane, iii. 362.

Tuke, Francis, in holy orders, viii. 227.

—— Mabel, wife of E. B. Drummond, viii. 227.

TULLIBARDINE, MURRAY, EARL OF (1606), i. 469-472.

Tullibardine, John, first earl of, i. 466, 469; viii. 410.

—— —— his wife, Katharine, or Margaret Drummond, i. 469; vii. 47; ix. 29.

—— William, second earl of, i. 470; viii. 410; ix. 29 bis.

—— —— his 1st wife, Cecilia Wemyss, i. 471; viii. 498.

—— —— his 2nd wife, Dorothy Stewart, i. 446, 471.

TULLIBARDINE, MURRAY, EARL OF (1628), viii. 410-415.

Tullibardine, Patrick, third earl of, i. 470, 471; viii. 411.

—— —— his 1st wife, Prudence *, viii. 412.

—— —— his 2nd wife, Elizabeth Dent, viii. 412.

—— James, fourth earl of, i. 474; iii. 573; viii. 414.

—— —— his 1st wife, Lilias Drummond, viii. 223, 414.

—— —— his 2nd wife, Anne Murray, i. 473; viii. 415.

—— —— his 3rd wife, Lilias Drummond, viii. 415.

TULLIBARDINE, MURRAY, EARL OF (1676), i. 474.

Tullibardine, John, fifth earl of, i. 474.

—— —— his wife, Amelia Anne Sophia Stanley, i. 475.

TULLIBARDINE, MURRAY, EARL OF (1696), i. 478.

Tullibardine, John, sixth earl of, i. 475, 478; iii. 354; iv. 37.

TULLIBARDINE, MURRAY, MARQUESS OF, i. 479-502.

Tullibardine, George Augustus Frederick John, sixth marquess of, i. 498.

—— James, second marquess of, i. 487; vii. 556 n.

—— John, first marquess of, i. 479.

—— John, eldest son of 1st duke of Atholl; styled marquess of, i. 480; ix. 29.

—— John, third marquess of, i. 489.

—— John, fourth marquess of, i. 495.

—— John, fifth marquess of, i. 498.

—— John George, eldest son of 7th duke of Atholl; styled marquess of, i. 500.

—— —— his wife, Katharine Marjory Ramsay, i. 500.

—— John James Hugh Henry, seventh marquess of, i. 499.

* Name unknown.

Tullibardine, William, 2nd son of 1st duke of Atholl; styled marquess of, i. 480.

—— master of, William Murray, eldest son of 1st earl of Tullibardine, i. 469.

TULLIBARDINE, MURRAY, LORD MURRAY OF, i. 469-501.

Tullibardine, Ada of, wife of Sir William Murray, i. 453, 454 n.; ix. 28.

—— Conghal of, i. 453 n.

—— Duncan of, i. 419.

—— Muriel of, wife of Sir Malise, steward of Strathearn, i. 453.

TULLIBODY, ALEXANDER, LORD ALEXANDER OF, viii. 173.

Tullideph of Tullideph, Walter, vi. 115.

—— Mary Margaret, wife of major-gen. Alexander Leslie, vi. 115.

Tullie, David, iv. 566.

—— —— his wife, Euphame Carmichael, iv. 566.

Tulloch of Bonnington, Dorothea, wife of Walter Wode, viii. 274.

—— of Montcoffer, Alexander, iv. 71.

—— —— his wife, * Forbes, iv. 71.

—— —— John, portioner, viii. 281.

—— —— his wife, Elizabeth Lyon, iv. 54; viii. 280.

—— of Tulloch, Walter, i. 110.

—— —— his wife, Marjorie Ogilvy, i. 110.

—— Elizabeth, dau. of John T., iv. 54.

Tullois of Pitkennetie, Thomas, v. 411.

Tunstall of Scargill and Wycliffe, Francis, iii. 298.

—— —— his wife, Cicely Constable, iii. 298.

—— Cuthbert, bishop of Durham, iv. 358.

Tunstall-Constable of Burton Constable, Cuthbert, nephew of last viscount Dunbar, iii. 298.

Turck, Johanna, wife of Sir Henry Livingston, vi. 449.

Turing of Foveran, Gilbert, i. 287.

—— —— his wife, Katharine Arbuthnott, i. 287.

—— —— Robert, viii. 56.

—— —— his wife, Helen Carnegie, viii. 56.

Turnbull of Bedrule, George, v. 59.

—— —— his wife, Janet Ker, ii. 230; v. 59.

—— —— Sir Thomas, iv. 472; v. 61; viii. 400.

—— —— Walter, iv. 473.

—— —— William, iv. 472.

—— —— his wife, Margaret Home, iv. 471.

—— of Bewlie, Robert, v. 73.

—— of Hassendean Bank, John, iv. 229.

—— of Minto, Sir John, 'out wyth swerd,' ii. 539; iv. 145, 147, 148, 150; vii. 366.

—— —— Walter, iv. 150.

—— Andrew, v. 69.

—— Esther, vii. 72.

—— James, advocate, ii. 277.

—— —— his wife, Erskine Monro, ii. 277.

* Name unknown.

* Name unknown.

Walters, Mary, wife of (1) Wm. Sarsfield, and (2) Wm. Fanshaw, i. 30.
—— Thomas, vicar of Boyton, vii. 155.
—— William, Haverfordwest, ii. 238.
—— —— his wife, Elizabeth Protheroe, ii. 238.
Waltheof, earl of Huntingdon, i. 3.
Waltheof of Allerdale, 2nd son of 1st earl of Dunbar, iii. 243.
—— —— his wife, Sigrid, iii. 244.
Waltheof, abbot of Croyland, iii. 244.
Walton of Fole, James, i. 400.
—— Margery, wife of John Aston, i. 400.
—— John, viii. 139.
—— Rosina, wife of Campbell James Dalrymple, viii. 139.
WANDELL, DOUGLAS, LORD, iv. 77-79.
Wandell, Archibald, first lord, iv. 77.
—— Archibald, second lord, iv. 78.
Wantage, Robert (Lindsay), V.C., K.C.B., lord, i. 524.
—— —— his wife, Harriet Loyd Jones, i. 524.
Warbeck, Perkin, the pretender, iv. 530.
—— —— his wife, Katharine Gordon, iv. 530.
Warburton of Winnington, Thomas, i. 376.
—— Jane, wife of duke of Argyll and Greenwich, i. 376.
Ward, William Humble (Ward), 10th baron, i. 392.
—— Alice, wife of M. P. G. D. Drummond, viii. 225.
—— Joseph, London, i. 410 n.
—— Julia Susannah, wife of (1) A. H. A. Anson, and (2) bishop Claughton, i. 392.
—— William C., viii. 225.
Warde, George, H.E.I.C.S., i. 492.
—— —— his wife, Anne Amelia Dashwood, i. 492.
Wardlaw of Hownam, Henry, vii. 326.
—— of Kilbaberton, John, iii. 64; ix. 63.
—— —— his wife, Margaret Cockburn, iii. 64.
—— —— Robert, ix. 113.
—— —— his wife, Margaret Carmichael, ix. 113.
—— of Otterston, Elizabeth, wife of Walter Leslie of Cowcairnie, vii. 291.
—— —— Isabella, vii. 291.
—— of Pitreavie, Sir Henry, viii. 178.
—— of Riccarton, James, ii. 144.
—— —— William, vi. 417.
—— —— his wife, Abellina Napier, vi. 417.
—— of Spot, Henry, iii. 276 n.
—— of Torrie, Andrew, vii. 290.
—— —— his contr. wife, Beatrix Leslie, vii. 290.
—— —— Andrew, vii. 296.
—— —— his 1st wife, Agnes Leslie, vii. 296.
—— —— Henry, vi. 539; vii. 326.
—— —— his wife, Margaret Oliphant, vi. 539.

Wardlaw of Torrie, Henry, iv. 457; vii. 281, 546; ix. 83.
—— —— his contr. wife, Grisel Leslie, vii. 281.
—— —— his contr. wife, Agnes Murray, iii. 502; ix. 83.
—— —— his 1st wife, Alison Home, iv. 457.
—— —— John, iii. 309; vii. 281.
—— Agnes, wife of Alex. Colville, ii. 549.
—— Christian, wife of * de Hay of Locherworth, viii. 422.
—— Elizabeth, wife of David Melville, iii. 92.
—— Elizabeth, wife of Sir Anthony Alexander, viii. 179.
—— Helen, wife of Sir James Makgill, and *probably* dau. of Thomas W. of Foulford, vi. 587.
—— Henry, bishop of St. Andrews, iii. 275, 276; iv. 564.
—— Isobel, wife of Sir A. Hepburn, ii. 144.
—— James, advocate, vi. 593.
—— —— his wife, Isobel Cuninghame, vi. 593.
—— Jonet, sister of Henry W. of Spot, iii. 276 n.
—— Jonet, dau. of Henry W. of Spot, iii. 276 n.
—— Margaret, sister of Henry W. of Spot, iii. 276 n.
—— Margaret, wife of William Maitland of Thirlestane, v. 289.
—— Margaret, wife of Henry Makgill, vi. 591.
—— Marion, wife of (1) Jas. Scrimgeour, and (2) Sir A. Hepburne, ii. 145; iii. 309.
—— Robert, v. 403.
—— —— his wife, Martha Fernie, v. 402.
—— William, brother of Henry W. of Spot, iii. 276 n.
—— * wife of Sir John Carmichael of Carmichael, iv. 564.
Wardlaw-Ramsay of Whitehill, Robert, captain, iii. 43.
—— —— his wife, Anne Lindsay, iii. 43.
—— —— Robert Balfour, viii. 471.
—— —— his wife, Louisa Jane Hay, viii. 471.
—— R. E., captain, viii. 472.
Wardrop, James, M.D., viii. 138.
—— —— his wife, Margaret Dalrymple, viii. 138.
—— John of, v. 329.
—— —— his wife, Mary, v. 329.
Ware, Samuel Hibbert, M.D., i. 493.
—— —— his wife, Charlotte Wilhelmina Murray, i. 493.
Warenne of Coventre, Reginald de, vi. 530; vii. 398.
—— Ada de, wife of Henry, earl of Northumberland and Huntingdon, i. 4; viii. 560 n.

* Name unknown.

FINIS

Printed by T. and A. CONSTABLE, Printers to His Majesty
at the Edinburgh University Press